CW00551963

The Preces Privatae of Lancelot Andrewes

Bishop of Winchester

Lancelot Andrewes

Translator: F. E. Brightman

Alpha Editions

This edition published in 2020

ISBN : 9789354047220

Design and Setting By
Alpha Editions
www.alphaedis.com
email - alphaedis@gmail.com

THE

PRECES PRIVATAE

OF

LANCELOT ANDREWES

BISHOP OF WINCHESTER

TRANSLATED

WITH AN INTRODUCTION AND NOTES

BY

F. E. BRIGHTMAN, M.A.

FELLOW OF S. MARY MAGDALEN COLLEGE, OXFORD

CANON OF LINCOLN

METHUEN & CO.

36 ESSEX STREET W.C.

LONDON

1903

PREFACE

A DESCRIPTION of the character of the present volume will perhaps at the same time serve as an excuse for a new version of an old and famous book.

1. The text which has been translated is that of the Oxford edition of 1675, corrected and supplemented by the MSS., especially the Laudian MS., which contains a considerable mass of Hebrew matter that was not represented in the edition of 1675, and the Harleian MS., the contents of which are almost wholly outside the scope of the edition of 1675 and have never as a whole appeared in English. To this is added the matter recovered from Stokes' *Verus Christianus*, which, while in many cases it represents only a preliminary form of what is contained in the other sources, yet includes some new passages, and throughout offers points of interest which seem worth preserving. The sources of the text are indicated in detail on the inner margin.[1]

2. In the translation the aim has been, where the original is drawn from the Septuagint or the Vulgate, to use the language of the Authorised Version and of the Psalter of the Book of Common Prayer, except in cases in which for any reason correction seemed necessary or desirable, or Andrewes elsewhere supplies a corrected rendering of his own. Where the text of the Septuagint or the Vulgate is altered, some attempt has been made to represent this in the English; but it has proved scarcely possible to carry out this plan consistently, and perhaps it was not worth while to attempt it in detail. Where the original text is quotation from the Hebrew of the Old Testament, the rendering of the Authorised Version has been corrected, largely in the direction of the Revised Version of 1881. Outside of quotations from Holy Scripture, the translation has been

[1] As a rule only the *ultimate* source is indicated; but it must be remembered that all that is in W and W is also in O.

made anew and the text adhered to as nearly as possible. But regard has been had to Andrewes' own rendering of such passages as occur elsewhere in his writings and to the language of the *Sermons* generally. Apart from this the influence of Cardinal Newman and Dr Neale will be obvious. No one who has made much use of their version will be either able or willing to ignore it. Very rarely a few words have been added to ease or complete the sense; and these are enclosed in pointed brackets.

3. The whole book has been rearranged for practical use, and redistributed, as far as possible in accordance with the Bishop's own scheme of devotion as given on pp. 12 sq. In the edition of 1675 and in versions dependent on it, the contents of the 'second part' are not only kept quite distinct from those of the first, but are wholly without arrangement: it would seem that Andrews' papers were printed without any attempt to put them in order, with the result that this part of the *Preces* has probably been little used as a whole. It is sometimes difficult to know exactly where to put a paragraph or fragment, but it may be hoped that the present arrangement will serve practical purposes. For titles, etc., which are printed in thick type and mark the arrangement of the text, I am responsible. The Greek MSS. have no titles, and those of the 'second part' are incomplete and unsystematic; and for the titles in former versions the editors have been mostly responsible.

4. Where the original is in Hebrew, the translation is printed in italic[1]; but no attempt has been made to mark the distinction between the Greek and the Latin of the original.

5. With regard to the arrangement of the lines of the text, the Laudian MS. has been taken as authoritative, and over the ground covered by its contents, its arrangement has been as far as possible almost exactly followed. Elsewhere, the arrangement of the current text has not been regarded as finally authoritative, but while it has been adhered to in general, it has been modified in detail in accordance with what seem to be the principles of the Laudian MS., and occasionally in accordance with mere

[1] *i.e.* everything printed in Italic represents Hebrew in the original, with the exception of the sub-titles on pp. 171-177.

convenience. The Hebrew of the Laudian MS. is not arranged like the Greek, but in general all the lines begin at the same level. Where a given passage is only in Hebrew this arrangement has been reproduced; but where the parallel Greek is added, this is indicated by the arrangement of the italic text in accordance with the Greek.

6. References to sources are added in the outer margin. The Scriptural references of course apply to the text of the original, and consequently they may not always be recognisable in the English Bible. But when the difference is a marked one, 'heb.,' 'sept.,' or 'vulg.' is commonly added to the reference. When the original is only in Hebrew the reference is printed in italic; but when the Greek is added, the reference is in ordinary type. An asterisk in the text indicates the end of the quotation; where no such indication is given, it must be understood that the reference applies to the whole of the text down to the end of the paragraph or to the next marginal reference. In a few cases a quotation from Holy Scripture occurring within a quotation from some other source is indicated by a subordinate reference enclosed in square brackets. A note of interrogation in the margin indicates that a passage appears to be a quotation, but its source has not been discovered. The books and editions indicated in the nonscriptural references are given in the index; but it may be well to repeat here that the Greek Liturgies (S. James, S. Basil, S. Chrysostom) are referred to in the edition used by Andrewes, printed by Morel at Paris in 1560; that '*Horae*' represents the Sarum *Horae* printed at Paris in 1514, and '*Prymer*' (without added date or publisher) represents the Sarum *Prymer* printed by Nicholas le Roux at Paris in 1537; and '*Heb. morn.*,' '*Heb. even.*,' etc., refer to the Synagogue morning and evening prayers, etc., as contained in *The Authorised Daily Prayer Book of the United Hebrew Congregations of the British Empire*, edited by the Rev. S. Singer, London, 1895.

7. The Notes are chiefly concerned with illustrating and explaining the text by the help of the other works of Andrewes, and treating the sources more fully than is possible in the margin. But some attempt at further exposition has been made where it seemed necessary, and occasionally an extended note has been written on the

origin and history of a topic or formula, where no convenient reference could be given to its treatment elsewhere, or it seemed possible to add anything to current accounts of things. Both in the Notes and in the Introduction, Andrewes' works are referred to as they are contained in the *Library of Anglo-Catholic Theology*, except in the case of the S. Pauls' and S. Giles' Lectures, which are referred to in ΑΠΟΣΠΑΣΜΑΤΙΑ *sacra*, London, 1657.

It remains to return my best thanks to the Rev. R. G. Livingstone, Rector of Brinkworth, for the loan of the Laudian MS., to the Master and Fellows of Pembroke College, Cambridge, for the loan of the MSS. in their possession, and to several friends for help in various ways, of which I hope they will accept this general acknowledgement.

F. E. B.

MAGDALEN COLLEGE,
NATIVITY OF S. JOHN BAPTIST, 1903.

CONTENTS

INTRODUCTION

THE *Preces Privatae* of Lancelot Andrewes, the peculiar heritage of the English Church from an age of astonishing fruitfulness and distinction in devotional literature,[1] was compiled for his own use and was not published till some years after his death. It is a collection of material to supply the needs, daily and occasional, of his own devotional life, providing for the great departments of the life of the spirit—faith and hope and love, praise and thanksgiving, penitence and petition. 'Of this reverend prelate,' says John Buckeridge, his second successor in the see of Ely, in his sermon at Andrewes' funeral,[2] 'I may say *Vita eius vita orationis*, "his life was a life of prayer"; a great part of five hours every day did he spend in prayer to God. . . . And when his brother Master Nicholas Andrewes died, he took that as a certain sign and prognostic and warning of his own death, and from that time till the hour of his own dissolution, he spent all his time in prayer; and his prayer book, when he was in private, was seldom seen out of his hands.' The *Preces Privatae* is a monument of these hours of devotion, in which he first tested for himself what he has bequeathed for us.

I

As sources of the text we still possess the three manuscripts from which the printed editions have been derived, besides a fourth of no independent value.

1. The most important of these is a copy given by the

[1] It is enough to notice here that the *Exercitia spiritualia* of S. Ignatius Loyola (1491-1556) were published in 1548; the *Combattimento spirituale* of Lorenzo Scupoli (1530-1610) in 1589; the *Vie dévote* of S. François de Sales (1567-1622) in 1618; and the *Paradisus animæ* of Jacob Merlo of Horst (1597-1644) in 1644.

[2] Andrewes *Sermons* v p. 296.

bishop himself to William Laud, which remained generally unknown until it was recovered from a dealer's stock and purchased in 1883 by Mr R. G. Livingstone, Fellow of Pembroke College, Oxford, and now Rector of Brinkworth in Gloucestershire. In form, it is a little paper book, 5 × 2½ in., of 188 pages with gilt edges, bound in white vellum and tied with four narrow green silk ribbands.[1] On the front cover is written in Laud's handwriting, 'My reverend Friend Bishop Andrews gave me this Booke a little before his death. W: Bath et Welles'; and this is repeated below in a later hand, the original inscription having meanwhile faded. The text is unfinished, ending abruptly on p. 168, early in the course of the Evening Prayers, and the last 20 pages are left blank. The Greek is beautifully and, except for the accentuation, for the most part correctly written; the Hebrew is scarcely beautiful and it is very incorrect. In the preface to his translation of the *Preces*, which will be referred to below, Richard Drake remarks, 'Had you seen the original manuscript, happy in the glorious deformity thereof, being slubbered with his pious hands and watered with his penitential tears, you would have been forced to confess, That book belonged to no other than pure and primitive devotion.'[2] It has been suggested[3] that the Laudian manuscript is the copy here referred to. But this is quite impossible: so far from being 'deformed' or 'slubbered' or 'watered,' the manuscript is quite clean and shows no signs of having been much used.[4] Neither is it probable that it is an autograph, as has been claimed for it.[5] Perhaps none of Andrewes' later Greek handwriting survives for comparison with the handwriting of the manuscript; but in a copy of Demosthenes,[6] given to Andrewes by Dr Thomas Watts, who nominated him to his

[1] The book in the bishop's left hand in his portrait in the Hall of Jesus College, Oxford, is of the same form and may in fact be his prayer book.

[2] *A manual of the private devotions and meditations of . . . Lancelot Andrews . . . by* R. D., B.D., 1648, preface.

[3] By Mr Rackham in R. L. Ottley *Lancelot Andrewes*, append. D, p. 216.

[4] None of the passages from Andrewes which Laud incorporated in his own *Devotions* are contained in this MS. See below, p. lviii.

[5] By Mr Medd in his edition of the Laudian text, p. xii.

[6] Formerly belonging to R. W. Church, Dean of S. Paul's, and now to the Bishop of Oxford.

scholarship at Pembroke Hall, there are Greek marginal annotations, apparently in Andrewes' handwriting, and this writing is quite unlike that of the present manuscript. It may of course be said that the character of his handwriting as an undergraduate is no test of what it would be in his old age, and this MS. was written after his translation to Winchester in 1618. But on the other hand, his English hand remained steady: the signatures and Latin notes in the Demosthenes are apparently in the same hand as the papers of his mature life; while the Greek is of a different type from that of the manuscript of the *Preces* and such as would not naturally develop into it. Nor does the writing of the manuscript appear to shew any signs of old age. But what seems to be quite decisive is the Hebrew text: this is singularly incorrect and often unintelligible without emendation; and it is inconceivable that it can have been written by anyone who really understood Hebrew and could say his prayers in it; while the mistakes are just such as would be made by a copyist who knew little or nothing of the language beyond the alphabet, and did not understand what he was writing. It is almost certain therefore that the manuscript was written for the bishop by an amanuensis; and it may be conjectured that it was copied expressly for presentation to Laud, while its unfinished condition suggests that the copying was interrupted in order that the dying prelate might make the gift with his own hand.[1] The subsequent history of the manuscript, until its recovery by Mr Livingstone, is unknown. The only details that survive are the signature 'J. Mandevile' written in an 18th cent. hand on p. 188, and an entry from an auction catalogue of the 18th cent. pasted inside the back cover (p. 205), running as follows, 'Fifth Days S... | Friday, Januar... | Lot MANUSCR... | 592 The Psalms in Greek in the handwriting of Archbishop Andrews, and presented by him to Archbishop Laud, and 10 others,' the date being torn off; while in the upper left hand corner of the slip is written, 'Mowing's Auction Rooms, Maiden Lane, Covent Garden, W. Bristow Auctioneer.' This MS. is represented in the margin of the present volume by the symbol L.

[1] Laud does not notice any visit to Andrewes in his Diary of this date, and he records his death quite shortly, under Sept. 21, 1626.

2. After describing 'the original manuscript' as above, Drake adds that he had 'the happiness to obtain a copy under the fair hand of his [the bishop's] amanuensis.' This copy survives, and is preserved in the Library of Pembroke College, Cambridge, with an entry written and signed by Richard Drake himself to the effect that it was copied and given to him by his friend Samuel Wright, who had been secretary to Andrewes while bishop of Winchester, and was then Registrar to Matthew Wren bishop of Ely.[1] In form, the manuscript is a paper book, $6 \times 3\frac{3}{4}$ in., of 170 pages with gilt edges, bound in brown calf tooled in gold. The text is beautifully written, and although the writing is rather larger than that of the Laudian manuscript, it is possible, but by no means certain, that the two manuscripts are by the same hand. But there is considerable difference in their contents. The occasional variations in reading and some additions in Wright's copy are of little importance. The only considerable additions are the paragraph on p. 123 of the MS. (p. 197 below), and the whole of the concluding pages, 146-168, for which the last 20 blank pages of the Laudian MS. were evidently intended.[2] But the omissions are some of them more serious. They are of four kinds: (1) omissions of passages presumably not contained in the MS. from which Wright copied; viz. pp. 6, 7 (pp. 13-15 below), p. 18 ll. 16-19 (p. 40 ll. 18-21 below): (2) passages of purely personal application, of no direct practical use to any-one but the bishop himself, pp. 47, 119, 124 (pp. 61, 272, 223 below): (3) most of the Hebrew passages, very few of which, and those generally only single words and lines, are retained; while a few are rendered into Greek or the corresponding Septuagint text is substituted: (4) most of the petitions for the departed. In many or most cases under the last three heads, it is evident that the omissions are of what was contained in the text which Wright had before him, since their position is commonly marked by spaces in his copy. And perhaps in the case of the Hebrew, it was intended to insert at least some of it afterwards, and throughout for the most part the Hebrew that is retained

[1] *Amicissimus meus Samuel Wright Lanceloto Wintoniensi Epo olim à chartis, nunc autem Matthaeo Eliensi à Registris, pretiosum hoc κειμήλιον suâ manu accuratè descriptum dono dedit mihi Richardo Drake*

[2] Below pp. 108-112, 266, 121-124, 3, 4.

has the appearance of having been written in afterwards, perhaps by a different hand. In the matter of the petitions for the departed, those on pp. 55, 71, 86 of the Laudian MS. (pp. 59, 68, 78 below) are omitted simply without warning; the text runs straight on.[1] That on p. 13 below occurs in a passage two pages in length, which, as was noted above, was perhaps not contained in the exemplar from which Wright made his copy; while the positions of the petitions on pp. 85, 128 of the Laudian MS. (pp. 76, 101 below) are marked by blanks in Wright's copy (pp. 70, 111); and the petitions, for living and dead on p. 33, and for the unburied on p. 41, of L (pp. 48, 51), are retained by Wright (pp. 29, 35). The purpose of these omissions is not difficult to conjecture. It may be supposed that Wright's copy was prepared for an edition adapted to more or less popular use; and it might well be thought that the purely personal allusions would be only distracting, and the Hebrew unintelligible except to a very few; while the prayers for the departed might be regarded as unlikely to be welcome to the current opinion of the moment (1642-1648). For, although a proposed condemnation of prayers for the dead in a draft Article had been rejected in 1563, yet there was a strong feeling against them in some quarters in the 17th century, witness Donne's Sermon lxxii in 1626,[2] and Sir Thomas Browne's curious treatment of them as a 'heresy' in the early pages of the *Religio Medici* in 1642; while all that Andrewes has to say of them, outside the *Preces*, is 'For *offering* and *prayer for the dead*, there is little to be said against it; it cannot be denied that it is ancient.'[3]

But the MS. does not remain exactly in the condition in which it left Wright's hands: two sets of additions have been made to it. First, Drake has added throughout a large number of marginal references to the Scriptural sources, and from time to time corrected the text by the Septuagint; and on a flyleaf he has written Dean Nowell's distich *Officium vespertinum*, with Latin and English renderings of his

[1] The decisive words of that on p. 86 (78) are omitted in Mr Medd's text and translation.

[2] *Donne's Works* iii. pp 388 sqq. (ed. Alford).

[3] *Answer to Cardinal Perron* ix.

own.[1] And secondly, the whole MS. has been worked over by a second hand (apparently not Drake's) and corrected by a copy akin to the Laudian MS., but probably not identical with it in contents; with the result that several of Wright's omissions, including the personal references, have been supplied, and some new matter, not found in L, is added (p. 3*).[2] All these restorations and additions were made before 1675, when they appear in the *editio princeps* of the Greek text; and all of them, except the contents of pp. 6, 7,[3] are earlier than 1648, since they are represented in Drake's translation. This MS. is referred to below by the symbol W and the work of the second hand by W².

3. In the Barham Library, now belonging to the Master of Pembroke College, Cambridge, is a third MS., a paper book, $5\frac{7}{8} \times 3\frac{3}{4}$ in., of 144 pages with gold edges, the last 10 being left blank, except that on p. 142 is written Nowell's distich with Drake's renderings. The hand writing is poor and unequal. The text was evidently copied from Wright's MS. before it had been worked over by the second hand, *i.e.* at least before 1648; and it has obviously no independent value. This MS. is represented below by the symbol B.

4. The Harleian MS. 6614, in the British Museum, is a paper book, $6\frac{1}{8} \times 4$ in., of 154 pages with gilt edges, bound in stamped leather with two clasps. Only 84 of the pages are written on; the rest are blank. A note on the first page, originally signed with the initials of an unknown 'J. W.,' now almost obliterated by those of an equally unknown 'V. M.,' which are also stamped on the binding, says that the MS. is 'ex manu propria Lancelotti Andrews Wintoniensis olim episcopo, sicut a fide dignis accepi.' But the handwriting, a somewhat bold and irregular 17th cent. script, with obvious mistakes of reading, is certainly not that of Andrewes. The text is wholly Latin, and consists of devotions, certainly by Andrewes, but not corresponding to anything in the Greek. Their authenticity is sufficiently proved by their character as compared with the other works of Andrewes, and by the fact that a confession of faith, of which fragments are found in the 'second part' of the first and subsequent editions of the *Preces*, here occurs in full.

This MS. is referred to below by the symbol H.

[1] Below p. 104. [2] Below p. 9. [3] Below pp. 13-15.

II

The first form in which any part of the original text of the *Preces privatae* was given to the world, was that of an appendix to some copies of the *Verus Christianus* of Dr David Stokes, published at the Clarendon Press in 1668.[1] In this appendix the author gives a series of specimens, some in Greek, some in Latin, and one rendered into English, derived from the papers of Lancelot Andrewes, which he had 'received from several hands' (p. 56). Some of these have never hitherto appeared elsewhere; others, as will be seen immediately, form part of the current editions, in some cases in a text more developed and finished than that of Stokes' appendix, which evidently in these cases reproduces a preliminary draft of what was afterwards worked up more carefully. In fact these extracts throw some light on the genesis of the prayers and make it clear that the matter of them grew under the bishop's hand. Matter derived from this source is indicated below by the symbol S in the margin.

The first comprehensive edition of the *Preces*, the *textus receptus*, was edited by Dr John Lamphire, Principal of Hart Hall, and published at the Clarendon Press in 1675, with the *imprimatur*, dated March 16, 1673, of the Vice-Chancellor, Dr Ralph Bathurst, President of Trinity, and under the title *Rev. Patris Lanc. Andrews Episc. Winton. Preces Privatæ Græcè & Latinè*. The sources of this edition are threefold: first, Wright's MS. as we have it, that is, after Drake had made his corrections and additions, and after it had been worked over by the second hand, forming 'pars prima' of the whole; secondly, matter supplied to the editor by Richard Drake from Andrewes' papers, mostly in Latin, and here forming the 'pars secunda'; and thirdly, Stokes' appendix, from which are derived the Greek meditations on 'the Last Judgment' and 'the Shortness of Human Life' appended to the 'pars

[1] The Brit. Mus. copy has the appendix: that of the Bodleian has not.

prima,' and perhaps some of the paragraphs of the second part which it has in common with Stokes. The Greek of the first part is accompanied throughout by a parallel Latin version printed on the opposite page. Two facts seem to shew that, if this Latin as a whole is not to be attributed to Andrewes, yet Lamphire at least used and incorporated the Latin of Andrewes' papers, so far as it went. For first, in a passage of which Stokes gives the Latin, Lamphire's Latin is identical with Stokes', while it does not exactly represent the parallel Greek;[1] and secondly, while Lamphire shews no signs of any knowledge of Andrewes' Latin sources, the Latin of his text agrees too closely with the sources to be an independent rendering of the Greek.[2] By way of appendix, Dr Lamphire has added, under a note,[3] the Greek Morning and Evening Hymns, *i.e.* the *Gloria in excelsis* and the Φῶς ἱλαρόν,[4] derived from Archbishop Ussher's *de Romanæ ecclesiæ Symbolo apostolico vetere*, published in 1647; and a Greek Ode on the Passion, written Ap. 19, 1633, by Thomas Master, Fellow of New College, apparently taken, along with the accompanying Latin version by Henry Jacob of Merton, from a pamphlet published at Oxford in 1658, under the title *D. Henrici Savilii τοῦ μακαρίτου, Oratio, coram regina Elizabetha Oxoniæ habita; aliæque doctiss. virorum opellæ posthumæ.*[5] This edition is referred to as O.

This text of the *Preces* was republished in two sizes in

[1] Lamphire p. 73 = Stokes p. 22 = pp. 59 sq., 269 below.

[2] See pp. 59 sq. (p. 52 ll. 20-30 below), 93 (69 ll. 27-37), 173 (277).

[3] P. 351: *Sequitur Hymnus Matutinus usûs antiquissimi in Ecclesiâ, ex MS.* Alexandrino *Bibliothecæ Regiæ. Accedit & Vespertinus, quia vetus. De utroque consulendus est Rev.* Usserius, *p.* 41, 43. *l.* de Symbolis. The text of the *Gloria in excelsis* is not in fact that of Cod. Alex.; see note on p. 23 l. 11 below.

[4] Below pp. 23, 104.

[5] This pamphlet contained also an English verse translation of the Ode by Abraham Cowley. T. Master, who was a friend of Lamphire's, had a considerable reputation as a writer of Greek odes. See *Dict. National Biog.* vol. xxxvii under his name. The Ode was published separately with an English translation in Eἰς τὴν τοῦ Χριστοῦ σταύρωσιν μονοστροφικά: *an ode on the Crucifixion of Christ: being a paraphrase of a Greek Hymn at the end of Bishop Andrewes' Devotions*, by R-t T-r, A.M. Greek and English. Edinb. 1742.

1828, with a new Latin preface, and some corrections and added references, by Peter Hall, under the title *Reverendi Patris Lanceloti Andrews episc: Wintoniensis Preces Privatæ Quotidianæ Græce et Latine: editio altera et emendatior* (London, Pickering); and an *editio tertia et emendatior* was issued by an anonymous editor and the same publisher in 1848, being Peter Hall's edition, with a short additional preface explaining that some rearrangements of the text of 1675 have been made and the references corrected. It was again independently edited in 1853 for the Library of Anglo-Catholic Theology, by Dr John Barrow, Principal of S. Edmund Hall, who collated Lamphire's text with Wright's copy and Stokes' appendix, and added as 'pars tertia' the Latin devotions of the Harleian MS., which were here printed for the first time. In 1865 Mr Frederick Meyrick, now Prebendary of Lincoln and Rector of Blickling, began a new edition with a beautifully printed issue of the Latin of the first part; in 1867 he added the Greek, in 1870 the second part, and in 1873 the third part. Again, in 1895, Mr Henry Veale, sometime Rector of Newcastle-under-Lyme, re-edited the first and second parts, with added headlines, marginal numberings, introduction, notes, etc., of no value.

Meanwhile, in 1892 Mr P. G. Medd, Rector of North Cerney, edited for the S.P.C.K. the text of the then recently recovered Laudian MS., supplying the blank at the end from Wright's copy, correcting the Hebrew, adding an apparatus of the readings of the Cambridge MSS. and the *textus receptus*, and in an introduction giving a history of the text. Unfortunately the reproduction of the text of L leaves something to be desired in point of accuracy.

III

So far we have been concerned with the MSS. and printed editions of the Greek and Latin of the *Preces*. But the book was given to the world in an English translation some time before any part of the original text was published.

In 1630 appeared *Institutiones piæ or directions to pray* by H. I. (London, Henry Seile). 'H. I.' is Henry Isaacson of Pembroke Hall, Cambridge, who lived with Andrewes for some time as his secretary. In the fourth edition of this work, published in 1655, after the date of Isaacson's death early in the same year, the title is altered to *Holy devotions with directions to pray . . . by the Right Reverend Father in God Lancelot Andrewes, late Bishop of Winchester ;* and in a new preface by Henry Seile the publisher, it is said: 'the true father and primary author of these Devotions was the glory of this Church, the great and eminent Andrews . . . and thus the parentage of this Book, which, like that of Cyrus, was, for divers years, concealed under a Shepherd's cottage, (a good and faithful Shepherd he was that concealed it) comes now to be vindicated to its own nativity: and the Child being of full age, desires to be known abroad in the world for her Father's daughter, the daughter of her true, not supposed Father.' In this form the book was re-issued several times up to 1684, and in 1834 it was rearranged and edited anew by W. H. Hale, Preacher of the Charterhouse. The new title and the statements of the preface are so far true to the facts, that the book certainly contains passages of considerable length which are found elsewhere among Andrewes' devotions; and other passages, which cannot be so verified, would seem from their method and character to be worked up from material supplied by him; and his influence is clear throughout. But the book as a whole cannot be ascribed to Andrewes. The form and style of the bulk of it is not in his manner. It has not seemed desirable to include in the present edition any of its contents, except what it has in common with other sources.[1]

In 1647 Humphrey Moseley published the *Private Devotions by the Right Reverend Father in God Lancelot Andrewes, late Bishop of Winchester*, a 12mo volume consisting of fragments of the matter which later editions have made familiar and a few things from the sermons, with very little, and that of no importance, which does not occur elsewhere. In range and general character it is quite unlike

[1] The *Institutiones piæ* is the source of what is attributed to Andrewes in Spinckes *The true Church of England Man's Companion to the Closet, or a complete Manual of Private Devotions* 1749 (frequently reprinted), and of the Litany in *A Litany and Prayers of the Holy Communion by Bp. Andrewes* London, Jas. Burns, 1844.

what has generally been known as 'Bp. Andrewes' Devotions.' On its publication, Richard Drake, who had been a scholar of Andrewes' College, 'finding' in it, as he says, 'a great invasion made upon' the bishop's 'honour,' 'resolved to pay' his 'due respects to his precious memory and to exercise so much charity, which' he 'had learned from his devotions, towards others, and not to engross to' his 'own private use and benefit, what' he 'was confident would be most serviceable and welcome to the Church of God,' but to publish an adequate version of the *Preces* from the copy he had obtained from Dr Wright. Accordingly the same publisher issued *A manual of the private devotions and meditations of the Right Reverend Father in God Lancelot Andrews, late Lord Bishop of Winchester : translated out of a fair Greek MS. of his Amanuensis by* R. D., *B.D.*, the preface being dated S. John Baptist's Day, 1648. This version represents Wright's MS. after most of the additions had been made by the second hand.[1] It was re-issued in *A manual of Private Devotions with a manual of directions for the Sick, by Lancelot Andrews, late Bishop of Winchester*, London, 1670; and subsequent editions appeared in 1674, 1682, 1692. In 1853 it was re-edited 'with corrections' in the *Churchman's Library*, and in 1854 by James Bliss in the *Library of Anglo-Catholic Theology*,[2] and a selection from it, with corrections, was published in 1855 and onwards in *A Manual of Private Devotions* (London, Masters).

Another translation, if so it can be called, made from the *editio princeps* of 1675, was published in 1730, under the title *Private Prayers translated from the Greek Devotions of Bp. Andrewes, with additions by Geo. Stanhope D.D.* Dr Stanhope, Dean of Canterbury, died in 1728, and this edition was published from his papers with a preface by J. Hutton, of King's College, Cambridge. It was re-edited by George Horne, Dean of Canterbury and President of Magdalen College, Oxford, afterwards Bishop of Norwich, between 1781 and 1790, and re-issued by the S.P.C.K. from 1808 onwards. Dr Stanhope's rendering can scarcely be called a translation : it is rather a grandiloquent paraphrase, with omissions and insertions and alterations which effectively obliterate the point and conciseness of the original. Its

[1] See above, p. xviii. [2] Andrewes *Minor Works*, pp. 223 sqq.

contents are chiefly the (Greek) morning and evening prayers, the morning prayers for a week, and the Dial. It was abridged and supplied with references by Burton Bouchier in *Prayers and offices of private devotion* (London, 1834); and reprinted as a whole, with part of Hutton's preface, an introduction, references, irrelevant notes, etc., and a supplement of prayers altered from some of those of the Book of Common Prayer, by Jos. Macardy in *The Heart: its meditations and exercises, comprising private prayers from the Greek devotions of Lancelot Andrews by George Stanhope, late Dean of Canterbury. Also from approved authorities an introduction, notes and supplement* (London, 1843). It was also the source of what is derived from Andrewes in *A few forms of morning and evening prayer, adapted for private and family devotion, from the works of Bishop Andrewes*, etc., by Stuart Corbett (London, 1827).

A new version was made by Peter Hall and published by Pickering in 1830, under the title *The Private Devotions of Lancelot Andrews, Bishop of Winchester, translated from the Greek and Latin . . . to which is added the Manual for the Sick by the same learned prelate: second edition corrected*, and it was re-issued in 1839, with additions to the preface.

In 1839 also, Edward Bickersteth, Rector of Walton, published a new translation of both the first and the second parts, with added titles and some emendations, in his work *The Book of Private Devotions, containing a collection of the most valuable early devotions of the Early Reformers and their successors in the Church of England.*

The 78th of the *Tracts for the Times*, published in 1840, consisted of *The Greek Devotions of Bishop Andrewes translated and arranged* by John Henry Newman, in a version of which R. W. Church has said that it is 'one of those rare translations which make an old book new.'[1] It embraces nearly the whole of the First Part, with some rearrangements, the object of which is not always clear. The version was re-issued with a preface and in a more tractable form in 1842 (Oxford, Parker). In 1844 John Mason Neale, in *Private Devotions of Bishop Andrewes translated from the Latin* (Oxford, Parker), completed the work with a version of the Second Part, omitting some fragmentary or perplexing

[1] *Pascal and other Sermons*, Lond. 1896, p. 86.

passages. This translation sometimes misses the sense: but it is not unworthy to stand beside Card. Newman's version of the Greek. The two were afterwards combined; and it is in this form that the Devotions have since been most easily accessible. These translations supplied the prayers for communion in *A Litany and Prayers of the Holy Communion* (London, Jas. Burns, 1844), and were the source of J. W. H. M[olyneux'] *Private prayers for members of the Church of England selected from the devotions of Bishop Andrewes* (London 1866, 1883), and formed the basis of *The Mantle of Prayer: a book of devotions compiled chiefly from those of Bishop Andrewes* (London, Masters, 1881) by A. N. with a preface by W. J. Butler, afterwards Dean of Lincoln.

In 1883 the late Edmund Venables, Precentor of Lincoln, revised these translations, chiefly in the way of substituting the language of the Authorised Version and the Prayer Book in quotations which Newman and Neale had re-rendered, and supplying Neale's omissions, and re-edited the whole, with a preface by J. R. Woodford, Bishop of Ely, and an interesting introduction of his own (*The Private Devotions of Lancelot Andrewes*, new ed., London, Suttaby, 1883). In 1896 Dr Alexander Whyte of S. George's Free Church, Edinburgh, in *Lancelot Andrewes and his Private Devotions: a biography, a transcript and an interpretation* (Edinburgh) rearranged a large part of the devotions, mainly following Newman and Neale's versions, and prefixed to them a depreciation of Andrewes and an interesting, but perhaps extravagant, appreciation of the devotions. And lastly, these versions are the basis of Mr J. E. Kempe's *Private Devotions of Bishop Andrewes selected and arranged with variations adapted to general use* (London S.P.C.K., 1897), in which the very large 'variations' were made 'with some reference to hints by Stanhope.'

Finally, in 1899 Mr Medd published an English translation of the Laudian MS. uniform with his edition of the text.

IV

The life of Lancelot Andrewes has often been written, and it is not proposed to rewrite it here. It is sufficient for the present purpose to recall the outlines of his history and the chief aspects of his character.

He was the son of John Andrewes, Master of Trinity House, and was born in 1555 in Thames St. in the parish of All Hallows Barking and baptized in the parish church by the Tower. He was sent first to the Cooper's Free School of Ratcliffe, in the parish of Stepney, under Master Ward, and then to the recently founded Merchant Taylors' under the headmastership of Richard Mulcaster. In 1571 he went up to Cambridge as a scholar of Pembroke Hall on the foundation of Dr Thomas Watts, Archdeacon of Middlesex, who nominated him to one of his six scholarships; and in the same year he was nominated by the Queen to a scholarship at Jesus College, Oxford, by the advice of the founder of the College. He took his degree in 1575, and was elected a fellow of Pembroke Hall in 1576; after which he resided till 1586, visiting his home for a month at Easter in each year; and during his holiday in 1580 he witnessed the earthquake which destroyed part of S. Paul's and, as we shall see, made a lasting impression on his mind. He was ordained deacon in 1580 and priest some time between this and 1585,[1] when he took his B.D. As Catechist of his College he lectured on the Decalogue, and the substance of his lectures is preserved in *The Pattern of Catechistical Doctrine*. In 1586 Henry Earl of Huntingdon, President of the North, made him his chaplain and took him with him to York, where, it is noticed, he reconciled many Roman Catholics to the English Church. Soon after, he became chaplain to Whitgift, Archbishop of Canterbury, and to the Queen. In 1589 Walsingham procured his presentation to the cure of S. Giles' Cripplegate, and to a prebend at Southwell, and later in the same year to the stall of S. Pancras in S. Paul's. Of his work at S. Giles' and S. Paul's, the S. Giles' sermons and the S. Paul's lectures on Genesis remain as monuments in the *Apospasmatia*.[2] In the same year, 1589, he was elected Master of his College in

[1] Sixteen years before his *Judgment of the Lambeth Articles* (*Cat. doct.* p. 294); so probably in 1580 or 1581.

[2] ΑΠΟΣΠΑΣΜΑΤΙΑ SACRA *or a collection of posthumous and orphan lectures delivered at St Pauls and St Giles his Church . . . never before extant* London, 1657.

succession to Fulke, and held the office till 1605. In 1597 he became a prebendary of Westminster, and in 1601 succeeded Goodman as Dean; and in this capacity he assisted, in the office belonging to the Dean of Westminster, at the Coronation of James I on S. James' Day 1603, the first coronation celebrated in English. In 1604 he took part in the Hampton Court Conference, where he was especially prominent in the defence of the sign of the cross in baptism;[1] and in the same year he was appointed one of the translators of what became the 'Authorised Version' of the Bible, published in 1611. In 1605 he was consecrated to the see of Chichester, in succession to Antony Watson, became Lord High Almoner, and resigned the Mastership of Pembroke Hall. While bishop of Chichester he began his controversy with 'Matthaeus Tortus,' Cardinal Robert Bellarmin, and published *Tortura Torti* in 1609, in which year he was translated to Ely, in succession to Martin Heaton, and here he continued the controversy by the publication of the *Responsio ad Apologiam Cardinalis Bellarmini* in 1610. On the death of Bancroft in this year, it was generally expected that Andrewes would succeed to the see of Canterbury; but this was not to be, and Abbot became archbishop. In 1618 Andrewes was translated to Winchester, as successor to James Montague, and in 1619 became Dean of the Chapel Royal. In 1621 he was one of the group of peers who attended Francis Bacon to accept the acknowledgment of his confession made to the Upper House; and in the same year, as a member of the commission in Abbot's irregularity, incurred by accidental homicide, he checked the severe judgment of his colleagues and secured an opinion favourable to the metropolitan. In the beginning of 1625 he was unable, through his own illness, to attend the King in his last sickness, and on Sept. 26 of the next year himself died, and was buried on Nov. 11 behind the high altar of S. Saviour's, Southwark, where his tomb and effigy are still to be seen.

In his preface to the *Holy devotions with directions to pray*—that is, the second edition of the *Institutiones piæ*—Henry Seile sums up the life of Andrewes in the words, 'Dr Andrews in the School, Bishop Andrews in the Pulpit,

[1] Cardwell *Conferences* p. 198.

Saint Andrews in the Closet.' And this represents the three conspicuous aspects of the life of the prelate, as scholar and theologian, ecclesiastic, and saint.

1. He was pre-eminently a scholar. His studiousness began in his early years, and was excessive. As a schoolboy he had to be forced to play games, and as an undergraduate he disliked both indoor and outdoor games and found his recreation in walking, whether with a companion with whom he discussed what interested him, or alone, occupying himself with the observation of nature, which continued to be his chief relaxation all his life long, and supplied the basis of a knowledge of natural science which was not merely dilettante but was recognised as something more by Francis Bacon, who notes that he had pretensions to some experiments.[1] At school he made brilliant progress in Latin, Greek, and Hebrew; and at Cambridge he was among the first representatives of the reviving Greek scholarship. His Easter holiday in London was generally devoted to getting some knowledge of a new language, with the result that he became a considerable linguist, till, in Fuller's whimsical words, he was 'so skilled in all (especially oriental) languages, that some conceived he might, if then living, have served as interpreter-general in the confusion of tongues.'[2] He was among the most considerable, if not himself the most considerable, of English scholars, in an age of great scholars, with something of an European reputation; the correspondent of Cluverius and Vossius, of Grotius, Erpenius and Heinsius, the closest friend of Casaubon, the literary censor of Bacon—his 'inquisitor,' as Bacon calls him—the associate of Selden, the friend and encourager of his brilliant juniors, George Herbert[3] and John Donne,[4] and the thoughtful and munificent patron of plenty of young and promising scholars, and, as Dean of Westminster, the keen promoter of the interests of Westminster School. After taking his master's degree, he devoted himself chiefly to Theology, and his lectures as Catechist of Pembroke Hall attracted large audiences from the whole University and the surrounding country. He was a man

[1] Bacon *Works*, ed. Ellis and Spedding, iv p. 63.
[2] Fuller *Church History of Britain* xi 17 § 46.
[3] I. Walton *Life of Mr George Herbert*.
[4] Jessop *John Donne* p. 51.

after the Second Solomon's own heart, and the King turned to him to defend him against the assaults of the great Bellarmin, who attacked the imposition of the oath on Roman Catholics after the Gunpowder Plot; with the result that against his will and inclination he became the official controversialist of the English Church, and proved its adequate defender when the guns of the new Jesuit learning were turned upon it. He also replied to Cardinal Perron's strictures on the Anglican position, and carried on a controversy with the protestant du Moulin. His library, so far as can be judged from that part of it which he bequeathed to Pembroke Hall, while chiefly theological, was yet of considerable range.[1] And his learning is conspicuous enough in his works, where, learned as they obviously are, and found to be still more so if anyone will be at the pains to examine their sources, he does not think it necessary, after the modern fashion, to give references for all he has to say. His extraordinarily minute knowledge of the Holy Scriptures is plain to everybody; and his command of it and of the rest of his learning, is such that it perhaps serves to conceal his originality. His wealth of reminiscence is such, and is so inwrought into the texture of his mind, that he instinctively uses it to express anything he has to say. To one to whom knowledge is so large an element in life and is itself so living a thing; whose learning is so assimilated as to be identified with his spontaneous self, and has become as available as language itself, originality and reminiscence become in a measure identical; the new can be expressed as a combination of older elements. But originality was scarcely the chief note of his mind. He is marked rather by great, solid and readily-available learning than by great original ideas. He was scholarly, historical, inductive, rather than speculative and creative. His imagination was collective and organising, as it were, rather than originative. It showed itself in new combinations of existing material, rather than in substantively new contributions. He took up what he found and fused it into a new whole, and that often with something of real poetic distinction. He was a scholar, with a scholar's instinct for analysis and sense of the value of words and appreciation of form. But he was not a *litterateur*. His English

[1] See the list in *Minor Works* p. cxiv. sqq.

style has been criticised, and justly. In formal composition he was not happy, so far as we have the means of judging. And in the period of his mature life, we have not much to judge from; for the great sermons are scarcely formal compositions, for all the pains he bestowed on them; they are rather exhaustive notes, written under the stimulus of a vivid imagination of a congenial audience, and in language not strictly literary but colloquial and in a way casual, and obviously different from what he used when he was writing to be read and not to be heard. It is clear, from what was said of him as a preacher, that his delivery was a very real part of the charm of his sermons; and perhaps no one could read them aloud with effect who did not possess a considerable faculty of dramatic interpretation. This applies chiefly to the great sermons which belong mostly to his later life. With the earlier ones the case is rather different; it seems clear that they are much more of the nature of formal compositions, and were not written under the same conditions. His audiences at S. Giles' and S. Paul's were not so congenial intellectually as the more educated audiences of the Court, and this probably reacted on his style; he had to compose his sermons, rather than to make notes, with the consequence that in form they were rather dull and unadorned. Besides, he was less experienced, and perhaps had not yet gained the colloquial confidence of his later years. But perhaps there is a reason for the defect of his English style quite apart from this. Isaac Williams has accounted for his own defective style by the fact that as a boy he habitually thought in Latin, and his written English was a translation of Latin thoughts.[1] It is probable that the same was the case more or less with Andrewes, and that Latin was his language of soliloquy; and he lived too habitually in the medium of other languages than his mother-tongue to leave his English style much chance. His sermons are full of Latin and Greek, and he gives precedence to the Vulgate in reciting his text. It was the habit of preachers of his day to interlard their sermons with Latin; and sometimes this degenerates into a mere trick with a result as ludicrous as that of Buckeridge's sermon at Andrewes' funeral, in which the Latin seems often to be nothing but a quite gratuitous trans-

[1] *Autobiography* pp. 5, 21.

lation of what is just going to be said in English. But this is not so with Andrewes; his Latin and Greek and Hebrew has a reason, whether as the *ipsissima verba* of what he is quoting, or as adding something to the point and clearness and exactness of what he is saying. His Latin composition, in the *Opuscula* and the controversy with Bellarmin, is perhaps livelier and readier than his formal English; but it is not the living, lucid, limpid tongue of the Middle Ages, but the artificial classicised Latin that resulted from the Renaissance. Of his Greek perhaps no specimen remains outside the Devotions.

2. As an ecclesiastic Andrewes was the most notable man of his day in England. He was rising under Elizabeth and might earlier have taken the lead if he had been willing to accept the bishoprics that were offered him at the price of the sacrilege which he loathed, the sacrifice of their revenues to the Tudor rapacity. Under James I he soon found his level. His experience was varied and representative. As Catechist of his College, as Chaplain to the President of the North and to Whitgift, as Vicar of S. Giles' and canon of Southwell, S. Paul's, and Westminster, and Dean of the last, and as bishop successively of Chichester, Ely and Winchester, he had experience of most of the possible spheres and conditions of ecclesiastical life. And in them all he represented a new type which was emerging after the degradation of the preceding period. What the general standard was and what he thought of it, can be gathered from his Convocation sermon in 1593,[1] where he holds up the mirror to the clergy, and especially to the bishops, and lashes their unworthiness—their sloth and neglect and indifference, their want of learning and the ineptitude of their preaching, their servility to the great, their low standard of life, their laborious solicitude for their own interests and neglect of those of their flocks and of the good of the Church, their indifference as well about error in doctrine and life as about the edification of the faithful, their spoliation of the Church and venal dispensations and general rapacity, their scandalous ordinations, their simony and sacrilege and the prostitution of ecclesiastical censures. This, and more, is what men think of them, and he tells them that it is true, and warns them that men's eyes are on them, and that if they will not attend to their flocks, their flocks will

[1] *Opuscula posthuma* pp. 29 sqq.

soon attend to them. It is interesting to compare this sermon with Colet's famous Convocation sermon eighty years before. After sixty years of professed reformation, the state of things is very much what it was; only Andrewes' picture is darker and his chastisement more severe. From this, and from the inquiries in his Visitation Articles something can be gathered of what he thought the standard of clerical life ought to be and of what he aimed at in his own life. There is not much recorded of the details of his ecclesiastical life. To the generality he would chiefly be known as a preacher and as the great preacher of his day. He was a 'painful' preacher, taking infinite trouble with his sermons; he said of himself that if he preached twice in a day, he prated once. Of his sermons, besides the famous 96, there survive the 19 on *Prayer and the Lord's Prayer*, the 7 on the *Temptation*, a number of parochial sermons at S. Giles', and the lectures on the early chapters of Genesis given partly at S. Paul's, partly at S. Giles'. Their learning and compact matter indicate the perhaps over-severe standard he applied when he complained of the ignorant ineptitude of contemporary preaching. But as the most notable preacher of his day, he used his opportunity to rebuke and counteract the 'auricular profession,' as he calls it, of an age which exaggerated the importance of preaching, and to insist that the hearing of sermons is not the chief part of religious observance, and that the Word is the stimulus to devotion and is useless unless it issue in this and in its central highest act, the communion of the Eucharist. Perhaps the only detail of his spiritual ministration which is explicitly recorded is that as Prebendary of S. Pancras, and therefore *ex officio* Penitentiary, he attended in the north aisle of S. Paul's in Lent in readiness for any who desired to consult him. It is needless to say that this resulted in a charge of 'popery.' In his sermon on *Absolution* he expounds the doctrine and bearing of the power of the keys. For the exercise of the 'key of knowledge' he had qualified himself while at Cambridge and had become 'well-seen in cases of conscience' and acquired a reputation as a casuist. His sense of the neglect of this key he expresses in another sermon. 'I take it to be an error . . to think the fruits of repentance, and the worth of them, to be a matter any common man can skill of well enough; needs never ask

St John or St Paul what he should do; knows what he should do as well as St Paul or St John either. And that it is not rather a matter wherein we need the counsel and direction of such as are professed that way. Truly it is neither the least, nor the last, part of our learning to be able to give answer and direction in this point. But therefore laid aside and neglected by us, because not sought after by you. Therefore not studied, but by very few, *quia nemo nos interrogat*, because it is grown out of request quite. We have learned, I know not where, a new, a shorter course, which flesh and blood better likes of. To pass the whole course of our life, and, in the whole course of our life, not to be able to set down, where, or when, or what we did, when we did that which we call repenting; what fruits there came of it; what those fruits might be worth. And but even a little before our death (and as little as may be), not till the world have given us over, then, lo, to come to our *quid faciemus?* to ask, "what we should do?" when we are able to do nothing. And then must one come, and (as we call it) speak comfortably to us, that is, minister to us a little Divinity laudanum, rather stupefactive for the present than doing any sound good; and so take our leaves to go meet with *ira ventura*. This way, this fashion of repenting, St John knew it not; it is far from his *fructus dignos;* St Paul knew it not; it is far from his *opera digna*. And I can say little to it, but I pray God it deceive us not.'[1] In the 16th of his Visitation articles is an inquiry as to the violation of the seal of confession.

In the sermons again Andrewes complains of the want of worship and its expression in his day. 'Now, adoration is laid aside, and with the most, neglected quite. Most come and go without it, nay they scarce know what it is. And with how little reverence, how evil beseeming us, we use ourselves in the church, coming in thither, staying there, departing thence, let the world judge. Why? What are we to the glorious saints in heaven? Do not they worship thus? Off go their "crowns," down "before the throne they cast them," and "fall down" themselves after, when they worship. Are we better than they? Nay, are we better than his saints on earth, that have ever seemed to go toc far, rather than to come too short in this

[1] *Sermon Repent. and Fasting* viii (i pp. 450 sq.).

point.'[1] 'Our religion and *cultus* must be uncovered, and a barefaced religion; we would not use to come before a mean prince, as we do before the King of kings and Lord of lords, even the God of heaven and earth. "The four and twenty elders fell down before Him that sat on the throne, and worshipped Him that liveth for ever, and cast their crowns before His throne." The wandering eye must learn to be "fastened on Him" and "the work of justice" and "peace." The worship of the "knees" "to bow" and "kneel before the Lord their maker." Our feet are to "come before his face; for the Lord is a great God and a great King above all gods." Jacob though he were not able to stand or kneel, yet because he would use some corporal service "leaned upon his staff and worshipped God." . . . This must be done as duty due unto God.'[2] Accordingly, Andrewes was the 'ritualist' of his day. In Prynne's indictment of Archbishop Laud, there is produced a plan of Andrewes' chapel, and a description of his altar with its lights and cushions, the canister for the wafers and the basin for the oblations, the cruet for the 'water of mixture,' the credence and provision for the lavatory, the censer and incense-boat, copes and altar-cloths and veil.[3] And in the *Notes on the Book of Common Prayer*[4] there is an elaborate ceremonial of the altar, which if carried out to-day, would perhaps even now be surprising. Henry Isaacson, Andrewes' chaplain and biographer, remarks on the impression produced by the worship of the chapel at Ely: 'the souls of many that *obiter* came thither in time of divine service, were very much elevated, and they stirred up to the like reverend deportment. Yea some that had been there were so taken with it, that they desired to end their days in the bishop of Ely's chapel.'[5] But he did not enforce his own standard of worship on other people; he was 'content with the enjoying without the enjoining.'[6]

[1] *Serm. Gunpowder Treason* ix (iv p. 374).

[2] *Serm. Temptation* (v p. 554): cf. *ib.* pp. 60, 231, i p. 262, *Opuscula posthuma* p. 49.

[3] See *Minor Works* pp. xcvii sqq.

[4] *Minor Works* pp. 151 sqq. Notice his frank assertion of the pagan analogues and origins of Christian ceremonies in *A discourse of ceremonies* (*Cat. doct.* p. 365 sqq.).

[5] *Minor Works* p. xiii.

[6] Fuller *Church History* xi 48.

3. The saintly character of the 'good bishop' was recognised by his contemporaries. His 'whiteness of soul' inspired reverence; and in the court of James I he alone could awe the royal chatterbox into some silence.[1] Those who knew him dwell upon his zeal and piety, as illustrated by his hours of private devotion, the worship of his chapel, and his strict observance of Lent and Embertides and the other fasts; his charity and munificence, as exemplified by his large and ever-increasing and thoughtful alms during his lifetime, and his imaginative bequests, which were characteristically minute in their application, on his death; his fidelity in the discharge of his public duties, in the maintenance and improvement of the property entrusted to him in his several benefices, in the distribution of his patronage, and his hatred of simony and sacrilege and usury, and in the exercise of the influence which his position gave him for the promotion of the right men; his gratitude to his benefactors, in his care for them, their memory and their families; his generous hospitality, especially to scholars and strangers; his affability and geniality, his 'extraordinary kindness' and 'wonderful memory' for persons and places, and his 'grave facetiousness'; and his modesty and humility.[2]

And all this was grounded in a large, clear and definite theology. 'From *nescitis* cometh no good; without knowledge the soul itself is not good. *Nescitis quid petatis*—no good prayer; *adoratis quod nescitis*—no good worship. And so, ignorant devotion, implicit faith, blind obedience all rebuked. Zeal, if not *secundum scientiam*, can not be *secundum conscientiam*.'[3] His theology is the Catholic Faith, neither pared away on the one hand, nor embellished with questionable deductions on the other. '*Compass Sion and go round about her*. For one Canon given of God, two testaments, three symbols, the four first councils, five centuries and the series of Fathers therein, fix the rule of religion.'[4] So stated this might no doubt easily be criticised; but in substance it represents the defensible position arrived at consciously or unconsciously by the English Church. It repre-

[1] *Ib.* 46.
[2] See *Minor Works* pp. xii-xxv.
[3] *Serm. Gunpowder Tr.* iii (iv p. 250).
[4] *Opuscula* p. 90; *Respons. ad Bellarm.* p. 26.

sents to Andrewes the proportionate Catholic religion—what he fought for in the confusions of his time, distinguishing it on the one hand from vain speculations and intrusions into what we do not and can not know, from vain imaginations and 'idiolatries' positive and negative, and on the other from dubious deductions claiming to be of faith. There are for him such things as *principal* doctrines, and 'there is no *principal dogma* in which we do not agree with the Fathers and they with us.'[1] Everything is not on the same level and equally essential. And so—'Blessed be God that among divers other mysteries about which there are so many mists and clouds of controversies raised in all ages and even in this of ours, hath yet left us some clear and without controversy; manifest and yet great; and again great and yet manifest. So great as no exception to be taken; so manifest as no question to be made about them. Withal, to reform our judgments in this point. For a false conceit is crept into the minds of men, to think the points of religion that be manifest to be certain petty points scarce worth the hearing. Those —yea those be great and none but those, that have great disputes about them. It is not so: τὰ μὲν ἀναγκαῖα &c. Those that are necessary He hath made plain: those that are not plain, not necessary. What better proof than this here? [1 Tim. iii 16.] This here a mystery, a great one —religion hath no greater—yet manifest and *in confuso* with all Christians. Zachary's prophecy and promise touching Christ, wherewith he concludeth his *Benedictus* (we hear it every day) shall not deceive us for this mystery: He came "to guide our feet into the way of peace." A way of peace then there shall be whereof all parts shall agree, even in the midst of a world of controversies. That there need not such ado in complaining, if men did not delight rather to be treading mazes than to walk in the ways of peace. For even still such a way there is, which lieth fair enough and would lead us sure enough to salvation, if leaving those other rough labyrinths we would but be "shod with the preparation of the Gospel of peace." Yea further the Apostle doth assure us that if whereunto we are come and wherein we all agree, we would constantly proceed by the rule, these things wherein we are "otherwise minded," even them would God reveal

[1] *Respons. ad Bellarm.* p. 70.

unto us. That is he maketh no controversy but controversies would cease, if conscience were made of the practice of that which is out of controversy. And I would to God it were so, and that this here and such other *manifeste magna* were in account. With the Apostle himself it was so . . . in that having been "ravished in spirit up to the third heavens and there heard wonderful high mysteries past man's utterance"; yet reckoned he all those nothing in comparison of this plain mystery here, nay "esteemed himself not to know anything at all" but this.'[1] In broad outline the theology which he preached, and in which he apparently hoped that the practice of that which is out of controversy would generally issue, is the Creed, professed by a Catholic Church, wherein the Holy Ghost, through a ministry of apostolic succession and divine right,[2] regenerates men in baptism, confirms them by the imposition of hands, absolves them by a second imposition of hands, in the exercise of the keys, 'the Church's act,' by which 'God ordinarily proceedeth'[3]; feeds them with the body and blood of Christ our Lord in the most holy mysteries of the Eucharist, which impart what they represent, in which there is at once a sacrifice and a communion.[4] In the Church, men, 'not trusting in their own righteousness,'[5] are to live in faith and hope and love, in a disciplined life of penitence and its fruits and obedience to the commandments, in prayer and fasting and almsgiving, bringing forth the fruit of the Spirit in order, peace and comeliness. With this as the clue he was free to range over the broad field of Holy Scripture and literature and experience, and to illustrate and expand and embellish it with all that knowledge and imagination could find there. In this he looked for that peace, of which he was 'avidior fortasse quam par est.'[6] In an age when men were for penetrating the mysteries of the divine predestination and making it the substance of religion, Andrewes strove to call them back to the 'plain mystery' of the Faith, and avowed that in the 16 years since he was

[1] *Serm. Nativity* iii (i p. 35); cf. *ib.* xi (i p. 191).
[2] *Opuscula posthuma*, pp. 183, 187; *Serm. Absolution* (v 92).
[3] *Serm. Pent.* v (iii 191), *Absolution* (v 93).
[4] *Serm. Res.* xii (ii 402), *Nativ.* xii (i 213); *Res.* vii (ii 300), *Imagin.* (v 66 sq.); and conclusions of Christmas, Easter, and Whitsunday sermons *passim*.
[5] See *Serm. Justification* (v. 106 sqq.). [6] *Opuscula posth.* p. 48.

ordained priest he had never ventured to discuss publicly or privately, or to preach on, predestination.[1] In an age which prated of faith, he insisted that the value of faith lay, not in itself, but in its object and its moral issues and the effort it inspires: 'of itself it is but a bare act, faith; a thing indifferent: the virtue and the value of it is from the object it believeth in; if that be right, all is right'[2]: 'neither fear, if it be fear alone, nor faith, if it be faith alone, is accepted of Him':[3] 'we must not lie still, like lumps of flesh, laying all upon Christ's shoulders.'[4] In an age of new ecclesiastical systems, he was content, and more than content, with the traditional system as he found it represented in the English Church, in so far as that was true to itself.

V

The purpose of recalling all this is to suggest what is likely to be found in the *Preces* and to indicate what is in fact found there and illustrate it by anticipation.

For the *Preces* are in a measure an autobiography. In his prayers, Andrewes is real, actual, detailed. He recounts, in thanksgiving and intercession, his circumstances and the conditions of his time: his devotion is brought to bear on his experience, and is marked by the absence of all vagueness and mere generality. He commemorates his birth in the City, 'of honest parentage,' in soundness of mind, senses and limb, in 'competent state' and 'honest fortune,' so as in after life never to have occasion 'either to flatter or to borrow'; in 'times of peace,' such as it was in the middle of the 16th century; his baptism at All Hallows and his religious bringing up; his two schools and 'gentle masters'; his College and the benefactors to whom he owed his education; his 'attentive pupils' and 'likeminded colleagues,' 'sincere friends' and 'faithful servants,' and all who had been of use to him 'by their writings, sermons, conversations, examples, rebukes, injuries.' He remembers an impressive event, like the earthquake of 1580; and to the end gives

1 *Judgment of the Lambeth Articles* (*Cat. doct.* p. 294).
2 *Serm. Pent.* xiii (iii 345); cf. *S. Giles' Lectt.* p. 544.
3 *Serm. Pent.* xii (iii 337).
4 *Serm. Tempt.* (v 483).

thanks and prays for all the cures and benefices he had held, and the souls who had been committed to his charge. And behind it all, he recalls his spiritual experience and his sense of the divine care and patience; his 'calling, recalling and further recalling manifold,' God's 'forbearance, longsuffering and long longsuffering, many times, many years.'[1]

And as the background of his own life, we catch sight of the large conditions of the world and the Church, the England and the Europe, the English Church and the Christendom, of his day. There is the Catholic Church and the unreclaimed world of 'pagans, Turks, Jews' beyond demanding her 'increase'; the long schism of East and West: the Eastern Church under the heel of the barbarian and crying for 'deliverance and reunion'; Western Christendom, torn and dislocated by the calamities of the 16th century, needing 'readjustment and pacification'; the British Church, 'keeping' indeed 'that which was committed to her, teaching the way of peace, maintaining,' in theory at least, 'order, stability and comeliness,' with 'pastors according to God's heart' as compared with those of the earlier years of Elizabeth; and yet not to be idealised, but all too imperfect in her attainment and wavering in her hold, and needing just the prayer for 'the restoration of the things that are wanting and the strengthening of the things that remain, which were ready to vanish away'[2]; a Christendom beset by the 'evils and troubles' which he probes and satirises and chastises in the Sermons—private interpretation, and innovation, the teaching of strange doctrine and doting about questions and making endless strifes, the dangers of heresies and schisms and scandals, of subservience to the civil power, indifference and contempt, arbitrary rule, robbery and simony and sacrilege, sectarianism and ignorance and the upstart pride of an unlearned clergy, and a meddling and censorious laity.[3] And in the civil sphere he has his eye on the commonwealths of the world and on his own, and their several estates and institutions; kings and lords and commons, magistrates, army and navy, education and commerce, farming, handicrafts, even the beggars. As an Englishman, we can see in him the glow of the pride and joy of the later years of

[1] Pp. 14, 61, 85 sq., 223 sqq., 272.
[2] Pp. 36, 60.
[3] Pp. 243, 268.

it sometimes leaves something to be desired in point of correctness; and in particular he shares with his contemporaries, the translators of the Authorised Version of the New Testament, a curious elementary defect in his inability to manage the combination of article, adjective and substantive, and seems unconscious that ὁ ἄνθρωπος ἀγαθός cannot mean 'the good man.'

Like much of the Sermons, the *Preces* are not original. In the whole mass of them there are comparatively few lines, perhaps none, that, considered apart, are wholly original: they are for the most part a mosaic of quotations. What has been said of Gray as a poet can be said, *mutatis mutandis*, of Andrewes as a devotional writer: 'Gray, if we may believe the commentators, has not an idea, scarcely an epithet, that he can call his own'; only the quotation must be continued —'and yet he is, in the best sense, one of the classics of English literature. He had exquisite felicity of choice; his dictionary had no vulgar word in it, no harsh one, but all culled from the luckiest moods of poets, and with a faint but delicious aroma of association; he had a perfect sense of sound, and one idea without which all poetic outfit (*si absit prudentia*) is of little avail—that of combination and arrangement, in short, of art.' [1]

The range of his materials and the use he makes of them, if it is inadequate to represent, yet suggests and illustrates, his learning. He seldom indicates the sources of his matter. The MSS. have a few original scriptural references; the greater part of the Harleian MS. gives the scriptural references with considerable fulness; and Drake has added a large number of references, one patristic, a few liturgical, the rest scriptural, in Wright's MS. Dr Lamphire gives a great many, mostly scriptural, in the Latin of the First Part; in the Second Part, the general indications of authors, sometimes misplaced, in the Reflexions on the several departments of devotion, seem to be original; but whether the references throughout the Second Part are original or are due to the editor cannot be determined. Later editors have dealt more fully with the scriptural sources; but no one seems to have attempted to trace the sources at all exhaustively. It is of course a task of some difficulty, and it must be more or less

[1] J. R. Lowell *My Study Windows*, 'Carlyle.'

a matter of accident, to distinguish them, nor is it always possible to say from which of two or more sources a given phrase or suggestion is in fact derived. But it is possible to indicate generally the range and character of the sources.

The first and principal source is Holy Scripture. For Andrewes devotion is the purpose of Holy Scripture. '*Thou hast magnified* 1. *thy Name and* 2. *thy Word above all things;* 1. His Name, and 2. His Word. His Name for our invocation, his Word for our instruction. And these two, as they are the highest things in God's account, so are they to be in ours. Not the Word only, which carrieth all away in a manner in these days, but his Name also no less. For in the setting them down, the Holy Ghost giveth the first place to the Name. . . . And the very hearing of the Word itself is that we may call upon His Name. *How shall they call on* his Name *whom they have not heard? How shall they hear without a preacher?* So that preaching and hearing of the Word are both ordained for the calling on of this Name.'[1] Accordingly Andrewes uses the whole Scripture as a treasury of devotion. William Law has said, 'If [people] were to collect the best forms of devotion, to use themselves to transcribe the finest passages of Scripture-prayer; if they were to collect the devotions, confessions, petitions, praises, resignations and thanksgivings which are scattered up and down in the Psalms and range them under proper heads as so much proper fuel for the flame of their own devotion; if their minds were often thus employed, sometimes meditating upon them, sometimes getting them by heart and making them as habitual as their own thoughts, how fervently would they pray, who came thus prepared to prayer.'[2] This on a large scale was Andrewes' method, and it is likely that Law had the *Preces* in view when he wrote. Anyone who knows anything of the *Sermons* will recognise Andrewes' astonishing knowledge of the Bible, in its original texts and in its principal versions and in its minute details, and his spontaneity and dexterity in the use of it. And the same is observable in the devotions. In the Greek parts of them he uses of course the original of the New Testament; and for the Old

[1] *Serm. Justification* (v 107).

[2] *Serious Call* xiv, quoted in this connexion by Dr A. Whyte in *Lancelot Andrewes* p. 34.

Testament he uses the Septuagint version, but here he frequently corrects the text by the Hebrew, or uses the Hebrew instead of or in addition to the Septuagint. In the Latin prayers, while his basis is the Vulgate, he habitually corrects it by the originals, or renders these anew, with or without reminiscences of the Vulgate in his mind. There is the same range of quotation as in the *Sermons*, the same imaginative skill in combination, the same appreciation of symbolical language, the same pregnant use of types. And in fact at times a commentary is needed to elucidate his meaning. Happily he generally supplies it somewhere in his other works; but sometimes it is impossible to be sure that one has caught his meaning or got to the bottom of an allusion, since his application of some passages seems to be determined by some ancient or mediæval comment on them or use of them. His quotations and allusions range over nearly all the books of the Bible: of the Old Testament all are used except perhaps Ruth, Obadiah, Nahum, Zephaniah and Haggai; of the Deutero-canonical books all but 1 and 2 (3 and 4) Esdras, the additions to Esther, Susannah, Bel, and the Maccabees—and here again he is making an implicit protest against the puritan 'imagination' that will tolerate no use of the Apocrypha;[1] of the New Testament he uses all the books except Philemon, and the 2nd and 3rd Epistles of S. John. The *Preces* point the way to a devotional concordance to the Bible; Andrewes develops whole subjects and turns them round, as it were, and observes them on all sides by collecting and arranging the allusions contained in the Holy Scriptures; he collects materials for whole departments and disposes them for meditation. And he thinks in terms of the Bible and its typical figures. The 'evils and difficulties' in Church and State alluded to above, are mostly recounted, not in abstract terms, but in the concrete form of the typical figures of Holy Scripture—Asshur, Jeroboam, Rehoboam and the rest.[2] And so it is elsewhere; like the *Sermons* the devotions are a study in the symbolism of the Bible; he delights in it and means something quite definite by it; it is no cover for vagueness or looseness of thought,

[1] *Serm. Worshipping of Imaginations* (v. 61).
[2] Below, pp. 243, 268.

but a deliberate form of expression. In short, he has brought the Sacred Scriptures in detail into definite relation with actual experience, and has studied them in this relation till he has found them typical throughout and in detail.

Next, Andrewes used existing devotional collections—those of the Synagogue, of the Eastern Church and of Latin Christendom. He uses them freely, either quoting them at length, or weaving together lines, phrases, words, picked up here and there over a whole book. But it is not merely a matter of direct quotation; he knows how to follow up a clue or a suggestion and to construct new forms on old models. And here as elsewhere, he freely modifies and adapts his material to the purpose he has in view.

The Prayers of the Synagogue had been frequently printed from 1485 onwards. Andrewes uses the rite of the Spanish Sephardim, in some points of detail differing from that of the German Ashkenazim, which has been adopted by the modern United Synagogue. His use of this source is not very frequent and is confined mostly to the prayers for Sunday and one or two of the forms of thanksgiving.[1]

Of the Greek Service-books he makes large use. They were easily accessible in his day; and in his own library he possessed the edition of the liturgies of S. James, S. Basil and S. Chrysostom published at Paris in 1560 by Morel under the title Λειτουργίαι τῶν ἁγίων πατέρων; the *Triodion*, containing the proper of Lent and the three preceding weeks, of 1614; the *Pentekostarion* (the proper of Eastertide) of 1602; and the *Menaea* (the service of the immovable feasts) of 1599-1614.[2] Of these he uses the first frequently, and the rest probably more often than it has been possible to trace, since they form so considerable a literature that it is difficult to note particular quotations. But the *Horologion*, which corresponds to the Western Breviary and was published frequently from 1509 onwards, has left a marked and easily recognised impress on the *Preces*.

Of the Latin Service-books, he makes some use of the *Missal*, of which he possessed copies according to the York

[1] Below, pp. 53-55, 201 sqq., 226.
[2] See *Minor Works*, pp. cxv (126), cxviii (309, 310).

and the Roman uses,[1] of the *Manual* or *Ritual*, of which he possessed a MS. copy according to the use of York,[2] and of the *Breviary*. But his principal source among the Latin books was that which was variously known as *Horae beatae Mariae virginis*, *The Primer*, *Horarium*, *Encheiridion* or *Hortulus animae*. This book consisted essentially of the additional offices which from the ixth century onwards became the customary supplement to the Services of the Canonical Hours, viz. the Offices of the B.V.M. and of the Dead, the Litany, and the Penitential and Gradual Psalms.[3] In the xvth century at least it was amplified by the addition of further devotions, traditional or new, Latin or vernacular, varying from country to country and from edition to edition, till it became a complete book of private prayers, the prototype of the manuals of daily devotions of modern times. In the xvith century in England it was several times reformed; and a reformed and authorised Roman *Horae* was issued in 1571. Andrewes used one of the editions of the Sarum *Horae* published at Paris for Fr. Byrckman in 1511 and onwards,[4] and apparently also some other edition, perhaps one of the *Prymers* of 1537.

Besides these public or official collections, Andrewes apparently used directly or indirectly the more strictly private collections which were current under the names of S. Augustine and S. Anselm; like the *Meditations*, the *Soliloquies* and the *Speculum* attributed to the former, a somewhat formless accumulation of intense mediæval monastic devotion[5]; and the *Prayers* and *Meditations* of the latter, which he certainly sometimes quotes through the medium of the *Horae*, and probably also directly. He certainly also made some use of the *Golden Litany*, a fine mediæval pleading of the Life and Passion, Resurrection and Ascension of our Lord; and of the *Golden Legend*, a companion to the Christian year, containing instructions on the seasons, fasts and festivals, and the lives of the Saints, compiled by Jacobus de Voragine in about 1275 and printed in 1470 and frequently afterwards. It

[1] See *Minor Works*, p. cxv (127, 128). [2] *Ib*. pp. cxv, cxviii.
[3] Mr Edmund Bishop in Mr Littlehales' edition of *The Primer* (E.E.T.S.).
[4] These editions alone contain the *O bone Jesu*, p. 169 below.
[5] See *Opera S. Aug*. ed. Bened. vi app. pp. 83, 103, 146.

was translated from the French version into English by William Caxton and published in 1483.[1]

It is needless to say that the Book of Common Prayer has contributed something to the *Preces*; but beyond this but little use is made of xvith century materials.

Besides Holy Scripture and the directly devotional inheritance of the Church, Andrewes draws more or less on a long list of writers. It is not possible to enumerate them exactly, since it is not always possible to say from which of several authors, who repeat one another, he quotes a particular passage; but his sources include the Rabbinical writings; 'the ancient Fathers and lights of the Church in whom the scent of this ointment,' of the Holy Ghost, 'was fresh and the temper true: on whose writings it lieth thick, and we thence strike it off and gather it safely'[2]: S. Irenæus, Tertullian, S. Cyprian, Arnobius, Lactantius, S. Jerome, S. Ambrose, S. Gregory of Nazianzus, S. Gregory of Nyssa, S. John Chrysostom, John Cassian, S. Augustine, S. Cyril of Alexandria, S. Fulgentius of Ruspe, Bede; mediæval writers like Theophylact, S. Bernard, Peter Lombard, S. Thomas Aquinas, Archbishop Bradwardine, Jean Gerson—and the notes below will suggest allusions to others; and pagan authors, Euripides, Cicero, Seneca—as the Apostles used them 'to provoke Christian men to emulation, by shewing them their own blindness in matter of knowledge, that see not so much as the heathen did by light of nature; or their slackness in matter of conversation, that cannot be got so far forward by God's law as the poor pagan can by his philosophy.'[3]

Consequently the *Preces* fall into line with the traditional system, and are for private devotion, only even more comprehensively in respect of their sources, what the Book of Common Prayer is in its way for the Church. They represent for the individual what it was the mission of Andrewes and his fellows to vindicate for the English Church—the inheritance of all the past, criticised by the best spirit of the Renaissance, adjusted to the proportion of Holy Scripture, and adapted to the needs of the present.

[1] Caxton's version has been edited by Mr F. S. Ellis in the *Temple Classics*, 1900, 7 vols.

[2] *Serm. Pentecost.* x (iii 287). [3] *Serm. Imaginations* (v 62).

It was noticed above that Andrewes had an interest in natural history, which was recognised by Bacon as not wholly amateur.[1] In the words of his biographer, 'he would often profess that to observe the grass, herbs, corn, trees, cattle, earth, waters, heavens, any of the creatures, and to contemplate their natures, order, qualities, virtues, uses, etc., was ever to him the greatest mirth, content, and recreation that could be: and this he held to his dying day.'[2] This side of his mind is also represented in the *Preces*. Each day of the week he commemorates the work of the day in creation, using the first chapter of Genesis as a framework in which to review the spectacle of nature, dwelling upon its details in language generally borrowed from other parts of the Bible. As prebendary of S. Paul's he chose the first four chapters of Genesis as the subject of a long course of lectures, which is still extant and in part forms a *Hexaëmeron* like those of S. Basil and S. Ambrose. From these lectures it is clear what was the character of his interest in nature; it was not ultimately scientific, but theological and moral. There is observation of the whole and of details, within the limits characteristic of his times; but it is used to illustrate the character of God and his operations, man and his duties. It is more like the interest of the Old Testament, than the modern scientific interest. He might say with Bacon, 'Thy creatures have been my books: but thy Scriptures much more. I have sought Thee in the courts, fields and gardens, but I have found Thee in thy temples'[3]; only he would add that he had found Him everywhere, and what he found in the temple he carried back to the fields.

Andrewes' scholarly temper, his sense of form and instinct for analysis, appears in the careful structure of the *Preces*. In his sermons on *Prayer* and in the *Catechistical doctrine* he has drawn out schemes of prayer in its several departments; and in the *Preces* he has other schemes, and one in particular which is developed with great and even exhaustive fulness of detail and articulation.[4] And the devotions themselves are constructed on strict plan; the more they are examined, the more close and exact the articulation is found to be. It is not only that in the general scheme of them the departments

[1] P. xxviii above.
[2] *Minor Works* p. vi.
[3] Church *Bacon* p. 138.
[4] Pp. 12 sq. below.

d

				WEDNESDAY	THURSDAY	FRIDAY	SATURDAY
Morning verse	S. Lk. i 78	Ps. v 3	Ps. lxiii 1	Ps. lxiii 7, 8	Ps. xc 14	Ps. lxxxviii 13	Is. xxxiii 2
Commemoration	1. Light 2. The Resurrection 3. Pentecost	1. Firmament 2. Angels 3. Water and atmosphere	1. Sea and Land 2. Plants 3. Minerals	1. Luminaries 2. Seasons 3. The Earthquake	1. Creeping things and Birds 2. The Ascension 3. The H. Eucharist 4. His Birthday	1. Beasts 2. Man and his education 3. The Promise and the Passion	1. The Sabbath 2. The Burial 3. Cessation from sin 4. The Departed
Penitence	General The Penitent. Pss.	Moses and Job S. Matthew Ps xiii	David and Solomon S. Luke Ps. xxx	Isaiah and Jeremiah SS. Paul and Peter Pss. xxxviii, lxix	Ezekiel and Daniel SS. James and John Ps. lxxvii	Minor Prophets The Passion Ps. lxxxv	Ps. lxxix, lxxxviii, vi Ezra and Manasseh Ejaculations from Gospels
Deprecation	Sins against Decalogue	Sins against Decalogue	Forms of sin	The vii capital sins	Sin in Heb., S. Jas. and S. John	Works of the flesh	Sin — guilt, stain, wound
Comprecation	1. Decalogue 2. Hedge of the Law	Decalogue	Godly sorrow (2 Cor. vii)	Virtues opposed to capitals	Beatitudes	Gifts, &c., of the Holy Ghost	Development of Faith (2 Pet. i)
Faith	Creed and its applications	Apostles' Creed	Apostles' Creed in abstract	Creed meditated	Creed from Holy Scripture	Creation, redemption, sanctification pleaded	The Holy Trinity and operations
Hope	Ps. lxv 5, &c.	Pss. xxxix 8, xxxi 1	Ps. lxv 5	Pss. xiii 5, cxxi 8, xxxvi 7, cxix 116	Ps. xxxiii 20, 21	Ps. cxix 49, 81	Ps. xx 4, 5, &c.
Intercession	H. Scripture and Liturgies	General	Scheme of heads	Liturgies of S. Bas. and S. James	Great Ektene (*Euchologion*).	Ektene (*Horologion*)	'Heavenly King' (*Horologion*)
Blessing	Aaronic (Num. vi)	Ps. lxvii 1, 6	Ps. cxxi 5, 7, 8	Ps. xc 17	2 Cor. xiii 14	*The Peace of God**	*Horae*
Commendation	*Horae*	*Horologion*	*Horae*	*Horae*	S. Jude 24, 25	Knox's prayer* *Anima Christi*	*Horae*
Praise and Thanksgiving	Of God (Heb. and *Lit. S. Jas.*)	The xiii Attributes (Ex. xxxiv 6); Ps. xxxiv 1; S. Lk. ii 14; the Angels	The Mercy of God	1 Chr. xxix 10-17	For blessings of life	Redemption (*Lit. S. Jas.* &c.) Rev. v 9, 12, 13, vii 10, 12	Eph. iii. 20, 21 The Saints Rev. xv 3-5, xix 5-7, xxi 3, 4

* On Friday, the Blessing and the Commendation seem to be in reverse order; but perhaps Knox's Prayer is the Blessing, and *Anima Christi* and *The Peace* the Commendation.

of devotion are represented in their order; but within these departments, the several acts imply a systematic use of the sources and are themselves articulated into their subordinate movements. The best specimen of external order and construction is the morning prayers for the week, which form the principal part of the finished devotions of the Greek MSS. The structure of these will be apparent from the accompanying table; and it will be seen that the whole is conceived on a plan, that the materials are used in a certain order, and that on several at least of the days certain subjects are more or less kept in view: Sunday, God—perhaps suggested by the service of ordinary Sundays in the Breviary; Monday, the Angels; Thursday, one's own life; Friday, the Passion; Saturday, the Departed.

But the structure is not merely an external scheme or framework: the internal structure is as close as the external. Andrewes develops an idea he has in his mind: every line tells and adds something. He does not expatiate, but moves forward; if he repeats, it is because the repetition has a real force of expression; if he accumulates, each new word or phrase represents a new development, a substantive addition to what he is saying. He assimilates his material and advances by means of it. His quotation is not decoration or irrelevance, but the matter in which he expresses what he wants to say. His single thoughts are no doubt often suggested by the words he borrows, but the thoughts are made his own, and the constructive force, the fire that fuses them, is his own. And this internal, progressive, often poetic structure is marked outwardly. The editions have not always reproduced this feature of the *Preces*, nor perhaps is it possible in any ordinary page to represent the structure adequately; but in the MSS. the intention is clear enough. The prayers are arranged, not merely in paragraphs, but in lines advanced and recessed, so as in a measure to mark the inner structure and the steps and stages of the movement. Both in form and in matter Andrewes' prayers may often be described rather as hymns.[1]

2. Andrewes' character as a priest is reflected in the devotions; they represent the background of his public ministry. If we consider him in the exercise of the *praecipuum*

[1] Cp. J. B. Mozley *Bishop Andrewes' Sermons* in *British Critic* xxxi, Jan. 1842, pp. 189 sqq.

munus epicoporum, as a preacher, it is not only that he admonishes himself with the words of S. Fulgentius, that it is rather by the piety of his prayers for himself and his flock than by fluency of speech that he will secure a willing intelligent and teachable hearing; that he can only deliver effectually what he has first received devoutly, and that it is only from the Truth that he can learn the truth; or that he prays the Word of the Father to give him the word and take the veil from his heart and touch his lips; but the *Preces* as a whole are closely related to the *Sermons* as a whole. It is a large part of the purpose of the notes of this edition to shew how close this relation is. The devotions are in fact an abstract of the sermons, the sermons a development and expansion of the devotions. The things which he delivers to the Church are the things in which he habitually 'exercises himself day and night'; they have been proved and tested in his own heart; and the essence of his public teaching is distilled into suggestion for his own devotion.

Two outstanding notes of the devotions correspond to two characteristics which have been noticed as recorded of Andrewes' ministration—his penitentiary work and his sense of worship. If we would understand in detail how he interprets the parts of penance—contrition, confession and satisfaction—and especially the first two of them—'the conditions required to be of the *quorum remittuntur*,' [1] in the exercise of 'the power of the thrice-holy keys'—it is in the great acts of penitence in the devotions that we can best find the interpretation; acts so intense in their consciousness of sin and their depth of self-humiliation as to be beyond the scope of most, even of devout people, and to require some abatement if they are to be at all generally used. And the sense of worship which he tried to express in one way in the services of his chapel, is expressed in another way in the acts of adoration and thanksgiving, which are characteristic of the *Preces*. These, notable for their breadth and minuteness, their variety and definiteness, are the expression and the discipline of a temper of thankfulness and worship which is not only meet and right and the bounden duty of every man, but is also the condition of his taking his place in and making his contribution to the common worship of the Church

[1] *Serm. Absolution* (v 98).

and 'giving thanks in his own order.'[1] It has sometimes been made a criticism on the *Preces* that they provide so small a proportion of devotion explicitly related to the worship of the Church in the Holy Eucharist and Communion. And of course they make no claim to completeness or proportion; they are after all rather a collection of specimens and models, than a rounded whole. But it may be worth while to recall two considerations. First, that specific 'devotions for holy communion' are of comparatively recent origin. The current western *Praeparatio* and *Gratiarum actio*, which grew up from the early middle ages onwards for the use of the celebrant, consist essentially of certain psalms and prayers which have no necessary relation to communion except as they are directed to it by the intention of the supplicant; while the more specific prayers, which are appended to the original forms, are attributed to S. Thomas Aquinas and S. Bonaventura in the 13th century, and the so-called 'Prayers of S. Ambrose,' now distributed over the days of the week, are also attributed to S. Anselm, and certainly with more probability, since they bear the impress of the 11th century rather than of the 4th.[2] And secondly, what the Church requires of communicants is not so much any exceptional form of devotion, as the tempers and virtues which form the basis and spring of the Christian character—faith and hope and love, penitence and thankfulness—; and the normal preparation for communion is the exercise of these virtues. And in fact specific 'devotions for holy communion' consist essentially of such acts, however their form may be affected by their immediate intention. The multiplied acts of faith and penitence and intercession and thanksgiving and petition for growth in grace in the *Preces*, therefore, largely supply the needs of the communicant. But the section devoted to the Holy Mysteries, drawn for the most part from the Greek Office of Preparation for Communion, provides a specimen of specific Eucharistic

[1] S. Clement of Rome 1 *Cor.* xli 1.

[2] The corresponding Greek Office, Ἀκολουθία τῆς ἁγίας μεταλήψεως, is no doubt also mediæval; in fact of the *Euchologia* contained in Dmitriewski's collection (Kiev 1901) the earliest copies which contain it are of the xvth. cent., though most of the material is of course older.

devotion, in extent bearing a proportion to the whole book perhaps as great as that of the like section to the whole in the devotional collections with which Andrewes was familiar, and fuller in devotional significance than its mere length might suggest, since the long list of the ends of communion, with which Andrewes expands what he derives from his Greek source,[1] seems to supply points of meditation on every aspect of the mystery.[2] The whole section, it seems clear, is intended not only for use in preparation for communion, but also and more especially for use at the celebration of the Holy Mysteries; and accordingly it has been distributed below under titles indicating its obvious intentions. It may be noted therefore that Andrewes provided for himself, as we all do more or less, a supplement to the Liturgy;[3] in fact he 'interpolated prayers from other rites'; and especially he 'restored that which is lacking,' by adopting from the Orthodox Eastern rite the paragraph, following the recital of the Institution in the Consecration, 'We therefore remembering,' the absence of any words corresponding to which forms a glaring and deplorable defect in the English rite since 1552; while happily it has been restored to the Scottish and American liturgies.

The theology of the *Preces* is that of the *Sermons*. Each day of the week Andrewes summarises it, more or less at length, in an act of faith; from Sunday to Wednesday in the Creed variously treated; from Thursday to Saturday in creed-forms woven out of passages of the Sacred Scriptures. But

[1] P. 122 l. 26-123 l. 14.

[2] The concluding paragraphs of most of the Christmas, Easter and Whitsunday Sermons contain masses of suggestion and material for meditation on the Eucharist in its relation to the mysteries commemorated on these festivals.

[3] Cp. Bp. Wilson *Sacra privata* Sunday: 'Private devotions at the altar, taken out of the most ancient Offices of the Church, to render our present Communion Service more agreeable to apostolic usage, and more acceptable (I hope) to God, and beneficial to all that partake thereof. Until it shall please God to put it into the hearts and power of such as ought to do it, to restore to us the first service of Edw. VI, or such as shall be more conformable to the appointment of Christ and His Apostles, and their successors. Which may the Divine Majesty vouchsafe to grant for His sake Who first ordained this Holy Sacrament. Amen.' Cp. also Archbp. Benson *Prayers public and private* pp. 170 sqq.

the fullest expression of it is in the expanded and meditated creed of the Harleian MS.[1] Here he gathers up and enlarges his treatment of the Creed elsewhere: —the conception of faith; its object, God, revealed and operating in the Incarnation and Life and Passion and Resurrection and Ascension of our Lord, working in us by the Holy Ghost, in the communion of a Catholic Church; its issue, a moral and spiritual growth corresponding to all the details of the divine revelation, each of which has some counterpart in the perfected Christian character.[2] And so he seems to assert once more, as he does more explicitly elsewhere,[3] the conviction that the Creed is central and all important, while what the men of his day mostly disputed about is at best secondary; and that peace and unity is to be sought in the first place, not by the way of controversy or of the mere enforcement of uniformity in secondary detail, but by a firm hold on what is central and in the main undisputed, and the positive and practical pursuit of its moral and spiritual issues. And it is in this sense that his Prayer for Unity 'Guide our feet into the way of peace,' etc.,[4] is to be understood.

3. Of the character of Andrewes, the devotions are necessarily the monument. They represent as a whole what he was and what he aspired to be; what men knew of him and what they could not know—'all the world's course thumb and finger failed to plumb.' They shew us the background, the spring, the force and inspiration of his public life and activity, the root of what men recognised in him: his piety, a serene and filial faith, a profound penitence, a living hope, a passionate love of God and a longing to be true to all he knew of Him; a large, detailed, imaginative charity, alive to all the varied conditions, needs and interests of peoples and individuals, resting on a keen alertness to all that experience had brought with it and the obligations created by it; a gratitude alive to all that God had done for him, whether immediately or through men and through nature; and a genial appreciation of life, its joys and its sorrows, and a belief in the possibility of its consecration.

[1] Below pp. 184 sqq. [2] Cp. *Serm. Of doing of the word* (v 200).
[3] See above p. xxxvi. [4] P. 259: see note on the passage.

VI

The qualities and significance of the devotions have been often appreciated, and from different points of view. And perhaps enough has been said already to indicate their chief characteristics. But a few paragraphs may be devoted to recalling two or three suggestive points.

And first, the method of the *Preces* is notable in two respects: first, in the orderly completeness with which they cover the departments of devotion—the exercise of Faith, Hope, Charity, Penitence, Petition, Deprecation, Intercession, Praise and Thanksgiving.[1] And perhaps this touches what most people are conscious of in their devotions—a lack of completeness through the inadequacy of at least one or other department of what ought to cover every side of their being and be the outgoing of themselves to all that is within their imaginative range. Andrewes may teach us how in our measure to make our devotional life complete and to determine its proportions, not by our own tastes and feelings at the moment, but by an objective standard of what ought to be. And secondly, the method of the *Preces* is instructive in the use of sources. It suggests the spiritual use of our interests and the consecration of them, by the appropriation of what they supply to us to the purposes of devotion. To Andrewes literature and nature and experience were a field in which he gathered fuel for devotion; in other words, he secured their moral and spiritual effectiveness by using what he found in them as the offering with which he drew near to God, through which he learned more of God and of his own possibilities. It is the trial of all our lives to bridge the interval between the world of everyday experience and the world of the spirit; and one way of doing something to effect it is deliberately to carry over the best we find in the one into the 'chamber' in which we do what we can to enter wholly into the other.

In the second place, Andrewes' detail may be noted, especially in the departments of Penitence, Thanksgiving

[1] In *Serm. Gowries* i (iv 7-9) he justifies and limits the place of Imprecation. The *Institutiones piæ* has a section of 'Imprecation'; but this is not represented in the *Preces*.

and Intercession. He had ancient and mediæval models for this; but perhaps in some respects he goes beyond his models. His Thanksgivings and Intercessions seem to embrace with more or less of explicitness every possible relation and circumstance of life. In his acts of Penitence he seems to strive to bring home to himself the seriousness of sin by every consideration he can bring to bear on it, to realise the mercy of God by the contemplation of every evidence he can find for it, and to appeal to it by every plea he can anywhere lay hold of. At the same time, in the matter of self-examination, where great minuteness may be, to some temperaments at least, a snare and a peril, whatever may have been his own practice, and whatever he may imply in what he says in the *Sermons*, the only form contained in the *Preces* which has any appearance of completeness is not a detailed inquiry into particular sins, but the suggestion of a positive ideal by which to try ourselves.[1] Again, it may be thought that the *Preces* are defective in the scope of their petitions—that there are many things we might naturally pray for, and many conditions in which we habitually find ourselves, which find no explicit recognition here; in other words, that the section of 'Comprecation' is meagre in comparison with the collection of occasional prayers in ordinary devotional books. But perhaps this is no real defect. In our devotions we are deliberately withdrawing from the detail of life and 'getting time' directly to 'seek first the Kingdom of God and His righteousness,' to habituate ourselves to the point of view from which we are called to look at life, and to realise anew the spirit which ought to inform its details. And at least the Lord's Prayer, except for a fraction of one of its petitions, has in view only large spiritual ends, and takes no notice of the mass of detailed desires and particular circumstances, which we are only too ready to look upon as the first subject-matter of our prayers. And the familiar practice of using the Lord's Prayer as often as occasion requires or suggests, and applying it for ourselves by special intention to particular conditions, is a healthy one. 'Hallowed be thy Name, thy Kingdom come, thy Will be done' covers and interprets all conditions 'in earth, as in heaven.'

[1] Below p. 105.

Another characteristic of the *Preces* is their compressed fulness, and the consequent demand they make on those who use them to do a great deal for themselves. It has been already noticed that for the most part they are a collection of select passages from the most sacred and authoritative sources, chosen, it may be assumed, for something in them which seemed to make them specially worth choosing and collecting. And these passages, so selected, are woven together into a close-textured whole, with the addition of no unnecessary words; with the result that they give us little, if anything, but solid matter. And again the forms of prayer sometimes consist of lists of words, phrases, synonyms, topics, and this sometimes without context or any external connexion with what goes before or follows. Consequently the *Preces* challenge reflexion, and if they are to be used as profitably as they obviously may be, must generally be regarded as matter for meditation, and sometimes, if they are to be used at all, must be treated as germs left to us to develop, rather than as prayers which can be recited as they stand. And the external arrangement, isolating as it does, by the use of lines, the several steps which go to make up the movement, at once suggests and encourages this use of the devotions.

And lastly, it may be added, the *Preces* are interesting. The feeling that this is so may be a personal one, which will not be generally shared. But at least, if a reminiscence may be pardoned, I can recall that one to whom I once gave a copy of Newman and Neale's version, told me that, on receiving it, he sat down and read the book through 'like a novel,' for the interest of it. This is probably not the common fortune of books of prayers. But the solid matter of the *Preces privatae*, the beauty of their materials, the picturesqueness and imaginativeness of treatment, their relation to the facts of the author's life, the originality and pointedness of their structural form, might well issue in such a result.

VII

In conclusion, a few notes may be added on the use and influence of the *Preces*.

Archbishop Laud incorporates several passages in his own *Devotions*; and he must have known the *Preces* apart from the Greek MS. which Andrewes gave him, since these passages are drawn from parts of the collection not contained in the Laudian MS.[1] Traces of their influence are perhaps to be recognised in Bp. Brian Duppa.[2] Bishop Ken possessed a copy of Drake's version (1682), which is preserved in the Library of the Cathedral Church of Wells. It shews no sign of much use, but its influence can easily be detected in his *Manual of Prayers*.[3] William Law knew the book and extracted from it in his own papers;[4] and it has been suggested above that the advice he gives in the *Serious Call* on the devotional use of Holy Scripture was suggested by the method of the *Preces*.[5] William Jones of Nayland recalls how George Horne, 'when he was a very young man,' as they were together 'upon a walk one summer's evening,' shewed him 'that precious composition of Bishop Andrewes, the first copy of which occurred to him in the Library of Magdalen College;[6] on which he set so great a value during the rest of his life, that while he was Dean of Canterbury, he published, after the example of the excellent Dean Stanhope, his predecessor, a handsome English edition of it.' And he adds that 'it happened sometime after Mr Horne had first brought the work into request, that a good number of copies of the Greek and Latin edition were discovered in a warehouse at Oxford, where they had lain undisturbed in sheets

[1] See *The private devotions of Dr William Laud*, ed. Faber, Oxford 1838, pp. 65, 146, 149, 150, 179, 185, 191 sqq., with which cp. below pp. 111 ll. 7 sq.; 134 l. 41-135 l. 8; 198; 273 ll. 2-10; 32 ll. 26-31; 33 ll. 37 sq.; 34 ll. 12-17; 31 ll. 31-33; 147 ll. 34, 36 sq.; 148 ll. 1, 3, 184 sqq. With Laud pp. 1 sq., 5 sq. cp. Andrewes *Minor Works* pp. 148, 147.

[2] See *A Guide for the Penitent*, London 1660; reprinted in *The Golden Grove . . by Jeremy Taylor*, Oxford 1836

[3] See the *Directions for those that are more grown in years*, esp. the penitential acts, where reminiscences of Andrewes are easily recognisable.

[4] See Dr A. Whyte *Characters and Characteristics of William Law*, pp. 320 sq., 326 sq., where pp. 25 ll. 28-30, 109 ll. 33-39 below are quoted.

[5] P. xliii above.

[6] The 1682 ed. of Drake's version, still in the Magdalen Library.

for many years.'[1] The saintly Alexander Jolly, bishop of Aberdeen, possessed copies of the *editio princeps* of 1675 and the 1823 issue of Horne's edition of Stanhope's version, which are preserved in the Library of the Edinburgh Theological College. After his wont, the bishop has used the flyleaves as a commonplace book of devotional extracts. But it is more especially since the beginning of the Oxford movement and the 78th of the *Tracts for the Times*, that the influence of the *Preces* has been marked. Not only have they often been republished, as we have seen, in text and translation, in whole and in part, but they have contributed largely to the compilation of a multitude of devotional works, like Dr Hook's *Private Prayers* (1836), the *Treasury of Devotion* (1869), or Dr Pusey's posthumous *Private Prayers* (1883); and perhaps few books of prayers in any way related to the Oxford movement have been quite uninfluenced by the *Preces*. And they have been not only extracted from, but also imitated: they have given a suggestion of method which has been followed up: witness *Supplications, Prayers, Intercessions and Thanksgivings for the use of Church Watchers and Church Workers*, edited by Nath. Keymer (Oxford, Mowbray, 1896), Mr Frere and Mrs Illingworth's *Sursum corda* (Oxford, Mowbray, 1898), or the Greek passages in Archbishop Benson's posthumous *Prayers Public and Private* (London, Isbister, 1899); or again, *An Horology, being a devout prayer for every hour of day and night*, with a preface by Alfred Gurney (London, Skeffington, 1897), and Mr Newbolt's *The Dial of Prayer, being devotions for every hour* (London, Longmans, 1897), consisting of Andrewes' *Dial*, supplemented so as to cover the twenty-four hours. The *Preces* are frequently quoted in Dr Pusey's Sermons; they formed the subject of an acute literary criticism by James Mozley,[2] and of a splendid appreciation in their relation to Bishop Andrewes'

[1] W. Jones *Memoirs of the life, studies and writings of the Right Reverend George Horne D.D. late Lord Bishop of Norwich* London 1795, p. 80. I have been unable to find a copy of the first issue of Horne's Stanhope, or the precise date of its publication. Jones adds that among his papers he found a MS. in which the *Preces* and the *Manual for the Sick* were combined, 'with improvements by the compiler'—'and I wish all the parochial clergy in the nation were possessed of it.'

[2] In *British Critic* xxxi, Jan. 1842, pp. 187-192.

life by R. W. Church;[1] Bishop James Woodford of Ely lectured on them in the series of lectures on *Companions for the devout life* at S. James' Piccadilly in 1876;[2] and Mr Ottley has devoted a chapter to them in his *Lancelot Andrewes* in the series of *Leaders of Religion*.[3]

But their influence in the last three-quarters of a century has not been confined within the limits of the Oxford Movement. And indeed it is impressive to recognise how wide their influence has been, and how a great devotional work can bridge over divergencies. Within a few years the *Preces* were translated and edited by a moderate, a leader of the 'evangelical' school and a leader of the Tractarians; by Peter Hall in 1830, by Edward Bickersteth in 1839, and by John Henry Newman in 1840. Both Dr Pusey and Archbishop Tait used them habitually.[4] In the last few years they have been edited not only by Mr Medd, but also by Mr Veale, whose introduction and notes are sufficient to shew that he belongs to a school not in sympathy with that of Andrewes, and by Dr Alexander Whyte of the Free Church of Scotland. And at the same time it is noticeable and characteristic that it is the 'evangelicals' of the English Church who are most reserved in their appreciation and most inclined to criticise in detail what they approve in general. Edward Bickersteth and Mr Veale find it necessary to make qualifications, while Dr Whyte is content to be enthusiastic.

[1] In Barry *Masters in English Theology* London 1877; reprinted in *Pascal and other Sermons* London 1896.

[2] *S. James's Lectures*: second series, London 1876.

[3] R. L. Ottley *Lancelot Andrewes* Lond. 1894, ch. x.

[4] *Spiritual Letters of E. B. Pusey* p. xii; Benham *Catherine and Crauford Tait* pp. 85, 392; cp. Davidson and Benham *Life of Archbishop Tait* vol. ii p. 596. The reference in the two latter is to the *Manual for the Sick*; but Archbishop Tait's copy of the *Preces* 'tattered and worn with constant use' is in the present Archbishop of Canterbury's possession. The copy of Peter Hall's version (1830), which Dr Pusey gave to Mrs Pusey on her birthday in 1836, is in the Library of the Pusey House.

ADDENDA

1. After most of this 'Introduction' was in type, Mr Henry Willett of Brighton most kindly called my attention to, and allowed me to examine, a hitherto unnoticed MS. in his possession. The volume is a paper book of 158 pages, in size approximately $5\frac{7}{8} \times 4$ in., bound in brown calf, tooled, partly in gold, with two clasps. On both covers are stamped the initials 'N. P.' The text, which occupies 156 pages, with occasional blanks, is written in a professional hand, which may be dated 1640-1650. It bears no title, but is evidently an English translation of a collection of Bishop Andrewes' devotions, and on examination it turns out to be closely related to Humphrey Moseley's *Private Devotions by Lancelot Andrewes*, published in 1647, which Drake's version was intended to displace.[1] Thus pp. 1-135, 145-156 of the MS. are apparently identical with pp. 1-130 of 1647, and pp. 137-144 of the MS. with pp. 152-160 of 1647; in other words, the MS. reproduces nearly all of what the collection of 1647 has in common with later editions of the *Preces*, and omits pp. 131-151 and 161 to the end, most of which is of a different character and in part consists of extracts from the sermons. The MS. therefore contributes no new matter. Dr Macray has been good enough to suggest to me that the initials 'N. P.' on the covers may be those of Nicholas Preston, who was prebendary of Winchester from 1645-1664. In his preface to the 1647 book, H. Moseley says: 'It appeares not as yet who translated this manuall of devotions: . . it is not improbable that wee are indebted to the same hand for the translation, to whom we owe the originall; since I could never yet learne that any have laid claim thereunto,'—scarcely a convincing argument.

2. To the Prayers for Holy Communion, below pp. 121 sqq., Drake adds as 'not in the Greek, but in the Latin MS.' (no longer extant)—after p. 123 l. 30, 'Let me so receive

[1] See above pp. xxii sq.

these mysteries, that I may be worthy to be ingrafted into thy body, which is the Church; that I may become one of thy members,[1] and Thou my Head: that I may remain with Thee, and Thou with me; that now, not I in myself, but Thou in me and I in Thee, and Thou my Head, may for ever continue in an indissoluble bond of love. Wash out the stains of my old and fresh sins; never let any sinful spot abide where so pure sacraments have entered.[2] Through this sacred mystery, which I here call to mind, bury me, already dead to this world, with Thee in Thy grave'; and before p. 124 l. 13 'It is good for me to hold me fast by God and to put my trust in the God of my salvation' [Ps. lxxiii 27].

[1] Cp. *Orat. S. Thomae Aq.* Omnipotens sempiterne Deus, ecce accedo — da mihi corpus unigeniti Filii tui. . . sic suscipere ut corpori suo mystico merear incorporari et inter ejus membra connumerari.

[2] *Canon missae* Corpus tuum Domine—ut in me non remaneat scelerum macula quem pura et sancta refecerunt sacramenta.

THE PRECES PRIVATAE

OF CHRISTIAN LIFE

I

1. What shall I do that I may inherit eternal life? S. Mk. x 17
   a. Keep the commandments. S. Mt. xix 17

2. What shall we do? Acts ii 37
   b. Repent and be baptized every one of you. 38

3. What must I do to be saved? Acts xvi 30
   c. Believe on the Lord Jesus Christ. 31

4. What shall we do then? S. Lk. iii 10
   a. He that hath {two coats / meat}, let him impart to him that hath none. (To the people) 11
   b. Seek no more than that which is appointed you. (To the publicans) 13
   c. Do violence to / accuse falsely } no man; be content with your wages. (To the soldiers) 14

Ps. xcix 6 Samuel among such as supplicate. W^{2} 1

1 Sam. xii 23 As for me, God forbid L 2
that I should sin against the Lord
in ceasing to pray
before Him for you,
and to teach you the way,
good and right.

Acts vi 4 But we will give ourselves continually to prayer
and to the ministry of the word.

Ps. lxv 2 Thou that hearest the prayer, W 2
unto Thee shall all flesh come * :
this also shall come.
3 But my misdeeds prevail against me :
o be Thou merciful unto my sins.

Ps. li 15 Thou shalt open my lips, o Lord,
and my mouth shall shew forth Thy praise.

POINTS OF MEDITATION BEFORE PRAYER

Thou art careful about many things: but one thing is S. Lk. x 41, 42
46 needful.

But we will give ourselves continually to prayer and to the ministry of the word. Acts vi 4

Watch ye and pray always, that ye may be accounted worthy to escape the things that shall come to pass. S. Lk. xxi 36

Love the Lord all thy life and call upon Him for thy salvation. Ecclus. xiii 14

Humble thy soul greatly: for the vengeance of the ungodly is fire and worms. *Ib.* vii 17

A man can receive nothing except it be given. S. Jo. iii 27

If He prayed that was without sin, how much more ought a sinner to pray: S. Cyp. *de or. dom.* 29

but God is a hearer, not of the voice, but of the heart. *Ib.* 4

More is done by groanings than by words: S. Aug. *ep.* cxxx 20

to this end Christ groaned, for to give us an ensample of groaning. Beda *expos. in Marc. ev.* vii 34

It is not that God desireth us to be suppliant or loveth that we lie prostrate: the profit thereof is ours and it hath regard to our advantage. Arnob. *adv. gent.* i 27

Prayer goeth up, pity cometh down. [S. Aug.] *serm.* ccxxvi (v app. 90 F)

God's grace is richer than prayer: God alway giveth more than He is asked. S. Amb. *expos. in Luc.* x 121

God commandeth that thou ask, and teacheth what to ask, and promiseth what thou dost ask, and it displeaseth Him if thou ask not: and dost thou not ask notwithstanding? S. Amb. (?)

Prayer is a summary of faith, an interpreter of hope. *Cp.* Tertull. *de or.* 1

It is not by paces but by prayers that God is come at. S. Aug. (?)

Faith poureth out prayer and is grounded in prayer. *Cp.* S. Aug. *serm.* cxv 1

Col. iv. 12 — Therefore go on to labour fervently in prayers

S. Lk. xviii 1 — always to pray and not to faint

S. Jo. iv 23 — in spirit and in truth.

Theophyl. *in S. Luc.* xviii (i 433 A) — Faith is the foundation and basis of prayer *: H 3

the foundation of faith is the promise of God.

S. Cyp. *de or. dom.* 31 — Lift up your hearts.

Ib. 2 — He that made us to live, the same taught us withal to pray.

Ecclus. xxxv 17 — The prayer of the humble pierceth the clouds.

S. Greg. Nyss. *de or. dom.* i (xliv 1124 B) — Prayer is colloquy with God.

CIRCUMSTANCES OF PRAYER

W² 3* 1. Time.

Always: S. Lk. xviii 1
without ceasing: 1 Th. v 17
at all times. Ps. xxxiv 1; Eph. vi 18
He kneeled upon his knees three times a day and prayed and gave thanks before his God, as he did aforetime. Dan. vi 10
In the evening and morning and noonday will I pray and that instantly: and He shall hear my voice. Ps. lv 18
Seven times a day do I praise Thee: Ps. cxix 164
1. in the morning, a great while before day S. Mk. i 35
2. when I was waking Ps. lxiii 7
3. at the third hour of the day Acts ii 15
4. about the sixth hour Acts x 9
5. at the hour of prayer, being the ninth hour Acts iii 1
6. at the eventide Gen. xxiv 63
7. by night, Ps. cxxxiv 2
at midnight. Ps. cxix 62; Acts xvi 25

W 4* 2. Place.

In all places where I record my name, I will come unto thee and I will bless thee. Ex. xx 24
Congregation. Secretly among the faithful and in the congregation. Ps. cxi 1
Closet. Enter into thy closet and when thou hast shut thy door pray in secret. S. Mt. vi 6
Upper room. He went up upon the housetop to pray. Asts x 9
Temple. They went up into the temple. Acts iii 1
Beach. On the beach. Acts xxi 5
Garden. In a garden. S. Jo. xviii 1
Bed. In their beds. Ps. cxlix 5
Desert. In a desert. S. Mk. i 35
Everywhere holding up holy hands without wrath and doubting. 1 Tim. ii 8

3. Accompaniments. L 8 W 8

Reference		Accompaniment	
S. Ja. iv 10	1. *a.*	Bending of the knee	Humiliation.
S. Mt. xvii 14	*b.*	kneeling-down	
S. Mt. xxvi 39	*c.*	on the face:	
Ps. xliv 25		my { soul is brought low, even unto the dust belly cleaveth unto the ground.	
S. Jo. xix 30; 1 Cor. vi 5 S. Ja. iv 9	2.	Bowing of the head: downcastness	Shame.
S. Lk. xviii 13; 2 Cor. vii 11	3.	Smiting of the breast	Indignation.
Job iv 14; 2 Cor. vii 11	4.	Trembling	Fear.
Rom. viii 26; 2 Cor. vii 10	5. *a.*	Groaning *:	Sorrow.
	b.	joining of the hands	
S. Jo. xvii 1; 2 Cor. vii 11	6. *a.*	Lifting up of the eyes	Vehement desire.
Ps. cxli 2; 1 Tim. ii 8	*b.*	hands	
1 Cor. ix 27; 2 Cor. vii 11	7.	Buffetting	Revenge.

SCHEMES OF PRAYER

rm. V p 357

The apostle saith PRAY WITH ALL MANNER OF PRAYER: therefore it is meet we should take notice how many kinds of prayer there are; wherein the apostle guides us when he says LET SUPPLICATIONS, PRAYERS, THANKSGIVING AND INTERCESSIONS BE MADE. *A preparation to prayer* vi. Eph. vi 18 1 Tim. ii 1

I

ut. Doct. p 100

Prayer is either
- petition
  - for ourselves
    - deprecation — SUPPLICATION
    - precation — PRAYER
  - for others — INTERCESSION
- thanksgiving — GIVING OF THANKS.

II

rm. V p 358

Prayer Intercession
- confession
  - of sins
    - confession of sins
    - supplication for pardon
  - of praise
    - for pardoning our sins
    - for bestowing his benefits
- petition
  - deprecation
  - comprecation

(all the above) { for ourselves / for others.

O 331

III

1. Prayer
   - Yea: LET IT COME UP — Acts x 4
   - Nay: CAST NOT AWAY — Ps. xxvii 10
2. Confession
   - of thanks: Song
   - of praises: Hymn
   - of Faith, of Hope, of Love.

O 316

IV

Exercise
by day or by night:

1. of penitence for evil things done,
2. of gratitude for good things received:

appertaining to special

age	if	an old man
vocation		in orders
estate		a bishop.

V

O 315

i. Address:

[S. Aug.] *Serm.* ccxxvi — LET PRAYER ASCEND:

Ps. xxvii 10 — CAST NOT AWAY.

ii. Confession of Sins:

lamentations: profession of penitence;
supplication: petition for pardon;
because,
for the sake of or
through,
according to:

Ps. lxvi 14, lv 18 — AND I WILL
TELL:

or thus:
profession of resolution, vow;
confession of weakness;
petition for grace;
through.

iii. Confession of Faith:
Hope.

iv. Confession of Benefits:
praise,
blessing,
thanksgiving: Creation,
nurture, government,
preservation, disposal.
Redemption,
conception
birth
life
passion and death
resurrection
ascension.
Inspiration.

v. Deprecation
of sin,
of punishment.

vi. Comprecation
of grace,
of reward.

vii. Intercession for the creation,
the human race,
the Church,
the commonwealth,
our own people,
ourselves.

viii. Blessing.

ix. Commendation.

L 5

VI

i. I have sinned. I confess. Have mercy { according to — Ps. li 1, cxix 58
for the sake of — Ps. lxxix 9
as: — Ps. cxix 132

I purpose. I am weak. Succour { for the sake of — Ps. lxxix 9
in. — Ps. xxxi 1

ii. Lord, I believe: help Thou mine unbelief — S. Mk. ix 24
increase littleness of faith. — S. Lk. xvii 5

iii. And now what is my hope? — Ps. xxxix 8
Is it not Thou?
Truly my hope is even in Thee.

iv. *a.* Open Thou mine eyes — Ps. cxix 18
and I shall see:
b. incline my heart — 36
and I shall fervently desire: — 20, 131
c. straighten my steps — 133
and I shall walk in the way of thy commandments. — 35

v. Let us beseech the Lord *. — *Gk. Litt.*

1. Creation,
the human race,
those aforetime fallen asleep,
those in the body
and compassed with infirmity. — Heb. v 2

2. Catholic,
eastern,
western,
British.

3. Bishops,
presbyters,
orders of clergy,
the Christloving people,
our own.

4. The commonwealths of the world,
christian,
neighbouring,
our own.

5. Those Thou hast given the
right to rule,
ours:
{counsel,
judicature:
{civil control,
armed force:
{commonalty,
succession:
education.

6. Nature,
good offices received,
ministry of carnal things:

charge, aforetime {college
parish
Southwell
S. Paul's
Westminster
Chichester
Ely:

at present {diocese of Winton
church
Chapel Royal
Almonry
six colleges.

7. Friendship,
christian charity,
neighbourhood,
promise,
mutual obligation,
lack of leisure,
entire want of intercessors,
those in extremities,
those assaying some achievement,
those doing good works,
those scandalised by me
any while.

vi. 1. Alleluia	{ *O give thanks unto the Lord*		Ps. cxxxvi 1
	{ *Praise ye the Lord*		Ps. cxxxv 1
with			
for.			Ps. cvi 5
2. Destroy not	*Al-tashḥeth*		Ps. lvii tit.
in			
in			
in.			
3. Hosanna	*Save now*		Ps. cxviii 25
in			S. Mt. xxi 9
in			
in.			
4.	*In the morning*		
Of the evening.			
5. At lamplighting,			
	By night.		Cant. iii 1

DAILY PRAYERS

Thou who hast put the times and seasons in thine own power : Acts i 7 : *Horolog.* p. 187
grant that we make our prayer unto Thee in a time Ps. xxxii 7
convenient and when Thou mayest be found,
and save us.

Thou who for us men and for our salvation wast born at Nic. Creed
dead of night :
give us daily to be born again by renewing of the Christmas collect : Tit. iii 5
Holy Ghost, till Christ be formed in us unto a Gal. iv 19 ; Eph. iv 13
perfect man,
and save us.

Thou who very early in the morning while the sun was yet S. Mk. xvi 2
arising didst rise from the dead :
raise us up daily unto newness of life, Rom. vi 4
suggesting to us ways of repentance which Thyself *Horolog.* p. 474
knowest,
and save us.

Thou who at the third hour didst send down thy Holy *Horolog.* p. 85
Ghost on the apostles :
take not away the same Spirit from us, [Ps. li 11]
but renew Him daily within us,
and save us.

Thou who at the sixth hour and on the sixth day didst nail *Horolog.* p. 93
the sins of the world with Thyself on the cross : [Col. ii 14]
blot out the handwriting of our sins which is
against us and taking it out of the way
save us.

Thou who at the sixth hour didst let down a great sheet from Acts x 11
heaven to earth, a figure of thy Church :
receive us up into it, sinners of the gentiles, Gal. ii 15
and with it receive us up together into heaven,
and save us.

S. Jo. iv 52 Thou who at the seventh hour didst will that the fever should leave the nobleman's son:
if aught abide of fever or of sickness in our soul,
take it away from us also,
and save us.

Horolog. p. 135 Thou who at the ninth hour for us sinners and for our sins didst taste of death:
Col. iii 5 mortify in us our earthly members and whatsoever is contrary to thy will,
and save us.

Acts iii 1 Thou who hast willed the ninth hour to be an hour of prayer:
hear us while we pray in the hour of prayer and make us to obtain our prayer and our desires,
and save us.

S. Jo. i 39, 41 Thou who at the tenth hour didst will thine apostle, whenas he found thy Son, to declare with great joy WE HAVE FOUND THE MESSIAS:
make us also in like sort to find the Messias and when He is found in like sort to rejoice,
and save us.

S. Jo. xix 38, 41 Thou who at eventide didst will to be taken down from the cross and buried in the tomb:
take away our sins from us and bury them in thy sepulchre,
Horolog. p. 473 covering with good works whatsoever we have committed ill,
and save us.

S. Mt. xx 6 Thou who didst vouchsafe even at the eleventh hour of the day to send men into thy vineyard and to fix a wage, notwithstanding they had stood all the day idle:
do unto us like favour and, though it be late, as it were about the eleventh hour, accept us graciously when we return to Thee,
and save us.

S. Jo. xiii 2; S. Mt. xxvi 26 Thou who at the hour of supper didst will to institute the most sacred mysteries of thy body and blood:

make us mindful of the same and partakers thereof, and that, never unto judgement but unto remission of sin and unto acquiring of the bequests of the new testament, 1 Cor. xi 34; S. Mt. xxvi 28

and save us.

Thou who late in the night didst by thy breathing confer on thine apostles the authority as well to forgive as to retain sins: S. Jo. xx 19, 22, 23

make us partakers of that authority, yet that it be unto remission, not unto retention, o Lord,

and save us.

Thou who at midnight didst awaken David thy prophet and Paul the apostle to praise Thee: Ps. cxix 62; Acts xvi 25

give us also songs by night and to remember Thee upon our beds, Job xxxv 10; Ps. lxiii 7

and save us.

Thou who with thine own mouth hast avouched that at midnight the Bridegroom shall come: S. Mt. xxv 6

grant that the cry THE BRIDEGROOM COMETH may sound evermore in our ears, that so we be never unprepared to meet Him, S. Jer. *Ep.* lxvi 10; Amos. iv 12

and save us.

Thou who by the crowing of a cock didst admonish thine apostle and make him to return to penitence: S. Mt. xxvi 75

grant us also at the same admonition to do the same, to wit to go forth and weep bitterly the things wherein we have sinned against Thee,

and save us.

Thou who hast foretold that Thou wilt come to judgement in a day when we look not for Thee and at an hour when we are not aware: S. Luke xii 46

make us prepared every day and every hour to be ready for thine advent,

and save us.

MORNING PRAYERS

S. Lk. i 78 Through the tender compassions of our God L 9
the Dayspring from on high hath visited us.

Ps. v 3 1. My voice shalt Thou hear betimes:
early in the morning *will I order my prayer and keep watch.*

Ps. lxiii i *a.* My God, my God, early will I seek Thee.

Ps. lxiii 7, 8 *b.* I have thought upon Thee when I was waking,
because Thou hast been my helper.

Ps. lxxxviii 13 2. Early shall my prayer come before Thee.

Ps. xc 14 3. O satisfy us with thy mercy and that betimes.

Is. xxxiii 2 4. Be Thou our arm every morning:
our salvation also in the time of trouble.

Ps. cxliii 8 5. O let me hear thy lovingkindness betimes in the morning,
for in Thee is my trust.

258 ON WAKING

Thou who sendest forth the light, createst the morning, Ps. xliii 3, lxxiv 17 vulg.
makest the sun to rise on the good and on the evil: * S. Mt. v 45
enlighten the blindness of our minds with the knowledge of the truth:
lift Thou up the light of thy countenance upon us, Ps. iv 7
that in thy light we may see light,* Ps. xxxvi 9
and, at the last, in the light of grace the light of glory.

352 THE MORNING HYMN

Glory be to God on high, *Gloria in excelsis*
and on earth peace,
goodwill towards men.
We praise Thee,
we bless Thee,
we worship Thee,
we glorify Thee,
we give thanks to Thee
for thy great glory,
o Lord, heavenly King,
God the Father almighty,
o Lord the only begotten Son
Jesu Christ,
and o Holy Ghost.
O Lord God,
Lamb of God,
Son of the Father,
that takest away the sins of the world,
have mercy upon us:
Thou that takest away the sins of the world,
receive our prayer:
Thou that sittest at the right hand of the Father,
have mercy upon us.
For Thou only art holy,
Thou only art the Lord,
Jesus Christ,
to the glory of God the Father. Amen.

A FORM OF MORNING PRAYER

L 11
W 9

Cp. *Horolog.* p. 175

Glory be to Thee, o Lord, glory be to Thee.

Horolog. p. 19

Glory be to Him that hath granted me sleep
for repose of weakness,
and for relief of the toils
of this travailling flesh.

Litt. S. Chrys. pp. 93, 101; *S. Ja.* p. 9.

1. To enter on this and every day,
a perfect holy peaceful healthful sinless day:
let us ask of the Lord.
Grant it, o Lord.
2. An angel of peace, a faithful guide,
a guardian of our souls and bodies,
tarrying round about me,*
and suggesting to me alway what things are wholesome:
let us ask of the Lord.

Ps. xxxiv 7

Litt. S. Chrys. pp. 93, 101; *S. Ja.* p. 9

3. The forgiveness and the remission
of all our sins
and of all our offences,
let us ask of the Lord.
4. What things are good and expedient for our souls,
and peace for the world,
let us ask of the Lord.
5. To accomplish the residue of our lifetime
in repentance and godly fear,
in health and peace,
let us ask of the Lord.

Phil. iv 8

6. Whatsoever things are true, whatsoever things are honest,
whatsoever things are just, whatsoever things are pure,
whatsoever things are lovely, whatsoever things are of

good report, if there be any virtue and if there be any praise, that we may think on these things* and practise these things,
let us ask of the Lord.

7. That the end of our life be christian, — *Litt. S. Chrys.* p. 93; *S. Ja.* pp. 10, 29
sinless, shameless,
and (if it like Thee) painless,
and a good defence at the appalling and fearful judgement-seat of Jesus Christ our Lord,
let us ask of the Lord.

Penitence

Superessential essence, nature uncreate, — Dion. Ar. *de div. nom.* i p. 439; *Horolog.* p. 43
Framer of the universe,
I set Thee, Lord, before me, — Ps. xvi 9
and to Thee I lift up my soul: — Ps. xxv 1
I worship Thee kneeling upon my knees, — S. Mk. xv 19
and I humble myself under thy mighty hand: — 1 S. Pet. v 6
I stretch forth my hands, — Ps. cxliii 6
my soul gaspeth unto Thee as a thirsty land:
I smite upon my breast, — S. Lk. xviii 13
and I say with the publican
God be merciful to me the mere sinner,
the chief of sinners: — 1 Tim. i 15
to the sinner beyond the publican, — S. Lk. xviii 13
be merciful as to the publican.

Father of mercies,* — 2 Cor. i 3
I beseech thy fatherly compassionateness,
despise me not 1. an unclean worm, — Cp. *Lay folks mass book* p. 127
2. a dead dog, — 2 Sam. ix 8
3. a rotten carcase. — Isa. xiv 19 vulg.
1. The workmanship of thy hands despise not. — Ps. cxxxviii 8; *Euchelog.* p. 229
2. Thine own image despise not,
albeit bearing brands of sin. — *Horolog.* p. 47
Lord, if Thou wilt Thou canst make me clean: — S. Mt. viii 2
Lord, speak the word only and I shall be made clean.* — 8
And Thou, my Saviour Christ, Christ my Saviour,
Saviour of sinners, of whom I am chief,* — 1 Tim. i 15
despise me not;
the price of thy blood,

thy namesake, despise not,
despise me not, o Lord:
Horae f. 59 but look upon me
with those eyes of thine
wherewith Thou didst look upon
the Magdalene at the feast,
Peter in the hall,
the robber on the rood:
so that
with the robber I may beseech Thee humbly
Remember me, Lord, in thy kingdom:
with Peter I may weep bitterly,
Jer. ix 1 and o that mine eyes were a fountain of tears
that I might weep day and night:
S. Lk. vii 47, 48 with Magdalene I may hear Thee saying
THY SINS ARE FORGIVEN THEE
and with her may love much,
because many sins, because many times so many
are forgiven me.

Lit. S. Ja. p. 3 And Thou allholy and good and quickening Spirit,*
despise me not:
Gen. ii 7 thy breath,*
thy holy things, despise not:
Ps. xc 13 but turn Thee again, o Lord, at the last
Ps. cvi 4 and {be gracious unto / visit} thy servant.

Thanksgiving

Tobit iii 11; 3 Child. 29 Blessed art Thou, o Lord,
our God,
the God of our fathers,
Amos v 8 that turnest the shadow of death into the morning
Ps. civ 30 and renewest the face of the earth:
Heb. even. p. 96 *that rollest darkness from the face of the light,*
that makest the night to pass, that bringest on the day:
Ps. xiii 3 that hast lightened mine eyes that I sleep not in death:
Ps. xci 5 that hast delivered me from terror by night,
6 from the pestilence that walketh in darkness:

that hast driven sleep from mine eyes, *Heb. morn.* p. 6
even slumber from mine eyelids :
that makest the outgoings of the morning and evening to Ps. lxv 8
praise Thee :
for I laid me down and slept and arose, Ps. iii 5
forasmuch as Thou, Lord, didst make me dwell Ps. iv 9
in safety :
for I awaked and beheld and my sleep was sweet Jer. xxxi. 26
unto me.

Comprecation

Blot out as a thick cloud of night my transgressions : Is. xliv 22 ; Hos. xiii 3 ; Wisd. ii 4
scatter as a morning cloud my sins.
Give me to be made a child of light and of the day, 1 Thess. v 5
to walk as in the day, soberly, purely, honestly. Rom. xiii 13
Vouchsafe to keep me this day without sin, *Horolog.* p. 71
upholding me when I fall, lifting me up what time I am Ps. cxlv 14
fallen :
that so I may never harden my heart Ps. xcv 8
in provocation or temptation
or in deceitfulness of any sin. Heb. iii 13
And furthermore deliver me this day Ps. xci 3
from the snare of the hunter,
from the noisome pestilence,
from the arrow that flieth by day, 5
from sickness, 6
from what destroyeth in the noonday.
From evil of {mine / the day} keep {the day / me}. S. Mt. vi 34
Let not my days be consumed in vanity, Ps. lxxviii 33
my years in misfortune.
One day telleth another : Ps. xix 2
let this day tell yesterday some knowledge or practice.
Make me to hear thy lovingkindness betimes in the morning, Ps. cxliii 8
for in Thee is my trust :
show Thou me the way that I should walk in,
for I lift up my soul unto Thee.
Deliver me, o Lord, from mine enemies, 9
for I flee unto Thee to hide me :
teach me to do the thing that pleaseth Thee 10

for Thou art my God:
let thy loving Spirit lead me forth into the land of righteousness.

Ps. cxliii 11 Quicken me, o Lord, for thy Name's sake,
and for thy righteousness' sake bring my soul out of trouble.

Wisd. i 5 Ps. xix 14	Put away from my soul thoughts that are without understanding.	But inspire good thoughts and acceptable in thy sight.
Ps. cxix 37 Prov. iv 25	Turn away mine eyes lest they behold vanity.	Let mine eyes look right on, and mine eyelids straight before me.
Ecclus. xxviii 24, xx 19; Prov. v 1 Is. l 5	Hedge mine ears about with thorns, that they give no heed to undisciplined words.	Waken mine ears morning by morning, and open mine ears to the discipline of the learned.
Ps. cxli 3 Col. iv 6; Eph. iv 29	Set a watch, o Lord, before my mouth, and keep the door of my lips.	Let my speech be seasoned with salt, that it may minister grace to the hearers.
1 Sam. xxv 31 Neh. xiii 31	Let no work be for grief unto me or offence of heart.	But let there be some work done for the which Thou mayest remember me for good.

Neh. xiii 22 And spare me according to
the greatness of thy mercy.

Commendation

Ps. xxxi 6; 1 Th. v 23 Into thy hands I commend my spirit, soul, body:
Thou hast created, redeemed, regenerated them,
o Lord of truth: *
and with me all mine and all things mine:
Thou hast bestowed them upon me, o Lord, in thy goodness.
Ps. cxxi 7 Preserve us from all evil,
preserve our souls, I beseech Thee, o Lord:
S. Ju. 24 keep us from falling and present us faultless
2 Tim. i 18 before the presence of thy glory in that day.
Ps. xix 14 *Let the words of my mouth and the meditation of my heart be alway acceptable in thy sight,*
o Lord my rock and my redeemer:

the beauty of the Lord our God be upon us : Ps. xc 17
and stablish Thou the work of our hands upon us,
yea, the work of our hands stablish Thou it.

LW Preserve my going out and my coming in, Ps. cxxi 8
from this time forth for evermore.

Prosper, I pray Thee, thy servant this day, Neh. i 11
and grant him mercy in the sight of * them that fall in with him.

O God, make speed to save me : Ps. lxx 1
o Lord, make haste to help me,*
L *o my God.*

LW O turn Thee unto me and have mercy upon me : Ps. lxxxvi 16
give thy strength unto thy servant,
and help the son of thine handmaid :
show some token upon me for good, 17
that I be not ashamed
in the sight of them that hate me :
because Thou, Lord, hast holpen me
and comforted me.

A SECOND FORM OF MORNING PRAYER

Ps. lxv 2 Thou that hearest the prayer,
unto Thee shall all flesh come.
Ps. lv 18 In the evening and morning and at noonday
will I pray and that instantly:
and Thou shalt hear my voice.
Ps. v 2 Unto Thee will I make my prayer, o Lord, betimes:
3 betimes shalt Thou hear my voice.
Ps. cxli 2 Let my prayer be set forth
in thy sight as the incense.
Ps. lxiii 7 I have thought upon Thee, o Lord, when I was waking,
8 because Thou hast been my helper.

Comprecation

Prymer, Rouen, N. le Roux, 1537, f. 17b I give Thee thanks, almighty Lord, everlasting God, who not for my merits, but of thy holy mercy, hast vouchsafed, to keep me in this night. Grant me, o Lord, so to pass this day in thy holy service that the dutifulness of my obedience may be pleasing unto Thee.

Lam. iii 41 I lift up my heart with my hands unto God in the heavens.
Ps. cxxiii 2 Behold even as the eyes of servants look unto the hands of their masters,
and the eyes of a maiden unto the hands of her mistress:
even so our eyes wait upon the Lord our God,
until He have mercy upon us.
Ps. cxix 132 O look Thou upon me and be merciful unto me,
as Thou usest to do unto those that love thy name.
Ps. xci 11 Give thine angels charge over me to keep me in thy ways.
Ps. xxv 3 Shew me thy ways
and teach me thy paths:

order my steps in thy word, Ps. cxix 133
and so shall no wickedness have dominion over me:
order my steps in thy paths, Ps. xvii 5
that my footsteps slip not.
O put into my mouth speech that is right and wellsounding, *Horae* f. 99
that all my words and looks and carriage,
and all my works be pleasing
to all men that see and hear me;
that I may find grace in all my speeches and petitions.

Penitence

O Lover of men, Tit. iii 4
very tenderly pitiful, S. Ja. v 11
Father of mercies, 2 Cor. i 3
rich in mercy toward all that call upon Thee: Rom. x 12; Eph. ii 4
I have sinned against heaven and before Thee, S. Lk. xv 18
neither am I worthy to be called a son, 19
neither am I worthy to be made an hired servant,*
no, not the lowest of them all.
But I repent, alas, I repent:
help Thou mine impenitence: Cp. S. Mk. ix. 24
and if there be any comfort of love, Phil. ii 1
for thy bowels of mercies, S. Lk. i 7, 8; Phil ii 1
for the multitude, Ps. li 1
for the riches of thy grace, Eph. i 7
for the exceeding abundance of thy mercies, Cp. Rom. v 20
for the great love wherewith thou didst love us, Eph. ii 4
be merciful to me a sinner, S. Lk. xviii 13; 1 Tim. i 15
be merciful to me of sinners { chief* / most miserable.
Deep calleth unto deep, Ps. xlii 9
the deep of our misery unto the deep of thy mercy. S. Bern. *Serm. Quadr.* iv 3
Where sin abounded let grace much more abound: Rom. v 20
overcome our evil with thy good: Rom. xii
let thy mercy rejoice against thy justice * S. Ja. ii 13
in our sins.
Yea, o Lord,
for above all things and before all things
I believe that Thou art the Christ, the Son of the living God, S. Mt. xvi 16

1 Tim. i 15 which didst come into the world to save sinners,
of whom I am chief: save me.
S. Jo. i 29 Thou that takest away the sins of the world,* take away my sins:
S. Lk. xix 10 Thou that didst come to redeem that which was lost,*
suffer not that to be lost which hath been redeemed of Thee.
Horae f. c. 3b From the remembrance of evil things:
that what things I have seen or heard from evil men
in the world I may not remember
nor ever tell to other;
that I may have in hatred every crooked way.*
Cp. *Horae* f. 78; Ps. ix 4; Heb. iv 16 I have deserved death:
but even now I appeal from the seat of thy justice
to the throne of thy grace.

Intercession

For the Catholic Church:
for the churches throughout the world:
their truth, unity and stability, to wit:
in all let charity thrive, truth live:
for our own church:
Tit. i 5 that the things that are wanting therein be supplied,
that are not right be set in order.*
Horae f. 47b that all heresies, schisms, scandals,
as well public as private, be put out of the way:
correct the erring,
convert the unbelieving,
increase the faith of thy church,
destroy heresies,
Horae f. 97b expose crafty }
crush violent } enemies.*
For the Clergy:
2 Tim. ii 15 that they rightly divide,
Gal. ii 14 that they walk upright,
2 Tim. ii 2 that while teaching others themselves may learn.*
For the People:
Rom. xii 3 that they think not of themselves more highly than the ought,*
but be persuaded by reason

and yield to the authority of superiors.
For Commonwealths:
their {stability and peace.
For the Kingdom,
municipality,
our city;
that they speed well and happily,
and be delivered from all peril and inconvenience.
For the King:
help him now, o Lord: Ps. cxviii 25
o Lord, send him now prosperity:
defend him with truth and favourable kindness as with a shield: *Lit. S. Bas.* p. 61
speak comfortably good things unto him
on behalf of the Church and thy people.*
For the prudence of counsellors,
equity, integrity of judges,
courage of the army,
temperance, holy simplicity} of the people.
For the rising generation,
whether in universities
or in schools,
that as in age so they may increase withal S. Lk. ii 52
both in wisdom and favour
with God and men.*
For them that make themselves beneficent
towards {things sacred, the poor and needy:
reward Thou them sevenfold into their bosom: Ps. lxxix 13
let their souls dwell at ease, Ps. xxv 12
and their seed inherit the land:
let them be blessed that consider the poor. Ps. xli 1
1. That it may please Thee to reward all our benefactors with eternal good things: Litan. Sarisb. *Horae* f. 129b
for the benefits which they have bestowed upon us on earth, *Horae* f. c. 7b
let them win eternal rewards in heaven.
2. That Thou vouchsafe to look upon and to relieve the miseries of the poor and of captives. Litan. Sarisb. *Horae* f. 129b

Horae f. 103b 3. That it may please Thee to remember with benign compassion the frail lapses of the flesh * and to support the falling.

Litan. Sarisb. *Horae* f. 129b 4. That it may please Thee to hold accepted the reasonable service of our obedience.

5. That it may please Thee to raise up our minds to heavenly desires.

6. That it may please Thee to turn back upon us the eyes of mercy.

7. That it may please Thee to deliver the souls of us and of our kinsfolk from eternal damnation.

Horae f. 76b 8. That together with them for whom I have prayed
or for whom I am in any sort bound to pray
and with all the people of God,
Cp. 2 S. Pet. i 11 it be granted me to be brought into thy kingdom,
Col. iii 4; Ps. xvii 16 there to appear in righteousness
and to be satisfied with glory:
Litan. Sarisb. We beseech Thee to hear us, good Lord.

Thanksgiving

Ps. cxlv 10 Let all thy works praise Thee, o Lord,
and thy saints give thanks unto Thee.
Ps. xcii 1 It is a good thing to give thanks unto the Lord,
and to sing praises unto thy Name, o most Highest;
2 to tell of thy lovingkindness early in the morning,
and of thy truth in the night season.
Ps. cxlv 1 I will magnify Thee, o God, my king,
and I will praise thy Name for ever and ever:
2 every day will I give thanks unto Thee,
and praise thy Name for ever and ever:
Rom. iv 17 who hast called the things which be not
as though they were:
Col. i 16 of whom were all things created that are in heaven and earth,
visible and invisible:
Heb. i 3 who upholdest all things by the word of thy power:
Acts xiv 17 who leavest not Thyself without witness in that Thou doest good, and givest us rain from heaven and fruitful seasons, filling our hearts with food and gladness:

forasmuch as all things continue unto this day according to Ps. cxix 91;
thine ordinance: for all things serve Thee: 2 Pet. iii 4
who, after deliberation had, Thyself with thine own hands Gen. i 26
didst form man of the dust of the ground and didst Gen. ii 7
breathe into his nostrils the breath of life:
and didst honour him with thine own image, *Lit. S. Bas.* p. 54
and gavest thine angels charge over him, Ps. xci 11
and didst set him over the works of thine hands, Ps. viii 6
and didst put him into the garden of Eden: Gen. ii 15
and when he despised thy commandments, notwithstanding *Lit. S. Ja.* p. 23
Thou didst not despise him
but didst open for him a door unto repentance and life, Acts xiv 27; xi 18
giving him an exceeding great and precious promise touching Gen. iii 15;
the saving Seed: 2 Pet. i 4
who hast instructed our race
by that which may be known of God, Rom. i 19
by the work of the law written in hearts,* Rom. ii 15
by the worship of sacrifices,
by the oracles of prophets,
by the melody of psalms,* S. Greg. Nyss. *in*
by the prudence of proverbs, *Pss.* 3
by the experience of histories:
who when the fullness of the time was come, Gal. iv 4
didst send thy Son;
which took on Him the seed of Abraham, Heb. ii 16
which emptied Himself, Phil. ii 7
and took upon Him the form of a servant:
which was made of a woman, Gal. iv 4
made under the law: *
by the oblation of his life
rendered the service of the law:
by the sacrifice of his death
took away the curse of the law: Gal. iii 13
by his death redeeming } our race: Cp. Rom. iv 25;
by his resurrection quickening } v 10
leaving nought undone that was needful, Is. v 4
that we might be made partakers of the divine nature: 2 Pet. i 4
who hath made manifest the savour of his knowledge in 2 Cor. ii 14
every place * by the preaching of the gospel:
bearing Himself witness Heb. ii 4
with divers signs and miracles,*

by marvellous sanctity of life:
by stupendous power,
Heb. xii 4; ix 22 even unto shedding of blood: *
by the incredible conversion of the whole world
unto faith
without inter-vention { of any authority
of any persuasion:
who hast made us children of the saints
Heb. xi 9 and heirs of the same calling:
1 Tim. iii 15 who hast given to thy Church to be a pillar and ground of the truth
S. Mt. xvi 18 to the end the gates of hell should not prevail against it:
1 Tim. vi 20 who hast given to ours to keep that which is committed to its trust,
Rom. iii 17 and to teach us the way of peace,
Col. ii 5; 1 Cor. xiv 40 and to keep order, stability and comeliness.
2 Sam. vii 13, 16 who hast stablished the throne of thy servant, our king:
Ps. cxlvii 14 who hast made peace in our borders
and filled us with the flour of wheat;
13 hast made fast the bars of our gates
and dost bless our children within us:
Ps. cxxxii 19 who hast clothed our enemies with shame:
Ps. xxi 6 who hast given us everlasting felicity
and dost make us glad with the joy of thy countenance:
Ps. cv 22 who hast informed our princes,
and taught our senators wisdom:
Jer. iii 15 who hast given us pastors according to thine heart
which feed us with knowledge and understanding:
Is. ii 4 who hast beaten swords into ploughshares
and spears into pruninghooks:
Ps. cxliv 14 for that there is no decay, no leading into captivity
and no complaining in our streets: *
who hast brought me forth into this life
Tit. iii 5 and hast brought me on to the washing of regeneration and renewing of the Holy Ghost:
Ps. xvi 12 and hast shewn me thy paths:
Wisd. xi 23 who hast winked at my sins because I should amend,
Is. lxiv 7 neither hast consumed me because of mine iniquities,
Is. xxx 18 waiting that Thou mightest shew graciousness in me:
Ps. xcv 8 who hast not suffered my heart to be hardened

but hast left pricking of heart Acts ii 37
remembrance of the last things Dt. xxxii 29
conscience of past sin : Heb. x 2
who hast opened to me a door of hope,* Hos. ii 15
when I confess and ask,
by the power of the mysteries and the keys :
who hast not cut off as a weaver my life with pining sickness, Is. xxxviii 12
nor from day even to night made an end of me,
nor taken me away in the midst of mine age, Ps. cii 24
but hast held my soul in life, Ps. lxvi 8
neither suffered my feet to slip :
for all these, &c.

A THIRD FORM OF MORNING PRAYER H 37

Commemoration

Ps. lxxiv 17 O Lord, the day is thine, and the night is thine:
Thou hast prepared the light and the sun:
Ps. cxix 91 they continue this day according to thine ordinance,
for all things serve Thee.
Ps. lv 18; xxxi 25 In the evening, in the morning and at noonday will I pray,
and that instantly,
and Thou, Lord, shalt hear the voice of my prayer:
Ps. v 2, 3 unto Thee, o Lord, will I make my prayer;
early in the morning will I make my prayer unto Thee,
and my voice shalt Thou hear.

Thanksgiving

Ps. cxix 12 Blessed art Thou, o Lord,
Am. v 8 which turnest the shadow of death into the morning,
Ps. civ 30 and dost renew the face of the earth:
Ps. xci 5, 6 which hast delivered us from terror by night,
from the pestilence that walketh
in the darkness:
Ps. xiii 3 which hast lightened our eyes that they sleep not in
death:
Heb. morn. p. 6 which hast made sleep to pass from our eyes
and slumber from our eyelids.

Petition

Is. xliv 22; Hos. xiii 3 Blot out, o Lord, as a thick cloud of night our transgressions
and as a morning cloud our sins:
1 Thess. v 5 make us children of the day and of the light:
Rom. xiii 13 grant us to walk chastely and soberly as in the day.
Te Deum Vouchsafe, o Lord, to keep us this day without sin.

Keep us from the arrow that flieth by day, Ps. xci 5
and from the sickness that destroyeth in the noonday: 6
deliver us from the hand of the hunter and from the noisome pestilence: 3
from the evil of this day keep us. S. Mt. vi 34
Today salvation and peace be to this house. S. Lk. x 5, xix 9
O let me hear thy lovingkindness, Ps. cxliii 8
for in Thee is my trust:
show Thou me the way that I should walk in,
for I raise my soul unto Thee.
Deliver me, o Lord, from mine enemies, 9
for I flee unto Thee to hide me:
instruct me to do what things are pleasing in thy sight, 10
for Thou art my God:
let thy loving Spirit lead me forth into the land of righteousness.
Regard thy servants and their works; Ps. xc 16; S. Lk. i 48
and the grace and glorious majesty of the Lord our God be upon us: Ps. xc 17
prosper Thou the work of our hands upon us,
o prosper Thou our handywork.
Set a watch, o Lord, before my mouth Ps. cxli 3
and keep the door of my lips:
let my speech be with grace, sprinkled with salt, Col. iv 6
that I may know how I ought to answer every man:
let the converse of my mouth and the meditation of my heart Ps. xix 14
be alway acceptable in thy sight,
o Lord my redeemer. 15
The Lord preserve our going out and coming in Ps. cxxi 8
henceforth and for evermore. Amen.

MORNING PRAYERS FOR A WEEK

I. SUNDAY

S. Lk. i 78 Through the tender compassions of our God,
the Dayspring from on high hath visited us.*

Commemoration

Horolog. p. 82; *Heb. morn.* p. 39 A. Glory be to Thee, o Lord, glory be to Thee,
which didst create the light and lighten the world.
Ps. cxviii 27 sept. vulg. God is the Lord who hath showed us light:
appoint ye a holiday with crowded folk,
yea, even up to the horns of the altar: *
the visible light { sun's beam,
flame of fire;
{ day and night
evening and morning:
the intellectual light,
Rom. i 19 { that which may be known of God *
what is written of the law
{ oracles of prophets
melody of psalms
admonition of proverbs
experience of histories:
Euchology. p. 289 the light whereof there is no eventide.
Rom. vi 4 B. By thy resurrection raise us up to newness of life,
Horolog. p. 474 suggesting unto us ways of repentance.
Heb. xiii 20, 21 The God of peace that brought again from the dead
that great Shepherd of the sheep,
through the blood of the everlasting covenant,
our Lord Jesus Christ:
make us perfect in every good work
to do his will,

working in us that which is wellpleasing in his sight,
through Jesus Christ,
to whom be glory
for ever.
C. Thou who on this day didst send down — *Horolog.* p. 85
thy thriceholy Spirit on thy disciples:
take It not withal from us, o Lord,
but renew It day by day in us who supplicate Thee.

Penitence

1. O Lord, full of compassion and mercy, — Ps. lxxxvi 15
longsuffering and plenteous in goodness:
I have sinned, I have sinned, o Lord, against Thee. — Ps. xli 4
Alas, wretched man that I am,* I have sinned, o Lord, against Thee: — Rom. vii 24
much and grievously have I sinned,
and that by observing lying vanities: — Jonah ii 8
L *and it profited me not.* — *Job xxxiii* 27
LW 2. I hide not anything: I make none excuses: — Josh. vii 19; Ps. cxli 4 sept.
I give Thee glory, o Lord, this day:
I acknowledge against myself my sins: — Ps. xxxii 5
indeed it is I that have sinned against the Lord, — Josh. vii 20
and thus and thus have I done.
O what have I done and Thou hast not requited me — Job xxxiii 27 sept.
the due reward of my sins: — S. Lk. xxiii 41
L *and it profited me not.* — *Job xxxiii* 27
LW 3. And what shall I say now or wherewith shall I open my mouth? — Is. xxxviii 15; Job xxxii 20
what shall I answer, for myself have done it?
Excuseless, defenceless, self-condemned am I. — Rom. ii 1; Tit. iii 11
My destruction cometh of myself: — Cp. Hos. xiii 9
o Lord, righteousness belongeth unto Thee, — Dan. ix 7
but unto me confusion of face.
Howbeit Thou art just in all that is brought upon me; — Neh. ix 33
for Thou hast done right and I have done wickedly.
4. And now what is my hope? Is it not Thou, o Lord? — Ps. xxxix 8
Yea, my hope is even in Thee,*
if I have hope of salvation, — 1 Th. v 8

Cp. *Euchol.* pp. 556, 373 — if thy love towards mankind overcome the multitudes of mine iniquities.

Ps. lxxviii 38, 39 — *But He is so merciful that He forgiveth iniquity* L
and destroyeth not:
yea many a time turneth He his wrath away
and suffereth not his whole displeasure to arise.

Ps. ciii 14 — *For the Lord knoweth whereof we are made*
He remembereth that we are but dust,

Ps. lxxviii 40 — *and He remembereth that we are but flesh,*
a wind that passeth away and cometh not again.

Ps. lxxxix 46 — O remember what my substance is, *remember how short my time is :* LW

Ps. cxxxviii 8 — *the work of thy hands,**
the image of thy countenance,
the price of thy blood,
the name from thy name,
Ps. lxxiv 1 — *the sheep of thy pasture,*
Acts iii 25 — *the son of thy covenant.*

Ps. cxxxviii 8; *Euchol.* p. 229 — The workmanship of thy hands despise not.
Ger[illegible] — Thine own image and likeness,
Ps. lxxxix 46 — hast Thou indeed made it for nought? *
For nought, if Thou destroy it.
Cp. Ps. xxx 9 — And what profit is there in my destruction?
Ps. xxxviii 16 — Thine enemies will triumph over me : *
o let them never triumph over me, o Lord :
grant not to thine enemies my destruction,
Cp. *Ps. viii* 2 — *because of thine enemies.* L
Ps. lxxxiv 9 — *Look upon the face of thine Anointed,* LW
Zech. ix 11; Heb. xiii 20 — and in the blood of thy covenant,
1 Jo. ii 2 — in the propitiation for the sins of the whole world,
S. Lk. xviii 13 — Lord, be merciful to me the sinner,
be merciful to me,* o Lord, of sinners
1 Tim. i 15 — chief, chiefest and greatest.
Ps. xxv 10 — For thy Name's sake be merciful unto my sin,
for it is great,*
for it is so great as none can be greater :
Acts iv 12 — for the sake of that Name of thine,

apart wherefrom there is none other under heaven
given among men
whereby we must be saved.

L *We have sinned and there is none to stand up in our behalf:* Heb. morn. p. 59
notwithstanding let thy great Name stand up for us
in the time of trouble.

LW May the Spirit Himself help our infirmities Rom. viii 26
and make intercession for us
with groanings which cannot be uttered.

For the Father's fatherly bowels,* Ap. const. viii 9
the Son's bloody wounds,
the Spirit's unutterable groanings, Rom. viii. 26

L *in wrath remember mercy and repent Thee of the evil.* Hab. iii 2; Joel ii 13

LW O Lord, hear: Dan. ix 19
o Lord, forgive:
o Lord, hearken and do and defer not
for thine own sake,
Lord, Lord my God.*

But as for me Cp. S. Chrys. Hom. 31 in Heb. 3; Ps. li 3; xxxviii 17; Job vii 2; x 1
I forget not my sins,
they are ever before me:
I count them up again in the bitterness of my soul,
I am anxious for them, *I am sorry,* Ps. xxxviii 18
I turn away and groan, Is. xxx 15 sept.
I have indignation, Cp. 2 Cor. vii 11
I have revenge,
I am weary of myself, Gen. xxvii 46
I abhor and buffet mine own self,* Job xlii 6; 1 Cor. ix 27
that not more, not more fully
do I repent, Lord. O Lord, I repent, Cp. S. Mk. ix 24
help Thou mine impenitence *
and more and still more
pierce, rend in pieces, grind to powder Ps. cix 15; Joel ii 13; Ps. cxlvii 3
my heart.

And remit, assoil, pardon all things Lit. S. Ja. p. 30
that are for grief unto me and offence of heart: 1 Sam. xxv 31
cleanse Thou me from my secret faults, Ps. xix 12
keep thy servant from presumptuous sins: 13
shew thy marvellous lovingkindness * Ps. xvii 7
upon the mere sinner,
and in due time say unto me, Lord,

S. Mt. ix 2 BE OF GOOD CHEER : THY SINS ARE FORGIVEN THEE,
2 Cor. xii 9 MY GRACE IS SUFFICIENT FOR THEE.
Ps. xxxv 3 Say unto my soul I AM THY SALVATION.
Ps. xlii 6 Why art thou so heavy, o my soul,
and why art thou so disquieted within me?
Ps. cxvi 7 Turn again then unto thy rest, o my soul,
for the Lord hath rewarded thee.
Penitent. Pss. vi 1 1. O Lord, rebuke me not in thine indignation:
neither chasten me in thy displeasure.
xxxii 6 2. I said I will confess my sins unto the Lord:
and so Thou forgavest the iniquity of my sin.
xxxviii 9 3. Lord, Thou knowest all my desire:
and my groaning is not hid from Thee.
li 1 4. Have mercy upon me, o God, after thy great goodness:
according to the multitude of thy mercies do away mine offences.
cii 13 5. Thou shalt arise, o Lord, and have mercy upon me:
for it is time that Thou have mercy upon me, yea the time is come.
cxxx 3 6. If Thou, Lord, wilt be extreme to mark what is done amiss,
who may abide it?
cxliii 2 7. Enter not into judgment with thy servant:
for in thy sight shall no man living be justified.

Comprecation

Ps. cxix 48 My hands will I lift up unto thy commandments which I have loved.
Ps. cxix 18 Open Thou mine eyes and I shall see,
Ps. cxix 36, 20 incline my heart and I shall desire,
Ps. cxix 133 order my steps and I shall walk
Ps. cxix 35 in the path of thy commandments.*
O Lord God, be Thou to me a God:
Ex. xx 3 (heb.); Is. xxvi 13 beside Thee let there not be to me another,
Deut. xxxii 39 none else, nought else with Thee.
Grant unto me
to adore Thee and to worship Thee
Cp. S. Jo. iv 24 i. in truth of spirit,

ii. in comeliness of body,
iii. in blessing of the mouth,
iv. in private and in public :
v. and to render
honour to them that have the rule, {to obey / to submit myself to} them ; Heb. xiii 17
natural affection to mine own, {to care / to provide} for them : 1 Tim. v 8
vi. to overcome evil with good : Rom. xii 21
vii. to win possession of my vessel in sanctification and honour : 1 Thess. iv 4
viii. to have my conversation without covetousness, Heb. xiii 5
being content with such things as I have :
ix. to follow the truth in love : Eph. iv 15
x. to desire not to lust, Ps. cxix 20 sept.
not to lust with concupiscence, 1 Thess. iv 5
not to walk after lusts. Ecclus. xviii 30; S. Jude 16

The Hedge of the Law

To bruise the serpent's head, Gen. iii 15
to remember the last things, Ecclus. xli 3 (Is. xlvii 7; Lam. i 9)
to cut off occasions, 2 Cor. xi 12
to be sober, 1 Pet. v 8
not to sit idle, Cp. S. Mt. xx 6
to refuse the evil, Cp. 1 Tim. v 11; Tit. iii 10
to cleave to the good, Rom. xii 9
to make a covenant touching the eyes, Job xxxi 1
to bring the body into subjection, 1 Cor. ix 27
to give oneself to prayer, 1 Cor. vii 5
to withdraw unto penitence. 2 Pet. iii 9

Hedge Thou up my way with thorns, Hos. ii 6; Ecclus. xxviii 24
that I find not the path
to follow after vanity : Prov. xxi 6
hold Thou my mouth with bit and bridle, Ps. xxxii 10 sept.
who come not nigh Thee :
o Lord, compel me to come in unto Thee. S. Lk. xiv 23

Faith

I believe, o Lord, in Thee
one God { Father / Word / Spirit :
that by thy natural affection and power
the universe hath been created :
Tit. iii 4 that by thy kindness and love towards mankind
Eph. i 10 the universe hath been summed up
in thy Word :
Nicene creed who for us men and for our salvation
S. Jo. i 14 was made flesh
S. Lk. i 31 was conceived, was brought forth,
Apost. creed suffered, was crucified,
died, was buried,
descended, rose again,
ascended, sat down,
will return again,* will recompense :
that by the onshining and operation
of thy Holy Spirit
hath been called out of the universal
Tit. ii 14 a peculiar people,
2 Thess. ii 13 unto a commonwealth after belief of the truth,
Cp. 2 Pet. iii 11 after holiness of conversation ;
that herein we partake
Apost. creed of the communion of saints } in the time present ;
of the forgiveness of sins }
Nicene creed that herein we look for
a resurrection of the flesh } in the time to come.
life everlasting }
S. Jude 20 This most holy faith
3 which was once delivered unto the saints,
S. Mt. ix 24 Lord, I believe,
help Thou mine unbelief,
Cp. S. Lk. xvii 5 increase Thou my littleness of faith :
and grant unto me
to love the Father for his natural affection,
to reverence the Almighty for his power :
1 Pet. iv 19 to Him as unto a faithful Creator to commit the
keeping of my soul in welldoing : *

from Jesus / Christ / the onlybegotten Son } to partake of { salvation, / unction, / adoption : — S. Mt. i 21; 1 Jo. ii 20; Gal. iv. 5, 6

to serve the Lord

for the conception — in faith,
the nativity — humility,
the sufferings — endurance and antipathy to all things touching sin,
the cross — to crucify occasions,
the death — to mortify the flesh,
the burial — to bury evil purposes by good works,* — *Horolog.* p. 473
the descent — to meditate on the things in hades, — Cp. S. Greg. Naz. *Or.* xlv 24
resurrection — on newness of life, — Rom. vi 4
ascension — to set my affection on things above, — Col. iii 2
sitting — on the better things at the right hand,* — Cp. Col. iii 1; Ps. xvi 12
return — to mind the fear of the second advent,
judgement — to judge myself or ever I be judged: * — Cp. 1 Cor. xi 31

from the Spirit to receive the breath
of the grace that bringeth salvation : — Tit. ii 11

in the Church / holy / catholic } to partake of { calling, / sanctification, / distribution,* — Heb. iii 1; Cp. Heb. xii 14; Heb. ii 4

and of the communion of the hallowed things,
prayers, fastings,
groanings, watchings,
tears, afflictions,

unto confidence of forgiveness of sins,
hope of resurrection / translation } unto life everlasting.

Hope

O Thou that art the hope of all the ends of the earth — Ps. lxv 5
and of them that remain in the broad sea :
o Thou in whom our fathers hoped, — Ps. xxii 4, 5
and Thou didst deliver them ;

for whom they waited and they were not confounded:
Ps. lxxi 4 my hope even from my youth,
Ps. xxii 9, 10 when I hanged yet upon my mother's breasts,
unto whom I have been left ever since I was born:
Ps. cxlii 6 be Thou my hope
Ps. cxli 5 B. yet and yet again
Ps. cxlii 6 and my portion in the land of the living.*
In thy nature,
in thy names,
in thy types,
in thy word,
in thy work is my hope:
Ps. cxix 116 let me not be disappointed
of this my hope.

Intercession

Ps. lxv 5 O Thou that art the hope of all the ends of the earth:
Neh. xiii 31 remember all thy creation for good;
Cp. Ps. cvi 4 o visit the world with thy compassions.
Job vii 20; cp. Wisd. xi 26 O Thou preserver of men, o Lord thou lover of man: *
remember all our race,
Rom. xi 32 and, as Thou has concluded all in unbelief,
on all have mercy, o Lord.
Rom. xiv 9, 8 O Thou that for this end didst die and come to life again,
that Thou mightst be Lord both of dead and living:
whether we live or whether we die we are thine,
Thou art our Lord:*
have mercy on quick and dead, o Lord.
Ps. ix 9; *Lit. S. Bas.* p. 62; *S. Ja.* p. 16 O succourer of the succourless, refuge in due time of trouble:
remember all that are in necessity,
and need thy succour.*
S. Jo. i 17; 1 Pet. v 10; Dt. xxxii 4; Is. lxv 16 O God of grace and truth:
2 Pet. i 12 establish all that stand in grace and truth:
Gal. vi 1; 1 Tim. vi 4 restore all that are sick of heresies and sins.
Ps. xxviii 9 O Thou wholesome defence of thine anointed:
Ps. lxxiv 2 remember thy congregations
which Thou hast purchased and established and redeemed of old:
Acts iv 32 o may the heart and soul of them that believe be one.

O Thou that walkest in the midst of the golden candlesticks : Apoc. ii 1
remove not our candlestick out of its place : Apoc. ii 5
set in order the things that are wanting, Tit. i 5
strengthen the things that remain, that Thou wast ready to cast away. Apoc. iii 2
O Thou Lord of the harvest : S. Mt. ix 38
send forth the labourers enabled of Thee into thy harvest. 2 Cor. iii 5
O Thou portion of them that wait at thy temple : * 1 Cor. ix 13
grant to our clergy
rightly to divide the word of truth, 2 Tim. ii 15
to walk uprightly therein : * Gal. ii 14
grant to the Christloving people
to obey and submit themselves to them. Heb. xiii 17
O King of the nations * unto the ends of the earth : Rev. xv 3
strengthen all the commonwealths of the whole world,
as thine institution, albeit the ordinance of man : Rom. xiii 2; 1 Pet. ii 13
scatter the peoples that delight in wars; Ps. lxviii 30
make wars to cease in all the world. Ps. xlvi 9
Lord, on whom the isles do wait and on whom they hope : Is. li 5; lx 9
deliver this island and all the country wherein we sojourn *Lit. S. Ja.* p. 9; *Lit. S. Chrys.* p. 100
from all tribulation, peril and necessity.
Lord of lords,* Prince of princes : Rev. xvii 14
remember all princes *Lit. S. Bas.* p. 61
to whom Thou hast given the right to rule on the earth : *
and o especially remember
our king preserved of God, *Euchology.* p. 21
and more and more work with him
and give him prosperity in all things :
speak comfortably unto him good things *Lit. S. Bas.* p. 61
in behalf of thy church
and of all the people :
bestow upon him profound peace that may not be taken away,
that in his serenity [Cp. Jer. xxix 7]
we may lead a quiet and peaceable life [1 Tim. ii 2]
with all godliness and honesty. *
O Thou of whom are the powers ordained : * Rom. xiii 1
grant unto them that are eminent at court
to be eminent both for virtue and for fear of Thee :
to the parliament thy holy prudence;

2 Cor. xiii 8 to our powerful men to have no power against the truth,
but for the truth ; *
to the judicature thy judgements, to judge all persons in
1 Tim. v 21 all causes without prejudice and partiality.
Is. xliv 6 O God of sabaoth (of the armies to wit) :
Horolog. p. 21 speed and strengthen all the Christloving army
S. Jude 20 against the foes of our most holy faith :
grant to our people
Rom. xiii 5 to be subject unto rule
not only for wrath but also for conscience' sake : *
to husbandmen and graziers, good seasons ;
to the fleet and fishermen, fair weather ;
to tradesmen, not to overreach one another ;
to mechanics, to work lawfully at their occupation ;
even down to the sordid craftsmen,
even down to the beggars.
God not of us only but also of our seed :
Ps cxlvii 13 ; S. Lk. ii 52 bless our children among us that they may increase
in wisdom as in stature withal,
and in favour both with Thee and with men.
1 Tim. v 8 ; 2 Tim. iii 3 Thou that willest we provide for our own and hatest them
that are without natural affection :
Rom. ix 3 remember, Lord, my kinsmen according to the flesh :
Esth. x 3 : Ps. cxxii 9 grant me to speak peace concerning them and to
seek to do them good. *
Thou that willest we requite them that do us good :
Neh. v 19 remember, Lord, for good * all
at whose hands I have received good offices :
Ps. xli 2 keep them alive and bless them upon earth
and never deliver them into the will of their enemies.
1 Tim. v 8 Thou that hast written that he that is careless of them of his
own house is worse than an infidel :
Ps. cvi 4 remember according to thy favour all in my household :
S. Lk. x 5, 6 peace be to my house,
the son of peace be upon all therein.
S. Mt. v 20 Thou that willest that our righteousness exceed the righteousness of sinners :
S.Aug.*Conff.* iv 9 grant unto me, Lord, to love again them that love me ;
Prov. xxvii 10 mine own friends and my father's friends
and friends' children never to forsake.

Thou that willest we overcome evil with good and pray for them which despitefully use us: * — Rom. xii 21; S. Mt. v 44
have mercy on mine enemies, Lord, as on myself
and bring them unto thy heavenly kingdom,* even as myself. — 2 Tim. iv 18

Thou which grantest the prayers of thy servants one for another:
remember, o Lord, for good, and grant mercy * — Neh. v 19; 2 Tim. i 18
to all them that bear me in mind in their prayers
and all I have promised to bear in mind in my prayers.

Thou that in every good work holdest accepted a ready mind: — 2 Cor. viii 12
them that for reasonable causes give not themselves to prayer — *Lit. S. Bas.* p. 62; 1 Cor. vii 5
remember, Lord,* as if they did pray unto Thee.

Thou shalt arise and have mercy on them that are in extreme necessity, for it is time that Thou have mercy, yea the time is come: * — Ps. cii 13
and Thou shalt have mercy on them, Lord, as on me withal when I am in extremities.

The infants, — Cp. *Lit. S. Bas.* p. 62
children,
youths,
young,
grown men,
old,
them that are in extreme age,
and helplessness; *

the hungry, — S. Mt. xxv. 44
thirsty,
naked,
sick,
prisoners,
strangers,* unfriended,
unburied; — *Lit. S. Ja.* p. 15

possessed
unto suicide,
vexed with unclean spirits; — *Lit. S. Bas.* p. 62
sick in soul,
or body,
weakhearted,
them that are past hope;
those in prison
and bonds,
the condemned to death;
orphans,
widows,
strangers,

them that travel by land
by water;
Cp. S. Mt. xxiv 19 with child,
giving suck;
Lit. S. Ja. p. 27 those in bitter thraldoms,
mines,*
galleys;
Lit. S. Bas, p. 61 those in solitude.
Ps. xxxvi 7 Thou, Lord, shalt save both man and beast:
how excellent is thy mercy, o God,
and therefore the children of men shall put their trust
under the shadow of thy wings.*

Blessing

Num. vi 24-26 1. The Lord bless us and keep us:
2. The Lord make his face to shine upon us
and be gracious unto us:
3. The Lord lift up his countenance upon us
and give us peace.

Commendation

Horae f. 100 I commend unto thee, o Lord,
my soul and my body,
my mind and my thoughts,
my prayers and all my vows,
Horae f. 40b, c. 6 my senses and my members,
my life and my death,
my brothers, sisters and their children,
friends and benefactors,
commended,
household, neighbours,
country and all Christian folk.

Praise and thanksgiving

Dion. Ar. *de div. nom.* i 1 Superessential essence,
Horolog. p. 43 nature uncreate,
Framer of the universe:
God *Gen.* i 1 *Creator* *Eccl.* xii 1 *Merciful* *Ex.* xxxiv 6, 7
Jehovah, the Name *Dt.* xxviii 58 *Possessor* *Gen.* xiv 10 *Gracious*

L

Most high	*Gen. xiv* 18	*Deliverer*	*Ps. cxxx* 8	*Longsuffering*
Lord	*Gen. xviii* 27	*Redeemer*	*Job xix* 25	*Abundant in goodness*
Almighty	*Gen. xvii* 1	*Preserver*	*Neh. ix* 6	*Keeping mercy for thousands*
Eternal	*Gen. xxi* 33	*Sanctifier*	*Ex. xxxi* 13; *Lev. xx* 8	*Forgiving iniquity and transgression*
Living, seeing me	*Gen. xvi* 14			*Repenting Him of the evil.*

Blessed, praised, celebrated, — *Heb. morning* p. 37
magnified, exalted,
*glorified, hallowed be thy holy Name**

LW[2] for godhead,
incomprehensibleness,
height,
lordship,
almightiness,
eternity,
providence.

L *The God of truth, the God of knowledge, the God of pardons*
*the Holy One, the God of hosts.** — *Dt. xxxii* 4; *Is. lxv* 16; 1 *Sam. ii* 3; *Neh.* ix 17; *Is. xl* 25; *Ps. lxxxiv* 13
Commemorated, lauded, extolled, honoured, uplifted
be my strong tower, — *Ps. lxi* 3
my stronghold, — *Ps. xliii* 2
my refuge, — *Ps. cxlii* 5

	LW[2]	
my strength	strength,	Ps. xviii 1
my rock	foundation,	
my fortress	refuge,	
my deliverer	deliverer,	
my God	God,	
my strong rock in whom I will trust	succourer,	
my shield	protection,	
my horn of salvation	horn of salvation,	
my high tower	helper.	

L *Blessed art Thou, o Lord our God, God of our fathers,* — *Heb. Pr. Bk.* p. 44
which givest sight to the blind, — *ib. p.* 6 [*Ps. cxlvi* 7]
makest the dumb to speak, — *ib. p.* 125
loosest the prisoners, — *ib. p.* 6 [*Ps. cxlvi* 7]
dost clothe the naked,

Ps. cxlvi 6 — *givest food to the hungry,*
Heb. Pr. Bk. p. 45 [*Ps. cxlv* 14] — *upholdest such as fall,*
ib. p. 6 [*Ps. cxlv* 14] — *liftest up those that are down,*
Ps. cxlvii 2 — *gatherest together the outcasts,**
deliverest the captives,
Heb. Pr. Bk. p. 45 — *sustainest the living,*
healest the sick,
quickenest the dead,
Ps. cxlvi 9 — *preservest the strangers,*
fatherless,
widow,
Ps. cxlvii 6 — *settest up the meek,*
Heb. Pr. Bk. p. 136 — *bringest down the haughty,*
liftest up the lowly,
Ps. cxlvi 8 — *lovest the righteous,**
dost compassionate sinners,
Heb. Pr. Bk. p. 44 — *bestowest loving kindnesses,*
ib. p. 136 — *answerest the meek when they cry unto Thee,*
ib. p. 45 — *dost establish thy faith with them that sleep in dust,**
teachest the way of repentance,
ib. p. 50 [cp. *Gen. xxxv* 3] — *answerest in time of trouble,*
ib. p. 49 — *makest salvation to flourish,*
ib. p. 45 — *rememberest thy creatures in mercy,*
ib. p. 251 [*Gen. ix* 15] — *thy covenant,**
the seed of thy beloved,
ib. p. 44 — *the pieties of the fathers,*
Hab. iii 2 — *mercy in wrath.*
Lit. S. Ja. p. 21 — Let us lift up our hearts unto the Lord. W
It is very meet and right, LW
fitting and our bounden duty *
Cp. *Lit. S. Bas.* p. 57 — in all things and for all things,
1 Cor. i 2; 2 Th. iii 16; cp. Eph. vi 18 — at all times, in all places, every way,
in every hour and country,
alway, everywhere, altogether,
to commemorate Thee,
Lit. S. Ja. p. 22 — to worship Thee,
to confess to Thee,
to praise Thee,
to bless,
to hymn,
to give thanks to Thee,

of all things * that are
creator nourisher
preserver governor healer
benefactor perfecter
Lord and Father,
King and God,
the wellspring of life and immortality, Lit. S. Ja. p. 22
the treasury of eternal goods,
whom the heavens hymn,
and the heaven of heavens,
the angels and all the heavenly hosts
without ceasing * 1 Th. v 17
crying one to another,
and we lowly and unworthy
under their feet,* Cp. Lit. S. Ja. p. 29
with them :
HOLY, HOLY, HOLY, Is. vi 3; Rev. iv 8; Te Deum
LORD GOD OF SABAOTH,
THE WHOLE HEAVEN AND THE WHOLE EARTH
ARE FULL
OF THE MAJESTY OF THY GLORY.*
BLESSED BE THE GLORY OF THE LORD FROM HIS PLACE. Ezek. iii 12

L **Prayer for Sunday**

Accept our rests : Heb. Pr. Bk. p. 139
hallow us by thy commandments :
give us our portion in thy law :
satisfy us with thy goodness :
gladden our heart with thy salvation
and purify our heart to serve Thee in truth
and make us to inherit in love and favour.

Give glory unto thy people, ib. p. 239
praise to them that fear Thee,
thanksgiving to them that seek Thee,
boldness to them that wait for Thee,
joy to thy land,
gladness to thy city,
flourishing of the horn to thy servant,
the ordaining of a lantern to thine anointed.

II. MONDAY

Ps. v 3 — My voice shalt thou hear betimes, o Lord:
early in the morning *will I order my prayer unto Thee and will keep watch.*

Commemoration

Ps. cxix 12 — Blessed art Thou, o Lord,
Gen. i 7 — who didst create the firmament of heaven,
1 K. viii 27; Ps. cxlviii 4 — the heavens and the heavens of heavens;
Lit. S. Ja. p. 8 — the heavenly hosts
Targ. Jerus. on Gen. i 26 — angels, archangels,
cherubim, seraphim:
Ps. cxlviii 4 — waters above the heavens,
Jer. x 13 heb. — vapours,*
exhalations,
whereof
Ps. cxxxv 7 — rains, clouds from the ends
dew, of the earth,
Ps. cxlviii 8; Jer. x 13 — hail, lightnings, thunders,
Ps. cxlvii 16 — snow like wool, winds out of treasures,
Ps. cxlviii 8 — hoar frost as ashes, storms,
Ps. cxlvii 16 — ice as morsels:
Gen. i 9 — waters under the heavens *
for drinking
washing.

Penitence

Of Moses
Lev. xxvi 40 — I will confess mine iniquities
and the iniquities of my fathers,
that I have trespassed and despised Thee, o Lord,
and have walked contrary unto Thee.
Ps. xc 8 — Set not, o Lord, my misdeeds before Thee
nor my secret sins in the light of thy countenance:
Num. xiv 19 — but pardon the iniquity of thy servant
according unto the greatness of thy mercy
as Thou hast forgiven him
from childhood even until now.

Of Job
I have sinned: what shall I do unto Thee, Job vii 20, 21
o Thou watcher of men?
why hast Thou set me as a mark against Thee,
so that I am a burden to myself?
O why dost Thou not pardon my transgression
and take away mine iniquity?
Deliver my soul from going down into the pit Job xxxiii 28, 24
for Thou hast found wherewith to be appeased.

Of the Canaanitish woman
Have mercy on me, o Lord, Thou Son of David: Mt. xv 22, 25, 27
Lord, help me:
yea, Lord, even the whelps eat
of the crumbs that fall
from their masters' table.

Of the debtor in ten thousand talents
Have patience with me, o Lord; Mt. xviii 26, 25, 32
or rather
I have not aught to repay, I confess unto Thee:
forgive me all the debt,
I beseech Thee.

How long wilt Thou forget me, o Lord, for ever? Ps. xiii 1-5a
how long wilt Thou hide thy face from me?
how long shall I take counsel in my soul,
having sorrow in my heart day and night?
how long shall mine enemy triumph over me?
Consider and answer me, o Lord my God;
lighten mine eyes
that I sleep not in death;
lest mine enemy say
I have prevailed against him:
lest mine adversaries rejoice when I am moved.
But as for me, in thy mercy do I trust:
L *let my heart be joyful in thy salvation:* *Ps.* xiii 5b, 6
I will sing unto the Lord because He hath dealt bountifully
with me.

Deprecation

Put away from me LW

Ex. xx 3-17 1. all irreligiousness and profanity,
all superstitiousness and hypocrisy,
2. idolatry and idiolatry,
Tertull. *de pudic.* 19 3. rash oath and curse,*
4. withdrawal from and indecency in worship:

5. swelling and heedlessness,
6. strife and wrath,
7. passion and corruption,
8. sloth and dishonesty,
9. leasing and insolence,
Lit. S. Ja. p. 31 10. every evil conceit,
every lascivious thought,
every shameful lust,
every unseemly thought.*

Comprecation

Grant unto me
1. Godfearingness and religion,
2. adoration and worship,
3. fair speech and faithfulness to mine oath,
4. comely confession in the assembly:

5. kindly-affectionedness and obedience,
6. patience and friendly-mindedness,
7. purity and sobriety,
8. contentedness and goodness,
9. truth and incorruptibleness,
10. *good imagining,*
continuance unto the end. W

Faith

Apost. creed I believe in God LW

i. Father, almighty, maker of {heaven and earth.

ii. And in *a.* Jesus
b. Christ
c. his onlybegotten Son
d. our Lord:

1. conceived of the Holy Ghost
2. born of Mary evervirgin
3. suffered under Pontius Pilate
4. crucified
5. dead
6. buried
    (1) descended into hell
    (2) risen again from the dead
    (3) ascended into heaven
    (4) set at the right hand
    (5) to return again therefrom
    (6) unto judgement both of quick and of dead.

iii. And in the Holy Ghost:
    a Church
    (1) holy
    (2) catholic
    (3) a communion of saints:
    1. forgiveness of sins
    2. resurrection of flesh
    3. life everlasting.

Hope

And now, Lord, what is my hope? Ps. xxxix 8
Truly my hope is even in Thee.
In Thee, o Lord, have I trusted; Ps. xxxi 1
let me never be confounded.

Intercession

Let us beseech the Lord * *Litt. patr.* p. 5 etc.
for the whole creation:
a supply of seasons { healthful, fruitful, peaceful:
for all our race:
{ not Christians
{ Christians
{ fallen asleep aforetime: { rest, light;
{ living: conversion of { atheists, ungodly, paynims, Turks, Jews:

for the restoration of them that are sick of { errors, sins;

S. Jo. i 17 confirmation of them to whom Thou grantest { truth, grace : *

for the succour and consolation

of all, men and women, suffering hardness in { dejection, sickness, resourcelessness, unsettlement;

for the thankfulness and sobriety

of all, men and women, that are in good case in { cheerfulness, health, resourcefulness, tranquillity:

for the Church Catholic,
its confirmation and increase:
eastern,
its deliverance and union:
western,
its readjustment and pacification:
British,
Tit. i 5 the restoration of the things that are wanting } therein:
Rev. iii 2 the strengthening of the things that remain * } therein:
for the episcopate, presbyterate, Christloving people:
for the commonwealths 1. of the world,
2. Christian and far off,
3. neighbouring,
4. ours:
for those in authority:
our king preserved by God,
the queen and the prince,
them that are eminent at court,
parliament, judicature, civil control, armed force,
commonalty, leaders of the commonalty,
husbandry, grazing, fishery,
commerce, trade, mechanical occupation,
even down to { the sordid craftsmen, the beggars:
for the succession:
the good education of all the royal seed,
of the scions of the nobility:

of those in universities,
in inns of court,
in schools,
in businesses in {town, country}:

for those commended to me by

1. kindred: brothers, sisters: * S. Ans. *Or.* 13
for the blessing of God upon them
and upon their children:
2. good offices received: * Cp. S. Ans. *u.s.*
for recompense on all of whom I have any time received good offices
and on them that minister unto me in carnal things:
3. charge: * S. Ans. *u.s.*
those educated
or yet ordained any time by me:
college, parish,
Southwell,
S. Paul's
Westminister;
the diocese of {Chichester, Ely, and this present,}
clergy, peoples, helps, governments; 1 Cor. xii. 28.
the deanery of the Chapel Royal,
the Almonry,
the colleges committed to me:
4. friendship: * Cp. S. Ans. *u. s.*
for them that love me
and some even unknown:
5. christian charity:
for them that hate me
and some even for the truth and righteousness' sake:
6. neighbourhood:
for them that dwell by me quietly and harmlessly:
7. promise: * S. Ans. *u.s.*
for them I have promised to bear in mind in my prayers:
8. mutual obligation:
for them that bear me in mind in their prayers
and beg as much of me: * Cp. S. Ans. *u.s.*

9. much occupation :

Lit. S. Bas. p. 62 for them that for reasonable causes * fail of calling upon Thee :

Horae f. 161b for them that have none to intercede for them individually : *
for them that at present are struggling in extreme necessity or deep affliction :
for them that are essaying some achievement,
whereby will come glory to thy Name
or some great good to the Church :

Lit. S. Ja. p. 15 for them that are doing good works *
either in respect of sacred things
or in respect of the needy :
for them that have any time been scandalised by me whether by deed or by word.

Blessing

Ps. lxvii 1, 6 God be merciful unto me
and bless me :
shew me the light of his countenance
and be merciful unto me :
God, even our own God,
God give me his blessing.

Commendation

Horolog. p. 16 Accept my entreaty :
direct my life unto thy commandments :
sanctify my soul,
purify my body,
rectify my thoughts,
cleanse my desires :

Horolog. p. 469 soul and body,
mind and spirit,
heart and reins,
renew me wholly,* o Lord :

S. Mt. viii 2 for if Thou wilt, Thou canst.

Praise

Ex. xxxiv 6, 7 Pesiqta *Eth qorbani* 57a

1. *The* Lord, *the* Lord,
2. *God,*
3. *full of compassion*
and

4. *gracious,*
5. *slow to anger*
and
6. *plenteous in mercy*
and
7. *truth,*
8. *keeping mercy for thousands,*
9. *forgiving iniquity*
10. *and transgression*
11. *and sin :*
12. *and He will by no means clear the guilty ;*
13. *visiting the iniquity of the fathers*
upon the children.

I will alway give thanks unto the Lord : Ps. xxxiv 1
his praise shall ever be in my mouth.
Glory to God in the highest : S. Lk. ii 14
on earth peace,
goodwill towards men.

The Angels charge : *Horae f.* 98
Archangels illumination :
Virtues marvels :
Thrones judgement :
Dominations benefaction :
Principalities government :
Powers against devils :
Cherubim knowledge :
Seraphim love.

In every imagination of our heart : *Gen. vi* 5
the words of our lips : *Ps. lix* 12
the works of our hands : *Dt. ii* 7
the ways of our feet. Cp. *Prov. iv* 26

III. TUESDAY

L 65
W 53

Ps. lxiii 1 O God, Thou art my God: early will I seek Thee.

Commemoration

3 Child. 3 Blessed art Thou, o Lord,
Gen. i 9 that didst gather together the water into sea,
that didst bring to light the earth,
Gen. i 11 that didst bring forth the shoots
of herbs and fruitbearing trees,
Gen. i 2 *Deep:*
Ps. xxxiii 7; lxxviii 14; 3 Child. 55, 56 the depths } as on an heap,
the sea }
lakes, rivers, fountains.
Gen. i 2 *Waste:*
3 Child. 52, 53 earth, continent, islands:
mountains, hills,* valleys:
arable, meadows, woods.
Gen. i 2 *Void:*
the green things,
bread,
grass:
herbs and flowers,
for food,
pleasure,
healing:
Gen. i 12 the trees
bearing fruit
Dt. xi 14 fruits * wine
oil *
spices:
for wood:
the things under the earth: stones
metals
and minerals:
coals,
Joel ii 30 blood and fire and pillars of smoke.

Penitence

Of David
Who can tell how oft he offendeth? Ps. xix 12, 13
O cleanse Thou me from my secret faults:
keep thy servant also from presumptuous sins,
so that they get not the dominion over me.
For thy Name's sake Ps. xxv 10
be merciful unto my sin,
for it is great.
My sins have taken such hold on me, Ps. xl 15, 16
that I am not able to look up:
yea they are more in number than the hairs of my head
and my heart hath failed me.
O Lord, let it be thy pleasure to deliver me,
make haste, o Lord, to help me.
Shew thy marvellous lovingkindness upon me, Ps. xvii 7
Thou that art the Saviour of them which put their trust in Thee.
I said, Lord be merciful unto me: Ps. xli 4
heal my soul for I have sinned against Thee.

Of Solomon
I have sinned, 2 Chr. vi 37
but I am ashamed, 2 Chr. vii 14
and I turn from my wicked ways,
and I return unto my heart, Bar. ii 30
and with all my heart I return unto Thee, 2 Chr. vi 38
and seek thy face 2 Chr. vii 14
and pray unto Thee saying 2 Chr. vi 37
I have sinned, I have done amiss, I have dealt wickedly,
I know, o Lord, the plague of my heart: 1 Ki. viii 38
and behold I turn unto Thee 2 Chr. vi 37
with all my heart
and with all my strength.
And now, o Lord, from thy dwelling place 2 Chr. vi 30
and from the throne of the glory of thy kingdom in heaven, Wisd. ix 10; 3 Child. 33
hear therefore the prayer 1 Ki. viii 38; 2 Chr. vi 19; vii 14; Ps. xli 4
and the supplication of thy servant,
and forgive thy servant
and heal his soul.

Of the Publican
S. Lk. xviii 13 God, be merciful to me the sinner ;
1 Tim. i 15 be merciful therefore to me, the chief of sinners.
Of the Prodigal
S. Lk. xv 18 Father, I have sinned against heaven and against Thee :
19 I am no more worthy to be called thy son :
make me one of thy hired servants,*
make me one or even the last
the least among all.

Ps. xxx 5 *HIS WRATH ENDURETH BUT THE TWINKLING OF AN EYE: IN HIS FAVOUR IS LIFE:*
WEEPING MAY TARRY FOR THE NIGHT, BUT JOY COMETH IN THE MORNING.

Ps. xxx 7, 8 *Thou didst hide thy face and I was troubled :*
I cried unto Thee, o Lord,
and unto the Lord did I make my supplication.
Ps. xxx 9-12a *What profit is there in my blood*
when I go down to the pit ?
Shall the dust give thanks unto Thee,
shall it declare thy truth ?
Hear, o Lord, and have mercy upon me :
Lord, be Thou my helper.
Thou hast turned me my mourning into dancing :
Ps. xxx 12b, 13 *Thou hast put off my sackcloth and girded me with gladness,*
to the end my glory sing praise unto Thee and keep not silence :
O Lord my God, I will give thanks unto Thee for ever.

Deprecation

Gen. vi 5 *Imagination*
Lev. iv 2 *error*
Gen. xxvi 10 *trespass*
Ex. xxxiv 7; Job xxxiv 37 *sin*
transgression
iniquity
Ezek. xvi 2 *abomination.*

Comprecation

2 Cor. vii 11 Carefulness
clearing of self

indignation
fear
vehement desire
zeal
revenge.

Faith

Belief. Apost. creed

Godhead
natural affection
power
providence.
Salvation
anointing
adoption
lordship :
conception
birth
sufferings
cross
death
burial :
descent
resurrection
ascension
session
return
judgement.
Breath
holiness
calling out of the
hallowing in the
universal :
communion of saints
hallowed things :
forgiveness of sins
resurrection
life everlasting.

Hope

Be Thou my hope,
Ps. lxv 5 o hope of all the ends of the earth
and of them that remain in the broad sea.

Intercession

Creatures:
men,
departed aforetime,
yet in the body,
compassed with infirmity.
Churches:
catholic,
eastern,
western,
British.
Episcopate,
presbyterate,
orders of clergy,
Christloving people.
Commonwealths:
of the world,
christian,
neighbouring,
ours.
Rulers:
kings,
religious,
ours.
Counsellors,
judges,
mighty men,
forces on {land, sea.
Commonalty,
succession,
education.
Those in the palace,
cities,
country.
Those concerned with souls,
bodies,
food,
clothing,

health,
things of this life.
< Those commended to me by >
nature,
good offices received,
charge
aforetime
at present,
friendship,
charity,
neighbourhood,
promise,
mutual obligation,
want of leisure,
entire neediness,
extremities.

Blessing

The Lord Himself be my keeper : Ps. cxxi 5, 7,
o Lord, be my defence upon my right hand.
The Lord preserve me from all evil :
yea the Lord be he that shall keep my soul.
The Lord preserve my going out
and my coming in,
from this time forth
for evermore.

Commendation

O Lord, Thou knowest and canst skill and willest *Horae* f. c.
the good of my soul :
wretched man that I am,
I neither know, neither can skill, neither (as I ought)
will it.
Do thou, o Lord, I beseech Thee,
in thine unspeakable loving affection
so take order concerning me
and so dispose,
as Thou knowest to be best liking unto Thee
and most expedient for me.

Praise

2 Th. i 11 Goodness,
Rom. v 20 grace,
Rom. v 8 love,
Tit. iii 4 kindness,
love towards mankind:
2 Cor. x 1 meekness,
gentleness:
Rom. ii 4 forbearance,
longsuffering:
1 Pet. i 3 mercy 1. great
Ps. li 1 2. and large:
Rom. xii 1 compassions,
Ps. li 1 1. multitude of compassions,
Col. iii 12 2. bowels of compassions:
Pr. Manass. tender pitifulness:
S. Jas. v 11 great pitifulness:
Mic. vii 18 in passing by,
Acts xvii 30 winking at,
Is. lvii 11 holding long peace
Neh. ix 28 heb. many times
ib. 30 many years:
Cp. Lam. iii 33; Ezek. xxxiii 11 unwillingly,
not willingly,
Ps. lxxviii 39 not whole,
Ps. ciii 10 not according to,
Ps. ciii 9 not always:
Hab. iii 2 mercy in wrath,
Joel ii 13 repenting him of the evil,
Is. xl 2 double,*
unto pardon,
reconciliation,
repropitiation.

L 77
W 63

IV. WEDNESDAY

I have thought upon Thee when I was waking, o Lord: Ps. lxiii 7 8
for Thou hast been my helper.

Commemoration

Blessed art Thou, o Lord,
who madest the two lights { sun / moon } Gen. i 16; Ps. cxxxvi 8, 9
greater and lesser:
the stars also { *Mazzaroth,* Job xxxviii 31
Arcturus, Orion, Pleiades, Job ix 9
the chambers of the south, }
for 1 light Gen. i 15
2 signs 14
3 seasons: * spring, summer, autumn, winter,
4 and to rule over day and night * { days 16
weeks
months
years. }

L The earthquake.

Penitence

LW Of Esay
Behold Thou wert wroth and we sinned: Is. lxiv 5c
L *in them have we been of long time and shall we be saved?* 5d
LW *For we all are become as one unclean*
and all our righteousnesses
are as a polluted garment:
and we all do fade as a leaf and our iniquities like the wind
do take us away.
But now, o Lord, Thou art our father: 8
we are the clay and Thou our potter; we are all the
work of thy hand.

Is. lxiv 9 *Be not wroth very sore, o Lord,*
neither remember iniquity for ever :
behold, look, we beseech Thee, we are all thy people.

Of Jeremy

Jer. xiv 7 *Though our iniquities testify against us,*
deal Thou with us for thy Name's sake :
for our backslidings are many : W
we have sinned against Thee.
Jer. xiv 9 *And Thou, o Lord, art in the midst of us* LW
and we are called by thy Name :
leave us not.
Jer. xiv 8, 9 O our hope, which art a saviour in time of trouble, W
why shouldest Thou be as a stranger in thy land
or as a wayfaring man that turneth aside to tarry for a night?
why shouldest Thou be as a man astonied,
as a mighty man that cannot save?
Jer. xxxi 34 Forgive, o Lord, our iniquity
and remember our sin no more.
Jer. xxxi 18, 19 *I have surely heard Ephraim bemoaning himself* L
Thou hast chastised me and I was chastised as a calf unaccustomed to the yoke :
turn Thou me and I shall be turned,
for Thou art the Lord my God.
Surely after that I was turned I repented,
and after that I was instructed I smote upon my thigh :
I was ashamed, yea even confounded,
because I did bear the reproach of my youth.

Of Saint Paul LW

Rom. vii 14 Lord, I am carnal,
sold under sin :
18 in me (that is, in my flesh) dwelleth no good thing :
15, 16 for the good that I would, that I do not,
but the evil which I would not, that do I.
I consent unto the law that it is good
22 and I delight in it after the inward man :
23 but I see another law in my members
warring against the law of my mind
and bringing me into captivity to the law of sin.
24 O wretched man that I am!

who shall deliver me from the body of this
death?
I thank God through Jesus Christ Rom. vii 25
that where sin abounded, Rom. v 20
grace did much more abound.
O Lord, thy goodness leadeth me to repentance: Rom. ii 4
o give me sometime repentance to recover myself 2 Tim. ii 25, 26
out of the snare of the devil
who am taken captive by him.

Of Saint Peter
The time past of my life may suffice me 1 Pet. iv 3, 4
to work the will of my lusts,
walking in lasciviousness, revellings, banquetings,
and in all other excess of riot.
Lamb without blemish and without spot, 1 Pet. i 19, 18
who didst redeem me in thy precious blood*:
in the very blood have mercy and save me:
as well in thy very blood
as in thy very name, Acts iv 12
beside which there is none other given amongst men
whereby we must be saved.

O God, Thou knowest my foolishness Ps. lxix 5
and my sins are not hid from Thee:
Lord, all my desire is before Thee Ps. xxxviii 9
and my groaning is not hid from Thee.
Let not them that wait on Thee be ashamed for my cause, Ps. lxix 6
o Lord LORD of hosts:
let not those that seek Thee be brought to dishonour through me,
o God of Israel.
L *But as for me, I make my prayer unto Thee, o Lord, in an* *Ps. lxix* 13
acceptable time:
answer me, o God, in the multitude of thy mercy, even in the truth
of thy salvation.
LW *Take me out of the mire that I sink not:* Ps. lxix 14-16
let me be delivered from them that hate me
and out of the deep waters:
let not the waterflood drown me,
neither let the deep swallow me up,
and let not the pit shut her mouth upon me.
L *Answer me, o Lord, for thy lovingkindness is good:* *Ps. lxix* 17-19

turn Thou unto me according to the multitude of thy compassions.
And hide not thy face from thy servant,
for I am in trouble: o haste Thee and answer me.
Draw nigh unto my soul, redeem it,
o ransom me because of mine enemies.

Deprecation

Pet. Lomb. *Sent.* ii 42; Dt. vii 1 — LW

Conceit	Amorite
Envy	Hittite
Wrathfulness	Perizzite
Surfeit	Girgashite
Lasciviousness	Hivite
Distractions of this life	Canaanite
the lukewarmness of Accidy	Jebusite.

Comprecation

1 S. Pet. v 5; Phil. ii 3 — Humility
S. Ja. ii 13; iii 17 — Mercy
1 Tim. vi 11; 1 S. Pet. ii 20 — Patience
1 S. Pet. iv 7 — Sobriety
1 Tim. iv 12; 1 S. Jo. iii 3 — Purity
Phil. iv 11; 2 Cor. ix 8; 1 Tim. vi 6 — Contentment
S. Mt. xxvi 41; Rom. xii 11; Heb. vi 11 — the readiness of Zeal.

Faith

I believe — W
in the Father — benevolent natural affection, — LW
almighty — saving power,
creator — providence unto { preserving / governing / perfecting } of the universe.

S. Mt. i 21 — In Jesus — salvation,
1 S. Jo. ii 20 — Christ — unction,
Eph. i 5 — the onlybegotten Son — adoption,
Lord — care:
in conception / birth } the cleansing of our unclean { conception / birth,
sufferings — what we ought that we might not

cross — the curse of the law — taken away: — Gal. iii 13
death — the sting of death * — 1 Cor. xv 56
burial — eternal corruption in the grave
in descent — whither we ought that we might not,
resurrection — as the firstfruits of them that slept, — 1 Cor. xv 20
ascension — to prepare a place for us, — S. Jo. xiv 2
session — so as to appear and make intercession, — Heb. ix 24
return — so as to receive unto Him his own, — S. Jo. xiv 3
judgement — to render to every man according to his works. — Rom. ii 6

In the Holy Ghost power from on high,* — S. Luke xxiv 49
from without and invisibly / but effectuously and evidently — transforming unto holiness:
in the Church — a body mystical
of such as are called out of all the world
unto a commonwealth according to faith and holiness: * — Cp. S. Isid. Pel. *Ep.* ii 246
in the communion of saints, of the members of this body
a mutual sharing in hallowed things,
unto confidence of forgiveness of sins,
hope of resurrection / translation — unto life everlasting.

Hope

But my trust is in thy mercy — Ps. xiii 5
from this time forth for evermore. — Ps. cxxi 8
How excellent is thy mercy, o God.* — Ps. xxxvi 7
If I have an hope it is in thy mercy:
let me not be disappointed of this my hope. — Ps. cxix 116

Intercession

Moreover we beseech Thee: — *Lit. S. Bas.* p. 61
remember all, o Lord, for good, — *Lit. S. Ja.* p. 27
have mercy upon all, o sovran Lord,
be reconciled to us all:
pacify the multitudes of thy people,
scatter offences,
bring wars to nought,
stop the uprisings of heresies:

thy peace and love
grant to us, o God our Saviour,
Thou that art the hope of all the ends of the earth.
Remember to crown the year with thy goodness;
for the eyes of all wait upon Thee
and Thou givest them their meat in due season:
Thou openest thy hand
and fillest all things living with thy goodness.
Lit. S. Bas. p. 61 Remember thy holy Church
that is from one end of the earth to the other,
and pacify her
which Thou hast purchased with thy precious blood,
and stablish her even unto the end of the world.
Remember them that bring forth fruit and do good works in thy holy churches and are mindful of the poor and needy:
recompense them
with thy rich and heavenly gifts:
grant them
for the things earthly, the heavenly,
corruptible, incorruptible,
temporal, eternal.
Remember them that are in virginity and purity and discipline,
and futhermore them withal that live in reverend wedlock,
in piety and fear of Thee.
Lit. S. Ja. p. 27 Remember every christian soul
afflicted and oppressed and struggling
and needing thy mercy and succour:
and our brethren that are in captivities and in prisons
and bonds and bitter thraldoms:
Lit. S. Ja. p. 16 supplying return to the wanderers,
health to the sick,
deliverance to the captives,
and rest to them that have fallen asleep aforetime.
Lit. S. Bas. p. 61 Remember religious and faithful kings
unto whom Thou hast given the right to reign on the earth:
and chiefly remember, o Lord,
our king preserved by God:
strengthen his kingdom,

subdue to him all that oppose,
speak comfortably unto him good things
in behalf of thy Church and all thy people:
bestow upon him profound peace and such as may not be taken away,
that in his serenity we may lead
a quiet and peaceable life with all godliness and honesty.
Remember, o Lord, every principality and power
and our brethren at court *
and them that are eminent in council and judicature
and all on land and sea waging thy wars for us.
Moreover vouchsafe to remember, o Lord, our fathers in holy things, the honourable presbyterate, *Lit. S. Ja.* p. 28, 27; *S. Chrys.* p. 78
and all the clergy rightly dividing the word of truth
and walking uprightly therein. Gal. ii 14
Remember, o Lord, them that are standing round about us *Lit. S. Ja.* p. 16
and praying with us in this holy hour,
their zeal and ready mind:
remember also them that for reasonable causes are absent, and *Lit. S. Bas.* p. 62
have mercy on them and us
after thy great mercy.
Fill our garners with all manner of good,
preserve our marriages in peace and unanimity,
nourish the infants,
train the youth,
strengthen the aged,
comfort the weakhearted,
gather together the scattered,
bring back them that have strayed, and knit them to thy holy and catholic and apostolic Church.
Enlarge them that are vexed with unclean spirits,
sail with the voyagers,
travel with the wayfarers,
champion widows,
shield orphans,
deliver captives,
heal the sick.
Them that are under trial and in mines and exiles and galleys
and in any affliction or necessity and sore beset,
remember, o God; and all that need thy great tender mercy,

and them that love us and them that hate,
and them that have charged us unworthy
to remember them in our prayers.
And all thy people remember, o Lord our God,
and on all pour out thy rich mercy,
unto all imparting their petitions unto salvation.
And them that we have not remembered
by reason of ignorance or forgetfulness or multitude of names,
Thyself remember, o God, which knowest the age and appellation of each,
which knowest every man from his mother's womb.
For Thou, o Lord, art the succour of the succourless,
and the hope of them that are past hope,
the saviour of the tempest-tossed,
the harbour of the voyagers,
the physician of the sick:
Thyself become all things to all men,
which knowest each one and his petition,
each house and its need.
Deliver, o Lord, this city
Lit. S. Chrys. p. 100 and all the country wherein we sojourn
Lit. S. Bas. p. 62 from famine, pestilence, earthquake, flood,
fire, sword, onset of aliens
and civil factiousness.
Stop the schisms of the churches,
assuage the ragings of the heathen,
and receive us all into thy kingdom, making us children of light:
and thy peace and love bestow upon us,
o Lord our God.
Lit. S. Ja. p. 29 Remember, o Lord God, all spirits and all flesh,
whom we have remembered and whom we have not remembered,
from righteous Abel unto this day that now is.
And for us, direct the end of our lives to be christian, wellpleasing,
and (if it like Thee) painless in peace,
Lord, o Lord,
gathering us together under the feet of thine elect,
when Thou wilt and as Thou wilt,
only without shame and sins.

Blessing

The glorious majesty of the Lord our God be upon us : Ps. xc 17
prosper Thou the works of our hands upon us,
o prosper Thou our handywork.

Commendation

Be, Lord, Cp. *Horae* f. 88b

within	me to	strengthen me,
without		preserve,
over		shelter,
beneath		support
before		direct,
behind		bring back,
round about		fortify.

Praise

Blessed art Thou, o Lord, the God of Israel, 1 Chr. xxix 10-13
our Father,
for ever and ever.
Thine, o Lord, is the greatness
and the might
and the glory
and the victory
and the majesty
and the praise Vulg.
W[2] and the strength : Sept.
LW *for all that is in the heaven*
and in the earth is thine.
At thy presence trembleth Sept.
every king and every nation.
Thine is the kingdom, o Lord,
and Thou art exalted as head
above all.
Both riches and honour come of Thee
and Thou rulest over all,
the ruler of all rule : Sept.
and in thine hand is power and might,
and in thine hand it is to make great
and to give strength unto all.

Now therefore, our God, we thank Thee
and praise thy glorious Name.
1 Chr. xxix 14-17 *But who am I and what is my house that we should be able to offer so willingly after this sort?*
for all things come of Thee and of thine own have we given Thee.
For we are strangers before Thee and sojourners as were all our fathers:
our days on the earth are as a shadow and there is none abiding.
O Lord our God, all this freewill offering cometh of thine hand and is all thine own.
I know also, my God, that Thou triest the heart and hast pleasure in uprightness:
as for me, in the uprightness of mine heart I have willingly offered all these things:
and now have I seen with joy thy people which are present here to offer willingly unto Thee.

L 93
W 77
V. THURSDAY

O satisfy us with thy mercy and that soon, o Lord. Ps. xc 14

Commemoration

Blessed art Thou, o Lord,
which broughtest forth of water Gen. i 20
moving creatures that have life,
and whales 21
and winged fowls,
and didst bless them, 22
so as to increase and multiply.*

The things touching the Ascension.
Set up thy self, o God, above the heavens Ps. cviii 5
and thy glory above all the earth.*
By thine Ascension
draw us withal unto Thee, o Lord, S. Jo. xii 32
so as to set our affections on things above, Col. iii 2
and not on things on the earth.*

By the awful mystery of the holy body and precious blood
in the evening of this day:
By the birthday
of thy humble servant:
Lord, have mercy.

Penitence

Of Ezekiel
Thou that didst say Ezek. xxxiii 11
As I LIVE (saith the Lord God)
I HAVE NO PLEASURE IN THE DEATH OF THE SINNER:
BUT THAT THE WICKED TURN FROM HIS WAY AND LIVE:
TURN YE, TURN YE FROM YOUR EVIL WAY,
FOR WHY WILL YE DIE, O HOUSE OF ISRAEL?

Lam. v 21 turn Thou us unto Thee, o Lord,
and we shall be turned:
Ezek. xviii 30 turn us from all our transgressions
and let them not be our ruin.

Of Daniel

Dan. ix 5 I have sinned, I have committed iniquity, I have done wickedly
from thy precepts and from thy judgements.
7 O Lord, righteousness belongeth unto Thee,
but unto me confusion of face
as at this day,
because of the rejection wherewith Thou hast rejected us.
8 O Lord, to us belongeth confusion of face
and to our princes, because we have sinned against Thee.
16 Thdt. O Lord, in all things is thy righteousness:
16 vulg. unto all thy righteousness,
let then thine anger and thy fury be turned away,
17 and cause thy face to shine
upon thy servant.
18 O my God, incline thine ear and hear:
open thine eyes and behold
my desolations.
19 O Lord, hear: o Lord, forgive: o Lord, hearken:
hearken, o Lord, and do and defer not,
for thine own sake, o Lord, o Lord my God:
for thy servant is called by thy Name.

Of James

S. Ja. iii 2 In many things we offend all:
S. Ja. ii 13 o Lord, let thy mercy rejoice against thy judgement*
in my sins.

Of John

1 S. Jo. i 8 If I say I have no sin, I deceive myself,
and the truth is not in me:
9 but I confess my sins many and grievous,
and Thou, Lord, when I confess art faithful and just
to forgive me my sins.
S. Jo. ii 1 But withal, touching this, I have an Advocate
with Thee unto Thee
thine onlybegotten Son, the righteous:

let Him be a propitiation for my sins, 1 S. Jo. ii 2
who is also for the sins of the whole world.

Will the Lord cast off for ever? Ps. lxxvii 7
and will He be favourable no more?
Is his mercy clean gone for ever? 8
doth his promise fail for evermore?
Hath God forgotten to be gracious? 9
hath He in displeasure shut up his compassions? Selah.
And I said, This is mine infirmity: 10
but I will remember the years of the right hand of the Most High.

Deprecation

Every weight Heb. xii 1
and sin that cleaveth so fast:
all filthiness S. Ja. i 21
and superfluity of naughtiness:
lust of the flesh, 1 S. Jo. ii 16
eyes,
pride of life:
every movement of flesh and spirit aliened from the will of thine holiness. *Lit. S. Ja.* p. 31

Comprecation

1. To be poor in spirit so as to have a share in the kingdom of heaven: S. Mt. v 3-11
2. to mourn so as to be comforted:
3. to be meek so as to inherit the earth:
4. to hunger and thirst after righteousness so as to be filled:
5. to be merciful so as to obtain mercy:
6. to be pure in heart so as to see God:
7. to be peaceable so as to be called the son of God:
8. to be ready for persecutions and reproaches for righteousness' sake so as to have my reward in heaven.

Faith

Coming unto God Heb. xi 6
I believe that He is,
and that He is a rewarder of them that diligently seek Him.

Job xix 25 heb. I know that my Redeemer liveth;
S. Mt. xvi 16 that He is the Christ the Son of the living God;
S. Jo. iv 42 that He is indeed the Saviour of the world;
1 Tim. i 15 that He came into the world to save sinners,
of whom I am chief.
Acts xv 11, 10 Through the grace of Jesus Christ we believe that we shall be saved
even as our fathers withal.
Job xix 26 sept. I know that on the earth shall stand my skin,
that endureth these things.
Ps. xxvii 15 I believe verily to see the goodness of the Lord
in the land of the living.

Hope

Ps. xxxiii 20 Our heart shall rejoice in the Lord,
because we have hoped in his holy Name: *
the Name
of the Father:
the Saviour, Mediator, Intercessor, Redeemer:
the double Paraclete,
the Lamb, the Dove.
Ps. xxxiii 21 Let thy merciful kindness, o Lord, be upon us,
like as we do put our trust in Thee.

Intercession

Lit. S. Chrys. p. 78 In peace let us beseech the Lord:
for the peace that is from above and the salvation of our souls:
for the peace of the whole world,
the stability of the holy churches of God
and the union of all men:
for this holy house and them that with faith and piety enter therein:
for our fathers in holy things, the honourable presbyterate, the diaconate in Christ and all clergy and people:
for this holy mansion and every city and country and them that dwell therein in faith:
for good temperature of the air, plenteous bearing of fruits of the earth and peaceful seasons:

for them that travel by land and by water, the sick, toilworn
and captives, and their safety.
Help, save, have mercy and preserve us, o God, by thy
grace.
Commemorating the allholy, immaculate, more than
blessed mother of God and evervirgin Mary,
with all saints,
let us commend ourselves and one another and all our
life unto Christ God:
unto Thee, o Lord,
for unto Thee is due glory, honour and worship.

Blessing

The grace of our Lord Jesus Christ — 2 Cor. xiii 14
and the love of God
and the fellowship of the Holy Ghost
be with me and with us all.
Amen.

Commendation

I commend as well myself as mine and all things mine
to Him that is able to keep me from falling — S. Jude 24
and to present me faultless before the presence of his glory,
to the only wise God and our Saviour,
to whom be glory and majesty
dominion and power
both now
and world without end.*

Thanksgiving

O my Lord, Lord,
for that I am, — S. Aug. *de civ. Dei* vii 31
that I am alive,
that I am rational: *
for nurture,
preservation,
governance:

for education,
citizenship,
religion :

Gerson *de x consid. in orando* (iii 693)
for thy gifts of { grace
nature
estate : *

for redemption,
regeneration,
instruction :
for calling,
recalling,
further recalling manifold :
for forbearance,
longsuffering,
long longsuffering towards me,
Neh. ix 28 many times,
30 many years,
until now :
for all good offices I have received,
good speed I have gotten :
for any good thing done :
for the use of things present,
Horolog. pp. 16, 90 thy promise
and my hope
touching the fruition of the good things
to come : *
for my parents honest and good,
teachers gentle,
benefactors alway to be had in remembrance,
colleagues likeminded,
hearers attentive,
friends sincere,
retainers faithful :
for all who have stood me in good stead
by their writings,
their sermons,
conversations,
prayers,
examples,
rebukes,
wrongs :

for all these things and all other, *Lit. S. Chrys.* p. 95
which I wot of, which I wot not of,
open and privy,*
what things I remember, what things I have forgotten withal,
things done to me after my will or yet against my will,* S. Chrys. *hom. vi in i Tim.* 1
I confess to Thee and bless Thee and give thanks to Thee,
and I will confess and bless and give thanks to Thee
all the days of my life.
Who am I and what is my father's house, 2 Sam. vii 18
that Thou shouldest look upon such a dead dog as I am? 2 Sam. ix 8
What reward shall I give unto the Lord Ps. cxvi 11
for all the benefits that He hath done unto me?
What thanks can I render to God again 1 Thess. iii 9
for all * things wherein
He hath spared me
He hath waited for me hitherto? Cp. 2 Sam. vii 18
HOLY, HOLY, HOLY Rev. iv 8
Thou art worthy, o Lord and our God, the Holy One, 11
to receive the glory and the honour
and the power:
for thou hast created all things,
and for thy pleasure they are
and were created.

VI. FRIDAY L 105 W 89

Ps. lxxxviii 13 Early shall my prayer come before Thee.

Commemoration

Ps. cxix 12 Blessed art Thou, o Lord,
Gen. i 24 which didst bring forth of the earth beasts and cattle
25 and everything that creepeth
29 for food
Gen. iii 21 clothing *
succour:

Gen. i 26 and didst make man,
in thine image,
to have dominion over the earth,
28 and didst bless him.
S. Cyr. Al. *Glaph. i in Gen.* p. 5 The forecounsel,
fashioning with thine own hand,
Gen. ii 7 *breath of life*,
Gen. i 27 image of God,
Ps. viii 6 setting over the works,
Ps. xci 11 charge to the angels concerning him,
Gen. ii 8 garden.

Heart	life	knowledge of God
reins	sensation	writing of the law
eyes	reason	oracles of prophets
ears	spirit	melody of psalms
tongue	freewill	admonition of proverbs
hands	memory	experience of histories
feet	conscience	worship of sacrifices.

Ps. cxix 12 Blessed art Thou, o Lord,
2 Pet. i 4; Gen. iii 15 for thy great and precious promise
S. Iren. *Haer.* v 23 § 2 on this day touching the quickening seed,
Eph. i 10; S. Jo. xix 14 and for the fulfilling of the same in fulness of the times
on this day.*

Blessed art Thou, o Lord, for the holy sufferings of this day.
By thy saving sufferings on this day
save us, o Lord.

Penitence

Of Osee
I have rebelled against Thee, o Lord, but I return unto Thee: Hos. xiii 16; xiv 1
I have fallen by mine iniquity:
but I take with me words 2
and I turn unto Thee saying
Forgive sin and receive prayer:
so will I render Thee the calves of my lips.

Of Joel
Spare, o Lord, spare, Joel ii 17
and give not thine heritage to reproach *
unto thine enemies.

Of Amos
O Lord, Lord, forgive: cease, I beseech Thee: Amos vii 2
by whom shall Jacob arise?
for he is small.
Repent, o Lord, for this: 3
this also shall not be. 6

Of Jonas
Observing lying vanities Jonah ii 8
I forsook my own mercy,
and I was cast out of thy sight: 4
when my soul fainted in me I remembered the Lord. 7
I will look yet again towards thy holy temple, 4
and it is Thou that shalt bring up my life from the pit. 6

Of Micah
Who is a God like unto Thee, that passest by the iniquity of the remnant of thine heritage? Mic. vii 18
Thou wilt not hold fast thine anger for ever,
because Thou delightest in mercy.
Turn again, have compassion upon us, o Lord: 19
subdue our iniquities,
and cast all our sins
into the depths of the sea,
after thy truth and after thy mercy. 20

Of Abacuc

Hab. iii 2 sept. O Lord, I have heard thy speech
and was afraid :
I considered thy works
and was astounded.
In wrath remember mercy.

Of Zachary

Zech. iii 3 Behold me, o Lord, clothed with filthy garments :
1 behold Satan standing at my right hand :
Zech. ix 11 and, o Lord, by the blood of thy covenant,
Zech. xiii 1 in the fountain opened to sprinkle
all uncleanness,
Zech. iii 4 cause my iniquity to pass away from me,
Is. vi 7 and purge my sins.
Zech. iii 2 Save me as a brand plucked out of the fire.

S. Lk. xxiii 34 Father, forgive me : for I know not,
indeed I know not, what I did *
in my sinning against Thee.
42 Lord, remember me in thy kingdom.*
Acts vii 60 Lord, lay not to mine enemies' charge their sins :
Lord, lay not to my charge my sins.

S. Lk. xxii 44 By the sweat bloody, in clots,
S. Mt. xxvi 38; S. Lk. xxii 44 the soul in agony,
Horae f. 70; S. Mt. xxvii 30 the head wreathed with thorns driven in with the rods,
the eyes filled with tears,
the ears full of opprobries,
the mouth given to drink of vinegar and gall,
the face shamefully befouled with spitting,
S. Jo. xix 17 the neck loaded with the burden of the cross,
Ps. cxxix 3; S. Mt. xxvii 26 the back ploughed with the weals and gashes of whips,
Ps. xxii 17 the hands and feet digged through,
Heb. v 7; S. Mt. xxvii 46 the strong crying ELI ELI,
Horae f. 70 the heart pierced with a spear,
S. Jo. xix 34 the water and blood flowing forth,
1 Cor. xi 24 the body broken,
S. Mt. xxvi 28 the blood outpoured.

Ps. lxxxv 1 *Lord, Thou hast been favourable unto thy land :*
Thou hast brought again the captivity of Jacob.

Thou hast forgiven the iniquity of thy people : Ps. lxxxv 2
Thou hast covered all their sin.
Thou hast taken away all thy wrath : 3
Thou hast turned thyself from the fierceness of thine anger.
Turn us, o God of our salvation, 4
and cause thine indignation to usward to cease.
Wilt Thou be angry with us for ever, 5
wilt Thou stretch out thine anger from one generation to another ?
Wilt Thou not turn again and quicken us, 6
that thy people may rejoice in Thee ?
Shew us thy mercy, o Lord,
and grant us thy salvation.

Deprecation

The works of the flesh : Gal. v 19-21

adultery	hatred	seditions
fornication	variance	heresies
uncleanness	emulations	envyings
lasciviousness	wrath	murders
idolatry	strife	
witchcraft		

drunkenness, revellings and such like.

Comprecation

The fruits of the Spirit : Gal. v 22, 23

love	longsuffering	faith
joy	gentleness	meekness
peace	goodness	temperance.

The Spirit of

wisdom	counsel	knowledge Is. xi 2
understanding	might	fear of the Lord.

The gifts of the Spirit : 1 Cor. xii 8
word of wisdom
word of knowledge
faith gifts of healing 9
working of miracles 10
prophecy
discerning of spirits
kinds of tongues
interpretation of tongues.

Faith

I believe
1. that Thou didst create me:
Ps. cxxxviii 8; *Euchology.* p. 229 the workmanship of thy hands
despise not.
Gen. i 26 2. that I am after thine image and likeness: *
thy likeness
suffer not to be blotted out.
1 Pet. i 18, 19 3. that Thou didst redeem me in thy blood: *
the price of the ransom
suffer not to perish.
4. that Thou didst make me a Christian after thine own name:
thine own namesake
think not scorn of.
5. that Thou didst hallow me in regeneration:
thine own hallowed thing
destroy not.
Rom. xi 24 6. that Thou didst engraft me in the good olivetree: W
1 Cor. xii 27 the member of the body mystical
Rom. xi 22 cut not off.

Hope

Ps. cxix 49 O think upon thy servant as concerning thy word, LW
wherein Thou hast caused me to put my trust.
81 My soul hath longed for thy salvation
and I have a good hope because of thy word.

Intercession

Horolog. p. 21 For the speeding and strengthening
of all the Christloving army
S. Jude 20 against the enemies of our most holy faith.
Horolog. p. 21 For our fathers in holy things,
and all our brotherhood in Christ.
For them that hate us and them that love us.
For them that pity and minister unto us.*
For them we have promised to have in mind in our prayers.
Horolog. p. 22 For deliverance of the prisoners.
For our fathers and brethren that are absent.
For them that voyage by sea.
For them that are laid low in sickness.

Let us pray
also for plenteous bearing of fruits of the earth
and for every soul of orthodox Christians.
Let us felicitate religious kings,
orthodox pontiffs,
the founders of this holy mansion,
our parents,
and all our forefathers and brethren
that have departed aforetime.

Commendation

Be unto me, o Lord, alway *Book of Com. Ord.* p. 191
thy mighty hand
for defence:
thy mercy in Christ
for salvation:
thine alltrue word
for instruction:
the grace of thy lifebringing Spirit
for comfort
until the end
and in the end.

Horae f. 62

Soul of Christ,	hallow	
body	strengthen	
blood	ransom	
water	wash	me.
stripes	heal	
sweat	refresh	
wound	hide	

Blessing

The peace of God, *Order of Communion* 1548
which passeth all understanding,
keep my heart and mind
in the knowledge and love of God.

Thanksgiving

Thou who when man transgressed thy commandment and fell *Lit. S. Ja.* p. 23
didst not despise him nor forsake, o Good,
but didst visit him in divers manners like a tender Father,

2 Pet. i 4 supplying unto him thy great and precious promise
Gen. iii 15 touching the quickening seed,
Acts xiv 27 opening to him the door of faith
Acts xi 18 and of repentance unto life:
Eph. i 10; Gal. iv 4 and in fullness of the times
didst send thy Christ himself,
Heb. ii 16 all to take on Him the seed of Abraham,
Eph. v 2 and in the oblation of life
to fulfil the obedience of the law,
and in the sacrifice of death
Gal. iii 13 to take away the curse of* it:
and in his death to redeem the world,
1 Cor. xv 45 and in his resurrection to quicken it:
S. Chrys. *ad eos qui scandalizantur* 8 Thou who doest all things*
so as to bring back our race to Thee,
2 Pet. i 4 to be made partaker of thy divine nature* and of the eternal glory withal:
Heb. ii 4; Gal. ii 14 Thou who hast borne witness with the truth of thy gospel
in many and diverse miracles,*
in the evermemorable conversation of thy saints,
in supernatural endurance of tortures,
in the more than marvellous conversion
Rom. i 5; xvi 26 of all the world to the obedience of faith*
without might, persuasion, force:
Heb. morn. p. 37 blessed, praised, celebrated,
magnified, exalted, glorified,
hallowed be thy Name*
the commemoration, the memory and every memorial of it
S. Jude 25 both now and for ever.

Rev. v 9 1. Thou art worthy to take the book
and to open the seals thereof:
for Thou wast slain and hast redeemed us unto God
by thy blood,
out of every kindred and tongue and people and nation.
12 2. Worthy is the Lamb that was slain
to receive the power and riches and wisdom and strength
and honour and glory and blessing.
13 3. To Him that sitteth upon the throne and to the Lamb
be the blessing and the honour and the glory and the power
for ever and ever. Amen.

4. Salvation to our God which sitteth upon the throne Rev. vii 10
and unto the Lamb.

5. Amen.
The blessing and the glory and the wisdom and the 1
thanksgiving and the honour and the power and the might
be unto our God for ever and ever.

VII. SATURDAY

L 121
W 10

Is. xxxiii 2 O Lord, be gracious unto us: we have waited for Thee:
be Thou our arm every morning,
and our salvation also in time of trouble.*

Commemoration

Ps. cxix 12 Blessed art Thou, o Lord,
Gen. ii 2, 3 which didst rest on the seventh day
from all thy works,
and didst bless and hallow it.*

The things touching the sabbath,
touching an intermittent rest,
S. Thom. Aq. *Summa* ii² 122 § 4 ad prim. touching the obsequies of Christ,
and the cessation from sins;
touching them that went to their rest aforetime.

Penitence

Ps. lxxix 5 *How long, o Lord, wilt Thou be angry for ever?*
shall thy jealousy burn like fire?
8 *Remember not against us the iniquities of our forefathers:*
let thy compassions speedily prevent us,
for we are brought very low.
9 Help us, *o God of our salvation*
for the glory of thy Name,
and deliver us and purge away our sins
for thy Name's sake.
Ps. lxxix 14 *So we thy people and sheep of thy pasture* L
will give Thee thanks for ever:
we will show forth thy praise to all generations.
Ps. lxxxviii 9 *Mine eye wasteth away by reason of affliction: I have called daily upon Thee, o Lord:*

I have spread forth my hands unto Thee.
Wilt Thou show wonders to the dead? *Ps. lxxxviii* 10
shall they that are deceased arise and praise Thee? Selah.
Shall thy lovingkindness be declared in the grave 11
or thy faithfulness in destruction?
Shall thy wonders be known in the dark, 12
or thy righteousness in the land of forgetfulness?
But unto Thee, o Lord, have I cried, 13
and in the morning shall my prayer come before Thee.
O Lord, why dost Thou cast off my soul? 14
why dost Thou hide thy face from me?
I am afflicted and ready to die from my youth up: 15
while I suffer thy terrors I am distracted:
for in death there is no remembrance of Thee: *Ps. vi* 5
in sheol who shall give thanks unto Thee?

B Of Ezra

LW I am ashamed and blush Ezra ix 6
to lift up my face to Thee, my God,
for mine iniquities are increased
over my head
and my trespass is grown up
unto the heavens.
Since the days of my youth 7
I am in a great trespass unto this day,
and I cannot stand before Thee because 15
of this.

Of Manasses

I have sinned above the number of the sands of the sea: Pr. of Manasses, from *Horologion* p. 164
my transgressions are multiplied,
and I am not worthy to behold and see the height of heaven for the multitude of mine iniquities:
neither have I any release, for I have provoked thy wrath
and done evil before Thee:
I did not thy will
neither kept I thy commandments.
Now therefore I bow the knee of mine heart,
beseeching Thee of grace:
I have sinned, o Lord, I have sinned,
and I acknowledge mine iniquities.

Wherefore I humbly beseech Thee,
forgive me, o Lord, forgive me,
and destroy me not with mine iniquities:
be not angry with me for ever by reserving evil for me,
neither condemn me into the lower parts of the earth:
for Thou art the God, even the God of them that repent,
and in me Thou wilt show all thy goodness:
for Thou wilt save me that am unworthy,
according to thy great mercy:
therefore will I praise Thee for ever.

S. Mt. viii 2 Lord, if Thou wilt Thou canst make me clean.
8 Lord, speak the word only and I shall be healed.
S. Mt. viii 25; S. Mk. iv 38 Lord, save us: carest Thou not that we perish?
S. Mt. ix 2 Say unto me BE OF GOOD CHEER: THY SINS ARE FORGIVEN THEE.
S. Lk. xvii 13 Jesus, master, have mercy on us.
S. Mk. x 47 Jesus, Thou son of David, have mercy on me,
S. Lk. xviii 38 Jesus, Thou son of David,
S. Mk. x 48 Thou son of David.
S. Mk. vii 34 Lord, say unto me EPHPHATHA.
S. Jo. v 7 Lord, I have no man.
S. Lk. xiii 12 Lord, say unto me THOU ART FREED FROM THINE INFIRMITY.
Ps. xxxv 3 Say unto my soul I AM THY SALVATION:
2 Cor. xii 9 Say unto me MY GRACE IS SUFFICIENT FOR THEE.

Deprecation.

All the

discomfitures	1 Cor. vi 7	debts	S. Mt. vi 12
shortcomings	1 Th. iii 10	sins	S. Mk. iii 28
falls	Ps. xxxv 6, lvi 13	miscarriages	Num. v 8; Jer. ii 5; 2 Esd. x 19
faults	(S. Ja. iii 2)	ignorances	Gen. xliii 12; Heb. ix 7
trespasses	Ps. xix 12; S. Mt. vi 14	iniquities	1 Sam. xxv 28, &c.
offences	Ex. xxiii 33; Is. viii 14; Rom. xiv 13, 20	impieties	Lev. xviii 17; Lam. i 14, iv 22; Dt. ix 27; 2 Pet. ii 6; Jude 15
transgressions	Ps. ci 4; Rom ii 23	pollutions:	Mal. i 7; Acts xv 20

the guilt

give condone, pardon, Eph. iv
forgive

pardon	*Jer. xxxi* 34	remit	S. Mt. vi 12
spare	*Joel ii* 17	spare	Joel ii 18; Rom. xi 21
cover	*Dt. xxi* 8	be propitious	Heb. viii 12
lay not	*Num. xii* 11	lay not to charge	Acts vii 60
impute not	*Ps. xxxii* 2	impute not	Ps. xxxii 2; 2 Cor. v 19
remember not	*Ps. xxv* 6	remember not:	Ps. xxv 6
	the soil		
cast behind us	*Is. xxxviii* 17	pass by	Rom. iii 25
*pass over**	*Mic. vii* 18	pass over	Mic. vii 18
turn away thine eyes		overlook, wink at	Wisd. xi 23; Acts xvii 30
cover	*Ps. lxxxv* 2	cover	Ps. lxxxv 2; S. Ja. v 20; 1 S. Pet. iv 8
wash	*Ps. li* 7	wash away	1 Cor. vi 11; Acts xxii 16
blot out	*Ps. li* 9	blot out	Ps. li 9; Acts iii 19; Col. ii 14
cleanse	*Ps. li* 2	make clean:	Ps. li 2; 1 S. Jo. i 7
	the hurt		
		put up with	Josh. xxiv. 19; Is. i 13
heal	*Ps. xli* 4	heal	Ps. xli 4
save from	*Ez. xxxvi* 29	save from	S. Mt. i 21
lift off	1 *Sam. xv* 25	take away	1 Sam. xv 25; S. Jo. i 29.
put away	2 *Sam. xii* 13	take off	1 S. Pet. ii. 24; Is. liii 12
bring forth from	*Ps. cxlii* 7	strip off	Heb. x 11
bring to an end	*Dan. ix* 24	bring to nought	Rom. vi 6
shut off		set aside	Heb. ix 26
		disperse	3 Mac. ii 19
let them not be found	*Jer. l* 20	let them not be found	Jer. l 20
let them not be		let them not exist.	

Comprecation

To supply 2 S. Pet. i 5
in faith virtue,
virtue knowledge,
knowledge temperance, 6
temperance patience,
patience godliness,
godliness love of the brethren,
love of the brethren charity;
and, forgetting not that I was cleansed from my old sins,
to give diligence to make my calling and election sure * by 10
good works.

Faith

I believe in Thee the Father:
Cp. Mal. i 6 behold then, if Thou be a father and we sons,
Ps. ciii 13 *like as a father pitieth his children, so pity us.*
I believe in Thee the Lord:
Cp. Mal. i 6 behold then, if Thou be Lord and we servants,
Ps. cxxiii 2 our eyes wait upon Thee our Lord,
until Thou have mercy upon us.
S. Mt. xv 27 I believe, that if we be neither sons nor servants, but whelps only,
it were lawful for us to eat of the crumbs that fall
from thy table.*
I believe that Christ is the Lamb of God:
S. Jo. i 29 o Lamb of God, that takest away the sins of the world,
take away mine withal.
1 Tim. i 15 I believe that Jesus Christ came into the world to save sinners:
Thou that camest to save sinners,
save even me, of sinners chiefest and greatest.
S. Mt. xviii 11 I believe that Christ came to save that which was lost:
Thou that camest to save that which was lost,*
never suffer that to be lost, o Lord, which Thou
hast saved.
Lit. S. Ja. p. 22 I believe that the Spirit is Lord and Giver * of life:
Gen. ii 7 Thou that gavest me a living soul,
Ps. xxiv 4 sept. grant me not to have received my soul in vain.*
I believe that the Spirit imparteth grace in his hallowed things:
2 Cor. vi. 1 grant me not to have received the grace of them in
vain
Lit. S. Bas. p. 65 nor the hope of thy hallowed things.
Rom. viii 26 I believe that the Spirit intercedeth for us with groanings
which cannot be uttered *:
of his intercession and these groanings grant me
to partake.

Hope

Ps. xxii 4 Our fathers hoped in Thee,
they trusted in Thee and Thou didst deliver them:
they called upon Thee and were holpen,
they put their trust in Thee and were not confounded *:
like as our fathers in the generations of old,
so withal deliver us, o Lord,
the while we put our trust in Thee.

Intercession

Heavenly King *Horolog.* p. 73
strengthen our faithful kings,
stablish the faith,
calm the nations,
pacify the world:
guard well this holy mansion:
our fathers and brethren
which have gone to their rest aforetime,
bestow them in the tabernacles of the righteous:
and as for us, receive us
in orthodox faith and repentance,
as good and a lover of man.

Blessing

Let the power of the Father shepherd me: *Horae* f. c. 2b
the wisdom of the Son enlighten me:
the operation of the Spirit quicken me.

Commendation

Preserve my soul, *Horae* f. 40
stablish my body,
upraise my senses,
direct my conversation,
compose my manners,
bless my actions,
perfect my prayers,
inspire holy meditations;
the sins done aforetime forgive,
the present correct,
the future prevent.

Thanksgiving

Now unto Him that is able to do exceeding abundantly Eph. iii. 20, 21
above all that we ask or think
according to the power that worketh in us,
to Him
be glory in the Church by Christ
throughout all ages
world without end.
Amen.

Heb. morning p. 37 Blessed, praised, celebrated,
magnified, exalted, glorified,
hallowed
be thy Name,* o Lord, and the commemoration
and the memory and every memorial thereof
for the
Horae f. 103b all-honourable senate of the patriarchs
ever-venerable quire of prophets
all-illustrious company of twelve apostles
evangelists
all-famous host of martyrs
conclave of confessors
doctors,
ascetics,
beauty of virgins,
sweetening of the world in infants
their faith
hope
toils
truth
blood
zeal
diligence
tears
chastity
goodliness.*
Glory be to Thee, o Lord, glory be to Thee,
glory to Thee which didst glorify them,
in whom we also glorify Thee.
Rev. xv 3 Great and marvellous are thy works,
Lord God almighty:
just and true are thy ways,
o King of the nations.
4 Who shall not fear Thee, o Lord
and glorify thy Name?
for Thou only art holy:
5 for all nations shall come
and worship before Thee,
for thy judgments are made manifest.
Rev. xix 5 Praise our God, all ye his servants
and ye that fear Him both small and great.

Alleluia, Rev. ix 6
for the Lord God omnipotent reigneth :
let us be glad and rejoice 7
and give honour to Him.
Behold the tabernacle of God is with men Rev. xxi 3
and He will dwell with them,
and they shall be his people
and God himself shall be with them,
and He shall wipe away all tears
from their eyes,
and there shall be no more death
nor crying
neither shall there be any more pain,
for the former things
are passed away.

EVENING PRAYERS

A. Nowell Thou that with darkness curtainst up the night W 170
With mercie veil our sins from Justice sight.

EVENING THOUGHTS O 260

Thou which givest evening to be the end of day,
whereby to bring to our mind the evening of life:
grant me alway to consider that, like as the day, so life flieth past:
Eccl. xi 8 grant me alway to remember the days of darkness that they are many;
S. Jo. ix 4 that the night cometh, when no man can work; *
to forestall the darkness by working,
S. Mt. xxv 30 lest we be cast into outer darkness;
S. Lk. xxiv 29 alway to cry unto Thee, Abide with us, o Lord,
for it is toward evening, and the day of our life is far spent.

THE HYMN OF THE LIGHTING OF THE LAMPS O 354

Horolog. p. 145 O gladsome Light of the holy glory of the immortal Father,
heavenly, holy, blest,
o Jesu Christ,
being come to the going down of the sun,
seeing the evening light,
we hymn the Father
and the Son
and the Holy Spirit of God.
Worthy art Thou at all times to be hymned with holy voices,
Son of God,
which givest life:
therefore the world doth glorify Thee.

S 39 O 349

ADMONITIONS AND PREPARATORY MEDITATIONS AT THE LIFTING OF THE MIND TO GOD AT EVENTIDE

In war there is a note
- of charge: fitted to action;
- of recall: whereby stragglers are called back.

So the human mind, like as in the morning it must be awakened, so at eventide as it were by a note of recall it must be called back to itself and its Captain

by
- scrutiny and inquisition or examination of self,
- prayers and thanksgivings.

A good man had liefer know his own infirmity than know the foundations of the earth and the topmost heights of heaven.* S. Aug. *de Trin.* iv 1

But that knowledge of a man's own infirmity is not procured save by diligent inquisition, without the which the mind is many times blind and seeth nought in its own concerns.

There are many lurkingplaces in the mind and many nooks. Cic. *pro Marcell.* 7

You must detect yourself or ever you amend yourself.* Seneca *ep. moral.* iii 7

A sore unknown waxeth worse and worse and getteth past cure. Cf. Virg. *Georg.* iii. 454

The heart is deceitful above all things:* Jer. xvii 9

the heart is deep and full of windings:

the old man is covered up in a thousand wrappings.

Therefore take heed to thyself.* Acts xx 28; 1 Tim. iv. 16

And this is most chiefly to be inquired into—

what hast thou today
- done / read
- said / written
- to
  - sort well with a Christian, a priest, a father, etc.
  - confirm faith, obedience
  - increase knowledge
  - or the government of
    - mind
    - body
  - work out the salvation of
    - thyself
    - others?

Gen. i 10 — We see God Himself none otherwise closing the several days of the first creation than with a review of the works of each day: AND GOD SAW THAT THEY WERE GOOD.

Cic. *de senect.* 11 — Cato required of himself an account of each day's business, and Pythagoras withal.

Auson. *Idyll.* xvi 15; Pythag. *aur. carm.* 40 — Ausonius saith out of Pythagoras:

Or thou compose thine eyes to slumber sweet,
of each day's acts review the tale complete.

Ps. lxxvii 6 — King David when the day was over meditated,
and searched out his spirits.*

Cp. Lucian *Hermotimus* 64; S. Aug. *Serm.* xx 2 — In this areopagitic nocturnal examination
look to it that thou show thyself, not the advocate of thy sins,
but the judge thereof:
and in the tribunal of thy mind say,
(say it with grief and indignation)

[Ps. li 3] — I ACKNOWLEDGE MY FAULTS, O LORD:

Ecclus. xxiii 2 — O WHO WILL GIVE SCOURGES TO MY MIND
THAT THEY SPARE NOT MY SINS?

1 Cor. xi 31 — If we would judge ourselves we should not be judged.

S. Greg. Nyss. *de orat. dom.* 1 — Prayer is { the guardian of them that sleep
the confidence of them that are awake:* }
for neither do we account him to be safe, whoso is not protected by the armour and the fortification of prayer.

Rightly therefore saith Rabbi J. touching the not putting off of penitence till the morrow:
Behold the hope of fruit and of salvation will be disappointed for evermore, if so be in this very night thou pluck not forth thy soul.

And an examination in this sort, if it be made for a measure of days, or at the least for one month, with penitence, will suffice to the gendering of a perfect habit of virtue.

167
V 143

A FORM OF EVENING PRAYER

Commemoration

Gotten past the day *Horolog.* p. 157
I give Thee thanks, o Lord.*
The evening draweth nigh:
make it bright.
There is an evening, as of the day,
so of life withal:
the evening of life is old age:
old age hath overtaken me:
make it bright.
Cast me not off in the time of age: *Ps. lxxi* 8
forsake me not when my strength faileth.

And even to old age I am He, *Is. xlvi* 4
and even to hoar hairs will I carry:
I have made and I will bear,
yea I will carry and will deliver.

L *Forsake me not, o Lord: o my God, be not far from me:* *Ps. xxxviii* 21 22
make haste to help me, o Lord my salvation.
LW Abide with me, o Lord, S. Lk. xxiv 29
for even now it is towards evening with me,
and the day is far spent *
of this travailling life.
Let thy strength be perfected 2 Cor. xii 9
in my weakness.
Departed and gone is the day:
going also is life,
the life lifeless.
Cometh the night,* S. Jo. ix 4
and cometh death withal,
the death deathless.

Near as the end of day,
so withal is the end of life.
Remembering it, therefore, we also
beseech Thee
Lit. S. Ja. pp. 10, 29 to direct the end of our life,
christian and wellpleasing,
sinless, shameless,
and (if it like Thee) painless,
in peace, o Lord, Lord,
gathering us
under the feet of thine elect,
when Thou wilt and as Thou wilt,
only without shame and * sins,
after we have prevented the night
by doing some good thing.
Near is judgement: W
Lit. S. Ja. p. 10 a good and acceptable defence
at the fearful and appalling judgement seat of Jesus Christ,
grant to us, o Lord.

Thanksgiving.

Ps. cxxxiv 2, 3 By night I lift up my hands
in the sanctuary and praise the Lord.
Ps. xlii 10 The Lord hath granted his lovingkindness in the daytime,
and for this cause even now in the night season do I sing of Him,
and make my prayer unto the God of my life.
Ps. lxiii 5 As long as ever I live will I magnify Thee on this manner,
and lift up my hands in thy Name.
Ps. cxli 2 Let my prayer be set forth
in thy sight as the incense,
and let the lifting up of my hands
be like as the evening sacrifice.
Tobit iii 11; 3 Child. 29 Blessed art Thou, o Lord our God,
the God of our fathers,
Cp. *Heb. even.* p. 96 who didst create changes of day and night,
Job xxxv 10 who dost supply to us occasions of songs in the night,
S. Mt. vi 13, 34 who hast delivered us from the evil
of this day;
Is. xxxviii 12 who hast not cut off like a weaver
my life,

nor from morning even to night
made an end of me.

Penitence

O Lord,
as days unto our days, Ps. lxi 6 sept.
so do we add unto our sins withal. 2 Chr. xxviii 13; Job xxxiv 37
The just man falleth seven times * a day, Prov. xxiv. 16
but I, the singular great sinner,
seventy times seven : S. Mt. xviii 22
a wonderful and horrible thing, o Lord! Jer. v 30
But groaning Is. xxx 15; Ps. cxix 101
I turn from my evil ways
and I return unto my heart, Bar. ii 30
and with all my heart I turn unto thee, Jer. xxiv 7; Dt. xxx 2
(God of penitents* and Saviour of sinners.) Pr. of Manas.
Yea evening by evening will I return,
from the inmost marrow of my soul, Eur. *Hippol.* 255
and out of the deep my soul calleth unto Thee: Ps. cxxx 1
I have sinned, o Lord, against Thee,* I have sinned Ps. xli 4
grievously against Thee :
alas, alas, woe, woe: o the wretchedness!
I repent, ah me, I repent: spare me,* o Lord: Neh. xiii 22
I repent, ah me, I repent:
help Thou mine impenitence. S. Mk. ix 24
Be favourable: spare me, o Lord: *Horae* f. 128b
be favourable have mercy upon me. *Euchol.* p. 22
I said, Be merciful unto me, o Lord: Ps. xli 4
heal my soul, for I have sinned against Thee.
Have mercy upon me, o Lord, Ps. li 1
after thy great goodness:
according to the multitude of thy mercies
do away mine offences *:
assoil the guilt,
heal the wound,
blot out the stains,
deliver from the shame,
pluck forth from the tyranny,
and make me not a public example. *Horolog.* p. 467

Ps. xxv 16 Bring Thou me out of troubles, o Lord:
Ps. xix 12 cleanse Thou me from secret faults,
13 keep thy servant also from presumptuous sins:
Wisd. iv 12 my wanderings of mind
Horolog. p. 17 and mine idle speaking
Acts vii 60 lay not to my charge.
Horolog. p. 489 Clear away the murk and noisome torrent
of foul and lawless thoughts.*

O Lord,
Hos. xiii 9 my destruction cometh to me of myself:
Primer 1604, f. 200b what things soever I have done amiss, mercifully forgive:
Ps. ciii 10 deal not with us after our iniquities,
neither reward us according to our sins.
Eng. Litany Mercifully look upon our infirmities
and for the glory of thine allholy Name
turn from us all the evils
and the troubles
which our sins (and we by reason of them)
have most righteously and worthily deserved.*

Petition

Cp. *Horolog.* p. 172 And to me, o Lord, in my weariness grant Thou rest,*
in my travail renew Thou strength.
Ps. xiii 3 Lighten mine eyes to the end I sleep not in death.
Ps. xci 5 Deliver me from terror by night
6 from the pestilence that walketh in darkness.*
Supply unto me wholesome sleep
and to get me through this night without fear.
Ps. cxxi 4 O keeper of Israel,
that didst neither slumber nor sleep ever yet,
7 preserve me this night from all evil:
yea, keep my soul, o Lord.*
Visiting me with the visitation of thine own,
Job xxxiii 15, 16 discover me my mind in visions of night: *
but if not (for I am not worthy, not worthy)
Cp. Wisd. xi 26 at least, o Lord Thou lover of man,*
let my sleep be to me a respite
as from toiling, so from sinning withal.
Rev. xvi 7 Yea, o Lord,*

and let me not in sleep imagine aught
that provoketh Thee
or yet defileth me.
Let not my loins be filled with illusions, — Ps. xxxviii 7 A, vulg.
but rather let my reins chasten me, — Ps. xvi 8
but without grievous fear. — Job xxxiii 16
Preserve me from the murky sleep of sin, — *Horolog.* p. 172
and every earthly and evil thought put to sleep within me.
Give me light sleep
and rid of
every imagining
fleshly and satanic.
The sleeplessness of mine unseen foes — *Horolog.* p. 159
Thou wottest, o Lord,
and the slackness of my wretched flesh,
o Thou that didst form me.
Let the wing of thy mercy shelter me:
awaken me at the time when Thou mayest be found,
at the time of prayer, — *Horolog.* p. 172
and give me to seek Thee early — Ps. lxiii 1
for thy glorifying — *Horolog.* p. 159
and service withal.

Intercession

Creation: the human race:
those in
tribulation and good case
error and truth
sin and grace.
Ecumenic:
Eastern: Western: our own:
prelates: orders of clergy: people.
Commonwealths of the earth:
the Christian: round about us: our own:
the king, the queen, the prince:
them that are eminent:
parliament, judicature, civil control, armed force:
commonalty,
husbandmen, merchantmen, artificers,
even to the sordid craftsmen
and beggars.

Those commended to me by
kindred,
good offices received,
ministry of carnal things,
charge {aforetime
now,
friendship,
christian charity,
neighbourhood,
my promise,
their earnest desire,
want of leisure,
sympathy for them in extremities.
merit,
good works,
scandal given,
having no intercessor.

Commendation

Ps. xxxi 6; 1 Thess. v 23 Into thy hands, o Lord, I commend myself
my spirit, soul, body:
Thou hast created and redeemed them,
o Lord, Thou God of truth: *
and with me, mine and all things mine:
Thou hast granted me them, o Lord,
in thy goodness.
Ps. cxxi 8; cxxxix 1 Preserve Thou my lying down and mine uprising
from this time forth for evermore:
Ps. lxiii 7 to remember Thee in my bed,
Ps. lxxvii 6 to search out my spirits;
Ps. cxxxix 18 to wake up and be present with Thee.
Ps. iv 9 I will lay me down in peace
and take my rest:
for it is Thou, Lord, only
that makest me dwell in safety.

A SECOND FORM OF EVENING PRAYER H 39

Commemoration

Ps. cxxxiv 2, 3 By night lift up your hands in the sanctuary
and praise the Lord.
Ps. lv 18 In the evening, in the morning and at noonday will I pray
and that instantly:
and Thou, Lord, shalt hear my voice.

The Lord hath granted his lovingkindness in the day time : Ps. xlii 10
therefore in the nightseason did I sing his praises
and made my prayer unto the God of my life.
Let my prayer be set forth in thy sight as the incense, Ps. cxli 2
and the lifting up of my hands as an evening sacrifice.

Thanksgiving

Blessed art Thou, o Lord, Ps. cxix 12
who hast created changes of day and night,* Cp. *Heb. even.* p. 96
and givest rest to them that are weary
and renewest strength to him that is spent :
who givest songs by night, Job xxxv 10
and makest the outgoings of the dayspring and evening to praise Thee : Ps. lxv 8
who hast delivered us from the arrow that flieth by day, Ps. xci 5
and the sickness that destroyeth in the noonday : 6
who hast not cut off as a weaver our life, Is. xxxviii 12
nor from day even to night made away with us.

Penitence

O Lord, as days unto days, Ps. lxi 6
so do we add sins to sins. 2 Chr. xxviii 13 Job xxxiv 37
The just man stumbleth seven times * in a day, Prov. xxiv 16
but we, miserable sinners,
seventy times seven.* S. Mt. xviii 22
Today also hath had his own
and shall receive his own.
But we return unto Thee Jer. xxiv 7
and all our bones say * We repent. Ps. xxxv 10
Let not the sun go down Eph. iv 26
upon thy wrath.
Lord, all our good works Is. xxvi 12
Thou hast wrought in us :
what thing soever we have done aright *Off.B.V.M.* 1573, p. 337
graciously behold.
Lord, our sin and our destruction Hos. xiii. 9.
are of ourselves :
what thing soever we have done wrong *Off.B.V.M.*
mercifully forgive.*
Behold the good,
pardon the evil.

Comprecation

Ps. cxix 12 Blessed art Thou, o Lord,
Ps. cxxvii 3 who givest thy beloved pleasant sleep,
Hos. ii 18 and to them that fear Thee to lie down safely.
Ps. xiii 3 Lighten our eyes,
that we sleep not in death :
Ps. xci 5 deliver us from the terror by night,
6 from the pestilence that walketh in darkness.
Ps. cxxi 4 Behold He that keepeth Israel
shall neither slumber nor sleep :
7 the Lord preserve us from all evil,
yea the Lord keep our souls.
Cant. v 2 Lord, I will sleep,
but my heart shall be awake.*
Visit me, o Lord, with the visitation of the saints,
Job xxxiii 15, 16 and discover mine ear in visions of night.*
Let my sleep be a respite,
as from toil, so from sin :
let me not in dreams think aught
to offend Thee or pollute me.
Cp. Ps. cxxxix 11 Grant me, Lord, to remember that with Thee
night is no night
and darkness is like the noonday light.*
Grant me, o Lord, when sleep flieth from mine eyes,
Ps. cxix 55 to remember thy Name in the night season,
that so I may keep thy law.
Ps. lxxvii 6 Grant me to commune in the night with my heart,
and to be sore exercised and to search out my spirits
Ps. xvi 8 and not to neglect the instruction of my reins *—
what I may do rightly, what more rightly,
how to be more acceptable to Thee,
how to be more pleasing unto men :
Ps. cxxxix 2, 12 that Thou art about my paths
and about my bed :
that my ways are thine :
(?) when my lamp is alight to see Thee,
when my lamp is quenched to see Thee.*
Grant me, o Lord, to think
of the long sleep,
the sleep of death,

the bed of the grave,
the mattrass of worms,
the coverlet of dust.

Commendation

I will lay me down in peace Ps. iv 9
and take my rest:
for it is Thou Lord only
that makest me dwell in safety.
Into thy hands, o Lord, Ps. xxxi 6
I commend my spirit,
for Thou hast redeemed me,
o Lord Thou God of truth.

S 51 A THIRD FORM OF EVENING PRAYER

Penitence

O Lord, as days unto days, Ps. lxi 6
so withal do we add sins to sins. 2 Chr. xxviii 13; Job xxxiv 37
The just man stumbleth seven times * a day, Prov. xxiv 16
but I, a singular great sinner,
seventy times seven. S. Mt. xviii 22
Nay but I return unto Thee, o Lord. Dt. xxx 2
O Lord Thou lover of man, Cp. Wisd. xi 26
that hast a golden censer: Rev. viii 3; Ex. xxix 18
add me thine incense unto this prayer
for a sweet-smelling savour before the throne,
and let the lifting up of hands be set forth Ps. cxli 2
for an evening sacrifice.
Lord the Almighty, Zech. i 6
all our works Thou hast wrought in us: Is. xxvi 12
if we have gotten any good success, receive it favourably, *Primer* 1604, f. 200 b.
o Lord abundant in goodness and very pitiful: Ex. xxxiv 6; S. Ja. v 11
but so many things as we have done amiss, pardon graciously, *Primer* 1604, f. 200 b.
for our destruction cometh of ourselves. Hos. xiii 9

Comprecation

Ps. xci 5, 6 Deliver me, o Lord, from the terror by night,
from the pestilence that walketh in darkness.
Ps. lxiii 1 Give me to seek Thee early,
Cp. *Horolog.* p. 159 even for thy praise and service.
Ps. cxxi 8; cxxxix 1 Preserve my lying down and my uprising
from this time forth even for evermore.
Job xxxiii 15, 16 Discover me my mind for meditation by night,
Ps. lxiii 7 so as to remember Thee upon my bed:
Ps. lxxvii 6 in the night to commune with mine own heart
and {to search out / to keep} my spirit: *
but if not this
(for I am not worthy,
I am not worthy, o Lord)
yet at leastwise,
Cp. Wisd. xi 26 o Lord Thou lover of * man,
let my sleep be to me a respite,
as from toiling, so from sinning withal.
Yea, o Lord, I beseech Thee, look upon me,
Horolog. p. 172 and put to sleep in me
every earthly and evil thought.
Horolog. p. 159 The sleeplessness of mine unseen foes, Thou wottest, o Lord:
the slackness of my wretched flesh
Thou knowest, which didst form me.
Let the wing of thy goodness shelter me:
Ps. xiii 3 lighten mine eyes
that I never sleep in death.*
Give me, o Lord, a good life, a good death,
and deathlessness:
2 Pet. i 14 for I know not, I know not, o Lord,
how soon is the putting off of my tabernacle.
Lit. S. Ja. pp. 10, 29 Wherein grant me, o Lord, that the end of life be christian,
sinless, shameless, and, if it like Thee, painless;
and a good defence
at the appalling and fearful judgment-seat of Jesus Christ;
Missale Sarisb. 1534, com. ss. f. 21 b. that I may hear the most sweet voice.
COME, YE BLESSED,
S. Mt. xxv 21 and that I may enter into thy joy *

and get fruition of the vision
of our Father which is in heaven.
Grant me sleep, o Lord, for repose of weakness *Horolog.* p. 19
and for relief of the toils
of this travailling flesh.
Into thy hands, o Lord, I commend myself Ps. xxxi 6
and all things mine:
preserve me, o Lord, Thou that art the keeper of Israel, Ps. cxxi 7, 4
that didst neither slumber nor sleep ever yet.

Blessing, thanksgiving and doxology

Blessed art Thou, o Lord God of our fathers, 3 Child. 29
that didst create changes of days and nights, Cp. *Heb. even.* p. 96
that hast delivered us from the evil of this day, S. Mt. vi 13, 34
that hast bestowed on us occasions of songs in the evening * Job xxxv 10
and to get us through the night fearlessly in hope:
for Thou art our light, salvation and strength of our life: Ps. xxvii 1
of whom then shall we be afraid? *
Glory be to Thee, o Lord, glory be to Thee,
for all thy divine perfections,
for thine inexpressible and unimaginable
goodness and mercy,
unto sinners and unworthy,
and to me
a sinner, of all most unworthy:
yea, o Lord,
glory and praise and blessing and thanksgiving
by the voices and concert of voices
as well of angels as of men
and of all thy saints in heaven
and of all thy creation withal on earth,
and under their feet
of me the sinner unworthy and wretched,
world without end.

ON GOING TO BED

O 256

Ps. cxix 55 Let me think upon thy Name in the night season,
and keep thy law:
[S. Aug.] *Serm.* ccxxvi let the evening prayer go up unto Thee,
and thy pity come down unto us,
Job xxxv 10 o Thou which givest songs in the night,
Ps. lxv 8 which makest the outgoings of the morning and evening to praise Thee,
Ps. cxxvii 3 which givest thy beloved wholesome sleep.

THE HOLY MYSTERIES

W 159 **AN ACT OF PREPARATION**

O Lord, *Horolog.* p. 468
I am not worthy, neither sufficient
that Thou shouldest enter beneath the filthy roof
of the house of my soul,
seeing it is all desolate and downfallen;
and Thou hast not with me a worthy place
to lay thy head.
But as Thou tookest upon Thee
to be laid in a cavern and a cratch of brute beasts:
as Thou didst not refuse
to be received even in the house of Simon the leper:
as Thou didst not repel
even the harlot like me, the sinner,
coming to Thee and touching Thee:
as Thou didst not abhor
her filthy mouth and polluted:*
neither the robber on the cross
confessing to Thee:
in like sort vouchsafe to accept me withal Cp. *Lit. S. Ja* p. 38; *Lit. S. Bas.* p. 66
the inveterate, miserable,
the singular great sinner,
to the touch and partaking
of the immaculate, awful, quickening
and saving mysteries
of thine allholy Body *Lit. S. Ja.* p. 34, 41
and precious Blood.

W 160 **AT THE LITURGY**

At the Offertory

Behold, o Lord our God, *Lit. S Bas.* p. 66
from heaven thy dwelling-place
and from the throne of the glory of thy kingdom,
and come to hallow us.

Thou that sittest on high with the Father,
and art here with us invisibly,
Lit. S. Bas. p. 58 come to hallow the gifts that are set forth,
ib. p. 61 and them for whom and them by whom and the ends whereunto
they are brought.
ib. p. 67 And give us communion
unto faith unashamed,
love without dissimulation,
keeping of the commandments,*
alertness for every spiritual fruit,
ib. turning aside of every adversary,
healing of soul and body:
ib. p. 65; *Horolog.* p. 467 with intent that we also, with all saints,
which have been wellpleasing unto Thee since the world began,
may be made partakers
of thine unalloyed and everlasting good things,
which Thou hast prepared for them that love Thee, o Lord:
in whom Thou art glorified
for ever.
S. Jo. i 29 O Lamb of God,
that takest away the sin of the world,*
take away the sin of me withal the mere sinner.
Unto a token of the fellowship,
a memorial of the dispensation,
1 Cor. xi 26 a showing forth of the death,
1 Cor. x 16 a communion of body and blood,
Heb. vi. 4 a participation of the Spirit,
S. Mt. xxvi. 28 remission of sins,
Lit. S. Bas. p. 67 a riddance of adversaries,*
quieting of conscience,
Cp. *Horolog.* p. 470 blotting out of debts,
cleansing of stains,
healing* of the sicknesses of the soul,
renewal of the covenant,
Horolog. p. 468. provision for the journey of ghostly life,*
increase of {enabling grace / winning comfort,
compunction of repentance,

illumination* of mind, — Cp. *Horolog.* p. 470
a preparatory exercise of humility,
a seal of faith,
fulness of wisdom,* — Ecclus. i 16; *Lit. S. Bas.* p. 67
a bond of charity,
a sufficient ground of almsgiving,
an armour of endurance,
alertness for thanksgiving,
confidence of prayer,
mutual indwelling, — S. Jo. vi 56
a pledge of resurrection, — 54
acceptable defence in* judgement, — *Horolog.* p. 468
a testament of inheritance,
a stamp of perfectness.

W 162

After the Consecration

Remembering therefore, o sovran Lord, even we,* — *Lit. S. Bas.* p. 57
(in the presence of thy holy mysteries)
the saving sufferings of thy Christ, — *ib.*
his quickening cross,*
right precious death,
three days' burial, — *ib.*
resurrection from the dead,
ascension into heaven,
session at the right hand of Thee the Father,
glorious and fearful coming—
we beseech Thee, o Lord,
that with the witness of our conscience clean, — *Lit. S. Bas.* p. 65; *Horolog.* p. 467
receiving our share of thy hallowed things,
we may be united to the holy body and blood of thy Christ,
and receiving them not unworthily
may have Christ indwelling in our hearts,
and be made a temple of thy Holy Ghost.
Yea, our God,
and make none of us guilty
of these thine appalling and heavenly mysteries
nor weak in soul or body
by reason of partaking of them unworthily:
but grant us,

unto our last and closing gasp,
worthily to receive an hope of thy hallowed things
Horolog. p. 468 unto
hallowing, enlightenment, strengthening,
lightening of the weight of my many sins,
a preservative against every diabolical operation,
a riddance and letting of my bad conscience,
mortification of the passions,
keeping of the commandments
an increase of thy divine grace,
and an appropriation of thy kingdom.

After the Blessing W 164

Lit. S. Bas. p. 68 Finished and perfected,
so far forth as is in our power,
o Christ our God,
is the mystery of thy dispensation.
For we have held the remembrance of thy death,
we have seen the figure of thy resurrection,
we have been filled with thine unending life,
we have had fruition of thine inexhaustible delight:
whereof in the world to come withal
be Thou pleased that we all
be accounted worthy.

2 Chr. xxx 18, 19 The Lord the good God
pardon everyone
that prepareth his heart to seek God,
the Lord God of his fathers,
though he be not cleansed
according to the purification of the sanctuary.

PENITENCE

OF PENANCE

O 338 I. Contrition

Bitterness of soul: Is. xxxviii 15
pricking of heart: Acts ii 37
a spirit or heart { rent / broken in pieces / crushed to powder }: Joel ii 13; Ps. li 17
godly sorrow: 2 Cor. vii. 10
throbbing of heart: 1 Sam. xxv 31
indignation. 2 Cor. vii 11

II. Confession

Acknowledgement: * Ps. li 3
Prayer deprecating { the past / the future }:

i. All have sinned. Rom. iii 23
   1. If Thou, Lord—who shall abide it? Ps. cxxx 3
   2. No man living shall be justified. Ps. cxliii 2
   3. He cannot answer one of a thousand. Job ix 3

ii. What then? For nought? Ps. lxxxix 46

iii. God hath granted repentance unto life.* Acts xi 18
   1. There is a place left for forgiveness,
      if sin only lie at the door. Gen. iv 7
   2. There remaineth a hope: Cp. Ezra x 2
      it shall not be a snare. Ps. lxix 23
   3. There is an healing: Dan. iv 27 marg.
      as it were { a city of refuge / a second plank. } S. Jer. *c. Pelag.* i 33; S. Jer. *Ep.* cxxx 9

iv. But God soliciteth
   by proclaiming: by complaining: Is. lv 7; i 2 sqq.; Jer. viii 4
   by swearing oath: by waiting: Ez. xxxiii 11; Is. xxx 18
   by promising { paradise to innocence / the kingdom of heaven / to penitence } if—
   by threatening unless.

III. < Satisfaction >

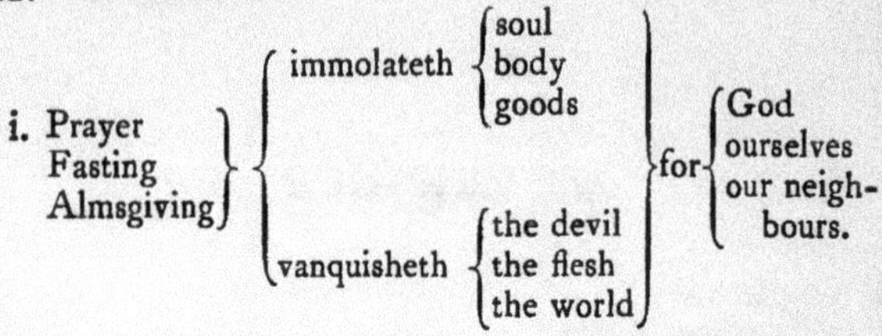

S. Bonavent. *in Sentt.* iv 15

ii. The seven Works of Mercy O 327

1. Corporal:

   Visit, feed, give drink, redeem, clothe, shelter, inter.

2. Spiritual:

   Teach, counsel, chastise, comfort, forgive, suffer, pray.

PENITENTIAL DEVOTIONS

O 345
H 3
S 6

BEFORE PENITENTIAL DEVOTIONS

O Lord, my heart is ready : Ps. cviii 1
so the Psalmist.
But, Lord, I fear that mine is not :
I desire indeed, and I grieve if it be not.
Would God it were ready ! woe is me that it is not !
O Lord, I dispose me and prepare :
help Thou my disposition and supply my preparation.
I will set my sins before me, Cp. Ps. li 3
that so they be not before Thee. Cp. Ps. xc 8

SELF-EXAMINATION

Penitence

Do I repent? Am I sorry? Am I ashamed? O 324
Am I grieved? Am I aghast? Am I aweary?

I had lief it were more, I fear lest, O 334
I grieve it is not, I were glad if.

Prayer

O 324

Ps. cxix 164 If not seven times like David;
Dan. vi 10 yet three times like Daniel?
1 Ki. viii 22 ff. If not, like Solomon, at length;
S. Lk. xviii 13 yet, like the Publican, shortly?
S. Lk. vi 12 If not for a whole night, like Christ;
S. Mt. xxvi 40 yet for a single hour?
S. Mk. xiv 35; Dan. ix. 3 If not on the ground, if not in ashes;
Cant. iii 1 yet not in bed?

Fasting

Jonah iii 8 If not in sackcloth;
S. Lk. xvi 19 yet not in purple and fine linen?
2 Sam. iii 35 If not wholly from all;
Dan. i 8 yet from dainties?

Alms

S. Lk. xix 8 If not, like Zacchee, fourfold;
Lev. v 16 yet, as the law is, with a fifth part overadded?
S. Mk. xii 41-44 If not like the rich;
yet like the widow?
S. Lk. xix 8 If not the half;
Dt. xxvi 12 yet the thirtieth part?
2 Cor. viii 3 If not beyond my power;
yet up to my power?

AN ACT OF PENITENCE

O 289 ### Address

Let prayer come up — *Horae* f. c. 3
come unto Thee — 2 Chr. xxx 27; Jonah ii 7
enter in — Ps. lxxxviii 1
appear in thy presence — Cp. Ps. cxli 2
find grace — Heb. iv 16
come before Thee: — Ps. cxix 169
and I ask that it return not unto me void: — *Horae* u. s.
but, according as thou knowest and canst and willest,
hear — Ps. cxix 149
incline thine ear — Ps. lxxxvi 1; Dan. ix 18
give ear and consider — Ps. lxi 1; x 15
understand — Ps. v 1
hearken — Ps. lxiv 1
remember to do. — Cp. Dan. ix 19

Do not cast away in displeasure — Ps. xxvii 10
hide thine eye — Is. i 15
hide thy face — Job xiii 24
cover thyself with a cloud — Lam. iii 44
shut up thine ear — Cp. Lam. iii 56
desert — Cp. Ps. xxxviii 21
forsake for ever — Ps. xxvii 11; xliv 23; cxix 8
abhor — Ps. xxii 24
hold thy peace — Ps. xxxix 13
sleep — Ps. xliv 23
go afar off — Ps. xxxv 22
be absent — Ps. xliv 23
take away lovingkindness — Gen. xxiv 27; Ps. lxxxix 33
suffer truth to fail
rebuke in displeasure — Ps. vi 1
chasten in indignation

Ps. li 11 cast away from thy presence
Wisd. ix 4 reject me from among thy children
Ps. li 11 take thy Spirit from me
Ps. lxxiv 20 forget for ever
Is. lxiv 9 be wroth very sore
Ps. xxvii 14 deliver me over } because of mine iniquities
Is. lxiv 7 consume me } because of mine iniquities
Hab. ii 3 tarry to return
Ps. xxvi 9 shut up my soul with the sinners.
Horae f. 177b Howsoever by thine allowance we suffer the power of the enemy for a season, let us not in any wise be swallowed up of his insatiable jaws.
Let the lion be vanquished by the feeble sheep,
the violent spirit by the feeble flesh.

Pleading

Ps. lxxxix 46 sept. O remember what my substance is:
Gen. xviii 27 that I am { dust and ashes
Is. xl 6 grass and a flower
Ps. lxxviii 40 flesh and a wind that passeth away
Job xvii 14 corruption and a worm,
Ps. xxxix 14 like a stranger and a sojourner,
Job iv 19 dwelling in a house of clay,
Gen. xlvii 9 days few and evil,
Cp. S. Mt. vi. 30 today and not tomorrow,
Cp. Is. xxxviii 13 in the morning and not so long as till evening,*
now and not presently,
Rom. vii 24 in a body of death,
Cp. 2 Pet. i 4 in a world of corruption,
1 S. Jo. v 19 lying in wickedness.
Ps. lxxiv 18 Remember this.

Confession

2 Sam. xii 13 I have sinned.
S. Mt. xxvi 73 Surely, o Lord, I also am one of them,
for my life bewrayeth me.
Prymer f. 145 I confess to Thee: for, if I will, I cannot hide it from Thee, o Lord.
Job xiv 4 Who can bring a clean thing out of an unclean?

I am a sinner { of an unclean seed / of an unclean womb :
in sin hath my mother conceived me : Ps. li 5
a root of bitterness Heb. xii 15
a slip of wild olive. Rom. xi 17

1. I have sinned, I have done amiss and dealt wickedly before Thee 2 Chr. vi 37
2. I have behaved myself forwardly in thy covenant. Ps. xliv 18
3. I have rejected the law Jer. vi 19
4. I have refused correction Prov. xv 32 ; Jer. v 3
5. I have vexed the Spirit Cp. Is. lxiii 10
6. I have walked after my devices Jer. xviii 12
7. I have gone over from evil to evil Cp. Jer. ix 3
8. neither have I feared Thee Cp. Jer. xliv 10
9. neither have I returned S. Lk. xv 17
10. not even when recalled Cp. Jer. vii 13
11. neither even when troubled Ps. cxix 67
12. but I have waxed hardened Heb. iii 13
13. I have provoked Thee 1 Kings xvi 33
14. and all these things Thou hast seen and hast held thy tongue. Ps. xxxv 22 ; l 21

Aggravation of Sin

Cp. *Prymer* f. 168

1. Measure of sin { harm / scandal
2. Quality
3. Repetition How oft ?
4. Continuance How long ?
5. Person Who ?
   age
   condition
   estate
   knowledge
6. Manner
7. Motive
8. Time
9. Place.

   1. Folly
   2. Ingratitude
   3. Hardness
   4. Contempt.

Kinds of Sin

- Is. v 18 — 1. Cords / ropes
- Ps. xxv 16; S. Jas. i 20 — 2. necessities / superfluities
- 3.
  - omission or deficiency:
    - leaving undone what we ought to do:
  - commission or excess:
    - doing what we ought not to do
- *Eucholog.* p. 378 — 4.
  - of the heart : within : in thought
  - of the mouth / of act : without : in word / deed*
- 5.
  - against God
  - against our neighbour
  - against our own body
- *Eucholog.* p. 378 — 6. unwitting / witting
- 7. unwilling / willing*
- 8. old / recent
- 9. in point of age
  - boyhood
  - youth
  - mature / advanced — age
- 10. once committed / often repeated
- *Eucholog.* p. 378; Ps. xix. 12; 1 Ti. v. 24 — 11. privy / open *
- 12.
  - of wrath
  - of concupiscence of the flesh / the world
- 13. by one not yet called / by one already called
- *Horolog.* p. 102 — 14. asleep, by night / awake, by day *
- Ps. xix. 13 vulg. — 15. one's own / others'
- 16. which I remember / which I have forgotten.

Horae f. c. 5b — What things soever from infancy even until now
even until this moment,

witting or unwitting,
within or without,
sleeping or waking,
in words, deeds, thoughts,
through the fiery darts of the enemy,
through the unclean desires of the flesh,
I have sinned against Thee,*
have mercy upon me, o God, and forgive me.

Contrition

	I am penitent	
1. I am sorry	sorrow	for the wound
2. I am ashamed	shame	spot, stain, filth
3. I am grieved	indignation	guilt
4. I am horrorstruck	fear	punishment
5. I am weary	I travail	thraldom, yoke.

1. Fear 2 Cor. vii 11
2. indignation
3. judgement 1 Cor. xi 31
4. revenge 2 Cor. vii 11
5. hatred S. Ju. 23
6. flight from occasion Gal. v 13
7. humiliation S. Ja. iv 10
8. smiting of the breast S. Lk. xviii 13
9. thigh Jer. xxxi 19
10. laying aside of excellency, sackcloth Jonah iii 6
11. fasting S. Mt. vi 16
12. prayer, devotion, commemoration 5
13. works of mercy.* 2

Grant me alway to grieve,
and alway of grief to rejoice. [S. Aug.] *de vera et falsa paenitentia* 28

Petition for Mercy

Have mercy
Look upon me and be merciful Ps. cxix 132
forsake me not Ps. xxvii 11
remember mercy Ps. xcviii 4
have mercy upon us and that soon Ps. lxxix 8

Is. lxiv 9 be not wroth

Hab. i 13; Is. lvii 17 regard not my sins neither have indignation

Eph. iv. 32 forgive

Is. lxiv 12; Ps. lxxvii 10 refrain wrath : put off wrath

Acts vii 60 lay not to charge

Ps. xxxii 2 impute not

Ps. lxxix 8 remember not

Ps. cxxx 3 be not extreme to mark

Ps. cxliii 2 enter not into judgement

Ps. xxvii 11 despise not

Ps. li 11 cast not away from thy presence.

Ps. lxxix 5 How long?

Ps. lxxvii 8 For ever?

Ex. xxxii 12 Be { easy to be appeased

Joel ii 13 easy to be approached

Ps. xc 13 easy to be entreated. }

Horae f. c. 5b Let not thy wrath come upon me,

but let thy grace, I pray thee, prevent me.*

Shew mercy unto me

Horae f. c. 8 now and in the hour of death.

Horae f. c. 7 Let not the fault of the flesh hurt me unto punishment:

yea let the compassionateness of affection profit me unto pardon*.

1. Guilt 3. Sickness

2. Stain 4. Thraldom

Dt. xxi 9 i. Guilt.

1 Cor. xi 34 Not unto condemnation.

Joel ii 17 1. Spare

S. Jo. i29; Is. vi 7 2. take away

2 Sam. xii 13 3. put away

3 Macc. ii 19 4. scatter

Wisd. xii 11 5. give pardon

Is. lxiii 7; S. Mt. vi 12 6. forgive

Is. lv 7 7. pardon

Ps. lxxix 9 8. deliver from punishment, condone

9. be merciful

2 Mac. viii 29 10. be reconciled

1 Kings viii 39 11. be propitiated.

Dt. xv. 21 ii. Stain, ill favour.

Ps. li 9 1. Turn thy face from sins;

Ps. xxvii 10 turn it not away from misery

2. pass by	Wisd. i 8; Mic. vii 18
3. wink at, overlook	Wisd. xi 23; Acts xvii 30
4. put up with, forbear	Rom. ii 4
5. cover	Ps. xxxii 1; lxxxv 2
6. wash	Ps. li 2
7. cleanse	Ps. xix 12
8. wash away	Acts xxii 16; Is. i 16
9. make white	Ps. li 7
10. put out, blot out.	Ps. li 9; Is. xliv 22
iii. Sickness, plague, the sickly hurt.	Is. i 6; xxx 26
1. Cure,	S. Lc. x 35
have a care	
2. heal	Job. v 18
3. recover,	Jer. xvii 14
make more remiss: save from:	S. Mt. i 21
root out: break not a reed.	S. Mt. xii 20
iv. Thraldom.	Rom. vi 16
Avenge rescue	S. Lk. xviii 5
deliver save.	S. Mt. vi 13; i 21

O 286 **Pleading of the divine mercy**

Through and for the sake of

1. { Name / glory of the Name	Ps. lxxix 9
2. { promised truth / intervention of an oath	Ps. lxxxix 3, 25; Heb. vi 17
3. comfort of love	Phil. ii 1
4. bowels of mercies	
5. great } mercy	Ps. li 1
6. good store } mercy	2 Sam. xxiv 14
7. old } mercy	Ps. lxxxix 48
8. plenteous } mercy	Ps. cxxx 7
9. everlasting } mercy	Ps. cxxxvi
10. exceeding } mercy	Eph. ii 4
11. marvellous } mercy	Ps. xvii 7
12. riches of mercy	Eph. i 7; ii 4
13. redundancy of mercy { excess / superfluity	Eph. i 8
14. supersuperfluity	1 Tim. i 14
15. superexcess	Rom. v 20

Eph. ii 7 16. extravagance
Ps. cxlv 9 17. triumph over all works
S. Ja. ii 13 18. over justice
19. the satisfaction and merits of Christ
Acts ix 31 20. the comfort of the Holy Ghost.

Lam. iii 22 Mercy

1. that we are not consumed
Ps. lxxix 8 2. preventing
Ps. xxiii 6 3. following
Ps. xxxii 11 4. embracing on every side
Ps. ciii 3 5. pardoning
4 6. crowning.

Eph. iii 18
{ Length 1. long
breadth 2. broad
depth 3. deep
height 4. high.

Ps. xxv 5 1. Ever of old
Ps. cxxxvi 2. for ever
Ps. cviii 4 3. reaching unto the heaven
Cp. Ps. lxxxvi 13 4. reaching unto hell
Rom. xi 32 5. to all *
6. tender.

Cp. S. Bern. *Serm.* 2 *in dom. vi p. Pent.* 3
I have put off penitence
and Thou hast prolonged patience,*
o mercy, a wellspring that can never be exhaust.

Mercy

Ps. lxix 117; cix 20 1. sweet
Ps. lxiii 4 2. better than life
Ecclus. ii 18 3. as great as is his majesty
S. Mt. xviii 22 4. until seventy times seven times
Wisd. xi 25 5. abhorring nothing which He hath made
Ps. cxlvii 9 6. neglecting neither the young ravens
S. Mt. x 29 nor the tiny sparrow
1 Tim. ii 4 7. willing all men to be saved
2 S. Pet. iii 9 8. not willing that any should perish
S. Lk. xv 5 9. bringing back the sheep on his shoulders
8 10. sweeping the house for a piece of silver
S. Mt. xviii 24, 32 11. forgiving a thousand talents
S. Lk. x 30, 34 12. binding up the wounds of the half-dead
S. Lk. xv 20 13. meeting with joy the wicked son
Jonah ii 10 14. delivering Jonas while he fled

15. receiving Peter when he denied	S. Jo. xxi 15
16. not casting out unbelieving Thomas	S. Jo. xx 27, 29
17. converting Paul albeit he blasphemed	1 Tim. i 13
18. delivering the woman taken in adultery	S. Jo. viii 11
19. admitting the Magdalene which was a sinner	S. Lk. vii 37ff
20. joining the robber to Thyself in paradise	S. Lk. xxiii 43
21. standing at the door and knocking	Rev. iii 20
22. the Master himself asking his servants	2 Cor. v 20
23. whose place is { the throne of grace	Heb. iv 16
{ the mercyseat of the ark	Ex. xxv 22
24. whose time is a day of salvation.	2 Cor. vi 2

O 297 **Purpose of Amendment**

I purpose

1. I am steadfastly purposed		Ps. cxix 106
2. I fervently desire		20
3. I long	vehement desire	2 Cor. vii 11
4. I am zealous	zeal	
5. I am in earnest	carefulness	
6. I plead	clearing of self:	
that {	1. I will turn away	Is. xxx 15 sept.
	2. I will forsake	Is. lv 7
	3. I will depart from	2 Tim. ii 19
	4. I will say, It sufficeth	1 S. Pet. iv 3
	5. not again henceforth : no longer:	2
that {	1. I will turn again unto Thee	Lam. iii 40
	2. I will turn my feet	Ps. cxix 59
	3. I will lift up my hands	48
	4. I will eschew	Ps. xxxiv 14
	5. I will bring to nought the desire	Cp. Ps. xxxiii 10
	6. I will make the crooked straight	Is. xl 4
	7. I will set a hedge.	Hos. ii 6

Confession of Weakness

I am weak

1. I do not what I would,	Rom. vii 15
do what I would not	16
2. children come to the birth	Is. xxxvii 3
3. the thoughts that arise in my heart allow me not	S. Lk. xxiv 38

Ps. lxix 1 — 4. billows come in even unto my soul
Rom. vii 23 — 5. the law of the members bringeth me into captivity
Is. xxxviii 14 — 6. o Lord, I am oppressed: undertake for me
Rom. vii 24 — 7. who shall deliver me?

Petition for help

		Bring help
Ps. lxx 1	1. O succour	O God make speed to save
Ps. lxix 1	2. aid	Save me, o God
Ps. lxviii 1	3. help	Let God arise
Ps. iii 7	4. convert	Up, Lord

Ps. cxix 176 — 5. seek
Ps. lxx 1 — 6. make speed to save
Is. xxxvii 17 — 7. open thine eyes and see
8. incline thine ears and hear
Ps. cxix 36 — 9. incline my heart
Job xxxvi 10 — 10. open mine ears
Ps. xiii 3 — 11. lighten mine eyes
Neh. vi 9 — 12. strengthen my hands
Ps. cxix 133 — 13. order my steps
Ps. xxvi 2 — 14. try out my reins
Ps. cxix 120 — 15. transfix my flesh
Cant. i 4 — 16. draw me after Thee
Ps. xxxii 10 — 17. hold me with a bit
Job xvii 3 — 18. put me in surety with Thee
2 S. Pet. ii 22 — 19. let me not to my vomit
1 Cor. x 13 — 20. let there be no temptation but such as is common to man
Ps. lxxxix 23 — 21. let the enemy not be able to do violence
Ps: lxix 16 — 21. let it not drown me.
Hos. ii 6 — Hedge Thou up with thorns: *

remove { occasions / scandals.

Comfortable words

Rest of soul

Gen. iv 7 — Hitherto sin watcheth before the door.
Gen. xviii 32 — I would not destroy it for ten's sake.
Gen. xxii 14 — In the mountain the Lord will provide.
Ex. xxxiv 6, 7 — The Lord, the Lord God, merciful and gracious, long-suffering and abundant in goodness and truth, who keepest

mercy for thousands, who forgivest iniquity, transgression and sin.

They shall pine away until they confess; Lev. xxvi 39, 40
when they shall be humbled then shall they pray, 41
and I will remember my covenant. 42

When evils are come upon thee and thou shalt turn unto Dt. xxx 1-3, 5, 6 genev.
thine heart and shalt return unto God, He will have compassion upon thee and will do thee good and will circumcise thine heart to love the Lord.

Why art thou so full of heaviness, o my soul, and why art Ps. xlii 14
thou so disquieted within me?

Put thy trust in God, for I will yet give Him thanks, which 15
is the help of my countenance and my God.

Turn again then unto thy rest, o my soul; for the Lord shall Ps. cxvi 7
reward thee.

Remember

O think upon thy servant as concerning thy words: wherein Ps. cxix 49
Thou hast caused me to put my trust.

O stablish me according to thy words that I may live: and 116
let me not be disappointed of my hope.

He will not alway be chiding: neither keepeth He his anger Ps. ciii 9
for ever.

He will not deal with us after our sins: nor reward us 10
according to our iniquities.

He was so merciful that He forgave us our misdeeds: so as Ps. lxxviii 38
not to destroy us.

He considered that we are but flesh: and that we are even a 40
wind that passeth away and cometh not again.

Mercy triumphing S. Ja. ii 13

Come now and let us reason together, said the Lord: Is. i 18
Though your sins be as scarlet, they shall be as white as snow; though they be red like crimson, they shall be as wool.

When thou shalt turn and groan, then shalt thou be saved. Is. xxx 15 sept.

The Lord will wait that He may be gracious unto you. 18

A bruised reed shall He not break and the smoking flax Is. xlii 3
shall He not quench.

I am He that blotteth out thy transgressions for mine own Is. xliii 25
sake, and will not remember thy sins.

I blot out as a thick cloud thy transgressions and as a cloud Is. xliv 22
thy sins: return unto me and I will redeem.

Is. xlvi 4 And even to your old age I am He: and even to hoar hairs
will I carry you: I have made and I will bear:
even I will carry and will deliver.
Is. liii 4 Surely He hath borne our griefs and carried our sorrows:
5 He was wounded for our transgressions, He was bruised for
our iniquities:
the chastisement of our peace was upon Him and with his
stripes we are healed.
6 All we like sheep have gone astray: we have turned everyone to his own way: and the Lord hath laid on
Him the iniquity of us all.
Is. lxv 24 And it shall come to pass that, before they call, I will
answer: and while they are yet speaking I will
hear.
Ez. xviii 23 Have I any pleasure at all that the wicked should die and
not that he should return from his ways and live?
30 Return ye and turn yourselves from all your transgressions:
so iniquity shall not be your ruin.
Ez. xxxiii 11 As I live, I have no pleasure in the death of the wicked:
but that the wicked turn from his way and live.
Turn ye, turn ye from your evil ways: for why will ye die,
o house of Israel?
12 As for the wickedness of the wicked, he shall not fall thereby in the day that he turneth from his iniquity:
19 and if the wicked turn from his wickedness and do that
which is lawful and right, he shall live thereby.
Is. lv 7 Let the wicked forsake his way and the unrighteous man his
thoughts: and let him return unto the Lord and
He will have mercy upon him: and to our God,
for He will abundantly pardon.

H 11 **ANOTHER ACT OF PENITENCE**

I confess to Thee, o Lord,
that I was conceived in unclean seed, Cp. Job xiv 4
warmed in iniquity in my mother's womb, Ps. li 5
a root of bitterness, Heb. xii 15; Dt. xxix 18 sept.
a wild vine of Sodom, Dt. xxxii 32
a generation of a viper, S. Mt. iii 7
a slip of wild olive, Rom. xi 24
a child of wrath, Eph. ii 3
a vessel of destruction: Rom. ix 22
a heart rebellious like a deceitful bow; Jer. v 23; Hos. vii 16
a mouth like an open sepulchre, Ps. v 10
pouring out foolishness; Prov. xv 2
having unclean lips; Is. vi 5
a tongue, a world of iniquity; S. Ja. iii 6
eyes evil, prone to lusts; Ecclus. xxxi 13
ears uncircumcised, like a deaf adder; Jer. vi 10; Ps. lviii 4
the forehead of a whore, like brass; Jer. iii 3; Is. xlviii 4
a neck hard like an iron sinew;
hands remiss unto good; Heb. xii 12
feet swift to evil. Prov. vi 18
What thing soever I have done is
either a spider's web Is. lix 5
or a cockatrice's egg.
I have sinned, o Lord, Ps. xli 4
against Thee, o Lord, against Thee.
In the sight of thine eyes I have not had in reverence 2 Chr. xxxiii 23 vulg.
thy presence:
I, by nature corruption and a worm,* Job xxv 6
a vile grain of dust:
by sin Satan's slave;* Cp. 2 Tim. ii 26
by vice viler than hell.

I have sinned
sins
in number many, drops,
Ps. xl 15 more than the hairs of my head :*
in form manifold :
in places manifold,
on every green field,
1 Kings xiv 23 under every green tree :
very often, repeated many times,
Jer. vi 7 as a fountain, waters,
so my heart, sins ;*
till wrought into a habit,
Is. i 18 scarlet,
1 Kings xxi 25; Rom. vii 14 sold ;
till wrought into nature,
Jer. xiii 23 a leopard's spots,
an Ethopian's skin ;
Cp. *op imperf. in Mat.* xxxvii till myself am not a sinner
but sin*.

I have sinned
sins
broad,
Jer. xxx 14 vulg. hard,
15 in quantity great,
Cp. Ps. lviii 3 long, from my mother's breasts,
Is. v 18 thick, cords of iniquity,
Hos. ix 9 deep,
Ps. xxxviii 4 heavy like { a burden
Jer. vi 29 lead,
Gen. xviii 21; 2 Chr. xxviii 9 reaching heaven itself with their cry.

I have sinned
sins
in quality worst,
Cp. Rom. vi 21 because for naught, for vain things,
Ez. xiii 19 for a handful of barley, a piece of bread :
Eph. iv 19 because with greediness,
Is. xxx 1 sin upon sin :
Cp. Ez. iii 8 because with an obstinate forehead :
Ez. vii 19 because for a stumblingblock : *

because ungrateful,
a dog to his vomit, 2 S. Pet. ii 22
a sow to her wallowing: *
because a Christian.

But for this cause, because
righteous art Thou and true are thy judgements, Ps. cxix 137
I eat the fruit of lies: Hos. x 13
for what fruit have I now in those things whereof I am ashamed? Rom. vi 21
empty cisterns holding no water: Jer. ii 13
my days are consumed in vanity and my years in anxiety of heart: Ps. lxxviii 33
Thou didst give me up to my own heart's lusts, to do those things which are not convenient: Rom. i 28; Ps. lxxxi 13
and now there is no health in my flesh because of thy displeasure, neither is their any rest in my bones by reason of my sin. Ps. xxxviii 3
Add to this the confusion that is before me and the shame which hath covered my face: Ps. xliv 16
yea my tossing heart and the trembling of my flesh, Ps. cxix 120, 52
because of thine everlasting judgements:
and in short a bitterness bitter more than death, Jer. ii 19; 1 Sam. xv 32
to have forsaken God and to be forsaken with Him.

Woe is me rebellious,
that I should do these things.
See, o Lord, how vile I am become, Lam. i 11
and now my soul doth loathe my life. Job vii 16; x 1
I am waxed numb by reason of the greatness of my grief. Fisher *Ps.* i
And what shall I say now, and wherewith shall I open my mouth? what shall I answer, seeing myself have done these things? Is. xxxviii 15; Job xxxii 20
to which of the saints shall I flee? Job v 1
Wretched and luckless man that I am! Rom. vii 24
who shall deliver me from the body of this death?
Forasmuch as I have not what else to do or say, 2 Chr. xx 12 vulg.
this alone remaineth, to turn mine eyes unto Thee.*
Unworthy am I to turn them, but I will turn them nothwithstanding.

Ps. cxxx 1 Out of the deep have I called unto Thee, o Lord:
Lord, hear my voice.
3 If Thou, Lord, wilt be extreme to mark what is done amiss,
o Lord, who may abide it?
Ps. cxliii 2 Enter not into judgement with thy servant:
for in thy sight shall no man living be justified.
Cp. *Horae* f. 78 Therefore, o Lord, I appeal
from Thyself to Thyself:
from Thee just to Thee merciful: *
from the bench of justice to the throne of grace:
from Thee as Judge to Thee as Father in Christ.
Admit, o Lord, this peaceful appeal:
unless Thou admit it, we perish:
S. Mk. iv 38 and, o Lord, carest Thou not that we perish?
1 Tim. ii 4 who wilt have all men to be saved,
2 S. Pet. iii 9 who willest not that any should perish.

Ps. cxix 94 1. Indeed, o Lord, I am thine:
therefore save me.
Ps. cxxxviii 8 The work of thy hands, I beseech Thee, despise it not.
Ps. cxvi 14 Thy servant, the son of thine handmaid: *
a wasteful servant: yet a servant.
Thy son; yea the price of thy Son's blood, that so I might receive adoption:
though I have lost the ingenuity of a son,
Thou hast not lost the affection of a father:
Cp. [S. Aug.] *Med.* 39 (S. Lk. xv 19) though I be wicked, a prodigal son,
yet a son notwithstanding.
Jer. xiv 9 We are called by thy Name:
Heb. xi 16 Thou art not ashamed to be called our God:
we are Christians:
for the purchased of thy Christ
we are named of Him.
Triodion, p. 25; S. Bern. *in fest. s. Martini* 2 Spare thy work,
spare thy Name,*
spare the price of thy blood—
if so be Thou wilt not spare us.

2. But I am a sinner:
S. Jo. ix 31 and God heareth not sinners.

Notwithstanding, remember, I beseech Thee, what my substance is: Ps. lxxxix 46
consider that I am but flesh and that I am even a wind that passeth away and cometh not again: Ps. lxxviii 40
acknowledge whereof we are made, whereof we are moulded: Ps. ciii 14
remember that we are but dust: *

dust, wind, flesh — frail, light, dissolved:

and Thou, Lord, wilt not pursue the stubble: Job. xiii 25
wilt Thou follow hard on a flea? 1 Sam. xxiv 14

3. Thy creature:
and now miserable;
yea, a suppliant of mine own will.
Spare a suppliant.
David spared Shimei, albeit accursed: 2 Sam. xix 22
and David was a man after thine own heart. 1 Sam. xiii 14
Thou therefore spare. Joel ii 17
BEHOLD NOW WE HAVE HEARD THAT THE KINGS OF ISRAEL ARE MERCIFUL KINGS: LET US THEN, I PRAY THEE, PUT SACKCLOTH ON OUR LOINS AND ROPES UPON OUR HEADS AND GO OUT TO MEET HIM AND SAY LET MY SOUL LIVE, I PRAY: PERADVENTURE HE WILL SAVE OUR SOULS. 1 Kings xx 31, 32
Is any king of Israel
more merciful than Thou?
Forasmuch as Thou, Lord, didst spare Ahab, who had given himself to sin, when he humbled himself: 1 Kings xxi 29
spare me too, I beseech Thee.
How long wilt thou be angry with thy people, Ps. lxxx 4
that supplicateth, offereth prayers?
Indeed, o Lord, I cover not my transgressions as Adam: Job. xxxi 33
I make none excuses in ungodly work:* Ps. cxli 4 vulg.
of mine own will I confess:
I have sinned, I have done amiss, 2 Chr. vi 37
I have dealt wickedly, I have been rebellious. Num. xv. 30
But I judge myself,* 1 Cor. xi 31

I consider,
I give sentence:
2 Cor. vii 11 — I take vengeance myself on myself.
Joel ii 17 — Spare, o Lord:
Dan. iii 39 (3 Child. 16); Ps. li 17 — receive the sacrifice
of a troubled spirit,
a broken heart,
S. Jo. xii 27 — a sore troubled soul,
Cp. Ps. lxxiii 20 — wounded reins,
a smitten conscience.

Ps. li 4 — 4. Against Thee have I sinned:
Ps. cii 13 — but, Lord, Thou wilt have mercy on some.
Ps. lxxxix 46 — Hast Thou made all men here for nought?
Cp. Num. xiv 15, 16; Wisd. xi 24 — Shall the enemy upbraid Thee that Thou hast created us to be slain, or hast made because Thou abhorrest, with intent to destroy and blot out, or that Thou art not able to save?
Ps. lxxiv 19 — Remember this, o Lord, how the enemy hath rebuked and how the foolish people hath blasphemed thy Name.
Rom. iii 23 — Everywhere all have sinned and neglected the glory of God.
Job ix 3 — If Thou wilt contend in judgement, even the most righteous cannot answer one of thousands.
Job xiv 4 vulg., iv 18 — Neither a child of a day old, neither the very stars are pure in thy sight, and in thine angels Thou hast espied folly.
Ps. cxxx 3 — If Thou willest to be extreme to mark what is done amiss, none shall abide it:
Ps. cxliii 2; S. Lk. xviii 14 — if to enter into judgement, none shall get him away justified therefrom.
Josh. vii 9 — And what shall be done unto thy great Name? *
what unto those riches of thy mercy?
what unto the blood of thy Son?
Gal. ii 21 — Shall He die in vain?
Fisher *Psalm.* i — Of a surety the world will perish, if so be Thou multiply not thy mercy to usward.
God forbid.
Rom. xi 32; Gal. iii 22 — Of a surety Thou hast concluded all under sin,
that Thou mightest be able to have mercy upon all: *

all { who have acknowledged their sins,
who have earned misery therefrom,
who desire to return to Thee with all their heart:
all these hast Thou made beloved in thy Beloved: Eph. i 6
and they, no pelting sinners,
but { Manasses in the Old Testament 2 Chr. xxxiii 13
Paul in the New: 1 Tim. i 15; Gal. i 13
that in them Thou mightest shew forth the excellency of thy compassion: 1 Tim. i 16; Pr of Manasses.
that Thou mightest open a door of hope Hos. ii 15; Acts xiv 27
to the chief of sinners. 1 Tim. i 15

5. Wherefore spare me, that desire to return to grace:
for what profit is there in my blood, when I go down into hell? Ps. xxx 9
shall any give Thee thanks among the dead or shall there be any in the pit to remember Thee? Ps. vi 5
shall thy wondrous works be known in the dark or thy righteousness in the land when all things are forgotten? Ps. lxxxviii 12
For of a surety the grave cannot praise Thee, death cannot celebrate Thee: they that go down into Is. xxxviii 18
the pit cannot hope for thy truth. The living, 19
the living, he shall praise Thee, as I do this day.
I shall not die: but I shall live and declare the works of the Lord. Ps. cxviii 17

6. Nay, if I know Thee well, o Lord, and thy character:
Thou art good to the good and welldeserving,
gracious to the strangers and undeserving,
merciful to the evil and illdeserving.
In this last I stand.
When there is none for whose sake Thou canst,
when there is nought for the sake whereof,
for thine own sake * Thou forgivest sins: Is. xlviii 11
so ready art Thou to pardon.

7. But David the prophet made bold to pray on this wise:
HAVE MERCY ON ME AS TOUCHING THY LAW: Ps. cxix 29 vulg.
as if the law itself proclaimed Thee gentle;
and in truth so it is.

Thy law out of thine own mouth speaketh on this wise :
Ex. xxxiv 6, 7 THE LORD, THE LORD GOD, MERCIFUL AND GRACIOUS, LONG-SUFFERING IN ABUNDANT GOODNESS, KEEPING MERCY FOR THOUSANDS, FORGIVING INIQUITY AND TRANSGRESSION.
Num. xiv 18 And by this very word of thine Moses thereafter adjured Thee to forgive the people.

Is. xxviii 21; Hab. iii 2 8. Moreover Esay and Abacuc, by reason of this property of thine, make bold to call mercy thy work :
as though to punish and to upbraid were foreign and abhorrent from thy character.

9. Moreover neither the law and the prophets alone :
nature itself persuaded Job thereof by the leading of thy Spirit :
Job xxxiii 23, 24, 26 IF THERE BE A MESSENGER WITH HIM, AN INTERPRETER, ONE AMONG A THOUSAND, TO SHOW UNTO MAN HIS RIGHTEOUSNESS ; THEN HE IS GRACIOUS UNTO HIM AND SAITH DELIVER HIM FROM GOING DOWN TO THE PIT, FOR I HAVE FOUND A RANSOM. THEN HE SHALL PRAY UNTO GOD AND HE WILL BE FAVOURABLE.
Ps. xxxiv 8 O taste and see how gracious the Lord is :
blessed is the man that trusteth in Him.*
His mercy is
Ps. cix 20 sweet,
Ps. lxix 17 comfortable,
Ps. lxiii 4 better than life.
The mercies of God—
Ps. v 7 good store,
1 Pet. iv 10 manifold,
Ps. cxxx 7 plenteous,
Ps. cxix 156 great,
Ps. ciii 12 broad,
rising up and going down of the sun ;
deep, an abyss ;
Ps. xxxvi 5 high { unto heaven,
Ps. cviii 4 above the heavens ;
Ps. xxv 5 eternal { before
Ps. ciii 17 after.

His mercies are above all his works : Ps. cxlv 9
above our sin : Cp. Rom. v 20
above his justice : S. Ja. ii 13
as his majesty is so is his mercy. Ecclus. ii 18
His salvation is infinite : for I know no end thereof. Ps. lxxi 13

The Father of mercies : * 2 Cor. i 3
it is natural to him :
God is called mercy itself : Ps. lix 17 vulg.
O name, whereunder none may despair. S. Aug. *in Ps. lviii* 17
Great is the whirlpool of my wicked works : but greater is the wide and deep gulf of the mercy of God, that hath no bottom. S. Chrys. *Or.* 2

1. But of what sort is He in kind?
Patient, Ex. xxxiv 6 ; Joel ii 13
longsuffering,
slow to anger ;
a long while refraining : Cp. Hos. xi 8
winking at the sins of men, because they should repent : Wisd. xi 23
enduring for forty whole years : Ps. xcv 10
but He was so merciful that He forgave their misdeeds, being quickly appeased, lest He should destroy them : Ps. lxxviii 38
how many a time He refrained his wrath withal and would not suffer his whole displeasure to arise. 39
IF THOU DIDST KNOW, EVEN THOU. S. Lk. xix 42
This is that mercy of God, that we are not all consumed. Lam. iii 22

2. Mild even in chastisement,
in such sort that even his judgement is not without mercy.* Hab. iii 2
Punishment is a part of mercy :
I CHASTISE THEIR SINS WITH RODS : Ps. lxxxix 32
MY LOVINGKINDNESS WILL I NOT TAKE FROM HIM. 33
Let it not be done unto us after our sins, neither let Him reward us according to our wickednesses. Ps. ciii 10

For a great offence a small punishment is enough to a father:

Hos. xi 8 How SHALL I SMITE THEE, EPHRAIM?

3. Placability.

Because easily is He appeased:

Ps. ciii 9 Neither will He alway be chiding, neither will He upbraid for ever.

Ps. xxx 5 His wrath is but a moment:

Is. liv 7 FOR A SMALL MOMENT HAVE I FORSAKEN THEE, BUT WITH GREAT MERCIES WILL I GATHER THEE.

Hab. iii 2 In very wrath He remembereth mercy,* and that easily and on scant occasion:

Ps. xciv 18 When I said, My foot hath slipt, thy mercy, o Lord, lifted me up.

Ps. xxxii 6 I said, I will confess my sins unto the Lord: and so Thou forgavest the iniquity of my sin.

Is. xlviii 11 As though we had nought, FOR MINE OWN SAKE said God.

2 Sam. xii 13 David said, I have sinned against the Lord: Nathan answered, The Lord also hath put away thy sin: thou shalt not die.

Joel ii 13 The Lord is merciful and gracious, slow to anger, of great kindness, repenting Him of the evil.

Is. xxx 18 God will wait that He may be gracious unto us.

4. Compassion.

For albeit deservedly, notwithstanding He feeleth with our calamity.

S. Lk. i 78 His mercies are called tender bowels:

Ps. cxi 4 in which kind God is merciful and gracious:

Ps. cvi 43 Nevertheless when He saw their misery,* He suffered with them.

Who heareth not only sinners, but withal, in the day of tribulation, them that in time of peace have thought scorn of Him.

But if He be sought even then when we are under a

Ps. lxvi 18 cross, even then He casteth not out our prayers from Him nor turneth his mercy from us.

5. Not pardon only, but even in profusion.

Like as David of his own will brought Absalom back; but at the first not to see his face: notwithstanding, at the last he admitted him to his kiss: 2 Sam. xiv 24, 33

like as the father, when the wicked son returned, not only forgave him, but withal made ready the best robe and the ring and the fatted calf: S. Lk. xv 20-23

He will have joy and triumph in heaven over one sinner that repenteth. S. Lk. xv 7

And not only for trifling mistakes,

but withal for grave crimes.

YE SAY IF A MAN PUT AWAY HIS WIFE AND SHE GO FROM HIM AND BECOME ANOTHER MAN'S; SHALL THAT WOMAN NOT BE GREATLY POLLUTED? SHALL HE RETURN UNTO HER AGAIN? BUT THOU HAST PLAYED THE HARLOT WITH MANY LOVERS: YET RETURN AGAIN TO ME, SAITH THE LORD. Jer. iii 1

Wherefore also He forgave the disciples that forsook Him, Peter who forsware him, the robber that reviled and the Jews that crucified. S. Jo. xx 17, 19, 21; xxi 15 ff.; S. Lk. xxiii, 43, 34

He is kind unto the unthankful and to the evil. S. Lk. vi 35

6. Neither pardon only, but grace withal,

- preventing Ps. lxxix 8
- following Ps. xxiii 6
- embracing on every side. Ps. xxxii 11

7. Moreover, what little work soever we do (that grace enabling us), He rewardeth abundantly. S. Chrys. *ad Theod. laps.* i 6

He crowneth us with mercy and lovingkindness. Ps. ciii 4

He is merciful, for He requiteth us both according to and beyond our good works. Ps. lxii 12

Neither doth He suffer a cup of cold water to go unrewarded. S. Mt. x 42

8. But neither is he merciful in nature alone, but in practice withal.

He hath taught us to have mercy and hath had the practice thereof ever of old. Ps. xxv 5

Therefore rightly do we appeal to Him:

Ps. xxii 4, 5 — Our fathers hoped in Thee, they trusted in thy mercy, neither were they confounded.

Ps. lxxvii 9 — Hath God now forgotten to be gracious and will He shut up his lovingkindness within Himself?

Hos. xiii 15 — The fountain is not become dry
Is. lix 1 — hand is not shortened
ear is not heavy.

Ps. lxxxix 48 — Where are thy old lovingkindnesses?

1 — My song shall be alway of the lovingkindness of the Lord.

2 — I have said, Thy mercy shall be established for ever.

9. Neither is it in practice alone that He is merciful, but in promise withal.

Ps. cxix 49 — David accosteth Him on this wise, O think upon thy servant as concerning thy word wherein Thou hast given me hope, and Thyself hast caused to put me my trust.

Rom. iii 3 — For what if some have been miscreant? Shall their unbelief make the faith of God of none effect?

Gen. xxvii 33 — If Isaac would not change his word;
Dan. vi 8, 9 — if not the Persian, the paynim;
S. Jo. xix 22 — if not the profane Pilate;
of a surety never will God.

Gen. xxxii 26 — I will not let Thee go except Thou bless me.

S. Mt. xv 27 — Lord, even the whelps eat of the crumbs which fall from their master's table.

Eph. i 10 — 10. But all these are summed up in Christ:

2 S. Pet. i 4 — in whom He hath given unto us exceeding great and precious promises,

2 Cor. i 20 — and in whom all the promises of God are yea and amen: *

whom it was enough even to name—

S. Lk. xviii 38 — Jesus, Thou son of David, have mercy on me.

S. Mt. i 21 — Jesus: this is His Name, because He saveth us from our sins:

Cp. S. Ans. *Med.* iii 9 — Lord, be not attent unto my sin, in such wise as thereby to forget thine own Name.

Son of David: who forgave Shimei his reviler and sworn foe. 2 Sam. xix 23
Thou also, o Lord, forgive.
O Christ, hear us: Cp.S. Aug. *Serm.* 382 *de S. Steph.* 2
O Christ, intercede with us:
O Christ, intercede for us.*
Expiate our sins:
make the Father propitious unto us:
give us what Thyself art:
say unto my soul I AM THY SALVATION Ps. xxxv 3

Neither shall it be in vain that thine apostle hath said:
This is a true saying and worthy of all men to be received that Christ Jesus came into the world to save sinners, of whom I am chief. 1 Tim. i 15
Where sin abounded, grace did much more abound. Rom. v 20
God hath concluded all under sin, that He might have mercy upon all. Rom. xi 32; Gal. iii 22
God herein commendeth his love towards us, forasmuch as while we were yet sinners, nay, his enemies, Christ died for us. Rom. v 8, 10

Neither in vain that a second apostle:
Christ hath once died for our sins, the just for the unjust, that He might bring us to God. 1 S. Pet. iii 18

Neither in vain a third:
Mercy hath overcome judgement. S. Ja. ii 13

Neither in vain a fourth:
If any man sin we have an Advocate with the Father, Jesus Christ the righteous: and He is the propitiation for our sins: and not for ours only, but for the sins of the whole world. 1 S. Jo. ii 1, 2

Neither shall it be in vain Thyself hast said:
COME UNTO ME, ALL YE THAT TRAVAIL AND ARE HEAVY LADEN, AND I WILL REFRESH YOU. S. Mt. x 28
I CAME NOT TO CALL THE RIGHTEOUS, BUT SINNERS TO REPENTANCE. S. Lk. v 32

These things have not been said in vain:
they cannot have been.

Ps. xciv 19 Wherefore in the multitude of the sorrows that I had in my heart, these thy comforts have refreshed my soul.

Heb. iv 16; Ps. xxxii 7 Wherefore let us come boldly unto the throne of grace that we may obtain mercy and find grace in a time when Thou mayest be found.

Dan. ix 17 Now therefore, o Lord our God, hear the prayer of thy servant and his supplications and cause thy face to shine.

S. Lk. xviii 13 Lord be merciful to me a sinner :

s. cxliii 7 hear me, o Lord, and that soon : for my spirit waxeth faint.

O 339
[S 7]

ANOTHER ACT OF PENITENCE

1. Behold me, o Lord,
behold me of sinners { greatest, worst, most miserable.
And what shall I say now or wherewith shall I open my mouth? Is. xxxviii 15
What shall I answer, seeing myself have done it, done it, done it?
I will recount to Thee all my sins
in the bitterness of my soul:
would God in bitterness most bitter. 17
O Lord God, by these things men live and in all these things 16
is the life of my spirit: so wilt Thou recover me
and make me to live.
For behold for my peace, 17
my bitterness was made most bitter.
But I, like a crane or a swallow, so did I chatter: 14
I did mourn as a dove.
But I beseech Thee, o Lord, according to all thy mercy, Dan. ix 16
that thy most righteous indignation and fury be turned away: *
forasmuch as I have sinned and that grievously,
I have sinned against Thee,
grievously and oftentimes I have sinned against Thee.

ii. O Father of mercies, 2 Cor. i 3
I beseech the fatherly bowels of thy compassions: * Phil. ii 1
and despise me not, { an unclean worm,
a dead dog, 2 Sam. ix 8
a rotten carcase. } [S.Aug.] *Solill.* 2

Horae f. 59 Nay look upon me, o Lord,
look upon me with those eyes
wherewith { Magdalene at the feast, Peter in the hall, the robber on the rood ;
that { with Peter I may weep, with the robber I may acknowledge, with Magdalene I may love,*
may love Thee much,
S. Lk. vii 47 very much, as to whom very many sins have been forgiven.*

Spare, o Lord, I pray, spare, spare a penitent :
at leastwise { disposed and desiring to be penitent,
Is. xxxviii 15 recounting his sins with bitterness,
indignant at himself for sins committed,
remembering thy most bitter passion and cleaving thereunto. }

Horae f. 128b Spare, o Lord : be favourable.
Spare me, o Lord : be favourable.
Ps. li 1 Have mercy upon me
S. Ans. *Med.* iii 11 forasmuch as it is not difficult to thy power,
nor illsorting with thy righteousness,
nor unwonted to thy clemency.*

Num. xi 5 iii. Is it so, that for leeks and garlick
Ps. lxxvii 26 I have forsaken angels' food ?
S. Lk. xv 16 Is it so that for swine's husks
I have forsaken the Father's table ?
Woe is me miserable, woe is me insensate !
Gal. iii 1 Who did bewitch me *
in this sort to play the fool ?
O if Thou but vouchsafe to receive me,
my mind is wholly to return :
for then it was better with me than now it is.
Therefore wholly confounded
Prymer f. 145 neither worthy to name
neither to call upon
neither in heart to think upon * } thy Name,
save by thine essential goodness,
but having affiance in that,

suppliant / downcast / prostrate } I return unto Thee :
neither ask I that Thou do,
save what Thou hast full oftentimes done,
doest right gladly :
what if Thou shalt not do again and again,
no flesh shall live,
none shall abide it. Ps. cxxx 3
Have mercy on a sinner,* an exceeding great sinner, S. Lk. xviii 13
and therefore needing exceeding great mercy.* S. Bern. *de div. serm.* xiii 1
And Thou hast mercy exceeding great,
and reaching unto the heavens, Ps. xxxvi 5
and rescuing from the nethermost hell.* Ps. lxxxvi 13
It is marvellous :
show thy marvellous lovingkindness,* to meward : Ps. xvii 7
the which, if Thou wilt glorify it unmeasurably, Cp. S. Chrys. *Orat.* ii
extend unto me.*
Nowhere, never in the pardon of any sinner whatsoever
either was it / either will it be } more glorious.
Lord, if Thou wilt that I withdraw from Thee, give me another Thee : S. Aug. (?)
else I will not let Thee go.
Let the Spirit of truth teach me the truth. S. Jo. xvi 13; xiv 26

iv. To Thee, o Lord, I confess *Prymer* f. 145
(forasmuch as, if I will, I cannot hide them) *
to Thee I confess my sins, exceeding many, great, grievous.
I profess that I grieve withal, the which Thou also knowest :
but I confess that I have sinned far more than is the grief which is present with me wherewith to weep for my sins.
Grief so great is lacking unto me, is plainly lacking :
I am far gone from what there ought to be.
I can sin much :
I cannot grieve much.
My dryness, my dryness! woe unto me! Cp. Is. xxiv 16
I cannot much, but I desire much :
for I know that even much is not great enough.

Would God such grief were with me :
yea would God even more.
But I cannot win it of myself.
Ps. xxii 15 I am dried up, dried up like a potsherd.
Woe unto me!
Jer. ix 1 Do Thou, o Lord, { increase / supply } the fountain of tears { which I have / which I have not—
Rom. viii 26 a melted heart, groanings which cannot be uttered.
2 Cor. viii 11, 12 In the meanwhile, forasmuch as there is with me a ready mind,
hold me accepted according to that I have,
not according to that I have not.*
Yet I will extend it, forasmuch as I cannot intend it more,
through all the years of my life.

v. So often backslidden, with what face, with what mind,
shall I now be able to return?
There is none wherewith : for wholly confounded
I walk / I sit / I lie down } covered with my confusion.
Neither should I dare to do aught,
Cp. [S. Aug.] *Solill.* 24 neither should I do aught, save despair outright
and do what despairing men do,
Ezra x 2 save that hope is still left.
What hope?
S. Mt. xviii 22 That even until seventy times seven times
Thou dost extend thy mercy :
[and beyond,]
Cp. Savonarola *in Psalm. l* 2 for this measure hast Thou commended unto us.
To us, that we grant it one to another—
and that Thyself grant not the same?
But Thou wilt grant it and much more :
for God forbid that Thou wouldest have more of perfection to be in us than is in Thyself!
that Thou wouldest have us to forgive till seventy times seven,
and wouldest it not Thyself!
forasmuch as thy mercy surpasseth ours,
as much as Thyself us.
Therefore having affiance in that thy mercy
that forgiveth at the least four hundred fourscore and ten times,

standing afar off,* I fling myself down, S. Lk. xviii 13
and most downcast, as is but right, and most humbly,
smiting that heart of mine,
that smiteth me not enough,

I say } again and again—
I redouble }

Be merciful, o Lord, {
to me a sinner,*
to me a most miserable sinner,
to me the chief of sinners, 1 Tim. 15
to me wholly sin, *Op. imperf. in Mat.* xxxvii
to me sin most exceeding, Rom. vii 13
}

o Thou unto whom is never supplication made without hope of pardon. Alcuin *Conf. fid.* i 18

vi. But dost thou ask that He be merciful, yet that thou grieve not?
I ask it not.
For I do grieve in some sort:
I am afraid indeed it is not enough:
I had lief it were more:
I were glad if it were more:
I grieve it is not more:
for I am fain I could more,
and I grieve I cannot more.
I confess that my grief needs grieving for,
and myself grieve that it so much needs grieving for.
And o who will give me to be able more to grieve and more fully?
Myself, if it were in me, would do it:
but it is not in me,
it is not in my power,
It is in me indeed to appraise that it should be more, fuller;
yea, and to will it were more, fuller:
to will is present with me, but how to perform I find not.* Rom. vii 18
Do Thou, o Lord, give; it is in Thee to give,
Thou that turnest even the hard rock into a standing water: Ps. cxiv 8

Jer. ix 1 give tears, give a fountain to my head:
Alcuin *Conf. fid.* iv. 18 give the grace of tears.
Is. xlv 8 Drop down, ye heavens, from above*
and water the dryness of my desert.
Give, Lord, this grace.
No gift were more grateful to me,
not were it great riches,
not were it even the best of things earthly,
than if Thou gavest me tears,
like Thou didst bestow on David of old or Jeremy,
like as on Magdalene or Peter.
Jer. xiii 17 At leastwise a dropping eye:*
let me not be wholly a flint.
Ps. vi 6 Not so as to be able to wash my bed,
S. Lk. vii 38 not to water thy feet,
Jer. ix 1 not plenteously like Jeremy,
S. Mt. xxvi 75 not bitterly like Peter,*
(notwithstanding, o that it might be!);
but supply at leastwise just one little tear or twain,
Ps. lvi 8 the which Thou mayest lay up in thy bottle,
the which Thou mayest note in thy book.*
But if I win not even so much as this, ah pumice!
ah me! indeed lime! boiling in cold water:
out of it, where it less behoveth, without warmth;
where it behoveth not, grieving enough:
where it chiefly behoveth, cold, dry, dead outright.
At leastwise impart to me some of the tears of thy Christ,
which He shed plenteously in the days of his flesh:
o impart to me of them.
In Him there are more than enough for me,
of the things whereof there are less than enough for me in myself.

L 4
W 4

ANOTHER ACT OF PENITENCE

Alas I have sinned against Thee, o Lord, I have sinned against Thee : Ps, xli 4
o what have I done and Thou hast not requited me the due reward of my sins. Job xxxiii 27 sept.
But I am ashamed, 2 Chr. vii 14
and I turn from my wicked ways,
and I return unto my heart, Bar. ii 30
and with all my heart I return unto Thee, 2 Chr. vi 38
and seek thy face, 2 Chr. vii 14
and pray unto Thee saying : 2 Chr. vi 37
I have sinned, I have done amiss, I have dealt wickedly :
I know, o Lord, the plague of my heart, 1 Kings viii 38
and behold I turn unto Thee 2 Chr. vi 37
with all my heart
and with all my strength.
And now, o Lord, from thy dwelling place, 30
from the throne of the glory of thy kingdom in heaven, Wisd. ix 10 ; 3 Child. 33
hear therefore the prayer 1 Kings viii 38 ; 2 Chr. vi 19 ; vii 14
and the supplication of thy servant,
and forgive thy servant
and heal his soul. Ps. xli 4

I do not presume so much as mine eyes S. Lk. xviii 13
to lift up unto heaven :
but standing afar off
I smite upon my breast
and say with the publican
God, be merciful to me the sinner :
to the sinner above the publican
be merciful as to the publican.
The thought of man shall make confession unto Thee : Ps. lxxvi 10 sept.
and the residue of his thought shall keep feast unto Thee.

AN ACT OF PENITENCE WITH A MEDITATION ON THE LAST JUDGEMENT O 224 [302 S 17

Father unoriginate, Son onlybegotten, Spirit lifegiving,
Ps. lxxxvi 15 full of compassion and mercy, longsuffering,
S. Ja. v 11 plenteous in goodness, very pitiful,
Horolog. p. 16; *Euchalog.* p. 270 that lovest the righteous and hast mercy on sinners,*
that passest by sins and grantest petitions,
Pr. of Manasses. God of penitents,*
Saviour of sinners:
Ps. lxix 5 [God, Thou knowest my simpleness
and my faults are not hid from Thee:
Ps. li 3 I acknowledge withal, and my sin is ever before me:
Job xxxi 33 I cover not my transgressions as Adam:
Ps. cxli 4 sept., vulg. I incline not mine heart to any evil thing,
to make excuses in sins;
Ps. xxxii 5 but I confess my sins,
Ps. ciii 1 and all that is within me
Ps. xxxv 10 and all my bones say
Job vii 20 I have sinned,
I have sinned against Thee, o Lord:
Ps. cxix 176 I have gone astray like a sheep that is lost:
Jer. xxxi 18 I have been stubborn like a bullock unaccustomed to the yoke:
Prov. xxvi 11; 2 S. Pet. ii 22 I have returned as a dog to his vomit,
and as a sow that is washed to her wallowing in the mire.
Josh. vii 19 I give glory to thee, o Lord, and make confession:]
20 I have sinned against Thee, o Lord,
and thus and thus have I done—.
Is. xlii 3; S. Mt. xii 20 [O Lord, quench not the smoking flax,
break not a bruised reed.
Ps. lxix 16 Let not the waterflood drown me,
neither let the deep swallow me up,
and let not the pit close her mouth upon me.
Ps. xxxviii 9 Lord, Thou knowest all my desire,
and my groaning is not hid from Thee:

Thou knowest, o Lord, that I speak the truth Rom. ix 1
in thy Christ and lie not,
my conscience also bearing me witness
in the Holy Ghost,
that I have heaviness and sorrow in my heart, 2
for that in such wise I have sinned against Thee; Job vii 20
that I am a burden to myself,
for that my grief is not greater; *Primer* 1545 f. KK. 3b
that I pray of Thee { a contrite heart, Ps. li 17
groanings that cannot be uttered,* Rom. viii 26
tears of blood.
Woe unto me for { my parchedness Cp. Is. xxiv 16
my hardness of heart S. Mk. xvi 14; cp. Rom. ii 5
my dryness of eyes.] Cp. Jer. ix 1
Woe woe! Alas alas!
How was I enticed by mine own lust! S. Ja. i 14
how I hated instruction Prov. v. 12
[and my heart despised reproof! *
Behold, o Lord,
that fearfulness and trembling are come upon me, Ps. lv 5
and the fear of death is fallen upon me.* 4
What manner fearfulness and trembling and sternness
and agony and last separation shall I see!
what confusion shall seize upon me!
with what darkness shall I be compassed!]
And I reverenced not neither stood in awe of
the incomprehensibleness of the glory,
the awfulness of the presence,
the fearfulness of the power,
the exactness of the righteousness,
the loveableness of the goodness.
I will call, if there be any that will answer me; Job v 1
unto which of his saints shall I turn?
O wretched man that I am! Rom. vii 24
who shall deliver me from the body of this death?
How fearful is thy judgement, o Lord! *Horolog.* p. 159.
when the thrones are set,
when the angels stand by,
when men are brought in,
when the books are opened,
when the works are searched,

when the thoughts
1 Cor. iv 5 the hidden works of darkness } are examined.
Horolog. p. 159 What judgement shall be in my cause?
who shall quench my flame,
who shall lighten my darkness,
if Thou have not mercy on me?
O Lord, as a lover of man,
give me tears,*
give me tens of thousands, give them today.
S. Cyr. Al. *in exitu animae* (V^2 404 sqq) For then shall be a judge incorruptible,
the judgement-seat appalling,
the defence excuseless,
the charges inevitable,
the punishment summary,
the gehenna unending,
the angels pitiless,
the hell enlarging her mouth,
the river of fire sweeping on,
of fire unquenchable,
the prison murky,
the darkness without ray,
the beds of live coals,
the worm sleepless,
the bonds indissoluble,
the chaos unmeasurable,
the wall impassable,
the weeping inconsolable;
none { standing by,
pleading my cause,
plucking me forth.*
Cp. S. Mk. ix 24 But I repent, o Lord: o Lord, I repent:
help Thou mine impenitence,*
and more and still more
pierce, rend in pieces,
grind to powder, [smite] my heart.
Behold, o Lord, I have indignation
myself with myself,
by reason of the { senselessness
profitlessness
hurtfulness and
perilousness } of passion:

that I abhor myself
by reason of the {
foolishness
uncomeliness and hideousness
baseness
shamefulness
and disgracefulness
} [of desire]:
that my confusion is daily before me Ps. xliv 16
and the shame of my face hath covered me.*
Woe! alas alas!
Ah me! how long?
Behold, o Lord, that myself I judge myself 1 Cor. xi 31
worthy, [liable and guilty] of eternal punishment, S. Mt. xxv 46
yea, and of all the difficulties of this world.* *Lit. S. Ja.* p. 8
[I have deserved death of Thee } , o Lord, { of Thee just, Cp. *Horae* f. 78
but even now I appeal to Thee } , o Lord, { to Thee merciful;
from the bench of justice to the throne of grace.* Ps. ix. 4; Heb. iv. 16
Admit, o Lord, this appeal:
unless Thou admit it, we perish:
and, o Lord, carest Thou not that we perish, S. Mk. iv 38
who wilt have all men to be saved, 1 Tim. ii 4
who willest that none should perish?] 2 S. Pet. iii 9
Behold me, o Lord, selfcondemned: Tit. iii 11
behold, o Lord, and enter not into judgement with thy servant. Ps. cxliii 2
[I am not worthy of any, even the least, of thy mercies: Gen. xxxii 10
I am not worthy to be made one of thy hired servants,* S. Lk. xv 19
even the lowest of them all:
I am not worthy of the crumbs that fall from thy table: S. Mt. xv 27
I am not worthy to touch the hem of thy garment.] S. Mt. ix 20
And now, o Lord,
I humble myself under thy mighty hand: 1 S. Pet. v 6
I bow my knees unto Thee, o Lord; Eph. iii 14
I fall on my face Josh. v 14
to the earth:
Let this cup pass from me. S. Mt. xxvi 39
I stretch forth my hands unto Thee, Ps. cxliii 6
[I do not presume to lift up so much as mine eyes to heaven,] S. Lk. xviii 13
I smite upon my breast,
upon my thigh. Jer. xxxi 19

Ps. cxxx 1 Out of the deep my soul calleth unto Thee,
Ps. cxliii 6 as a thirsty land unto Thee;
Ps. xxxv 10 and all my bones
Ps. ciii 1 and all that is within me:
Ps. cxxx 1 Lord, hear my voice.
Ps. li 1 [For thy great mercy's sake,
the multitude of thy compassions:
Ps. xxv 10; lxxix 9 for thy Name's sake,
for the glory of thy Name,
be merciful unto my sin,
for it is great,*
for it is very great.
Ps. li 1 For the multitude,
the great multitude,
Eph. i 7; ii 4 the riches,
Rom. v 17 the abundance,
1 Tim. i 14; Rom. v 20 the superabundance,
of thy mercies,
S. Lk. xviii 13 be merciful to me, o Lord, the sinner,
Lord, o Lord, be merciful
1 Tim. i 15 to me, the chief of sinners.
S. Ja. ii 13 O Lord, let mercy rejoice against thy judgement *
in my sin.
Rom. v 20 O my Lord, where my sin abounded,
let thy grace much more abound.
Dan. ix 19 O Lord, hear;
o Lord, forgive;
hearken, o Lord;
o Lord, hearken and do;
do and defer not,
for thine own sake.]

O 239 AN ACT OF PLEADING

Two things I recognise in myself, o Lord; *Horae* f. 74
the nature which Thou hast made,
the sin which I have added.
I confess that by my fault I have disfigured nature:
but do Thou remember that I am a wind,
that passeth away and cometh not again.
For of myself I cannot come again from sin.
Alas! take Thou away from me what I have done;
let that abide in me which Thou hast made;
that so, that perish not which Thou hast redeemed with thy
precious blood.
Alas! let not my wickedness destroy Cp. S. Anselm *Med.* ii 8
what thy goodness hath redeemed.
O Lord my God, if I have so done as to be thy criminal, S. Anselm *Med.* iii 9 (*Horae,* f. c. v)
yet could I so do as not to be thy servant?
If thereby I have done away mine innocence,
yet have I thereby withal destroyed thy mercy?
If I have wrought that for which Thou mightest condemn
me,
yet hast Thou also lost that whereby Thou art used to
save?
'Tis true, o Lord, my conscience deserveth condemnation; S. Anselm *Med.* iii 11 (*Horae,* f. c. v)
but thy mercy overtoppeth all offence.
Spare therefore,
forasmuch as it is not { difficult to thy power / illsorting with thy justice / unwonted with thy loving kindness } to spare the wrongdoer. Job ix 28 vulg.
Thou that hast { created / redeemed } me, do not { destroy / condemn } me. S. Anselm *Med.* ii 8 (*Horae* f. c. v)
Thou that hast created me by thy goodness,
let not thy work perish by mine iniquity.
Acknowledge in me that is thine,
and take away from me that is mine.

Horae f. 61b Look upon me luckless,
o affection unmeasurable;
upon me wicked,
o mercy extended to all.
Feeble I come to the Almighty,
wounded I speed to the Physician.
Keep for me the graciousness of compassion,
who so long hast held suspended the sword of vengeance.
Blot out the numerousness of my crimes,
renew the multitude of thy compassions.

Prymer f. 145b How much soever I be

<table>
<tr><td>unclean
blind
sick
or even dead</td><td>}, Thou canst {</td><td>cleanse
enlighten
heal
upraise</td><td>} me.</td></tr>
</table>

Of what sort soever I be, whether good or bad,
I am alway thine.

<table>
<tr><td>If Thou {</td><td>cast me out
think scorn of me</td><td>}, who will {</td><td>receive
regard</td><td>} me?</td></tr>
<tr><td>Thou canst {</td><td>remit
spare</td><td>} more than I can {</td><td>commit
sin.</td><td></td></tr>
</table>

Horae f. 103b Let not noisome delights oppress me:
at leastwise let not perverted habit crush me.

Horae f. 81 From evil and unlawful desires,
from vain noisome unclean thoughts,
from deceits of malignant spirits,
from pollutions of mind and body.

ANOTHER ACT OF PLEADING

O 261

i. As regards God

1. *The Nature of God*

Because the Lord is full of compassion and mercy, Ps. ciii 8
longsuffering and of great goodness:
He will not alway be chiding, 9
neither keepeth He his anger for ever:
He hath not dealt with us after our sins, 10
neither rewarded us according to our wickednesses:
for look how high the heaven is in comparison of the earth; 11
so great is his mercy also toward them that fear Him:
look how wide also the east is from the west; 12
so far hath He set our sins from us.
Yea, like as a father pitieth his own children, 13
even so is the Lord merciful unto them that fear Him.
Because the Lord is good and gracious, Ps. lxxxvi 5
and of great mercy unto all them that call upon Him:
the Lord is loving unto every man, Ps. cxlv 9
and his mercy is over all his works.
Because He delighteth in mercy: Mic. vii 18
He is the Father of mercy: 2 Cor. i 3
He is mercy: Ps. lix 17 vulg.
to Whom {to have mercy is his proper work *Horae* f. 130b
to punish is a foreign and a strange act. Is. xxviii 21

2. *The Name of God*

Let the power of my Lord be great according as He hath proclaimed saying: Num. xiv 17, 18 (cp. Ex. xxxiv 6)
The Lord is longsuffering and of great mercy,
forgiving iniquity and transgression.

a. *The Name of the Father*

S. Jo. xx 17 I ascend to my Father
and your Father.
S. Lk. xv 20 The Father of the prodigal son.
Josh. vii 9 And what shall be done unto thy great Name?

b. *The Name of Christ*

S. Jo. i 29	Lamb in figure.	Behold the Lamb of God.
Job xix 25	Redeemer	I know that my Redeemer liveth.
S. Jo. iv 42	Saviour	We know that this is indeed the Saviour of the world.
1 Tim. ii 5	Mediator	One mediator between God and men.
1 Jo. ii 1	Advocate	We have an Advocate with the Father.
Heb. vii 25	Intercessor	
26	High Priest	

c. *The Name of the Holy Ghost*

S. Mt. iii 16	Dove in figure.	He saw the Spirit of a God descending like a dove.
1 Jo. ii 27	Ointment or Anointing.	As the Anointing teacheth you.
S. Jo. xvi 7	Comforter.	If I go not away, the Comforter will not come.

3. *The Promise of God*

Ps. cxix 49 O think upon thy servant as concerning thy word.
wherein Thou hast caused me to put my trust;
Tit. i 2 which God that cannot lie promised,
Heb. vi 17 with the confirmation of an oath:
Rom. iii 3 whose faith the unbelief of men shall not make without effect,
2 Tim. ii 13 but, if we believe not, He abideth faithful: He cannot deny Himself.

4. *The Practice of God*

Ps. xxii 4 Our fathers hoped in Thee:
they trusted in Thee and Thou didst deliver them.
Ps. xxv 5 Call to remembrance, o Lord, thy tender mercies
and thy lovingkindnesses which have been ever of old.
Ps. lxxxix 48 Lord, where are thy old lovingkindnesses?
Ecclus. ii 10 Look, ye sons, at the generations of old and see:
did ever any trust in the Lord and was confounded?
or did any abide in his fear and was forsaken?

ii. AS REGARDS OURSELVES : RELATIVELY TO GOD

1. *The Work and Creation of his hands*

Despise not Thou the work of thine own hands. Ps. cxxxviii 8
We are the clay and Thou our potter Is. lxiv 8
and we are all the work of thy hand :
Thou abhorrest nothing which Thou hast made. Wisd. xi 24

2. *The Image of his Countenance*

Blot not out.
Let us make man in our image, after our likeness : Gen. i 26
which is renewed in knowledge, Col. iii 10
after the image of Him that created him.

3. *The Price of his Blood*

Hold not cheap.
Ye are bought with a great price, 1 Cor. vi 20
with the precious blood of a Lamb without blemish 1 Pet. i 19
and without spot.

4. *Invocation of the Name : passively*

Think no scorn of the impress.
We are called by thy Name : Jer. xiv 9
for thy people are called by thy Name : Dan. ix 19
a vessel to bear thy Name. Acts ix 15

5. *A Member of the Body of Christ*

Cut not off.
Ye are the Body of Christ and members in particular : 1 Cor. xii 27
know ye not that your bodies are members of Christ? 1 Cor. vi 15
What? know ye not that your body is the temple of the 19
Holy Ghost which is in you?

6. *His Property in Christ*

I am thine : o save me. Ps. cxix 94
Behold, o Lord, how that I am thy servant : Ps. cxvi 14
I am thy servant and the son of thine handmaid.
We are all thy people : Is. lxiv 9
carest thou not if we perish? Yea, thou carest. S. Mk. iv 38
An unprofitable servant : a servant notwithstanding. S. Lk. xvii 10
A lost son : notwithstanding, a son. S. Lk. xv 24

iii. AS REGARDS OURSELVES: RELATIVELY TO OURSELVES

1. *The weakness of our nature*

Ps. vi 2 For I am weak.
Ps. lxxxix 46 O remember what my substance is.
Ps. lxxviii 40 For He considered that they were but flesh,
and that they were even a wind that passeth away
and cometh not again:
Ps. ciii 14 for He knoweth whereof we are made,
He remembereth that we are but dust.
15 The days of man are but as grass,
for he flourisheth as a flower of the field:
16 for as soon as the wind goeth over it, it is gone,
and the place thereof shall know it no more.

2. *The misery of our condition*

Ps. lxxix 8 We are come to great misery:
Ps. cvi 43 nevertheless, when He saw their adversity,
He heard their complaint.

iv. AS REGARDS OURSELVES: RELATIVELY TO OUR DUTY

1. *Penitent*

Ps. li 17 Because a broken and contrite heart, o God,
Thou wilt not despise:
Ps. xxxviii 18 for I will confess my wickedness
and be sorry for my sin.

2. *Suppliant*

Ps. lxxxvi 3 Forasmuch as I have called daily upon Thee:
Ps. lxxx 4 how long wilt Thou be angry with thy people that
prayeth?
S. Mt. xviii 32 I forgave thee all that debt because thou desiredst Me.

3. *Because we forgive*

S. Lk. vi 37 Forgive and ye shall be forgiven:
S. Mk. xi 25 and when ye stand praying forgive if ye have aught against any,
that your Father also which is in heaven may forgive
you your trespasses:
26 but if ye do not forgive, neither will your Father which is in
heaven forgive you your trespasses.

4. *Because we purpose henceforth*

My soul breaketh out for the very fervent desire, Ps. cxix 20
that it hath alway unto thy judgements:
my hands will I lift up unto thy commandments, 48
which I have loved.
I have vowed and have firmly purposed, 60, 106
to keep thy commandments.
Who desire to fear thy Name. Neh. i 11
The servant shall be punished who neither prepared neither did. S. Lk. xii 47

V. AS REGARDS THE EVIL ELSE ENSUING

1. *No advantage*

What profit is there in my blood, Ps. xxx 9
when I go down to the pit?
Shall the dust give thanks unto Thee, 10
or shall it declare thy truth?
For in death no man remembereth Thee, Ps. vi 5
and who will give Thee thanks in the pit?
Dost Thou shew wonders among the dead, Ps. lxxxviii 10
or shall the dead rise up again and praise Thee?
shall thy lovingkindness be shewed in the grave, 11
or thy faithfulness in destruction?
shall thy wondrous works be known in the dark, 12
or thy righteousness in the land where all things are forgotten?
For the grave cannot praise Thee, death cannot celebrate Thee: Is. xxxviii 18
they that go down into the pit cannot hope for thy truth.
The living, the living, he shall praise Thee. 19

2. *In vain*

Hast Thou made all men for nought? Ps. lxxxix 46
Enter not into judgement with thy servant, Ps. cxliii 2
for in thy sight shall no man living be justified.
If Thou, Lord, wilt be extreme to mark what is done amiss, Ps. cxxx 3
o Lord, who shall abide it?
If he will contend along with Him, Job ix 3
he cannot answer one of a thousand.

3. *The triumph of foes*

Joel ii 17 Give not thine heritage to reproach,
that the heathen should rule over them:
wherefore should they say among the people
Where is their God?
Ps. lxxiv 19 Remember this, o Lord, how the enemy hath rebuked
and how the foolish people hath blasphemed thy Name:
24 the presumption of them that hate Thee increaseth ever more and more.
Ex. xxxii 12 The Egyptians will say, For mischief did He bring them out, to slay them in the mountains and to consume them from the face of the earth:
Num. xiv 16 the Canaanites will say, Because the Lord was not able to bring this people into the land which He sware unto them, therefore He hath slain them in the wilderness.

vi. AS REGARDS THE GOOD ENSUING

1. *The glory of the Name*

Ps. lxxix 9 For the glory of thy Name, o Lord,
deliver us:
4 so we that are thy people shall give Thee thanks for ever,
and will alway be showing forth thy praise from generation to generation.

2. *The conversion of others*

Ps. li 13 Then shall I teach thy ways unto the wicked,
and sinners shall be converted unto Thee.

3. *Example*

1 Tim. i 16 Howbeit for this cause I obtained mercy, that in me first Jesus Christ might shew forth all longsuffering for a pattern to them which should hereafter believe on Him to life everlasting.

4. *God Himself*

Is. xliii 25 I blot out transgressions for mine own sake.
Dan ix 19 Hear, hearken, defer not,
for thine own sake.

He whom God hath set forth to be a propitiation. Rom. iii 25
Look upon the face of thine Anointed: Ps. lxxxiv 9
turn not away the presence of thine Anointed. Ps. cxxxii 10

5. *On the ground of the stock* <*of Christ*>

Have mercy on me, Son of David: S. Lk. xviii 39
and David said to Shimei, Thou shalt not die: 2 Sam. xix 23
and he sware to him.

6. *On the ground of the office* <*of Christ*>

The Spirit of God is upon Me because He hath anointed Me: Is. lxi 1 (S. Lk. iv 18)
the Lord hath sent Me to preach good tidings to the meek,
to bind up the brokenhearted.
I am come to call sinners. S. Mt. ix 13
God sent the Son that the world through Him might be saved. S. Jo. iii 17

A CONFESSION OF WEAKNESS S 20 O 232

Ps. vi 2 Have mercy upon me, o Lord, for I am weak:
Ps. lxxxix 46 sept. o remember what my substance is:
Ps. lxxviii 40 consider that I am but flesh,
even a wind that passeth away and cometh not again:
Ps. ciii 15 my days are but as grass, as a flower of the field;
16 for as soon as the wind goeth over me, I am gone,
and my place shall know me no more.
Gen. xviii 27 For I am but dust and ashes,
Gen. ii 7; Is. xl 6 earth and grass,
Ps. lxxviii 40; Gen. ii 7 flesh and breath,
Job xxv 6 corruption and a worm.
Heb. xi 13 As a pilgrim in the earth,
Job iv 19 dwelling in a house of clay,
Gen. xlvii 9 heb. of days few and evil,
Cp. S. Mt. vi 30 today and not tomorrow,
Cp. Ps. xc 6 in the morning and not so long as till night,
Rom. vi 6 in a body of sin,*
Cp. 2 Pet. i 4 in a world of corruption,
Job xiv 1 of few days and full of trouble;
2 coming forth like a flower he fleeth
and like a shadow he continueth not.
Lit. S. Ja. p. 30 Remember this, o Lord, and remit, forgive:
Ps. xxx 9 for what profit is there in my destruction
or when I go down to the pit?
Ps. li 1 For the multitude of thy compassions,
Eph. i 7, ii 4; Rom. v 20; 1 Tim. i 14 for the riches and exceeding abundant superfluity
of thy mercies; *
for whatsoever either Thou lovest or we must remember;
Dan. ix 19 and before and above all things for thine own sake,
for thine own sake,* o Lord, and thy Christ's;
S. Lk. xviii 13; 1 Tim. i 15 Lord, be merciful to me the chief of sinners.
S. Ja. ii 13 O my Lord, let mercy rejoice
against judgement in my sin.

O Lord, hear; Dan. ix 19
o Lord, forgive;
o Lord, hearken;
o Lord, hearken and do;
do and defer not, for thine own sake;
defer not, o Lord my God.

AFTER PENITENTIAL DEVOTIONS S 13 O 344

O my Saviour Christ, my Saviour,
who will give me to die
or ever I offend Thee anew,
Christ my Saviour, o my Saviour?
O Lord, let a new law of life
prove that a new Spirit hath come upon me.
For true penitence is a new life
S. Hilary *in Ps. cxviii* 17 §13 (p. 347 E) and a true confession is to be penitent without ceasing,*
keeping a perpetual Sabbath
from sin and the { occasion / fuel / danger } of it.
Cp. S. Ans. *Orat.* 10 For like as penitence destroyeth old sins,
in like sort do new sins destroy penitence.

CONFESSION
OF FAITH, OF HOPE, OF CHARITY

FAITH

O 334 ACTS OF FAITH

I believe

DAVID'S. To see the goodness of the Lord in the land of the living. Ps. xxvii 15

PAUL'S. That Christ Jesus came into the world to save sinners. 1 Tim. i 15

JOHN'S, That if any man sin, we have an Advocate with the Father, Jesus Christ the righteous: 1 S. Jo. ii 1
and He is the propitiation for our sins and for the whole world. 2

PETER'S. That Thou art the Christ, the Son of the living God. S. Mt. xvi 16

NATHANAEL'S. That Thou art the Son of God, the King of Israel. S. Jo. i 49

THE SAMARITANS'. That this is indeed the Christ, the Saviour of the world. S. Jo. iv 42

MARTHA'S. That Thou art the Christ, the Son of God, which should come into the world. S. Jo. xi 27

THE EUNUCH'S. That Jesus Christ is the Son of God. Acts viii 37

OF THE COUNCIL OF THE APOSTLES AND ELDERS. We believe that it is through the grace of Jesus Christ the Lord we shall be saved. Acts xv 11

ANDREW'S. I have found the Messias, which is, being interpreted, the Christ. S. Jo. i 41

We have believed in Christ Jesus, that we might be justified by the faith of Christ and not by the works of the law. Gal. ii 16

That there is one God and one Mediator between God and men, Christ Jesus, who gave Himself a ransom for all. 1 Tim. ii 5, 6

That faith worketh with our works and by our works is perfected. S. Ja. ii 22

THE CREED MEDITATED

H 4
O 307

S. Mk. ix 24 — I believe, o Lord: help Thou mine unbelief: — H

Apost. Creed — i. in God

1. the Father
2. Almighty
3. Maker of heaven and earth:*

in the Father, natural affection;
the Almighty, saving power;
the Creator, providence
for the preservation,
governance,
perfecting or consummation
of all things.

Apost. Creed — ii. in Jesus
Christ
his onlybegotten Son
our Lord:

1 Tim. iii 16; Constant. Creed. — in the great mystery of godliness, — HO
that for us men and for our salvation
God was manifest in the flesh,*
Man God,
Son of the Father,
anointed of the Spirit,
our Lord
because {Creator / Redeemer.

Apost. Creed — 1. That He was conceived, — H
to cleanse the uncleanness of the conception of our nature:

2. that He was born,
to cleanse the uncleanness of the birth of our nature:

3. that He suffered,
what things we ought,
that we might not suffer:

4. that He was crucified,
to take away the curse of the law: Gal. iii 13
5. that He died,
to take away the sting of death: 1 Cor. xv 55 sq.
6. that He was buried,
to take away the corruption of bodies in the tomb:
7. that He descended into hell,
whither we ought,
that we might never descend:
8. that He rose again from the dead,
to raise up along with Himself our nature, Eph. ii 6
being made the firstfruits of them that sleep: 1 Cor. xv 20
9. that He ascended into heaven,
to prepare a place for us, S. Jo. xiv 2
where we had no right:
10. that He sitteth at the right hand of the Father,
to appear continually Heb. ix 24; vii 3
and make intercession for us: Heb. vii 25
11. that from thence He shall come again, S. Jo. xiv 3
to receive us:
12. that He shall be the judge,
at the consummation of all things. S. Mt. xxiv 3; Acts iii 21

iii. in the Holy Ghost:
and in Him
power from on high sanctifying S. Lk. xxiv 49
and quickening unto immortality; Cp. Rom. viii 11
from without and invisibly,
but effectuously and manifestly
operating upon us 1 Cor. xii 6
by illumination of righteousness,
infusion of grace,
in reproof, S. Jo. xvi 8
teaching, S. Jo. xiv 26
bearing with,
help Rom. viii 26
witnessing with; Rom. viii 16; Heb. ii 4
the gifts 1 Cor. xii 8-10
the fruits Gal. v 22, 23
of this Spirit.

iv. the Holy Catholic Church,
Col. i 18 the mystical body of Christ the Head,
of those whom the Spirit calleth
out of all the world,
2 Th. ii 13 unto belief of divine truth,
2 Pet. iii 11 unto holiness of conversation:
of all the members of this body
a mutual participation
unto a communion of saints,
and remission of sins
in the present;
unto hope of resurrection and translation
to the life everlasting.

I believe, o Lord: supply Thou the deficiencies of my faith;
that Thee
the Father I may love,
the Almighty I may reverence,
1 S. Pet. iv 19 to Thee as unto a faithful Creator I may commit my soul:
that to thy Word and only Son HO
I may continually in memory give thanks,
as unto the cleanser of our nature
in the {conception and birth;
as unto the deliverer of persons
in the sufferings,
cross,
death;
as unto the triumpher
over hell in the descent,
over death in the resurrection;
Heb. vi 20 as unto our forerunner
in the ascension;
1 S. Jo. ii 1 unto our advocate
in the session;
Cp. Heb. xii 2 unto the restorer of our faith
in the second advent:
Rev. ix 11; S. Mt. i 21 who to the Destroyer opposeth Himself as Saviour, O
Abaddon Jesus,
Rev. xii 9; 1 Tim. ii 5; 1 Jo. i 2 Satan, the Adversary } Mediator,

the Devil
the Slanderer } Advocate,
the Accuser Intercessor, Rev. xii 10; Rom. viii 34
him that leads us captive Redeemer: 2 Tim. ii 26; Rev. v 9

HO that Christ Himself may be formed in us, Gal. iv 19
that so we may be made conformable Rom. viii 29
H to his image,* in works;
his conception, in faith;
his birth, in humility:
for his sufferings
to have sympathy with Him, Cp. 1 Pet. iv 1
as suffering for us;
to suffer for his sake, Phil. i 29
when it is his goodpleasure;
to have antipathy for sin
as the cause of these sufferings;
to take vengeance on, 2 Cor. vii 11
to crucify, Gal. v 24
to mortify, Col. iii 5
to bury, Col. ii 12
sin in ourselves:
to be made conformable
to his descent into hell,
by descending into hell in often meditation; Cp. S. Greg. Naz. *Or.* xlv 24
to his resurrection
by rising to newness of life; Rom. vi 4
to his ascension
by minding and seeking those things which are above and the things which accompany salvation; Col. iii 1, 2; Heb. vi 9
to his judgement
by judging ourselves, 1 Cor. xi 31, 32
that we be not condemned
with the world:
HO what time we are cold in prayer
and are needing some grace and heavenly consolation,
to remember
thy seat,
thine appearing,
thine intercession;

what time we are plenteous in affection
and evil concupiscence,
never to forget
Lit. S. Ja. p. 10. thy tremendous and appalling judgement-seat,
S. Jer. *Ep.* lxvi 10 and that continually in our ears may ring
the sound of the last trump: *
that for the sake of thy Christ,
we may receive of Thee, o anointing Father,
1 S. Jo. ii 20, 27 thine unction,
Tit. ii 11 the grace of the Holy Ghost that bringeth salvation,
2 Cor. ix 15 thine unspeakable gift,
in wholesome compunction,
clear knowledge,
Rom. viii 26 fervent prayer,
Rom. v 5 shedding abroad of love,
Eph. i 13 / Rom. viii 16 / Eph. i 14 witnessing { of seal / and / of earnest: O
1 Th. v 19 that I never quench the Spirit, HO
Acts vii 51 nor ever resist Him,
Eph. iv 30 grieve Him
Heb. x 29 do despite:
that in thy Church we be called,
Catholic, as parts thereof,
living, in vow and will;
that we be partakers of an holy communion
in holy persons,
actions,
prayers,
liturgies:
unto faith of remission of sins,
unto hope of { resurrection / translation } to the life everlasting.

S. Lk. xvii 5 Lord, increase my faith,
S. Mt. xvii 20 as a grain of mustard seed;
S. Ja. ii 20 not dead,
S. Mk. iv 17 enduring but for a time,*
1 Tim. 5 feigned,
Rom. iii 31 making void the law; H

but a faith
working by love, Gal. v 6
working with works, S. Ja. ii 22
a supplier of virtue, 2 S. Pet. i 5
living, Cp. S. Ja. ii 17, 20, 26
overcoming the world, 1 S. Jo. v 4
most holy. S. Jude 20
Amen

THE HOLY TRINITY

The works of
- the Creator — Righteousness,
- the Redeemer — Mercy,
- the Holy Ghost — holy Breathing.

CHRIST

I.

A summing up of the articles of the Faith

	Faith		
Conception	Birth	Circumcision	
	Epiphany	Baptism	
Fasting	Temptation	Sufferings	
	Cross	Death	Burial
Descent	Resurrection	Ascension	
	Session	Return	Judgement:

make me of these a partaker.

II.

What things I believe are for my sake
I recount, I give thanks for, I urge, I remember,
I commemorate, I offer or pray that Thou offer:
I beseech Thee make me a partaker of them and apply them to me:

by
- what things Thou hast done,
- what things Thou hast suffered,
- oblation, Eph. v 2
- sacrifice:

by
- emptying, Phil. ii 7
- humiliation, 8
- incarnation, S. Jo. i 14
- conception in the womb: S. Lk. ii 21

S. Mt. i 18 by birth,
S. Lk. ii 21 circumcision, firstfruits of blood,
S. Mt. iii 16 baptism,
S. Mt. iv 2 fasting,
3 ff. temptation,
S. Mt. viii 20 not having where to lay thy head:
S. Mt. xxi 18 by hunger,
S. Jo. iv 6 weariness,
7 thirst,
S. Lk. vi 12 watching,
S. Jo. vii 20, &c. insult:
Heb. xii 2 by endurance,
S. Mt. xxvi 50 seizure,
55 apprehension as a robber,
S. Jo. xviii 12 bonds:
S. Mt. xxvi 36 by the things that befel in Gethsemane,
S. Jo. xix 13 Gabbatha,
17 Golgotha:
Phil. ii 8 by obedience unto death,
S. Lk. xii 50 straitening unto the cross.

THE HOLY GHOST O 260

S. Jo. xiv 16 Comforter, another
1 S. Jo. ii 20, 27 Anointing
Eph. iv 30 Seal
2 Cor. i 22; v 5 Earnest.

THE BEATITUDE OF THE FAITHFUL O 324

Thomas

S. Jo. xx 28 My Lord and my God.
29 Blessed are they that have not seen and yet have believed.
Ps. xxxii 6 I said I will confess my sins unto the Lord,
Ps. xxxviii 18 and be sorry for my sin.
S. Lk. xii 38 And if he shall come in the second watch
or come in the third watch
and find them so,
blessed are those servants.

HOPE

O 333 ACTS OF HOPE

In Thee, o Lord, have I put my trust : let me never be put to confusion, Ps. xxxi 1
o my hope { when I hanged yet upon my mother's breasts Ps. xxii 9
even from my youth. Ps. lxxi 4
My flesh doth rest in hope. Ps. xvi 10
Thy word, wherein Thou hast caused me to put my trust. Ps. cxix 49
He shall have hope in the end. Jer. xxxi 17
The valley of Achor, a door of hope. Hos. ii 15
Hope maketh not ashamed : by hope we are saved. Rom. v 5 ; viii 24
The Lord of hope fill us. Rom. xv 13
If He slay me, I will trust. Job xiii 15
Thou that art the Saviour of them which put their trust in Thee. Ps. xvii 7
We have hoped in thy sacred Name. Ps. xxxiii 20
Under the covering of thy wings, under the shadow, under the feathers. Ps. xxxvi 7 ; lvii 1 ; xci 4
Thou, Lord, art my hope : Ps. xci 9
my trust is in Thee, Ps. lxii 7
Thou that art the hope of all the ends of the earth. Ps. lxv 5
O put thy trust in God. Ps. xlii 15

CHARITY

AN ACT OF CHARITY

O 336

T. Bradwardine *de virtute causarum* i 1 cor. 39

Thyself, o my God, Thyself for thine own sake, above all things else I love. Thyself I desire. Thyself as my last end I long for. Thyself for thine own sake, not aught else whatsoever, alway and in all things I seek, with all my heart and marrow, with groaning and weeping, with unbroken toil and grief. What wilt Thou render me therefore for my last end? If Thou render me not Thyself, Thou renderest nought: if Thou give me not Thyself, Thou givest nought: if I find not Thyself, I find nought. To no purpose Thou rewardest me, but dost wring me sore. For, or ever I sought Thee, I hoped to find Thee at the last and to keep Thee: and with this honied hope in all my toils was I sweetly comforted. But now, if Thou have denied me Thyself, what else soever Thou give me, frustrate of so high an hope, and that not for a little space but for ever, shall I not alway languish with love, mourn with languishing, grieve with mourning, bewail with grief, and weep for that alway I shall abide empty and void? Shall I not sorrow inconsolably, complain unceasingly, be wrung unendingly? This is not thy property, o best, most gracious, most loving God: in no sort is it congruous, no wise it sorteth. Make me therefore, o best my God, in the life present alway to love Thyself for Thyself before all things, to seek Thee in all things, and at the last in the life to come to find and to keep Thee for ever.

PRAISE, BLESSING, THANKSGIVING

S 30 O 348 REFLEXIONS ON PRAISE AND THANKSGIVING

PRAISE IS NOT SEEMLY IN THE MOUTH OF SINNERS Ecclus. xv 9

FOR THY SAINTS LIKE IT WELL: *i.e.* the saints like it well and Ps. lii 10
God likes it best from them: from such as can
worship Him with holy worship.

ALL THY WORKS PRAISE THEE, O LORD, AND THY SAINTS GIVE Ps. cxlv 10
THANKS UNTO THEE: *i.e.* all may confess the truth;
but "thy saints give thanks unto Thee": they have
more ties of greater thankfulness and are fitter to
express it, which others have not the skill to do.

BLESSED IS HE THAT CAN REJOICE IN THEE: *i.e.* he is a happy Ps. lxxxix 16
man that hath learned that art in which we shall
never excel till we are fitted for the quire above:
for who can sing the Lord's song in a strange land? Ps. cxxxvii 4

ALL SACRIFICE IS TOO LITTLE FOR A SWEET SAVOUR to Him. Judith xvi 16

WE MAY SPEAK MUCH AND YET COME SHORT: THEREFORE EXALT Ecclus. xliii 27,
HIM AS MUCH AS YOU CAN. Put forth all your 30
strength and be not weary: for you can never go
far enough.

WOE UNTO THEM THAT KEEP SILENCE TOUCHING THEE, O LORD; S. Aug. *Conf.* i 4
FORASMUCH AS EVEN THEY THAT ARE FULL OF WORDS
ARE BUT DUMB.

PRAISE (or *PSALM*) *IS SILENT UNTO THEE*: that is, it attaineth Ps. lxv 1
not to thy works, hath rather silence than words
and seemeth but to proceed out of the mouth of Ps. viii 2
sucklings.

AS IT WAS YOUR MIND TO GO ASTRAY FROM GOD, SO BEING Bar. iv 28
RETURNED SEEK HIM DOUBLE AS MUCH: as aforetime
in sins, so now in good works and praises let us
abound unto God.

BUT WHO AM I, O LORD [GOD, AND WHAT IS MY HOUSE THAT 2 Sam. vii 18
THOU HAST BROUGHT ME HITHERTO?]

BEFORE PRAISE AND THANKSGIVING S 31 O 333 349

I

Horae f. 176b Make me, o Lord, to give myself unto mine own penitence
2 S. Pet. iii 9 and to thy praises, to withdraw unto penitence and blessings.
Ps. xxi 13 Be Thou exalted, Lord, in thine own strength : O
so will we sing and praise thy power.
Ps. cxlv 10 Let thy works praise Thee, o God :
and thy saints give thanks unto Thee.
Horae f. c. 3 Open my mouth to bless thy holy Name : S O
Ps. li 15 Thou shalt open my lips, o Lord,
and my mouth shall show thy praise.
Horae f. 146 But for me, o Lord, sinning and not repenting,*
and so utterly unworthy,
it were more becoming to lie prostrate before Thee
and with weeping and groaning
to ask pardon for my sins,
than with polluted mouth to praise Thee.
Howbeit, trusting in thy huge goodness, I give praise :
o accept the praises I desire to sing,
I, an unworthy sinner, indeed unworthy ;
Horae f. 75 but would God I were devout and grateful unto Thee.
Horae f. 96 To Thee I give thanks, Thee I worship, I praise, I bless and O
Thee I glorify.
Rev. iv 11 Thou art worthy, o Lord* God, to receive praises and thanks, whom I, a sinner, am not worthy to call upon neither so much as to name or in my heart to think upon.
Horae f. 101 Thee I call upon, I worship, Thee, with the whole affection of my heart, I bless now and for evermore.

W 123 II

Thou, o God, art praised in Sion Ps. lxv 1
and unto Thee shall the vow be performed.
Thou art worthy, o Lord our God the Holy One, Rev. iv. 11
to receive glory and honour
and power.
Thou that hearest the prayer Ps. lxv 2
unto Thee shall all flesh come: *
this withal shall come.
But my misdeeds prevail against me: 3
o be Thou merciful unto my sins: *
that I may come to give thanks unto Thee
with all thy works
and with thy holy ones.
O Lord, Thou shalt open my lips Ps. li 15
and my mouth shall show
thy praise.

ACTS

AN ACT OF ADORATION O 325

Horae f. 100b O God the Father of heaven,
who hast marvellously created the world out of nothing,
who dost govern and uphold heaven and earth with thy power,
who didst deliver thine onlybegotten for us unto death:
O God the Son, Redeemer of the world,
who didst will to be incarnate of a virgin,
who hast washed us from our sins by thy precious blood,
who rising from the dead didst ascend victorious to heaven:
O God the Holy Ghost, the Comforter,
who didst descend upon Jesus in the form of a dove,
who coming upon the apostles didst appear in fiery tongues,
who dost visit and confirm with thy grace the hearts of the saints:
Horae f. 101 O sacred, highest, eternal, blissful, blessed Trinity,
Horae f. 78b alway to be praised, yet alway unspeakable:
Horae f. 101, c. 2b O Father good,
O Son loving,
O Spirit kind,
whose { majesty is unspeakable,
power is incomparable,
goodness is inestimable:
whose { work is life,
love is grace
contemplation is glory:
Deity, Divinity, Unity, Trinity:
Thee I worship, Thee I call upon,
with the whole affection of my heart I bless now and for evermore.

O 335

DOXOLOGIES

Glory to God in the highest, on earth peace, S. Lk. ii 14
goodwill towards men.
Hosanna to the Son of David. S. Mt. xxi 9
Blessed is the King of Israel, S. Jo. xii 13
that cometh in the Name of the Lord:
peace in heaven and glory in the highest. S. Lk. xix 38
Blessed be the kingdom of our father David, S. Mk. xi 10
which cometh in the Name of the Lord.
Hosanna in the highest.
Holy, holy, holy, Lord God almighty, Rev. iv 8
which was and is and is to come.

OF THE ANGELS

Worthy is the Lamb that was slain, Rev. v 12
to receive the power and riches and wisdom and strength and honour and glory and blessing.

OF ALL CREATURES

The blessing and the honour and the glory and the power be unto Him that sitteth upon the throne and unto the Lamb for ever and ever. Rev. v 13
Amen. 14

OF THE MARTYRS

The salvation to our God which sitteth upon the throne and unto the Lamb. Rev. vii 10
Amen. The blessing and the glory and the wisdom and the thanksgiving and the honour and the power and the might be unto our God for ever and ever. Amen. Rev. vii 12

OF THE XXIV ELDERS

We give Thee thanks, o Lord God almighty, which art and wast and art to come, because Thou hast taken unto Thee the great power and hast reigned. Rev. xi 17

EPITHALAMIUM

Rev. xix 5 Praise our God, all ye his servants and ye that fear Him, both small and great.

7 Let us be glad and rejoice and give honour to Him, for the marriage of the Lamb is come.

9 Blessed are they which are called unto the marriage-supper of the Lamb.

L 139 AN ACT OF PRAISE

I will extol Thee, my God, the King, Ps. cxlv 1
and I will bless thy Name for ever and ever :
every day will I bless Thee
and I will praise thy Name for ever and ever :*
today will I praise Thee,
yea, o Lord, both today and all the days of my life.

Thou art my God and I will give thanks unto Thee : Ps. cxviii 28
my God, I will exalt Thee.
I will sing unto the Lord as long as I live, Ps. civ 33
I will sing praises unto my God while I have my being :
let my meditation be sweet unto Him. 34
I will bless the Lord at all times : Ps. xxxiv 1
his praise shall be continually in my mouth.
I will give thanks unto the Lord with my whole heart, Ps. cxi 1
in the council of the upright and in the congregation.

Thy Name, o Lord, endureth for ever : Ps. cxxxv 13
thy memorial, o Lord, throughout all generations :
blessed be the Name of the Lord, Ps. cxiii 2
from this time forth for evermore :
from the rising up of the sun unto the going down of the same, 3
the Lord's Name be praised.
Who can tell forth the mighty acts of the Lord Ps. cvi 2; cxxxix
—if I should count them they are more in number than the sand— 18
or show forth all his praise?
Blessed be the Lord God, Ps. lxxii 18
who only doeth wondrous things :
and blessed be his glorious Name for ever, 19
and let all the earth be filled with his glory : amen, amen.
Blessed be the Lord God : Ps. cvi 48
let all the people say Amen.

Ps. civ 31 *Let the glory of the Lord endure for ever,*
let the Lord rejoice in his works.
Ps. cxlv 21 *My mouth shall speak the praise of the Lord.*
Ps. cl 6 *Let everything that hath breath praise the Lord,*
Ps. cxlv 21 *let all flesh bless his holy Name for ever and ever.*
Ps. ciii 22 *Bless the Lord, all ye his works,*
in all places of his dominion :
Ps. xxxiv 3 *o magnify the Lord with me,*
and let us exalt his Name together :
Ps. lxix 24 *let heaven and earth praise Him,*
the sea and everything that moveth therein.
Ps. lxvi 3 *All the earth shall worship Thee*
and sing to Thee : they shall sing unto thy Name :
Ps. xlix 2 *both high and low,*
Heb.Sabb.Morn. p. 126 *they shall bless Thee, shall praise Thee, shall extol Thee ;*
every stature shall stoop unto Thee,
every knee shall bow unto Thee,
every eye shall look up to Thee,
Cp. *Gen. xiv* 22 *every hand shall be lifted unto Thee,*
Heb.Sabb.Morn. p. 126; *Ps. cxix* 32 *every mouth shall give thanks to Thee,*
every heart shall be enlarged to Thee,
all that is within me shall bless,
all my bones shall say
Ex. xv 11 *Who is like unto Thee, o Lord, among the gods,*
who is like unto Thee, glorious in holiness,
fearful in praises, doing wonders ?
Ps. xxxv 10 *who deliverest the poor from him that is too strong for him,*
the needy and him that hath no helper.
Ps. cvi 42 *Many a time did He deliver them :*
but they were rebellious in their counsel and were brought down in their iniquity :
43 *nevertheless He regarded their distress, when He heard their cry.*

Ps. lxxxvi 9 *All nations whom Thou hast made shall come*
and worship before Thee, o Lord,
and shall glorify thy Name.
Ps. xcvi 7 *Give unto the Lord, o ye kindreds of peoples,*
give unto the Lord 'Glory is his Name' :
Ps. cxlviii 12 *old men and young,*
let them praise the Name of the Lord :
Ps. xlix 2 *both high and low,*

rich and poor together ;
let Israel now say, *Ps. cxviii* 2
let the house of Aaron now say, 3
the council of the upright, the saints *Ps. cxi* 1 ; *cxlix*
and the meekhearted *Ps. cxlix* 4
Bless the Lord, o my soul, *Ps. ciii* 1
and all that is within me bless his holy Name :
bless the Lord, o my soul, 2
and forget not all his benefits :
who forgiveth all thine iniquity, 3
who healeth all thy diseases,
who redeemeth thy life from the pit, 4
who satisfieth thy mouth with good things. 5
Blessed be the Lord which daily beareth our burden, *Ps. lxviii* 19
even the God which is our salvation.
God is unto us a God of deliverances, 20
and unto Jehovah the Lord belong the issues from death.

ANOTHER ACT OF PRAISE

O 311

Ps. lxxxix 16 Blessed is the people, o Lord, that can rejoice in Thee:
they shall walk in the light of thy countenance.
17 Their delight shall be daily in thy Name, o Lord:
and in thy righteousness they shall make their boast.
Ps. cxlv 21 My mouth shall speak the praise of the Lord:
and let all flesh give thanks unto his holy Name for ever and ever *
and everlastingly world without end.
Ps. xxxiv 3 O praise the Lord with me:
and let us magnify his Name together.
Ps. lxvi 14 O come hither and hearken to me, all ye that fear God:
and I will tell you what things He hath done for my soul.
Ps. lvii 12 Set up Thyself, o God, above the heavens:
and thy glory above all the earth.
Ps. cxi 1 I will give thanks unto Thee, o Lord:
secretly among the saints
and in the congregation.
Horae f. c. 3 Open my mouth to bless thy holy Name:
Horae f. 176b make me to give myself unto thy praises:
Ps. cxxxviii 1 even before the gods will I sing praise unto Thee.*
Receive the praises I desire to sing,
I a sinner unworthy, indeed unworthy—
Horae f. 75 but would God they might be devout and pleasing unto Thee:
Rev. iv 11 Thou art worthy, o Lord, to receive them.
Ps. cxviii 28 Thou art my God and I will thank Thee:
I will praise Thee:
Ps. civ 33 I will sing unto the Lord as long as I live:
I will praise my God while I have my being.
S. Lk. ii 14 Glory to God in the highest,
on earth peace,
good will towards men.

Glory, blessing, virtue, power, — Rev. v 12-14; vii 10, 12
honour, thanksgiving, riches, holiness,
praise, wisdom, might, and salvation
be unto our God that liveth for ever,
that sitteth upon the throne,
and unto the Lamb that was slain.
Amen. Alleluia. — Rev. xix 4
Hosanna in the highest. — S. Mt. xxi
Blessed is He that cometh in the Name of the Lord.

PRAISE OF THE DIVINE ATTRIBUTES O 269

For

1. Excellency of majesty

S. Jo. xvii 5 Glorify Thou Me, o Father, with thine own self,
with the glory which I had before the world was.
Gen. xiv 18 Melchizedek was the priest of the Most High God.

2. Exaltedness

Eccles. v 8 For there is Another higher than the highest.

3. Eternity

Gen. xxi 33 Call on the Name of the Everlasting God.

4. Omnipresence

Jer. xxiii 24 Do not I fill heaven and earth? saith the Lord.

5. Omniscience

Ps. cxxxix 6 Whither shall I go from thy Spirit or whither shall I go
from thy presence?
7 If I climb up into heaven Thou art there:
if I go down to hell Thou art there &c.
S. Jo. xxi 17 Thou knowest all things.
1 K. viii 39 For Thou, even Thou only, knowest the hearts of all the
children of men.

6. Omnipotence

S. Lk. i 37 With God nothing is impossible.
Gen. xvii 1 I am the Almighty God.

7. Depth of Wisdom

Rom. xi 33 O the depth of the riches both of the knowledge and wisdom
of God:
how unsearchable are his judgements and his ways past finding
out!

8. Unshaken Truth

The truth of the Lord endureth for ever. Ps. cxvii 2
Heaven and earth shall pass away, but my words shall not pass away. S. Mt. xxiv 35

9. Exact Righteousness

His righteousness endureth for ever. Ps. cxi 3

10. Wellspring, ocean, abyss of Mercy

One deep calleth another Ps. xlii 9

a. Mild, to pass by, to wink at

I beseech you by the meekness and gentleness of Christ. 2 Cor. x 1
I will not destroy it for ten's sake. Gen. xviii 32
Thou passest by transgressions. Mic. vii 18
The times of ignorance God winked at. Acts xvii 30

b. Forbearing, longsuffering

Or despisest thou the riches of forbearance and long-suffering? Rom. ii 4

c. Merciful

He was so merciful that He forgave their misdeeds and destroyed them not. Ps. lxxviii 38

d. Punishing unwillingly

O Ephraim, what shall I do unto thee? Hos. vi 4
o Judah, what shall I do unto thee?
Many times didst Thou deliver them; yet many years didst Thou forbear them: Neh. ix 28, 30
and for thy great mercies' sake 31
Thou didst not utterly consume them.
He doth not deal with us after our sins, Ps. ciii 10
nor reward us according to our wickednesses.
She hath received of the Lord's hand Is. xl 2
double for all her sins.
Yea, like as a father pitieth his own children, Ps. ciii 13
even so is the Lord merciful unto them that fear Him.

e. Sympathising

Repenting Him of the evil. Joel ii 13

f. Soon ceasing

Ps. ciii 9 He will not alway be chiding :
neither keepeth He his anger for ever.

g. Prone to pardon

S. Mt. xviii 32 I forgave thee all that debt because thou desiredst Me.

h. Reconciliation

2 Cor. v 19 Reconciling the world unto Himself,
not imputing the trespasses of the world.

i. Propitiation

S. Lk. xv 22 Bring forth quickly the best robe and put it on him,
and put a ring on his hand,
23 and bring hither the fatted calf, &c.

k. Kind

S. Lk. vi 35 For He is kind unto the unthankful and to the evil.

l. Munificent

S. Mt. xx 9 Allowing a day's wages for an hour's work :
S. Lk. xxiii 43 Today shalt thou be with Me in paradise.

Ps. cxlvi 7	Opening the eyes of the blind	loosing the prisoners,
Heb. P.B. p. 6; Ps. cxlv 14	clothing the naked,	lifting up those that are down,
Ps. cxlv 14; *Heb. P.B.* p. 45	upholding such as fall,	healing the sick,
Ps. cxlvii 2; *Heb. P.B.* p. 137	gathering together the outcasts,	sustaining the living,
Ps. cxlvi 6; *Heb. P.B.* p. 137	giving food to the hungry	quickening the dead,
Heb. P.B. p. 136	bringing down the haughty,	lifting up the lowly,
Heb. P.B. p. 50	delivering the captives,	helping in time of trouble.

Ex. xv 11 Who is like unto Thee, o Lord,
glorious in holiness,
fearful in praises,
doing wonders?

S 36 AN ACT OF PRAISE

Blessed be God
the creator, preserver and governor of all things :
whose kingdom is an everlasting kingdom, Dan. iv 3
and his dominion is from generation to generation.
He is the blessed and only Potentate, 1 Tim. vi 15
King of kings and Lord of lords,
who only hath immortality, 16
dwelling in the light unapproachable :
and though He hath his dwelling so high, Ps. cxiii 5
yet He humbleth Himself to behold
the things that are in heaven and earth.
That taketh the wise in their own craftiness : Job v 13
that putteth down the mighty from their seat, S. Lk. i 52
and exalteth the humble and meek :
that filleth the hungry with good things, 53
and the rich He sendeth empty away.
Lord, what is man, Ps. cxliv 3
that Thou hast such respect unto him,
or the son of man,
that Thou so regardest him ?
Blessed be the God of the spirits of all flesh, Num. xvi 22
in whom we live and move and have our being : Acts xvii 28
who will have all men to be saved 1 Tim. ii 4
and to come to the knowledge of the truth :
not willing that any should perish, 2 S. Pet. iii 9
but that all should come to repentance :
for his thoughts are not our thoughts, Is. lv 8
neither our ways his ways :
forasmuch as He is God and not man,* Hos. x 9
(*i.e.* as God exceeds man,
so do his mercies exceed the mercies of man).

Ps. cvii 21 O that men would therefore praise the Lord for his goodness
and offer unto Him the sacrifice of thanksgiving
and tell out his works with gladness!
22 O give thanks unto the Lord, for He is gracious:
and his mercy endureth for ever.
Ps. cvi 1 Who can express the noble acts of the Lord? *
(but who would not desire to express them?)
2 It is good to keep close the secret of a king:
but it is honourable to declare the works of
Tob. xii 11 God.
Rev. xix 7 Let us all be glad and rejoice and give honour to Him:
Ps. lxiii 6 as for my soul, it shall be satisfied, even as it were with
marrow and fatness:
Ps. lxxi 7 therefore let my mouth be filled with thy praise:
that I may sing of thy glory and honour all the
day long.
Rev. iv 8 This is the happiness of the iv creatures in the Revelation:
they rest not day and night saying
HOLY, HOLY, HOLY, LORD GOD ALMIGHTY
WHICH WAS AND IS AND IS TO COME.

O 273 CREATION, PROVIDENCE AND REDEMPTION

For
- light — Gen. i 3
- waters and sky — 6, 7
- earth and plants — 9-12
- lights — 14-18
- fishes and fowl — 20, 21
- wild beasts and beasts of burden — 24, 25
- the holy Sabbath. — ii 2, 3

For
- the framing of man
  - after deliberation had — i 26
  - with his own hands — *Euchology.* p. 557
- divine breath — Gen. ii 7
- image — i 27
- dominion over the creatures
- care of the angels over him — Ps. xci 11
- setting in paradise — Gen. ii 8
- sinning, yet not forsaken. — iii 9

For
- the promise of the Seed — iii 15
- that which may be known of God — Rom. i 19
- the work of the law written in hearts * — ii 15
- the oracles of prophets
- the melody of psalms
- the prudence of maxims
- the experience of histories.

For
- birth
- nurture
- preservation
- government
- education
- civil estate
- religion.

For
- redemption
- the great mystery of godliness — 1 Tim. iii 16
- emptying — Phil. ii 7
- humiliation — 8; Acts viii 33
- taking hold of the seed of Abraham * — Heb. ii 16

union with it
Eph. v 2 oblation of life
sacrifice of death.*

For all { the good things He did / the evil things He suffered } from the cratch to the cross.

For
Eph. i 10; iii 2 the whole dispensation
S. Jo. i 14 the holy incarnation
S. Lk. ii 7 the nativity in poverty
12 the laying in the cratch
21 the circumcision, subjecting to the law
the firstfruits of blood
S. Mt. i 21; S. Lk. ii 21 the lovely name JESUS
S. Mt. ii 11; Gal. ii 15 the manifestation to sinners of the gentiles
S. Lk. ii 22 the presentation in the temple
S. Mt. ii 14 the flight into Egypt *
the oblation of life
S. Lk. ii 46 1. the longing to hear
2. the eagerness to ask
51 3. the humility of obeying his parents.

For
S. Mt. iii 13 the most sacred baptism
Golden Litany the appearing therein of the Trinity
S. Mt. iv 1-10 the fasting
the temptation
viii 20 the want, so as that He had not where to lay his head
Golden Litany the hunger and thirst
cold and heat
Acts x 38 often weariness while he went about doing good
Golden Litany watchings } in prayer
S. Lk. vi 12 continuings all night } in prayer
Golden Litany the meek conversation
Heb. xii 3 amid the contradiction of sinners,
S. Lk. iv 29 when He was to be cast down headlong
for a good word;
S. Jo. x 31, 33 when He was to be stoned
for a good work:
for that He willed to be insulted
S. Jo. viii 48 to be called { a Samaritan
S. Mt. xi 19 a glutton
S. Jo. vii 20 a demoniac
S. Mt. xxvii 63 a deceiver;
21 to be put lower than Barabbas.*

For
- sermons, homilies * — *Golden Litany*
- conversations, discussions
- intercessions, prayers
- ensamples
- signs * — *Golden Litany*
- the sacraments
- the keys
- the blessings wrought by all the graces and compassions of thy miracles. — *Horae* f. 74

For the parables of
- the two debtors — S. Lk. vii 41
- the man halfdead — x 30
- the publican and the pharisee — xviii 10
- the servant in debt — S. Mt. xviii 23
- the stray sheep — S. Lk. xv 3
- the lost piece of money — 8
- the prodigal son — 11
- the called at the eleventh hour. — S. Mt. xx 1

For the sayings

FOR GOD SENT NOT HIS SON INTO THE WORLD TO CONDEMN THE WORLD; BUT THAT THE WORLD THROUGH HIM MIGHT BE SAVED. S. Jo. iii 17

I CAME NOT TO JUDGE THE WORLD, BUT TO SAVE THE WORLD. S. Jo. xii 47

I AM NOT COME TO CALL THE RIGHTEOUS, BUT SINNERS TO REPENTANCE. S. Mt. ix 13

THE SON OF MAN IS NOT COME TO DESTROY MEN'S LIVES, BUT TO SAVE THEM. S. Lk. ix 56

THE SON OF MAN IS COME TO SEEK AND TO SAVE THAT WHICH WAS LOST, S. Lk. xix 10

AND TO GIVE HIS LIFE A RANSOM FOR MANY. S. Mt. xx 28

COME UNTO ME, ALL YE THAT TRAVAIL AND ARE HEAVY-LADEN, AND I WILL REFRESH YOU. S. Mt. xi 28

HIM THAT COMETH TO ME, I WILL IN NO WISE CAST OUT. S. Jo. vi 37

FATHER, FORGIVE THEM, FOR THEY KNOW NOT WHAT THEY DO. S. Lk. xxiii 34

TODAY SHALT THOU BE WITH ME IN PARADISE. 43

I WILL GIVE UNTO THIS LAST EVEN AS UNTO THEE. S. Mt. xx 14

For the ensamples:

the Canaanitish or Syrophenician woman, S. Mt. xv 22; S. Mk. vii 26
the woman of Samaria, S. Jo. iv 7
the woman with an issue of blood, S. Mt. ix 20

S. Jo. viii 3 — the woman taken in adultery,
S. Lk. vii 37 — Mary Magdalene,
S. Lk. xix 2 — Zacchee,
S. Lk. xxiii 40 — the Robber,
S. Lk. xxii 61, 62; S. Jo. xxi 15 — Peter,
S. Jo. xx 24 — Thomas,
1 Tim. i 16 — Paul,
S. Jo. iii 1; xix 39 — Nicodemus—

S. Lk. xv 2 — THIS MAN RECEIVETH SINNERS:

Heb. xii 3 — them that contradicted,
S. Lk. iv 29 — them that would cast down headlong,
S. Jo. viii 59; x 31, 32 — them that twice would stone
for a good work,
S. Lk. xxii 65; S. Mt. xxvii 39 — them that blasphemed,
S. Jo. xviii 40 — them that preferred Barabbas,
S. Lk. xxiii 34 — crucifiers of the gentiles.

For the death of Christ:

Phil. ii 8 — 1. his obedience unto the death of the cross
S. Lk. xii 50 — 2. his straitening desire.

S. Mt. xxvi 36, S. Jo. xix 13, 17 — For the things which he suffered in { Gethsemane, Gabbatha, Golgotha:

Acts ii 24 — 1. the pain, pangs
Heb. xii 2 — 2. the shame } of the cross.
Gal. iii 13 — 3. the curse

S. Mt. xxvi 21 — 1. For that He willed to be betrayed
2. by his own disciple:
S. Mt. xxvi 15 — 3. for that He willed to be sold
4. for thirty pieces of silver.
S. Jo. xii 27 — 1. For that He willed to be troubled in soul,
Horae f. 75b — 2. to be very heavy,
3. to be sore amazed,
4. to be exceeding sorrowful, unto death,
5. to be in an agony,
Heb. v 7 — 6. to send forth strong crying,
7. to shed tears,
S. Lk. xxii 44 — 8. to sweat great drops of blood,
even unto the bedewing of the earth.

1. For that He willed that the disciples should fall asleep, S. Mt. xxvi 40
2. to be betrayed by the kiss of one of them, S. Lk. xxii 48
3. that the rest should be offended and turned to flight, S. Mt. xxvi 31, 56
4. to be left alone, S. Jo. xvi 32
5. to be denied of Peter S. Mt. xxvi 69
6. with strong oath 74
7. and curse.

For that He willed to be subjected to the power of darkness. S. Lk. xxii 53

1. For that He willed that hands should be laid on Him, S. Mk. xiv 46
2. to be arrested as a robber, S. Lk. xxii 52
3. to be bound, S. Jo. xviii 12
4. to be led away, 13
5. to be hurried to 1. Annas
   2. Caiaphas 24
   3. Pilate S. Mt. xxvii 2
   4. Herod S. Lk. xxiii 7
   5. Pilate anew 11
   6. the judgement-hall S. Jo. xviii 28
   7. Gabbatha S. Jo. xix 13
   8. the gibbet. 16

Thou that wast silent before the judge, *Horae* f. 132b
refrain my mouth :
Thou that didst will to be tied with bonds,
refrain my hands.*

For that Thou didst will
i. 1. to be smitten with a slap before Annas, S. Jo. xviii 22
ii. 2. to be accused before Caiaphas, S. Mt. xxvi 62
3. to be assailed of false witnesses, 60, 61
4. to be condemned of blasphemy, 65, 66
5. to be derided in many sorts *Horae* f. 75b
6. to be insulted of the servants,
7. to be buffetted,
8. to be smitten with the palms of the hands,
9. to be blindfolded,* S. Mk. xiv 65
10. to be cudgelled,
11. to be spat upon, S. Mk. xiv 65
12. to be mocked, S. Lk. xxii 63
13. to be blasphemed. 65

Horae f. 70		1. The head crowned with thorns, smitten with a reed,
		2. the eyes suffused with tears,
		3. the ears filled with revilings,
		4. the mouth given gall and vinegar to drink,
		5. the face foully daubed with spittings,
		6. the back ploughed with whips,
		7. the neck bowed down with the cross,
		8. the hands outstretched,
		9. the knees bent for prayer,
		10. the feet affixed with nails,
		11. the breast tossed with grief,
		12. the heart bored through with a spear,
		13. the blood flowing plenteously all over,*
S. Mt. xxvi 38; xxvii 46		14. the soul sorrowful and the agonising cry Eli Eli.
S. Lk. xxiii 5	iii.	1. To be accused before Pilate of sedition,
S. Mt. xxvi 70		2. to be denied of his own,
S. Jo. xviii 40		3. to be put lower than Barabbas,
Horae f. 75b	iv.	4. to be sent bound to Herod,
		5. to be arrayed in a white robe,
S. Lk. xxiii 11		6. to be had in mockery,
Horae f. 75b	v.	7. to be sent back to Pilate,
		8. to be demanded instantly for death,
		9. to be condemned to a most shameful death,
S. Lk. xxiii 25		10. to be delivered to the will of the soldiers,
Horae f. 75b		11. to be arrayed in purple,
		12. to be crowned with thorns,
		13. to be mocked with a sceptre of reed,
		14. to be hailed on bended knee,
		15. to be called king in derision,
		16. to be spat upon in the face,
		17. to be smitten on the head with a reed,
		18. to be stripped of the purple,
	vi.	19. to be bound to a pillar in the judgement-hall,*
		20. to be beaten with rods,
S. Mt. xxvii 26		21. to be scourged,
S. Lk. xii 50		22. to be baptized with a baptism of blood,
1 S. Pet. ii 24		23. to suffer stripes,
Is. liii 5		24. wounds,
S. Mt. xxvii 22, 23		25. to be required with clamour for the cross,
S. Jo. xix 5		26. to be exhibited as a mournful spectacle

BEHOLD THE MAN!

27. to be once more demanded urgently with clamour, *S. Jo. xix 6*
28. to be condemned to the cross, S. Mt. xxvii 26
vii. 29. to be loaded with the cross, *Horae* f. 75b
30. to be led to the place of punishment,
31. to sink under the cross, *Golden Litany*
32. to be given myrrh to drink, *Horae* f. 75b
33. to be stript naked, shame S. Mt. xxvii 35
34. to be outstretched on the cross, grief *Horae* f. 75b
35. to be fast fixed with nails,
36. to have his hands and feet digged, Ps. xxii 17
37. to be set in the midst between robbers, *Horae* f. 75b
38. to be reckoned with the transgressors,
39. to be mocked of the passers by,
40. to be blasphemed by the very robbers on Golgotha, S. Mt. xxvii 44
viii. 1. to be forsaken of God, 46
2. to be derided when He called upon God, 47
3. to thirst, *Horae* f. 75b
4. to be given vinegar to drink,
5. to bow his head,
6. to give up the ghost, S. Jo. xix 30
7. to have his side bored through with a spear, *Horae* f. 75b
8. to be blasphemed when dead, S. Mt. xxvii 63
9. to be called a deceiver,
10. unknown tortures. *Golden Litany*

By thy pains, which I unworthy here recount, *Horae* f. 73
deliver my soul from the pains of hell.

The seven last words of Christ:

1. FATHER, FORGIVE S. Lk. xxiii 34
2. WOMAN, BEHOLD THY SON S. Jo. xix 26
3. TODAY SHALT THOU BE WITH ME IN PARADISE S. Lk. xxiii 43
4. ELI, ELI S. Mt. xxvii 46
5. I THIRST S. Jo. xix 28
6. IT IS FINISHED 30
7. FATHER, INTO THY HANDS, ETC. S. Lk. xxiii 46

1. Thou who didst will thy glorious head should be wounded, *Horae* f. 59b
by it forgive
what sin soever I have wrought by the senses of my head.

2. Thou who didst will thy sacred hands should be digged,
by them forgive
what sin soever I have wrought by unlawful touch,
unlawful operation.
3. Thou who didst will thy precious side should be bored through,
by it forgive
what sin soever I have wrought by unlawful thoughts in the heat of lust.
4. Thou who didst will thy blessed feet should be fastened,
by them forgive
what sin soever I have wrought by the going of feet swift to evil.
5. Thou who didst will thy whole body should be distent,
by it forgive
what sin soever I have evilly wrought by the means of all my members.*

And I, Lord, am wounded in soul:
behold { the multitude
the length
the breadth
the depth of my wounds,
Is. i 6 from the crown of the head to the sole of the feet,
and by thine heal mine
1. The precious death,
S. Jo. xix 34 2. the opening of the side,
3. the issues of blood and water,
S. Mt. xxvii 58 4. the begging of the body,
S. Lk. xxiii 53 5. the deposition from the cross,
S. Mt. xxvii 60 6. the burial in another's grave,
Lit. S. Bas. p. 57 7. for three days: *
Horae f. 95ab by all these I urge Thee and I ask Thee,
I beseech Thee to vouchsafe to offer all these
for me to thy Father:
all the bitternesses Thou didst suffer,
the charity* above them all wherewith Thou didst suffer.

Transfiguration

Col. ii 15 1. The triumph over principalities and powers of darkness in Himself and the making a show of them,

2. the mighty resurrection, — *Lit.* 1549

3. the appearance
- 1. to the Magdalene — S. Jo. xx 14; S. Mk. xvi 9
- 2. to the women — S. Mt. xxviii 9
- 3. to Peter — S. Lk. xxiv 34; 1 Cor. xv 5
- 4. to them going towards Emmaus — S. Lk. xxiv 13
- 5. to the ten without Thomas — S. Jo. xx 19
- 6. to the eleven — S. Jo. xx 26; S. Mk. xvi 14
- 7. at the Sea of Tiberias — S. Jo. xxi 1
- 8. to James — 1 Cor. xv 7
- 9. to the five hundred — 6
- 10. in Bethany, — S. Lk. xxiv 50

4. the glorious ascension, — *Golden Litany*
5. the session at the right hand, — *Lit. S. Bas.* p. 57
6. the distribution of gifts, — Eph. iv 8
7. the abiding intercession for us, — Heb. vii 25
8. the return to judgement.

For the Holy Ghost

O come, Creator Spirit, come; — *Veni Creator*
make Thou the minds of thine thy home:
replenish Thou with heavenly dower
the hearts created by thy power.

In the Old Testament
- 1. the brooding on the waters — Gen. i 2
- 2. the sending forth into the living — Gen. i 20; ii 7
- 3. the inspiration of man
  - Bezaleel — Ex. xxxi 2, 3
  - the lxx elders — Num. xi 25
- 4. the descent upon the prophets. — 1 Sam. x 10

The visible advent — *Golden Leg.* Pent.

A SHADOW. 1. The oncoming and overshadowing in the conception of Christ — S. Lk. i 35

A DOVE. 2. The coming in the shape of a dove on Christ in the baptism — *Golden Legend* Pent.

A BREATH. 3. On the apostles in the breath of Christ after the resurrection

FIERY TONGUES. 4. in fiery tongues after the ascension.

The invisible advent

1. on them gathered together in prayer — Acts iv 31
2. on Cornelius — Acts x 44
3. on the xii Ephesians. — Acts xix 6, 7

Visitation henceforth from time to time:

1.	in vocation	1. avocation from sin	calling out
		2. evocation from the world	calling back
		3. revocation from relapse	calling back again
2.	invocation		calling upon
3.	advocacy		calling to.

1 Cor. xii 4	Division of	1. gifts
5		2. administrations
6		3. operations.

Is. xi 2, 3 Gifts of the Spirit,*
Works,
Gal. v 22, 23 Fruits.

S. Jo. xvi 8-11 1. The compunction wrought of Him reproving,
1 S. Jo. ii 20, 27 2. the anointing of Him teaching,
S. Jo. xiv 26 3. recalling to mind,
Rom. v 5 4. the shedding abroad of love,
Rom. viii 26 5. the helping of our infirmity in praying,
16 6. the witnessing with us of our adoption,
Eph. i 13; iv 30 7. the sealing in the sacraments,
2 Cor. i 22; Eph. i 14 8. the earnest of experience.

	1. Visiting	to visit the heart
Rom. viii 9, 11; 1 Cor. iii 16	2. Indwelling	
	3. Cleansing	
	4. Enlightening	illumination
Eph. iii 16	5. Strengthening	
	6. Adorning	
Gal. iii 3	7. Perfecting	onleading.
S. Jo. xvi 13		1. Guide to truth
2 Pet. i 5		2. supplying of virtue.

O 272 FOR THE ANGELS AND THE SAINTS

For
Angels, exercising care of men: *Horae* f. 98
Archangels, by their enlightening announcing greater things
(WITH THE VOICE OF THE ARCHANGEL): (1 Th. iv 6)
Virtues, doing wonders
(VIRTUES BEING MADE SUBJECT UNTO HIM): (1 Pet. iii 22)
Powers, warding off devils by command:
Principalities, advanced in government:
Dominations, doing good by dispensing of gifts:
Thrones, exercising judgement in session:
(ALL THINGS WERE CREATED BY HIM, WHETHER THEY BE THRONES OR DOMINATIONS OR PRINCIPALITIES OR POWERS): (Col. i 16)
Cherubim, radiant with knowledge
(HE PLACED CHERUBIM AT THE EAST OF THE GARDEN OF EDEN): (Gen. iii 24)
Seraphim, glowing with love
(ABOVE IT STOOD THE SERAPHIM: EACH ONE HAD SIX WINGS; WITH TWAIN): (Is. vi 2)
Morning stars, *Horae* f. 102
rulers of the world,
lovers of men,
highest ministers of the divine will.
The perseverance of angels: *Horae* f. 103b
climbing from strength to strength *Horae* f. 98b
to be joined with their quires.

Patriarchs Faith, *Horae* f. 103b
Prophets Hope,
Apostles Toils,

Evangelists	
Martyrs	Blood,
Confessors	Zeal,
Doctors	Studies,
Ascetics Therapeuts	Tears,

Horae f. 102b flowers of purity

Virgins { flowers of purity / heavenly jewels / consorts of the immaculate Lamb,

Horae f. 103b beauty

Horae f. 103 flowers of the church

Innocents { beauty / flowers of the church / mirrors of virtues / tabernacles of the Holy Ghost.

Horae f. 102 Whose faith was strong and their life approved ;

Horae f. 103 in whose { heart was charity / mouth was verity / life was piety.

L 142 W124 A PARTICULAR THANKSGIVING

My soul doth praise the Lord
for the good things He hath done to
the whole creation,
all our race,
LW² the commonwealth of the world,
the Church at large;
the churches } severally,
the commonwealths } severally,
the church } among us;
the commonwealth } among us;
the orders in either,
the persons in the orders;
the city,
the church wherein I was baptised,
the two schools,
the university,
the college;
the parish whereof I was put in charge,
three churches
Southwell,
S. Paul's,
Westminster;
three dioceses
Chichester,
Ely,
Winchester;
house,
kinsfolk,
them that shew mercy,
them that serve,
neighbours,
friends,
those commended.

For the things wherein Thou hast shewed mercy LW
to myself,
in soul,
body,
the things of this life ;
touching gifts of grace,
nature,
estate :
touching all good offices I have received,
good speed I have gotten aforetime,
now :
touching any good office I have done
anywhile :
health, W
good repute,
sufficiency ;
safety,
liberty,
quiet.

Is. xxxviii 12 *Thou hast not rolled up like a weaver my life :* LW
from day even to night Thou hast not made an end of me.
Job x 12 He hath granted me life * and breath
even unto this hour :
Ps. lxxi 15 *which hath entreated me well from youth and hitherto*
Is. xlvi 4 *even to hoar hairs :*
Ps. lxvi 8 *which holdeth my soul in life*
*and suffereth not my feet to be moved,**
delivering me from perils, sicknesses,
poverty, thraldom, public shame,
evil chances :
Horolog. p. 466 not giving me over to be destroyed
with mine iniquities :
on every wise awaiting
my conversion : *
leaving in me
Bar. ii 30 return into my heart,
Dt. xxxii 29 remembrance of the last things,*
some shame, horror, grief
touching the sins I have wrought aforetime,
fuller and greater, greater and fuller, LW[2]
more still and more, o Lord :

LW supplying unto me good hopes
touching the remission of them,
through penitence and the works thereof,
by the power of the thriceholy
keys and sacraments
that are in thy Church.

L *I am not worthy of the least of all the mercies* Gen. xxxii 10
and of all the truth which Thou hast shewed
unto thy servant.
What is thy servant? for who am I, o Lord God, and what is my house— 2 Sam. vii 18, 20
Thou heardest me, o God—for Thou hast brought me thus far? Ps. xcix 8
the dead dog—and what can thy servant say more unto Thee? 1 Sam. xxiv 14
such a man as I—and Thou knowest thy servant, o Lord God: * Neh. vi 11

LW that day by day
for these thy benefactions unto me Cp. *Lit. S. Chrys.* p. 95
which I remember— 2 Macc. ix 26
and that for other withal, exceeding many, forgotten Ps. lxxviii 12
by reason of their multitude and by reason of my forgetfulness, *Lit. S. Bas.* p. 62
as well those done unto me willing, knowing, asking Cp. S. Chrys. *hom. vi in 1 Tim.* i
as those done to me not asking, at unawares, unwilling: *
I confess and give thanks to Thee
I bless and praise Thee as is due and every day,
and I vow with all my soul,
and with all my mind I vow:
Glory be to Thee, o Lord, glory be to Thee,
glory to Thee and glory to thine allholy Name
for all thy divine perfections
therein:
for thine inexpressible and unimaginable goodness
and mercy to sinners and unworthy
and to me of all sinners
altogether most unworthy:
yea, o Lord, for these and for the rest
glory and praise and blessing and thanksgiving
by the voices and concert of voices
as well of angels as of men
and of all thy saints in heaven
and of all thy creation whether in heaven or on earth,
and under their feet

of me the unworthy and miserable sinner,
    thy lowly creature,
both now, in this day and hour,
and every day unto my last gasp,
and unto the end of the world
and for ever and ever.

Heb.Sabb.Morn. p. 125 *We are not sufficient*
to give Thee thanks, o Lord our God,
and to bless thy Name, o our King,
for one of the thousand thousands of thousands
or of the tenthousand times tenthousand
of the bounties, signs and wonders,
which Thou hast wrought with us
and with our fathers of old time. L

(?) *Behold I now at this hour*
bless praise celebrate
thy holy Name:
and Thou, o Lord, from this time forth for evermore,
wilt purify me, direct me, stablish me,
write me for life in the book of life.

Is. xlii 3 *The smoking flax quench Thou not.*

H 31 ANOTHER PARTICULAR THANKSGIVING

A joyful and pleasant thing it is to be thankful.* Ps. cxlvi 1
Unworthy before,
let me not be ungrateful after.
The soul that blesseth shall be made fat. Prov. xi 25 vulg.
When thou hast eaten and art full, Dt. viii 10
then thou shalt bless the Lord thy God
for the good land which He hath given thee.
Blessed be the Lord (of Jethro) Ex. xviii 10
I will sing unto the Lord (of Moses and the Israelites) Ex. xv 1
Thou art my God, Ps. cxviii 28
and I will thank Thee
and I will praise Thee.
Blessed be the God and Father of our Lord Jesus Christ, 1 S. Pet. i 3
which according to his abundant mercy hath begotten
us again unto a lively hope by the resurrection of Jesus
Christ from the dead.
Blessed be the God and Father of our Lord Jesus Christ Eph. i 3
who hath blessed us with all spiritual blessings in
heavenly places in Christ.
Blessed be the Lord God of Israel: S. Lk. i 68
for He hath visited and redeemed his people.
Blessed be the God and Father of our Lord Jesus Christ, 2 Cor. i 3
the Father of mercies and God of all comfort, who 4
comforteth us in all our tribulation.
I will give thanks unto the Lord with my whole heart: Ps. cxi 1
secretly with the faithful and in the congregation.
I will give thanks unto Thee, for I am wonderfully made: Ps. cxxxix 13
marvellous are thy works, and that my soul knoweth
right well.
My bones are not hid from Thee: 4
though I be made secretly and fashioned beneath in the
earth.

Ps. cxxxix 15 Thine eyes did see my substance, yet being unperfect:
and in thy book were all my members written,
16 when as yet there was none of them.
Job x 8 Thy hands have fashioned me together round about:
10 Thou hast poured me out as milk,
and curdled me like cheese:
11 Thou hast clothed me with skin and flesh,
and hast knit me together with bones and sinews:
12 Thou hast granted me life and favour,
and thy visitation hath preserved my spirit.
Ps. xvi 8 I will bless the Lord for giving me understanding.
Gen. xxxii 10 O Lord, I am not worthy of the least of all the mercies
and of all the truth which Thou hast shewed unto thy
servant:
for with my staff I passed over this Jordan and now I am
become two bands.
Ps. lxvi 7 O praise our Lord, ye peoples:
and make the voice of his praise to be heard:
8 who holdeth my soul in life:
and suffereth not my feet to slip:
Ps. xcii 4 for Thou, Lord, hast made me glad through thy works:
and I will rejoice in giving thanks for the operation of
thy hands.
Ps. ciii 1 Praise the Lord, o my soul:
and all that is within me, praise his holy Name:
2 praise the Lord, o my soul:
and forget not his benefits:
3 who forgiveth all thy sins:
and healeth all thine infirmities:
4 who saveth thy life from destruction:
and crowneth thee with mercy and lovingkindness:
5 who satisfieth thy mouth with good things:
making thee young and lusty as an eagle.
Ps. xxx 12 Thou hast turned my heaviness into joy:
Thou hast put off my sackcloth and girded me with
gladness:
13 that I may sing of thy praise without ceasing:
o my God, I will give thanks unto Thee for ever.
Ps. lxxi 18 O what great troubles and adversities hast Thou shewed me!
and yet didst Thou turn and refresh me:
yea, and broughtest me from the deep of the earth again:

Thou hast brought me to great honour : Ps. lxxi 19
and comforted me on every side.
My lips will be fain when I sing unto Thee : 21
and so will my soul whom Thou hast delivered.
My tongue also shall talk of thy righteousness all the day long: 22
o my God, who is like unto Thee? 17
Blessed be the Lord, even the God of Israel: Ps. lxxii 18
which only doeth wondrous things:
and blessed be the Name of his Majesty: 19
and all the earth shall be filled with his Majesty. Amen.
Blessed be the Name of the Lord: Ps. cxiii
from this time forth for evermore.
Blessed be the glory of the Lord from his place. Ezek. iii 12
Glory and honour and blessing Rev. iv 9
and power Rev. v 12
and divinity and wisdom
and strength and authority 13
and salvation Rev. vii 10
and glory and thanksgiving * 12
and praise
be unto the holy and undivided Trinity
for ever and ever. Amen. Rev. vii 12

For that {
I am Cp. *Hort. an.* 1516 f. 79.
I am alive
endowed with reason
civil
a christian
free, ingenuous
of honest stock
in possession of { mind, senses, limbs }
brought up
liberally educated
lettered :
}

for goods of { nature, estate, grace : }

for deliverance { from peril, from infamy, from disquiet : }

for { health
competent estate :

for { redemption
regeneration
catechism
calling
thy patience
my compunction
hope of pardon
prevention
care
good offices we have received
aught we do well
present consolation
future confidence :

for { parents good and honest
masters
benefactors
friends, relations
their children
faithful retainers :

for all who by { writings
sermons
conversations
prayers
examples
rebuke
injuries
have stood me in good stead :

for all these
and for all things else
known } or { unknown
open } or { privy
the which we remember } or { the which we forget,
I confess to Thee and will confess
bless } and { will bless
give thanks } and { will give thanks
all the days
of my life.

O 313 **ANOTHER PARTICULAR THANKSGIVING**

Sinning as I do, o Lord, and not repenting,* *Horae* f. 146
and so utterly unworthy,
it would better beseem me to lie prostrate before Thee,
and with weeping and groaning
to require the pardon of my sins,
than with polluted mouth to praise Thee.
Notwithstanding, trusting in thine essential goodness—
Blessed art Thou, o God,
which didst create me and bring me forth into this life,
and didst take order with me
that I should be
a living soul and not aught insensible, *Hort. an.* 1516 f. 79
a man not a brute, Diog. Laert. i 1 § 7
a civil man not a barbarian,*
free not a thrall,* *Heb. morning* p. 5
legitimate not a bastard,
of honest parentage not a sorry egg of a sorry crow, Erasmus *Adagia* s. v. *Originis*
well found not a dullard, Cp. *Hort. an.* u. s.
with senses } entire { and not blind nor deaf,
members } entire { and not halt nor maimed,
brought up not exposed,
lettered not a mechanic,
a christain not a paynim,* Cp. *Heb. morning* p. 5
delivered from perils } not swallowed up of { them
from infamy } not swallowed up of { it,
in days of peace* not tossed about in storms, Cp. *Hort. an.* f. 78b
of honest estate so as not to have need either to flatter or yet to borrow,
set at large from many sins,
endowed with gifts of { grace { redemption
vocation
nature
estate :

1 S. Pet. i 3 which according to thine abundant mercy
hast begotten us again unto a lively hope
by the resurrection of Jesus Christ,
4 to an inheritance incorruptible
and undefiled
and that fadeth not away,
reserved in heaven for us:
Eph. i 3 who hast blessed me with all spiritual blessings
in heavenly places
in Christ:
2 Cor. i 4, 5 who hast comforted me in all my tribulation:
for as the sufferings of Christ have abounded in me,
so my consolation also aboundeth
by Christ.
Dan. ii 23 I thank Thee and praise Thee, o Thou God of my fathers,
who hast given me wisdom and might
after some measure,
and hast made known unto me what I desired
of Thee,
and hast made known unto me the
matter.*

A work of the hands, a price of the blood,
an image of the countenance, a servant of purchase,
an impress of the name, a son of adoption,
a temple of the Spirit,
a member of the Church.

S 34 ANOTHER PARTICULAR THANKSGIVING

Glory be to Thee, o Lord,
for that {
I am
I am alive
I am rational :
for {
nurture
preservation
goverance :
for {
education
citizenship
devotion
religion :
for {
redemption
regeneration
instruction :
for my calling {
first
manifold
last :
for {
good offices I have received
any good speed I have gotten :
for {
thy promise
my hope
} touching the good things to come :
for gifts of {
nature
estate
grace :
for {
my parents honest and good
teachers
benefactors ever to be remembered
colleagues likeminded
hearers attentive
friends sincere
retainers faithful :

for {patriarchs
prophets
apostles
evangelists
martyrs
confessors
doctors of the Church :}

for all who by {writings
sermons
conversations
prayers
examples
reproofs
injuries} have stood me in good stead :

for all these and all things else
which we wot of, which we wot not of,
open and privy,
what things are remembered of me, what things are forgotten withal,
the things done to me when willing or yet against my will,
I confess to Thee and will confess,
I bless Thee and will bless,
I give thanks to Thee and will give thanks,
all the days of my life.

O 316 **CONCLUSION OF THANKSGIVING**

O Lord, I am not worthy of the least of all the mercies and of all the truth which Thou hast shewed unto thy servant: Gen. xxxii 10
and what can I say more unto Thee? 2 Sam. vii 20, 18
for Thou, Lord, my Lord, knowest thy servant. ix 8
Who am I, o Lord, thy servant, and what is my house,
that Thou shouldest look upon such a dead dog as I am,
that Thou hast loved me hitherto?
What reward shall I give unto the Lord Ps. cxvi 11
for all the benefits that He hath done unto me?
What thanks can we render to God again 1 Th. iii 9
for all the joy wherewith we joy before Him?
Thou that hast vouchsafed unto me, o Lord, on this holy day and at this hour to lift up my soul and to praise Thee and to offer the glory that is due unto Thee: *Lit. S. Bas.* p. 46; Ps. cxliii 8
do Thou thyself, o Lord, accept of my soul this spiritual sacrifice, and receiving it unto Thee on to thy spiritual altar, vouchsafe in requital thereof to send upon me the grace of thy most holy Spirit. *Lit. S. Bas.* p. 51; *S. Ja.* p. 19
Visit me in thy goodness: *Lit. S. Bas.* p. 46; *S. Ja.* p. 42, 8
forgive me every sin, as well voluntary as involuntary:
deliver me from eternal punishments; yea, and from all the distresses of this world:
transform my thoughts unto piety, *Lit. S. Ja.* p. 6, 20; *S. Bas.* p 47; *S. Ja.* p. 12
hallow my spirit, soul and body,
and grant me to worship and to please Thee
in piety and holiness of life,
even unto the last end of life.
Now unto Him that is able to do exceeding abundantly above all that we ask or think, according to the power that worketh in us: Eph. iii 20
unto Him be glory in the Church in Christ throughout all ages, world without end. 21
My soul shall be satisfied even as it were with marrow and fatness, when my mouth praiseth Thee with joyful lips. Ps. lxiii 6

DEPRECATION

332 A DEPRECATION

Like as Thou didst deliver the fathers, so deliver us, o Lord.

Like as our fathers in the generations of old— Cp. *Manuale Sarisb.* de extrema unctione

Noah from the flood, Gen. vii 13
Abraham from Ur of the Chaldees, Gen. xi 31
Isaac from being slaughtered for a sacrifice, Gen. xxii 12
Jacob from Laban and Esau, Gen. xxxi 17; xxxii 11
Joseph from the { slander of his mistress Gen. xxxix 21
prison, Gen. xli 14 }
Job from his temptations, Job xlii 10
Moses from { Pharaoh Ex. xii 31
stoning, Ex. viii 26; xvii 4 }
The people from { the Red Sea Ex. xiv 30
Babylon, Ezra i 1 }
David from { Saul, Goliath 1 S. xviii 11 &c.; xvii 50
Keilah, Ahitophel 1 S. xxiii 13; 2 S. xvii 14
Absalom, Doeg, Sheba, 1 S. xxii 9; 2 S. xviii 15; xx 22 }
Elias from Jezebel, 1 K. xix 3
Ezekias from { Rabshakeh 2 K. xix 35
his sickness, 2 K. xx 5 }
Esther from Haman, Esth. vii 10
Joash from Athaliah, 2 K. xi 2
Jeremy from the dungeon, Jer. xxxvii 17
the Three Children from the furnace, Dan. iii 26
Jonas from the whale's belly, Jon. ii 10
the Disciples from the storm, S. Mt. viii 26
Peter from Herod's prison, Acts xii 10
Paul from shipwreck, stoning, the beast— Acts xxvii 43; xiv 20; xxviii 5
so deliver us withal, o Lord, Ps. xxii 4
the while we put our trust in Thee.

A DEPRECATION OF THE DIVINE WRATH O 33

Dan. ix 16 I beseech Thee, o Lord, according to all thy mercy,
let thy most righteous indignation be turned away from * me,
for that {most often, most greviously / most greviously, most often} I have sinned against Thee:
chiefly what sins {most freshly / most lately} I have sinned against Thee:
let it be turned away from me, from my parents,
brothers, sisters,
my reverend lord, and my family,
relations, friends, neighbourhood, country,
the whole Christian people.
Amen.

L 149
W129

A LITANY OF DEPRECATION

Thou hast brought up my life from the pit. *Destroy not: deliver me.* *Jonah ii* 6; *Ps. lvii* tit. *Ps. lix* 1

Father who didst create, him Thou didst create—
Son who didst redeem, him Thou didst redeem—
Spirit who didst regenerate, him Thou didst regenerate—
destroy not. Ps. lvii *tit.*
Remember not, Lord, remember not mine offences, *Horae* f. 122b
nor the offences of my forefathers,
neither take Thou vengeance of their sins and mine:
spare us, o Lord, {them / me}:
spare thy people and among thy people thy servant,
whom Thou hast redeemed with thy precious blood,
and be not angry with us for ever.
Be favourable, be favourable, spare us, o Lord: Litan. Sarisb. *Horae* f. 128b
and be not angry with us for ever. Ps. lxxxv 5
Be favourable, be favourable, have mercy upon us, o Lord: *Euchlog.* p. 517
and be not angry with us full sore. Is. lxiv 9
Nay, o Lord,
deal not with me after my wickednesses, Ps. ciii 10
neither reward me according to my sins:
but after thy great goodness deal Thou with me,
and reward me according to the multitude of thy mercies. Ps. li 1
After the same great goodness
and according to that multitude of mercies,
as Thou didst unto our fathers in the generations of old,

by whatsoever is dear unto Thee,
Eng. Lit. from all evil and mischief,
in all time of necessity,*
arise, rescue, save me, o Lord:
from this present evil and mischief
in this present season—
Ps. lvii *tit.* *destroy not,*
Ps. lix 2 *deliver me:*
deliver me, o Lord,
and destroy not.

On the bed of sickness,
Litan. Sarisb. *Horae* f. 129 in the hour of death,
in the day of judgement,*
in that appalling and fearful day,
rescue, o Lord, and save me.
From seeing the face of the Judge overcast,
S. Mt. xxv 33 being set on the left hand,
S. Lk. xiii 27 hearing the appalling voice DEPART FROM ME,
2 Pet. ii 4 being bound in chains of darkness,
S. Mt. xxv 30 being cast into outer darkness,
Rev. xiv 10 being tormented in the bottomless pit of fire and brimstone,
11 where the smoke of the torments goeth up for ever:
be favourable, be favourable,
Heb. morn. p. 49 spare us,
have mercy upon us,*
deliver and save us, o Lord,
and destroy us not for ever.
Nay, o Lord.

And that it be not,
put away from me, o Lord,
S. Mk. xvi 14; iii 5; vi 52 hardness of heart, blindness of heart,
Eph. iv 19 being past feeling after sinning, despising of thy threatenings,
1 Tim. iv 2; Rom. i 28 searing of conscience, the reprobate mind,
S. Mt. xii 32; S. Mk. iii 29 the sin against the Holy Ghost,
1 S. Jo. v 16 the sin unto death,
Prymer f. 167b the four crying sins,
the six that forerun the sin against the Holy Ghost.

Deliver me

from the dangers and difficulties of the world — *Lit. S. Ja.* p. 8
pestilence, famine, war, — *Lit. S. Bas.* p. 62
earthquake, flood, conflagration,
plague of immoderate rains,* drought, rainlessness, — *B.C.P.* 1604
blasting, mildew,* — 2 Chr. vi 28; 1 K. viii 37
stroke of thunder, lightning, tempest,
epidemics and evil diseases
and unforseen death: — Litan. Sarisb. *Horae* f. 129
from evils and troubles in the Church:
private interpretation,* — 2 Pet. i 20
innovation touching the sacred things,
the teaching of a different doctrine, — 1 Tim. i 3
doting about questions and making endless strifes, — 1 Tim. vi 4; i 4
from heresies, schisms, scandals public, private:
making gods of kings, — Acts xii 21-23
the flattery of the people,
indifferency of Saul, — 1 Sam. xiii 8-14
contempt of Michal, — 2 Sam. vi 20
fleshhook of Hophni, — 1 Sam. ii 13
breaking up of Athaliah, — 2 Chr. xxiv 7
priesthood of Micah, — Judg. xvii 12, 13
fraternity of Simon and Judas, — Acts viii 18, 19; S. Mt. xxvi 15
doctrine of such as are unstable and unlearned, — 2 Pet. iii 16
pride of novices, — 1 Tim. iii 6
a people striving with the priest: — Hos. iv 4
from anarchy, multiplicity of rulers, tyranny: — Hom. *Il.* ii 204
Asshur, Jeroboam, Rehoboam, Gallio, Haman: — Hos. xi 5; 1 Ki. xii; Acts xviii 14; Esth. vii
the shrewd practice of Ahitophel, — 2 Sam. xv 31; xvi 21
the redelessness of them of Zoan, — Is. xix 11
the legislation of Omri, — Mic. vi 16
the adjudication of Jezreel, — 1 Kings xxi 13
the overflowings of Belial, — Ps. xviii 3
the plague of Peor, — Num. xxv 5
the valley of Achor:* — Josh. vii 26
pollution of blood or seed,
invasion of aliens, — *Lit. S. Bas.* p. 63
internal * factiousness,

deprivation of the honest and good
that are in authority,
uprising of the evil and knavish
to be in authority:
Aristoph. *Plut.* 969 from a life unlivable,*
in dejection, weakness, infamy, resourcelessness,
jeopardy, thraldom, unsettlement:
from a death
in sin, shame, tortures,
madness, foulness,
a violent death, by treachery,
unforeseen,
undying.

Ps. *lx* 11 *Give us help against the adversary:* L
for vain is the help of man.

O 250 ANOTHER LITANY OF DEPRECATION

Behold, o Lord our God, from thy dwelling place on high, *Lit. S. Bas.* p. 60
and from the throne of the glory of thy kingdom:
Thou that hast thy dwelling on high and yet beholdest the Ps. cxiii 5
things that are lowly:
behold and destroy not, o Lord: Ps. lvii *tit.*
nay, deliver us from evil.* S. Mt. vi 13
From all evil and misfortune,
deliver us.
As Thou didst our fathers in former ages,
deliver us.
By whatsoever is sweet unto Thee or dear,
deliver us.
In all our distress,
deliver us.
From evils of the world that is to be, *Manuale Sarisb.* de extr. unctione
from thy wrath,*
but still more
from thy failing to be wroth,
from eternal damnation.* Litan. Sarisb. (*Horae* f. 128b)
From all the terrors of the world to come,
from the Judge's face downcast,
from being placed on the left hand, S. Mt. xxv 33, 41
from hearing the appalling and tremendous voice
Depart from Me,
from being cast into outer darkness, S. Mt. xxv 30
from eternal chains under darkness, S. Jude 6
from the bottomless pit of fire and brimstone, Rev. xx 3; xiv 10, 11
where the smoke of the torments goeth up for ever.*
Be favourable. Spare us, o Lord. Litan. Sarisb. (*Horae* f. 128b)
Have mercy upon us.
Deliver us
and let us never be confounded. Ps. xxxi 1
From ghostly evils:

Horae f. 129; S. Mk. xvi. 14 — from blindness and hardness of heart *
which leadeth to impenitence,

Ezek. iii 8 / Is. xlviii 4 — from { softness / hardness } of forehead,

1 Tim. iv 2 — from a seared conscience *
and failure to grieve after we have sinned,

Rom. i 28 — from a reprobate mind,*
from contempt of thy threatenings,

1 S. Jo. v 18 — from the sin unto death

S. Mk. iii 29 — and against the Holy Ghost:
be favourable and deliver us, o Lord.

S. Cyr. Al. *in exitu animae* (v[2] 409 sqq.)

Chaff, tares,	grieving,
on the left hand,	withering,
in the storm,	fading,
the fire that is not quenched,	lamenting,
flames,	being condemned,
gehenna,	being reviled,
the overflowings of Belial,	wasting,
chains of darkness,	sorrow,
exile of the reprobate,	gnashing of teeth :

miserable,
thrice miserable,
with devils in darkness,
below
in the bottomless pit, whereat even the devil himself trembleth and is aghast.*

In the vision of God, in the turning away of his face.

S. Cyr. Al. *u.s.* p. 411

It is hard	to be sundered from the saints,
harder	God,
inglorious	to be bound,
full of anguish	to be cast out,
grievous	to be cast forth into the fire,
bitter	to call and not to be succoured,
pitiless	to beg for a drop of water and not to get it.*

Rescue { from all evil and misfortune,
1 Tim. vi 5 — from men of corrupt mind, }
Ps. lxxxiii 8 — from Asshur,
1 K. xii 28 — Jeroboam,
1 K. xii 13, 14 — Rehoboam,
Josh. vii 24 — the Valley of Achor,

from the evil spirit of the men of Shechem : Gen. xxxiv 23
from all scandal, grief, infamy : *Horae* f. 68
from {a deceitful tongue / perverse lips / snares : * *Horae* f. 40b
from all enemies {visible, invisible / bodily, ghostly : *Horae* f. 74b
from {vices and sins / lusts and temptations : *Horae* f. 40b
from the assault of devils, Litan. Sarisb. (*Horae* f. 128b)
from the spirit of fornication,
from the longing after vainglory,
from all uncleanness of mind and body,
from anger and illwill,
from polluted thoughts,
from blindness of heart.

Thou who saidst to thine angel as he was destroying *Horae* 1494, f. 45; [2 S. xxiv 16]
It is enough ; stay now thine hand :

in prayers and vows, *Horae* f. 39b ; S. Ans. *Or.* 1
distresses and perils,
infirmities and necessities,
temptations and tribulations,

< deliver us. >

COMPRECATION

L 155
W 135

A PRAYER FOR GRACE

Hosanna *save now* S. Mt. xxi 9; Ps. cxviii 25
in the highest: *in the heights.* *Ps. cxlviii* 1

Remember me, o Lord, with favour: *Ps. cvi* 4
o visit me with thy salvation:
that I may see the prosperity of thy chosen, 5
that I may rejoice in the joy of thy nation,
that I may glory with thine inheritance.
L *Men shall say* *Ps. lviii* 11
Verily there is a God that judgeth in the earth.
For He cometh, for He cometh to judge the earth. *Ps. xcvi* 13
LW But when the Judge cometh,
some shall see His face gladsome, Job xxxiii 26
they shall be set at the right hand, S. Mt. xxv 33, 34
they shall hear the most sweet voice COME YE BLESSED, *Horae* f. 69
they shall be caught up in the clouds, to meet the Lord, 1 Th. iv 17
they shall enter into the joy,* S. Mt. xxv 21
they shall win fruition of the vision Him,
they shall be ever with Him. 1 Th. iv 17
They alone, only they are blessed among the sons of men:
o give me, the last, the last place there,
under their feet,
under the feet of thine elect,* *Lit. S. Ja.* p. 29
the last among them all:
and that this may be
let me find grace in thy sight, Gen. xxxiii 15
so as to have grace Heb. xii 28
to serve Thee acceptably
with reverence and godly fear: *
and let me find withal the second grace,

2 Cor. vi 1 so as that grace
not to receive in vain,
Heb. xii 15 not to fail of it,
1 Tim. iv. 14 nay but not to neglect it,
Gal. v 4 so as to fall from it;
2 Tim. i 6 but to stir it up,
2 S. Pet. iii 18 so as to grow in it,
Cp. Acts xiii 43 nay but to persevere in it
unto the end of my life.
1 Th. iii 10 And, o perfect for me that which is lacking of thy gifts:
S. Lk. xvii 5 of faith: increase my littleness of faith: *
of hope: stablish trembling hope:
S. Mt. xii 20 of love: kindle its smoking flax:
Rom. v 5 shed abroad thy love in my heart,
S. Aug. *Conff.* iv 9 withal to love Thee,
my friend in Thee,
mine enemy for Thee.
S. Ja. iv 6 Thou that givest grace to the humbleminded,
to me withal give grace to be humbleminded:
Dt. xxxi 6; Ps. ciii 13; cp. ix 10 Thou that never failest them that fear Thee,
Ps. lxxxvi 11 *unite my heart to fear thy Name:*
ib. sept. let my heart be glad that I may fear Thee,
Job iv 6 *my fear, my confidence.*
S. Lk. vi 31 As I would that men should do unto me,
let me also do even so to them:
Rom. xii 3 not to think of myself more highly than I ought to think,
but to think soberly:
S. Greg. Naz. *Or.* xi 5 (i 244 E) let me fear one thing only, the fearing aught more than
Thee.

O 253 ANOTHER PRAYER FOR GRACE

Horae f. 93

Drive away the lust of gluttony ; give the virtue of abstinence :
put to flight the spirit of fornication ; give the love of chastity :
quench the greediness of the world ; give poverty of spirit :
refrain headstrong wrathfulness ; kindle gentleness in me :
take away the sorrow of the world ; increase ghostly joy :
drive away boastfulness of mind ; grant compunction of heart.*

Give strength of faith
Give security of hope
Give defence of salvation.
Give contempt of the world.

They shall enter into joy, S. Mt. xxv 21
full joy, S. Jo. xvi 24
the joy which shall not be taken away : S. Jo. xvi 22
on the right hand S. Cyr. Al. *de exitu animae* (v^2 409 sq.)
in tranquillity
in places green
in places dewy
in paradise
in refreshment
in the bosom of Abraham
in the tabernacles of the saints.

To rejoice, to sit at God's right hand,
to be glad,
to keep holiday,
to be glorified,
to be blessed,
to enjoy delights,
psalm,
song,
rest,
honour,
eternity,
the Tersanctus
with angels,
in light,
on high,
in heaven.*

Eph. vi 14-18 The girdle, the helmet,
the breastplate, the shield,
the shoes, the sword,
over all, prayer.

Horae, f. c. 3b Grant me the power and the opportunity of welldoing,
that before the day of my decease*
I may at all adventure effect some good thing,
whereof the fruit may remain:

Ps. xvii 16; Col. iii 4 that I may be able to appear with righteousness
and be satisfied with glory.

Horae f. 132b Thou which didst add fifteen years to the life of Ezekias,*
grant me so much space of life,
at the least unto such measure,
that I may be able therein to deplore my sins.*
And grant me a good end—
what is above every gift—

Horae f. 66b a good and holy end of life,
a glorious and joyful resurrection *

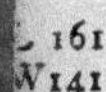

ANOTHER PRAYER FOR GRACE

One thing have I asked of the Lord, that will I seek after : *Ps. xxvii* 4
that I may dwell in the house of the Lord all the days of my life,
to behold the beauty of the Lord and to inquire in his temple :
that I may hearken to the voice of thanksgiving *Ps. xxvi* 7
and tell of all thy wondrous works.
Two things have I asked of Thee : *Prov. xxx* 7
deny me them not before I die.
Remove from me vanity and lies : 8
give me neither poverty nor riches,
feed me with the food that is needful for me,
lest I be full and deny Thee and say Who is the Lord? 9
or lest I be poor and steal and use profanely the Name
of my God.
Let me be instructed both to abound, Phil. iv 12
let me be instructed withal to suffer need,
and in whatsoever state I am, therewith to be content : * 11
and beside what I have,
neither to desire, neither ever to expect, Cp. S. Ans. *Or.* 16
aught earthly, temporal, corruptible.*
A good life in religion, gravity, all purity and ingenuity,
in cheerfulness, health, fair fame,
sufficiency, security, freedom, tranquillity.
A good death,
deathlessness.

ON ENTERING CHURCH L 3 W3 O 323

Ps. v 7 1. But as for me, I will come into thine house,
even upon the multitude of thy mercy:
and in thy fear
will I worship toward thy holy temple.
Ps. xxviii 2 2. Hear, Lord, the voice of my humble petitions,
when I cry unto Thee:
when I hold up my hands
towards the mercyseat of thy holy temple.
Ps. xlviii 8 3. Let us wait for thy lovingkindness, o God,
in the midst of thy temple.
Lit. S. Bas. 62 Remember, o Lord, the brethren that stand round about us,
Lit. S. Jas. 16 and are praying with us at this hour,
their earnestness and ready mind.
Lit. S. Bas. 62 Remember withal them that for reasonable causes are absent,
and have mercy on them and us
according to the multitude of thy mercy, o Lord.
Horolog. p. 22 Let us felicitate religious kings, LW
orthodox pontiffs,
the founders of this holy mansion.*
Glory be to Thee, o Lord, glory be to Thee:
glory be to Thee which didst glorify them,
in whom we also glorify Thee.
2 Chr. vi 40 Let thine eyes be open
and thine ears be attent
20 to hearken unto the prayer which thy servant prayeth toward this place
where Thou hast put thy Name.
Ps. xxvi 8 Lord, I have loved the habitation of thine house, O
and the place where thine honour dwelleth:
7 that I may shew the voice of thanksgiving,
and tell forth all thy wondrous works.

One thing have I desired of the Lord, which I will require, Ps. xxvii 4
even that I may dwell in the house of the Lord
all the days of my life,
to behold the fair beauty of the Lord,
and to visit his temple.
My heart hath talked of Thee, I WILL SEEK THE LORD: Ps. xxvii 9
I have sought Thee and thy face:
thy face, Lord, will I seek.
Open me the gates of righteousness, Ps. cxviii 19
that I may go in and give thanks unto the Lord.

BEFORE PREACHING

O 322 S. Lk. v 4 sqq.

World	Sea
Men	Fishes
Church	Boat
Preacher	Fisher
Word	Net.

S 3
O 345

Admonition

Let the preacher labour to be heard gladly, intelligently, obediently. And let him not question that he can do this better by the piety of his prayers than by the fluency of his speech. By praying for himself and for them he is going to address, let him be a bedesman or ever he be a teacher: and approaching devoutly, before he put forth a speaking tongue, let him lift up to God a thirsty soul, that so he may give out what from Him he hath drunk in, and empty out what he hath first replenished. S. Fulgent. *ad Monim.* I

Therefore of our very Lord and Master I cease not to ask that, whether by the utterances of his Scriptures or by the converse of brethren or by the inward and sweeter teaching of his inspiration, He will vouchsafe to learn me what things I can in such sort put forth and in such sort assert, that in my statements and assertions I may alway tarry fast in the Truth. Of this very Truth itself I ask to be taught the many more things I wot not of, of whom I have gotten the small store I wot of.

The very Truth I ask, mercy preventing and following, to learn me what things soever I know not, that ought to be known unto the soul's health: to keep me safe in the truths I know; to assist me in the things wherein, as a man, I am deceived; to confirm me in the truths wherein I waver, and to deliver me from things false and noisome, and to make those things, which more than aught else are pleasing in the sight of the Truth itself, in such sort to come forth out of my mouth, that they may be acceptable unto all the faithful: through Jesus Christ our Lord and Saviour.

Prayer O 322

Ps. cxix 18 Open Thou mine eyes that I may understand the wondrous things of thy law.

2 Cor. iii 14-16 Take away, o Lord, the veil of my heart while I read the Scriptures.

Ps. cxix 12 Blessed art Thou, o Lord: o teach me thy statutes*:
give me a word, o Word of the Father:
1 Sam. x 26 touch my heart:
Eph. i 18; S. Lk. xxiv 45 enlighten the understandings of my heart:
Ps. li 15; lxxi 7 open my lips and fill them with thy praise.

Cp. *Missale* ad evang. Be Thou, o Lord, in my spirit and in my mouth:
in my mouth that lawfully and worthily I may shew forth* thine oracles
Lit. S. Ja. p. 4 by the hallowing power of thy thriceholy Spirit.

O Thou coal of double nature, which in the tongs didst touch the lips of the prophet and take away his iniquity: touch my lips, who am a sinner, and purge me of every stain* and make me skill to shew forth thine oracles.

Ps. li 15 O Lord, open Thou my lips and my mouth shall show forth thy praise.

Is. l 4 Lord, o Lord, give me the tongue of the learned that I may
Eph. vi 20 know what manner word I ought to speak and
Eph. iv 29 may speak what word soever is to the use of edifying, that Thou mayest minister grace to the hearers.

Eph. vi 19 Let utterance be given me, that I may open my mouth.

Ps. lxxxi 11 I open my mouth wide, o Lord: do Thou fill it.

L 157
W139

FOR PLENTY AND PEACE

W Hosanna in things on the earth
LW *The eyes of all wait upon Thee,* *Ps. cxlv* 15
and Thou givest them their meat in due season:
Thou openest thine hand, 16
and satisfiest the desire of every living thing.
Thou hast crowned the year of thy goodness: *Ps. lxv* 12
L *thy paths drop fatness.*
Blessed of the Lord be our land, *Dt. xxxiii* 13
LW *from the precious things of heaven, from the dew,*
and from the deep that coucheth beneath,
and from the precious things of the fruits of the sun, 14
and from the precious things of the growth of the moons,
and from the summit of the ancient mountains, 15
and from the precious things of the everlasting hills,
and from the precious things of the earth and the fulness thereof, 16
L *and the goodwill of Him that dwelleth in the bush.*
LW Good seasons, good temperature of the air, *Lit. S. Chrys.* p. 79
plenteous bearing of fruits of the earth,*
good habits of body,
and peaceful seasons. *Lit. S. Chrys.* p. 79

L 157
W137

FOR UNITY

Give light to them that sit in darkness S. Lk. i 79
and in the shadow of death:
guide our feet into the way of peace;
that so we be likeminded one toward another: Rom xv 5
and, if in anything we be otherwise minded, Phil. iii 15, 16; Gal. vi 16
to walk by the same rule whereto we have already attained:
to maintain order, Col. ii 5
decency, stedfastness:
rightly to divide, 2 Tim. ii 15
to walk uprightly, Gal. ii 14
to edify: 1 Th. v 11
with one mind and one mouth to glorify God. Rom. xv 6

FOR NATIONAL PROSPERITY L 160 W139

Good government, good counsel,
fair order, right dealing,
ready obedience,
just retribution, plentiful resource.

Fruitful procreation, happy bearing,
goodly progeny,
wholesome nurture, sound education.

Ps. cxliv 12 **1.** *Whose sons are as plants grown up in their youth,*
2. *our daughters as corner stones hewn after the fashion of a palace:*
13 **3.** *our garners are full,*
4. *affording all manner of store,*
5. *our sheep bring forth thousands and ten thousands in our fields:*
14 **6.** *our oxen are well laden:*
7. *there is no breaking in and no going forth*
8. *and no outcry in our streets:*
15 *happy is the people that is in such a case,*
happy is the people whose God is the Lord.

GRACE BEFORE MEAT O 260

Ps. cxxxvi 25 Thou that givest food to all flesh,
Ps. cxlvii 9 which feedest the young ravens that cry unto Thee
Gen. xlviii 15 and hast nourished us from our youth up:
Acts xiv 17 fill our hearts with food and gladness
Heb. xiii 9 and establish our heart with thy grace.

BEFORE A JOURNEY S 38 O 326

Gen. xxiv 12 Send me good speed this day:
Ex. xxxiii 15 if thy presence go not with me,
carry me not up hence.
Thou who didst speed the way
Gen. xxiv 7 of Abraham's servant } by the leading of { an angel
S. Mt. ii 9 of the Wise Men } { a star:

Thou who didst preserve
Peter amid the waves, S. Mt. xiv 31
Paul in shipwreck : Acts xxvii 44
be with me, o Lord, and speed my way :
bring me on my way,
bring me to my journey's end,
bring me home again.
Let God arise, Ps. lxviii 1
and let his enemies be scattered.
Depart from me, ye wicked : Ps. cxix 115
I will keep the commandments of my God.

INTERCESSION

REFLEXIONS BEFORE INTERCESSION

2 Cor. ix 15

THANKS BE TO GOD FOR HIS UNSPEAKABLE GIFT

The apostle saith it is an unspeakable gift of God when many succour one another with mutual offices and mutually pray one for another and give thanks.

MOREOVER AS FOR ME, GOD FORBID THAT I SHOULD SIN BEFORE THE LORD IN CEASING TO PRAY BEFORE HIM FOR YOU, saith Samuel. 1 S xii 23

In the present world we know that we can be helped by prayers; but when we come before the judgement-seat of Christ, neither Job neither Daniel neither Noah can make request for us, but every man beareth his own burden. S. Jer. *in Gal.* vi 6 (vii 523 C)

THE SPIRIT MAKETH INTERCESSION FOR US WITH GROANINGS WHICH CANNOT BE UTTERED Rom. viii 26

'The Spirit maketh intercession for us with groanings unutterable:' is thy spirit or mine 'unutterable,' which oftentimes is naught, oftentimes is cold? Nay, but forasmuch as there is no day, no moment when supplication is not being made to God by the saints,* by one in more fervent sort, by another more lukewarmly; and forasmuch as all go to make up one Dove, it is herefrom that the groanings proceed which cannot be uttered, to wit from all the groanings in common, which are of advantage to all who are constituted in the body of the Church. S. Aug. *c. Max.* i 9 (viii 684 B)

Who prayeth for others laboureth for himself. *Prymer* Regnault 1537 f. 145b

If thou make request for thyself alone, alone wilt thou make request for thyself:
if thou pray for all, they will pray for thee. S. Amb. *de Cain et Abel* i 9 §39 (i 201 E)

A SCHEME OF GENERAL INTERCESSION W154

Lit. S. Chrys. p. 99	World	Inhabited earth
	Church*	Kingdom
	Throne	Altar
	Parliament	Lawcourts
	Colleges	Workshops.
Cp. *Lit. S. Bas.* p. 62	Infants	grown men
	children	well stricken
Lit. S. Ja. p. 15	youths	those in old age
	young men	and helplessness.*
Lit. S. Bas. p. 62	Possessed	wayfarers
	dispirited	voyagers
	sick	with child
	in bonds	giving suck
Lit. S. Ja. p. 16	orphans	in bitter thraldoms
	widows	in solitude
S. Mt. xi 28	strangers	heavyladen.

S 25 A GENERAL INTERCESSION

Let us beseech the Lord * *Lit. S. Ja.* p. 5
for the whole creation and all things living;
for the eyes of all wait upon Thee, Ps. cxlv 15
and Thou givest them their meat,
who feedest the young ravens: * Ps. cxlvii 9
for seasons fruitful / peaceful:
for human kind (Jews, Turks, paynims):
for all men and women
who are under trial, in mines, galleys, exiles: * *Lit. S. Bas.* p. 62
who are
either suffering hardness in dejection / weakness / resourcelessness / unsettlement:
or in prosperous case in cheerfulness / health / resourcefulness / quiet:
for all Christendom
and Christians in particular
whether dowered by Thee, o God, with grace and truth,
or sick of sins or heresies:
for the union of the holy churches of God; *Lit. S. Ja.* p. 15
for
the settlement of this church
all the sacerdotal order amongst us
all the clergy rightminded
and rightly dividing the word of truth * 2 Tim. ii 15
all the Christloving people:
for
the stability of all kingdoms of the world
the stability of our / every kingdom, country, city:

for our deliverance from
- *Lit. S. Ja.* p. 9 — all tribulation
- *Lit. S. Bas.* p. 62 — famine, pestilence, war, fire, flood, earthquake, peril
- *Lit. S. Ja.* p. 8 — all the difficulties of this world
- B.C.P. 1604 — the plague of immoderate rains* and of dearth
- *Lit. S. Bas.* p. 63 — invasion of aliens and civil war
- *Eng. Litany* — sedition and privy conspiracy *
- epidemic sicknesses and unforeseen death:

from
- anarchy, multiplicity of rulers, tyranny
- 1 K. xii 28, 8 — the rule of Jeroboam or Rehoboam
- 2 K. xvi 11; Judg. xvii — the priesthood of Urijah or Micah
- 1 K. xxi 11; Mic. vi 16 — the judgement of Jezreel or Omri
- 2 S. xvi 23 — the counsel of Ahitophel
- S. Mt. xxvi 14-16; Acts viii 18 — the fraternity of Judas Iscariot and Simon Magus:

Lit. S. Bas. p. 64 — stop the schisms of the churches,
assuage the ragings of the heathen:
Acts iv 32 — let the heart and soul
of the multitude of them that believe be one.*
Lit. S. Ja. p. 5 — Let us beseech the Lord *
for the whole commonwealth among us:
for our king preserved of God;
defend him with truth and favourable kindness as with a shield;
speak comfortably good things unto him
on behalf of the Church and thy people:
for the parliament, judicature and all the court, the army and the fleet:
for the education of the children and the young.
Lit. S. Ja. p. 5 — Bless, o Lord.*
For them that are essaying some achievement
whereby thy thriceholy name will be glorified.
Lit. S. Ja. p. 15 — For them that are doing good works for thy holy churches,
and remembering the poor and needy: *
preserve them in the evil day,
comfort them when they lie on the bed of sickness.
Ps. xli 3 — make Thou all their bed in their sickness.

For all, men and women, commended to me by
- kindred according to the flesh: (Rom. ix 3)
  - be favourable to them, o Lord:
- neighbourhood
- good offices received:
  - requite, o Lord:
- care
- friendship
- christian charity
- my promise
- their lack of leisure:
  - have mercy, o Lord.

For them that at present are in profound and extreme tribulation and straits and sore needing thy succour and consolation: (Cp. *Lit. S. Ja.* p. 16)
heal those that are broken in heart (Ps. cxlvii 3)
and give them medicine to heal their sickness.

S 22 ANOTHER GENERAL INTERCESSION

Hear us, o Lord:
for the whole creation—
seasons: wholesome, fruitful, peaceful:
for the race of mankind—
the conversion of Jews / Turks / paynims to the knowledge of the truth:
for the succour and consolation of all
with whom it fareth ill in mind or body,
who are in want / perplexed:
for sobriety and moderation on the part of those
who are of tranquil mind / of vigorous body / in affluence / of unperplexed purpose
for all Christians
who are in truth and grace,* (S. Jo. i 17)
that they be confirmed therein;
who are in error and sin,
that they return into the way:
for the churches throughout the world,
that they be in truth and stability;

for our church,
that all heresies, schisms and scandals { public / private } be put out of the way:
for the clergy,
2 Tim. ii 2 — that while teaching others, themselves may learn;
2 Tim. ii 15; Gal. ii 14 — that they rightly divide, walk uprightly:
for the people,
Rom. xii 3 — that they think not of themselves more highly than they ought to think,*
that they be persuaded by reason and yield to authority:
for commonwealths and their stability and peace;
for the kingdom, municipality, our city:
Ps. cxviii 25 — o Lord { *save now* / *send now prosperity*: * }
for prudence of counsel,
equity of judgement,
courage of the army:
for yeoman, merchantmen, handicraftsmen, even down to sordid crafts and the beggars:
for the rising generation whether in universities or in schools,
S. Lk. ii 52 — that, as in age, so they may increase in wisdom withal, and in favour with God and man: *
for those whom { kinship / neighbourhood / beneficence / friendship / christian charity / our promise } commendeth to us:
for those { whom some difficulty presseth / who, pressed by evils of business, cannot pray / who have commended themselves to our prayers / on whom is laid the care of Church or State or family: }
for those who show themselves beneficent
toward { things sacred / the poor and needy; }
Ps. lxxix 13 — reward Thou them sevenfold into their bosom,
Ps. xxv 12 — let their souls dwell at ease and their seed inherit the land.
Litan. Sarisb. (*Horae* f. 129b) — That it may please Thee to reward all our benefactors with eternal good things:
that Thou vouchsafe to behold and relieve the miseries of the poor and of captives:

that it may please Thee to remember with benign compassion the frail lapses of the flesh: *Horae* f. 103b
that it may please Thee to hold accepted the reasonable service of our obedience: Litan. Sarisb. (*Horae* f. 129b)
that it may please Thee to raise up our minds to heavenly desires:
that Thou vouchsafe to turn back upon us the eyes of thy mercy:
that it may please Thee to deliver our souls from eternal damnation:
we beseech Thee to hear us, good Lord.

310 A SHORT INTERCESSION

O God of truth withal and Prince of peace, Dt. xxxii 4; Is. lxv 16; ix 6
let there be peace and truth in our days: Is. xxxix 8
let there be one heart and one soul Acts iv 32
unto the multitude of them that believe.
O Thou that breakest not a bruised reed, S. Mt. xii 20
neither quenchest smoking flax:
stablish all that stand in truth and grace,* S. Jo. i 17
restore all that fall through heresies and sins.
I beseech thee, o Lord, in all thy mercy, Dan. ix 16; (cp. *Horae* f. c. 7b)
that thy wrath be taken away
from this city,
from this house,
for that we have sinned against Thee:*
that this place along with all the country Thou wouldest comfort, tempering justice with mercy.* Cp. Hab. iii 2
Grant me to love again them that love me,* S. Aug. *Conff.* iv 9
albeit unknown to me,
and bring them into thy heavenly kingdom,
even as myself:
and grant me to shew them the mercy of God
in my prayers:
that with them for whom I have prayed,
or in any sort am bound to pray, *Horae* f. 76b
and with all the people of God,
an entrance may be granted me into thy kingdom Cp. 2 S. Pet. i 11
there to appear in righteousness, Col. iii 4; Ps. xvii 16
there to be satisfied with glory.

A SCHEME OF PARTICULAR INTERCESSION L 135 W119

Do well, o Lord:
Ps. cxxv 4; li 18 visit with thy mercies
thy whole creation world
all our race inhabited earth
the commonwealth of the world:
the Church at large Christendom
the churches } severally:
the commonwealths }
the church } among us fatherland
the commonwealth }
the orders in either sacerdotal
the persons in the order
the king's
the prince's W2
the succession: LW
the city
the parish All Hallows Barking
the two schools
the university
the college:
the parish of S. Giles: LW2
Pembroke Hall:
the churches
of Southwell
S. Paul's
Westminister:
the dioceses
of Chichester
Ely
Winchester: W2
house LW
kinsfolk
those that have mercy
those that serve
neighbours
friends
commended.

O 326 **FOR THE QUICK AND THE DEAD**

Thou which art Lord at once of the living and of the dead; *Horae* f. c. 7b and f. 133
whose are we whom the present world yet holdeth in the
flesh;
whose are they withal whom, unclothed of the body, the
world to come hath even now received:
give to the living mercy and grace, *Horae* f. c. 8; 2 Esd. ii 34, 35;
to the dead rest and light perpetual: Is. xxxix 8
give to the Church truth and peace,
to us sinners penitence and pardon.

O 255 **FOR OUR COUNTRY**

Of the fruits of the earth and of the fulness thereof:
bless our ingathering,
make peace in our borders, Ps. cxlvii 14
fill us with the flour of wheat,
satisfy our poor with bread, Ps. cxxxii 16
make fast the bars of our gates, Ps. cxlvii 13
bless our children within us;
clothe our enemies with shame; Ps. cxxxii 19
bestow temperate weather, *Horae* f. 7b
grant the fruits of the earth;
drive away fleshly desires;
restore health to the sick,
grant restoration to the fallen,
to voyagers and wayfarers,
a prosperous journey and an haven of safety;
to the afflicted, joy;
to the oppressed, relief;
to captives grant liberty: *
sanity of mind,
soundness of body,
strength of faith,
security of hope,
defence of salvation.

FOR THE CLERGY L 159

Dt. xxxiii 8 *Thy thummim and thy urim are with thy godly one,*
whom Thou didst prove at Massah,
with whom Thou didst strive at the waters of Meribah :
9 *who said of his father and his mother*
I have not seen him :
neither did he acknowledge his brethren,
nor knew he his own children :
for they have observed thy word
and keep thy covenant.
10 *They shall teach Jacob thy judgements*
and Israel thy law :
they shall put incense before Thee
and whole burntofferings upon thine altar.
11 *Bless, Lord, his substance,*
and accept the work of his hands :
smite through the loins of them that rise up against him,
and of them that hate him, that they rise up no more.

Num. vi 24 *The Lord bless thee and keep thee :*
25 *the Lord make his face to shine upon thee*
and be gracious unto thee :
26 *the Lord lift up his countenance upon thee*
and give thee peace.

27 *I have put thy name upon thy people :*
do Thou bless them, o Lord.

FOR THOSE IN AFFLICTION AND PERIL O 337

For the wounded in spirit, the sick in mind, the perplexed.
For them that are in peril of their life, them that are sick,
them that are receiving medicine.
For captives, prisoners, them that are condemned to death.
For the poor, the oppressed, the desolate.
For strangers, orphans, widows.
For them that are with child, those in labour, infants.
For them that are abroad, voyagers, wayfarers,
in any sort in jeopardy,
especially them that pray not.

COMMENDATION

L 134
W120

A COMMENDATION

I commend unto Thee, o Lord,
my soul and my body, *Horae* f. 100, 40b
my mind and my thoughts,
my vows and prayers,
my senses and my members,
my words and my deeds,
my life and my death:

impulses,
occasions,
purposes,
endeavours,
going out and coming in,
downsitting and uprising:

my brothers and sisters
their children
my benefactors
wellwishers
household
neighbours
country
all Christian folk.

THE LORD'S PRAYER

A PREFACE TO THE LORD'S PRAYER

S 29 And last,
vouchsafe, o Lord, to remember *Lit. S. Bas.* p. 63
according to the multitude of thy mercies
mine unworthiness,
the inveterate sinner, *Lit. S. Bas.* p. 50
thine unworthy and unprofitable servant:
condescend, o Lord, to mine infirmities, *Lit. S. Ja.* p. 18
and cast me not away from thy presence,
neither loathe my * filthiness;
but after thy graciousness *Lit. S. Ja.* p. 25
and thine unspeakable love towards mankind,*
remove mine iniquities:
do not by reason of me and of my sins *Lit. S. Ja.* p. 25; *S. Bas.* pp. 63, 50
refrain thy readiness to hear
and thy grace from* { this / and every }
my service and prayer:
do not so, o Lord, but account me worthy, *Lit. S. Ja.* p. 31
o sovran Lord, which lovest mankind,
without condemnation, with clean heart and contrite soul,
with face unashamed and hallowed lips,
to make bold to call upon Thee
the holy God and Father which art in heaven
and to say
O 317 Our Father, S. Mt. vi 9-13
which art in heaven,
1. thy { name — be hallowed
2. thy { kingdom — come
3. thy { will — be done,
as in heaven
so also in earth.
4. Give us this day — our daily bread,

5. and forgive us our trespasses,
as we forgive
them that trespass against us :
6. and lead us not into temptation,
7. but deliver us from evil.
For thine is the kingdom,
the power and the glory,
for ever and ever.
Amen.

327 THE LORD'S PRAYER PARAPHRASED

Our Father

1. Holy art Thou: *Heb. Pr. Bk.* p. 45; Phil. ii 9
holy is thy Name above every name,
to be had in sanctification and with all veneration Cp. Ps. lxxxix 8
of all and of some much more than of others,
and of me principally beyond many.
Notwithstanding I have not so had it,
neither so much as in me lay have gone about so to do:
woe to wretched me, that I have not,
I frankly confess.

I heartily grieve { in heart / in mind / in soul / in spirit.

Humbly I ask pardon, humbly grace,
that henceforward I speak, do, live in such sort Cp. S. Chrys. *hom.* xix *in Mat.*
that thy Name be hallowed:
would God of others withal because of me.

2. Thy kingdom, the principal point of my desires,— Cp. S. Greg. Nys. *de or. dom.* iii
that I may come thereto in a state of glory, Ludolphus *vita Christi* i 37 § 5
let it come to me here in a state of grace.*
In the kingdom of things earthly here
let me by thy grace do somewhat,
that in the kingdom of heaven there
I attain unto some place, even the last,
under the feet of thy saints. Cp. *Lit. S. Ja.* p. 29

3. Let the will of { the flesh / man } depart from me: S. Jo. i 13

let thy will { holy / righteous / gracious } be done { by this earth / from this earth, Cp. Rom. vii 12
the which I am,
as it is in heaven.

4. Give what things are for { health
peace
sufficiency :
Ps. lxxviii 26 give angels' food unto eternal salvation.
5. Forgive me my debts,
the huge sum of debts,
shameful falls,
often relapses,
daily wallowings.
Dan. ix 7 To Thee, o Lord, belongeth righteousness, and to me confusion of face.
Hos. xiii 9 my destruction cometh to me of myself:
Ps. cxxx 3 if Thou, Lord, wilt be extreme to mark what is done amiss,
o Lord, who may abide it ?
4 But there is mercy with Thee :
7 with God there is mercy,
with God is plenteous redemption :
and He will deliver from all sins : *
deliver me, o God, from mine,
Ps. lxxxvi 13 deliver my soul from the nethermost hell.
Ps. xlii 9 Deep calleth unto deep *
to deliver from the deep.
But there are other things withal, the which I feel less—
not less grievous, peradventure more grievous,
whereof I ask to be enlightened,
that so I be able to confess them.
6. And lead not,
S. Cyp. *de or. dom.* 25 suffer me not to be led,
S. Mt. xxvi 41 suffer me not to enter, into temptation,*
mindful of and pitying my frailty
and mine infirmity so oftentimes proved.
7. But deliver me from evil,
evil in myself and the flesh
and the surprises thereof:
evil devil and his suggestion :
Engl. Litany evils of punishment which most righteously
and most worthily I have deserved:
evils of the world to come;
S. Aug. (?) there spare, here burn, here cut, o Lord :*
evils of the world that now is;

here also spare:
evils of this world
and the things that befall therein:
evils of this disease,
wherewith I struggle:
evils of business,
wherein I am entangled:
evils past, present and to come: *Missale Rom.* can. *Libera*
from all these deliver me,* o Lord,
and save me thy servant, for ever,
even last among the last.

PARAPHRASES OF THE LORD'S PRAYER FROM THE OLD TESTAMENT

318 I Moses

1. Let thy name be called upon of us. Gen. iv 26
2. Be Thou our shield Gen. xv 1
and our exceeding great reward.
3. What word soever proceedeth from Thee, Num. xxiv 13
let it not be in us to speak aught against it,
whether good or bad.
4. Give us bread to eat, Gen. xxviii 20
and raiment to put on.
5. And now pardon the iniquity and the unrighteousness of thy servants. Num. xiv 19
6. And, o Lord, let us not think anxiously in our hearts all the day long. Deut. xxviii 32; Lev. xxvi 16 (?)
7. And let not evils take hold of us. Deut. xxxi 17

319 II Job

1. Blessed be thy name i 21
both now and for ever.
2. Make not hypocrites to reign over us xxxiv 30
by reason of the sluggishness of thy people.
3. Like as seemeth good to Thee, o Lord, so be it. i 21
4. Let not thistles grow instead of wheat, xxxi 40
nor cockle instead of barley.
5. I have sinned: what shall I do unto Thee, o Thou preserver of men? vii 20

Job xxxi 1 6. I will make a covenant with my senses:
why then should I look upon evil?
v 19 7. Six times deliver me out of troubles:
yea the seventh time let no evil touch me.

MOSES

III O 319

Ex. xxviii 36 1. Holiness unto the Lord.
Ex. xix 6 2. Let us be made unto Thee a kingdom of priests.
Num. xxvii 21 3. Let us go in and go out at thy commandment.
Deut. viii 3 4. Let us not set our life in bread only,
but in every word that proceedeth out of thy mouth.
Ex. xxxiv 7 5. Forgive our iniquities, transgressions and sins.
Ex. xvii 9 (Ps. xcv 8) 6. Not into provocation, not into temptation.
Ex. xii 3 7. From the destroying angel and every deadly plague,
deliver us, o Lord.

PSALMS

IV O 320

cxiii 2 1. Blessed be thy Name now and for evermore:
3 thy Name be praised from the east unto the west.
cxlii 6 2. Be unto us a hope and a portion in the land of the living.
cxliii 10 3. Teach us to do the thing that pleaseth Thee, for Thou art our God:
let thy loving Spirit lead us forth into the land of righteousness.
cxlv 15 4. The eyes of all wait upon Thee, o Lord,
that Thou mayest give them their meat in due season:
16 open Thou thine hand
and fill all things living with plenteousness.
li 1 5. Have mercy upon us, o God, after thy great goodness:
according to the multitude of thy mercies, do away our sins.
lxxxix 23 6. Let never the enemy be able to do us violence,
nor the son of wickedness hurt us.
xci 10 7. Let not evils come upon us,
neither any plague come nigh our dwelling.

SOLOMON

V O 32c

Prov. xviii 10 1. Let thy Name be unto us a strong tower:
let us run thereunto and be safe.
Prov. viii 15; xxi 1 2. By Thee kings reign: let their hearts be in thy hand as the watercourses, to turn them whithersoever Thou wilt.
Bend them unto good, o Lord.
Prov. xix 21 3. Let not many devices be in our hearts:
but let thy counsel abide and be done, o Lord.

4. Two things have I required of Thee: deny me them not before I die: Prov. xxx 7
give me neither poverty nor riches: 8
give me things convenient and sufficient.
5. Who can say with confidence, I am clean from sin? Prov. xx 9
Be merciful unto Thy servants, for they have sinned against Thee and heal their souls. 1 Ki. viii 50; 2 Chr. vii 14
6. Remove my way from occasion of sinning: Prov. v 8
let me not come nigh to the gates of the house thereof.
7. Send not a cruel messenger unto us: Prov. xvii 11
but let all evils be put far away from our houses. 13

) 321 VI PROPHETS

1. Let not Thy Name be blasphemed among the gentiles through us. Is. lii 5 (Rom. ii 24)
2. Let all nations and kings that serve not thy kingdom perish and be utterly desolated. Is. lx 12
3. Let thine every counsel stand and all things that Thou hast decreed be performed. Is. xlvi 10
4. Give seed to him that soweth and give the stay of bread for food. Is. lv 10; iii 1
5. Be not wroth with us very sore, neither in time remember our sins: Is. lxiv 9
behold, see, we beseech Thee, we are all thy people.
6. Let us not any while set the stumbling block of our iniquity before our eyes. Ezek. xiv 3, 4
7. Set not thy face against us for evil. Ezek. xv 7; Jer. xxi 10

NOTES

The references are to page and line; titles, other than headlines, being included in the reckoning of the lines.

P. 3. *Serm. Repent.* viii (i 440) 'For that somewhat is to be done is so sure as ye shall not find any man in the mind or way to repent, but ever his first question is "What must I do?" And that even by the very instinct of reason. "Lord, what wilt Thou have me to do?"—St Paul's first words, when he began (Acts ix 6). *Quid oportet me facere?*—the gaoler's first words, being now a convert, to St Paul, when he began (Acts xvi 30). As much as to say, Somewhat I am to do, if I knew what. Thrice together you have this question here immediately after. *Quid faciemus?* say the Publicans: "What shall we do?" say the Soldiers: "What shall we do?" say all the people to St John when they come to the "baptism of repentance" (S. Lk. iii 10-14).'

P. 4. 12. 'Sacrifice' and 'oblation,' θυσία and προσφορά, used in Eph. v 2, of our Lord's offering of Himself, represent in Ps. xl 8 (Heb. x 5) *zebaḥ* and *minḥah*, *i.e.* the bloody and the unbloody offering. Andrewes frequently applies the words respectively, as here, to the sacrifice of sorrow and death and that of joy and life. See below, pp. 35, 94, 189, 212; and note on p. 35 l. 30.

P. 7. 24. See *Serm. Pentecost* xiv (iii 376).

—— 31. *Serm. Prayer* v (v 350) 'and this prayer is *breviarium fidei*: it teacheth us to believe those things which we pray for.' Tertull. *de Or.* 1: ut revera in oratione (the Lord's Prayer) breviarium totius evangelii comprehendatur. Cp. *Cat. doct.* p. 105.

—— 32. *Non passibus sed precibus itur ad Deum* is quoted as from S. Augustine in *Serm. Prayer* iii (v 321). Cp. *Cat. doct.* p. 97.

—— 33. This loses something of its point by the loss of the play on the words *fundit* and *fundatur*. S. Aug. *serm.* cxv 1: fides fundit orationem, fusa oratio fidei impetrat firmitatem, is the closest parallel I have found.

P. 8. 4. Theophylact *in S. Luc.* xviii πάσης προσευχῆς βάθρον καὶ κρηπὶς ἡ πίστις· εἰ μὴ γὰρ πιστεύσει ὁ ἄνθρωπος ὅτι ὃ ἐὰν αἰτήσῃ λήψεται πρὸς τὸ συμφέρον ματαία ἡ προσευχὴ ἣν ποιεῖται (i 433).

—— 6. *Sursum corda*, which introduces the preface of all liturgies, is found first in the *Hippolytean canons* 3 (of the 2nd or 3rd cent.) and S. Cyprian *de Orat. dom.* 31.

P. 8. 10. S. Greg. Nyss. *de Or. dom.* i Θεοῦ ὁμιλία. *Serm. Prayer* vi (v 352) 'there are three uses of prayer: one . . the use of dignity and perfection, when men do converse and enter into familiarity with God, by abstracting their minds from human affairs.' Cp. S. Chrys. *hom.* xxx *in Gen.* 5 ἡ γὰρ εὐχὴ διάλεξίς ἐστι πρὸς τὸν Θεόν: S. Aug. *Enarr. in Ps.* lxxxv 7 (iv 905 F) oratio tua locutio est ad Deum: quando legis Deus tibi loquitur: quando oras Deo loqueris.

Pp. 9, 10. Cp. *Serm. Prayer* vi (v 354 sqq.), v (v 349), *Resurrect.* ix (ii 334).

P. 10. 12. Reading χειροπλεξία for χειροπληξία.

—— 14. *Serm. Res.* iv (ii 249) '"to hold up the hands" *habitus orantis:* the meaning of which ceremony of lifting up the hands with prayer is *ut pro quo quis orat pro eo laboret* "what we pray for we should labour for."'

P. 11. With these schemes cp. Origen's τόποι τῆς εὐχῆς in *de Oratione* 33. The first of them is developed in detail in *Cat. doct.* pp. 100 sqq. Cp. S. Aug. *Ep.* cxlix 12-14: Cassian *Collat.* ix 9: S. Bern. *hom.* xxv *de divers.*: S. Thom. Aq. *Summa* ii² 83 § 17. In *Serm. Prayer* vi (v 359), following Cassian *Collat.* ix 17, Andrewes shows how our Lord used the several sorts of prayer.

P. 12. This scheme is illustrated by the morning prayers for the days of the week below, pp. 40 sqq.

—— 12. Cp. *Cat. doct.* p. 104 [the third part of thanksgiving is] 'Annunciation, to tell it to others what God hath done for us, Ps. lxvi 16 . . in the congregation Ps. cxi 1 . . yea, to all nations Ps. lvii 9 . . yea, to all posterity Ps. xxii 31 . .'

P. 13. Scheme VI: with i compare pp. 131-140; with iv, p. 44; with v, pp. 32 sq., 59 sq., 68 sq., 269 sq., 272.

—— 30. Τοῦ Κυρίου δεηθῶμεν is a bidding in the Greek rite generally corresponding to the Western *Oremus:* see *Euchology.* p. 131, etc.

P. 14. 19, 20. Κράτος, βία. The words are probably suggested by the names of the two spirits who nail Prometheus to the rock in the *Prometheus vinctus* of Æschylus. The exact meaning here intended is not clear. Newman renders by 'army, police'; but this, besides being too concrete and too much narrowing the application, at least by the exclusion of naval force, seems to reverse the order of the words. The rendering in the text would seem to be in the direction of the meaning intended. Cp. p. 33 l. 19, 60 l. 33, 68 l. 28.

—— 22. 'Succession' *i.e.* the rising generation: p. 33 l. 22, 60 l. 39 sqq., 68 l. 31 sq., 270 l. 27.

—— 24 sqq. The relations and conditions by which several classes of persons are commended to our prayers. Cp. pp. 61, 69, 112, 269 sq.

—— 27 sqq. See Introduction, p. xxvi sq.

P. 14. 38. *I.e.* the Colleges of which as bishop of Winchester he was *ex officio* visitor, viz. New College, Magdalen, Corpus Christi, Trinity, S. John's in Oxford, and Winchester College.

P. 15. 13 sqq. *Serm. Gunpowder Tr.* ii (iv 225) 'All the Psalms are reduced to them, even to those two words: Hallelujah and Hosanna, praises and prayers: Hallelujah, praises for deliverance obtained; Hosanna, prayers for obtaining the like upon the like need'; *ib.* p. 239 'and now shall we stay here and end with Hallelujah, and cut off Hosanna quite? I dare not: I seldom see Hallelujah hold long, if Hosanna forsake it and second it not.' Hence vi 1-3 represent respectively Thanksgiving, Deprecation, Comprecation.

—— 14, 15. 'With' angels and men, cp. pp. 55, 202 sq., 225: 'for' benefits received.

—— 16. Title of Pss. lvii-lix, lxxv. Cp. *Serm. Gowries* vii (iv 164), *Gunpowder Tr.* iii (iv 242).

—— 17 sqq. 'In . . in . . in' cp. p. 242 ll. 11-14.

—— 20-23. 'In' *i.e.* *ἐν ὑψίστοις*, prayer for eternal blessings, p. 251; 'in . . in' *i.e.* *ἐν ἐπιγείοις*, for earthly blessings, p. 259, in body and soul. Cp. S. Bern. *Serm.* v *in Quadrages.*

—— 24. *In the morning = Saḥarîth*, the title of the Jewish Morning Prayer.

—— 26. 'At lamplighting' = *ἐπιλύχνιος*. The prayers at lamplighting, *τὸ ἐπιλυχνικόν*, *lucernare* or *lucernarium*, are the origin of vespers or evensong. The first part of the Greek Vespers (*ἑσπερινός*) is still so called; and the hymn *Φῶς ἱλαρόν* (p. 104) is the 'epilychnian hymn.'

P. 19. The verses of the Dial are all constructed on the plan of the Greek *troparia*, *i.e.* the verses of which the hymns, which form a great part of the choir services, are composed. Those for the 3rd and the 6th hours, and the first of those for the 9th, are the characteristic *troparia* of the Greek terce, sext, and nones respectively. The verses, which are somewhat promiscuously arranged in the text, are here put into order.

—— 2. The *ἀπολυτίκιον* of Sept. 1 (*Horolog.* p. 187) begins *ὁ πάσης δημιουργὸς τῆς κτίσεως, ὁ καιροὺς καὶ χρόνους ἐν τῇ ἰδίᾳ ἐξουσίᾳ θέμενος.*

—— 15. From the prayer Ὁ *μόνος καθαρός* of Symeon Metaphrastes in the *Ἀκολουθία τῆς ἁγίας μεταλήψεως* (the office of preparation and thanksgiving for Communion).

P. 20. 26. Imitated from *θάψον μου διὰ τῶν ἀγαθῶν λογισμῶν τὰ πονηρὰ διαβούλια* in the same prayer. Cp. p. 47 l. 11.

P. 21. 3. Cp. *Serm. Resurrect.* xviii (iii 102) '*Quicquid testamento legatur, sacramento dispensatur* "what the testament bequeatheth, that is dispensed in the holy mysteries."'

—— 20. S. Jer. *Ep.* lxvi 10: sive legas sive scribas, sive vigiles sive dormias, Amos tibi semper buccina in auribus sonet.

P. 22. These, except the last, are the ejaculations prefixed to the morning prayers for the several days of the week below, in the order of their occurrence, except that those for Thursday and Friday are reversed.

P. 23. 9. On 'the light of grace' and 'the light of glory' see *Serm. Pentec.* xiv (iii 316); and cp. S. Thom. Aq. *in Ps.* xxxv 9, and *Summa* i 12 § 5. Cp. *S. Paul's Lectt.* pp. 214, 176.

—— 11. See Introduction p. xx. In the earliest copies (that of *Ap. constt.* vii 47, where the text has been seriously modified by the editor, and that of *Codex Alexandrinus* of the Greek Bible) *Gloria in excelsis* or the 'Great doxology' is described as 'the morning prayer' or 'the morning hymn': and this represents its most widespread use, as part of Matins or Lauds. In the Roman rite, as in our own, it is used only in the mass. On its history see *Church Quarterly Review* xli, Oct. 1885. Lamphire's note says that the text is derived from *Cod. Alexandrinus* (A), but it differs from it in reading *μονογενὲς* for *μονογένη*, and in omitting *ἐλέησον ἡμᾶς* before *πρόσδεξαι*; but agrees with Ussher's text (*de Rom. eccl. symb.* p. 41).

P. 24. 2. *Δόξα σοι* is a common ejaculation in the *Horologion.*

—— 3 sqq. From the second prayer of S. Basil *Σὲ εὐλογοῦμεν* in Matins. Cp. *Ap. constt.* viii. 37 *ὁ ποιήσας ἡμέραν πρὸς ἔργα φωτὸς καὶ νύκτα εἰς ἀνάπαυσιν τῆς ἀσθενείας ἡμῶν.*

—— 7 sqq. The latter part of an *ektene* or litany in frequent use in the Byzantine liturgy and offices. The text here is generally that of Lit. S. Jas., which has borrowed the litany.

P. 25. 12. 'Superessential essence,' *οὐσία ὑπερούσιος* (Newman 'Essence beyond essence'). *Ὑπερούσιος* is a characteristic word of the Dionysian writings, describing the divine essence as transcending all being, so as to be in this sense 'not being,' and as the source and ground of all being (*Ep.* i: *ὑπὲρ οὐσίαν ὑπεριδρυμένος*: *de div. nom.* i *ὑπερούσιος οὐσία . . αἴτιον μὲν τοῦ εἶναι πᾶσιν, αὐτὸ δὲ μὴ ὂν ὡς πάσης αἰτίας ἐπέκεινα*). Its source is Neoplatonic: cp. Plotinus *Ennead.* v 4 § 1 *ὃ δὴ ἐπέκεινα λέγεται εἶναι οὐσίας* (Plato *Rep.* vi 509): Proclus *Instit. theol.* 138 *καὶ ὅλως πρὸ τῆς οὐσίας τὸ ὑπερούσιον ὂν . . καὶ ἐν ταῖς ἀρχαῖς ἄρα τοῦ ὄντος ἐπέκεινα εὐθὺς τὸ μὴ ὂν ὡς κρεῖττον τοῦ ὄντος καὶ ἕν*: *Plat. theol.* iii 20 *τὸ μόνως ὑπερούσιον καὶ ὑπερὸν . . . ὑπεροσύιος ὕπαρξις.* Cp. Clem. Al. *Strom.* v 11 p. 689: Orig. *c. Cels.* vi 64, *in Joan.* xix 1: S. Jo. Dam. *de fide orth.* i. 13. See p. 52.

—— 12, 13. *Ἄκτιστε φύσις ὁ τῶν ὅλων δημιουργὸς* the opening words of a *troparion* in Lauds.

—— 26. *Serm. Prayer* ii. (v 318). 'The sins which we commit against God are many; therefore He is the Father, not of one mercy, but *Pater misericordiarum.* The Apostle Peter tells us that the mercy of God is *multiformis gratia* (1 Pet. iv 10). So that whether we commit small sins or great, we may be bold to call upon God for mercy: "According to the multitude of thy mercies have mercy upon me" (Ps. li|1). For as our sins do abound, so the mercy of God whereby He pardoneth and is inclined to pardon us, is *exuberans gratia* (Rom. v 17).' Cp. *Pentec.* xiv (iii 371).

P. 25. 28. Simmons *Lay Folks Mass Book* (E.E.T.S.) p. 127 'wel may I Ioyeful for he makith . . . me a stynkynge worme for to taste of heuenly delyte.'

—— 32 sq. From the Lauds of Saturday: *εἰκών εἰμι τῆς ἀρρήτου δόξης σου, εἰ καὶ στίγματα φέρω πταισμάτων· οἰκτείρησον τὸ σὸν πλάσμα δέσποτα.*

P. 26. 3 sqq. From the collect *Benignissime domine Jesu* after the seven prayers of S. Gregory: also *Orat. post commun.* in *Hort. an.* Lyons 1516, f. 168.

—— 20. *Πανάγιον καὶ ἀγαθὸν καὶ ζωοποιόν*: the usual epithets of the Holy Ghost in Greek doxologies.

—— 28-30. This address is very common in the Synagogue service book.

—— 33 sq. From a prayer at the beginning of the Hebrew evening service: in part founded on Job xvii 12. The second line is found in A*p. constt.* viii. 34 *ὄρθρου μὲν εὐχαριστοῦντες ὅτι ἐφώτισεν ἡμᾶς ὁ Κύριος παραγαγὼν τὴν νύκτα καὶ ἐπαγαγὼν τὴν ἡμέραν.*

P. 27. 11. Cp. *Serm. Pentec.* ix (iii 269) 'But I, saith God, let Me take it in hand, let Me blow with my wind and "I scatter thy transgressions as a mist and make thy sins like a morning cloud to vanish away."' But neither this nor the text is found, as it stands, in the Bible. Cp. Ken *Manual*, Morning Prayers, 'O do away as the night my transgressions, scatter my sins as the morning cloud'—which is probably borrowed from Andrewes. Cp. *Serm. Pentec.* ix (iii 266) 'The Scriptures speak of sin sometime as of a frost; otherwhile as of a mist or fog that men are lost in, to be dissolved and so blown away': *Repent.* iii (i 349) 'O the damp and mist of our sin! so great that it darkeneth not only the light of religion which God teacheth, but even the light of nature which her instinct teacheth.'

—— 15. This line is rendered by Andrewes himself from the verse of *Te Deum*, and is not in the form found among the versicles following the *Gloria in excelsis*, *Horolog.* pp. 71, 168.

—— 19. I.e. *Meribah* and *Massah* (R.V.). *Serm. on the Temptation* iv (v 513) 'As before the devil brought Him to the waters of Meribah, where the children of Israel did murmur and tempt God; so now he brings Him to the temptation of Massah, that is presumption, wantonness, and delicacy.'

—— 32. *I.e.* let me today make some advance in knowledge or practice on yesterday.

P. 28. 21. *Serm. Repentance* iv (i 361) 'After we once left our first way which was "right," there takes us sometimes that same *singultus cordis*, as Abigail well calls it, a "throbbing of the heart."' *Pentec.* vi (iii 204) 'Eschew them [greater sins] for that they breed *singultum et scrupulum cordis*, "the upbraiding or vexing of the heart," as Abigail excellently termeth it.' Cp. *S. Paul's Lectt.* p. 140.

P. 28. 32. S. Chrys. *Orat.* 2 (xii 803 B) καὶ τοὺς ἀδελφοὺς οὓς σὺ δέδωκας.

P. 30. 9 sq. *Serm. Repentance* v (i 390) 'We feel this or we feel nothing, that dull is our devotion and our prayers full of yawning, when the brain is thick with the vapour and the heart pressed down with the charge of the stomach; and that our devotion and all else is performed, as Tertullian saith, *pollentiori mente* and *vivaciore corde*, "our wits more fresh, our spirits more about us" [*de ieiun.* 6], while we are *in virgine saliva*, yet in "our fasting spittle"; when fasting and prayer are not asunder, but we serve God in both. Our morning prayer, that that is the "incense," saith the Psalm; our evening is but "the stretching out of our hands" in comparison of it, faint and heavy.'

—— 14 sqq. This collect is also in *Hortulus animae* Lyons 1516, f. 76.

P. 31. 5 sqq. The prayer *pro locutione accepta* in *Hort. an.* 1516 f. 183 b; and used before the Gospel in the missals of York (Maskell *Anc. Lit. of Ch. of Engl.* p. 66) and Evesham (Wilson *Liber Evesham.* c. 7).

—— 31 sq. Cp. S. Bernard *Confessio* init.: abyssus profundissima miseriæ meæ abyssum invocat altissimæ misericordiæ tuæ: Theophylact *in Ps.* xli (iv 550) τὸ ἄμετρον τῶν ἡμετέρων ἁμαρτιῶν τὸ ἄμετρον τῶν σῶν ἐπικαλεῖται οἰκτιρμῶν (so Euthymius *in loc.*): Savonarola *in Ps.* li 1 (printed in *Prymer* Rouen 1536, and translated in *A goodly prymer* 1535).

P. 32. 8 sqq. See also *Horae* 1494 f. 3; *Prymer* 1537 f. 11 b.

—— 14 sq. *Horae* f. 78 'O bone iesu si merui miser peccator de vera tua iusticia penam eternam pro peccatis meis grauissimis: adhuc appello confisus de tua iusticia vera ad tuam misericordiam ineffabilem.' Cp. F. Bacon *Works*, ed. Ellis and Spedding vii p. 260: 'in Him, O Lord, we appeal from thy justice to thy mercy.' Cp. pp. 146, 167. *Serm. Pentec.* iii (iii 152) '*Sedens in solio iustitiæ* as to some, "in his tribunal seat of strict justice": there sitting sentence will proceed otherwise than *si adeamus thronum gratiæ*, if we have access to Him in his "throne of grace," where we may "obtain mercy and find grace." And St James brings us good tidings that *supexaltat* etc.; the throne of grace is the higher court, and so an appeal lieth thither, to whom He will admit.' Cp. *Serm. Repent.* viii (i 436), *Gunpowder Tr.* vii (iv 328).

—— 24 sqq. From *A general and deuowte prayer for the gode state of our moder the churche milylante here in erth* Omnipotens et misericors deus.

P. 32. 30 sq. From the prayer to S. Gabriel *Precor et te o princeps:* also in *Horae* 1494 f. 70.

—— 36 sqq. *Spittle Sermon* (v 15) 'There is yet of this feather another kind of exalting ourselves above that we ought, much to be complained of in these days. St Paul calleth it "a stretching of ourselves beyond measure" (2 Cor. x 14). Thus if a man be attained to any high skill in law, which is a gift of God; or if a man be grown wise, and experienced well in the affairs of this world, which is also his good blessing; presently by virtue of this they take themselves to be so qualified as they be able to overrule our matters in divinity, able to prescribe Bishops how to govern and Divines how to preach; so to determine our cases as if they were professed with us; and that, many times affirming things they know not and censuring things they have little skill of. Now seeing we take not upon us to deal in cases of your law or in matters of your trade, we take this is a stretching beyond your line; that in so doing you are a people that control the priest (Hos. iv 4); that you are too high when you set yourselves over them that "are over you in the Lord" (1 Th. v 12); and that this is no part of that sober wisdom which St Paul commendeth to you (Rom. xii 3), but of that cup-shotten wisdom which he there condemneth. Which breaking compass and outreaching is, no doubt, the cause of these lamentable rents and ruptures in the Lord's net in our days. For "only by pride cometh contention," saith the Wise Man [Prov. xiii 10]. Which point I wish might be looked upon and amended. Sure it will mar all in the end.' *Concio ad clerum* (*Opuscula* p. 49) Idem ille *Populus* noster quam porro procax? ut non modo *Artifices*, sed et *mulierculæ* iam, et operæ tabernariæ, immiscere se quæstionibus Ecclesiasticis, et quasi in Synodo, sic in officina aliqua abundare istud in Ecclesia, deesse illud, nimis petulanter decernere.

P. 33. 13-16. From the great intercession of the liturgy of S. Basil (*Litt. E. and W.* p. 407).

—— 15. 'Comfortably' εἰς τὴν καρδίαν: cp. Is. xl 2.

—— 20 sq. *Serm. Spittle* (v 14) 'And not only this passing the ability is dangerous to the overturning of a commonwealth, but the passing of a man's condition too; and tendeth to the impoverishing and at last to the overthrow of the estate also. 1. Whether it be excess of diet; as when, being no magistrate, but plain Master Nabal, his dinner must be "like to the feast of a king" (1 Sam. xxv 36). 2. Or whether it be in excess of apparel, wherein the pride of England now, as "the pride" of Ephraim in times past, "testifieth aginst her to her face" (Hos. v 5). 3. Or whether it be "in lifting up the gate too high" (Prov. xvii 19), that is, in excess of building. 4. Or whether it be in keeping too great a train, Esau's case, that he go with "four hundred" men at his tail (Gen. xxxii 6), whereas the fourth part of the fourth part would have served his father well enough. 5. Or whether it be in perking too high in their alliance; the bramble's son in Lebanon must match with the cedar's daughter (2 Kings xiv 9). These are evidences and signs set down to prove a high mind: see and search into yourselves, whether you find them or no.' Cp. Green *English People* vii 5 'It was not wholly with satisfaction that either Elizabeth or her ministers watched the social change which wealth was producing around them. They feared the increased expenditure and comfort which necessarily followed it, as likely to impoverish the land and to eat out the hardihood of the people. "England spendeth more on wines in one year," complained Cecil, "that it did in ancient times in four years."' See also *Opuscula* p. 49.

P. 34. 1 sq. From the prayer *Omnes sancte virgines*.
—— 12 sqq. From the *Domine Iesu Christe fili Dei vivi*.

P. 35. 3 sq. *S. Paul's Lect.* p. 93: 'There is a partition wall, there is a difference, between this work of man and all the former. The stile now is changed, *fiet & fit* into *faciamus*: God before was a Commander, now he is a Counsellor: *Quis est* (saith a Father) *qui formabitur ut tanta sit opus prospectione.* Before with saying *fit & fiat, facta sunt*: but here in *faciamus* is deliberation, for that he now makes him, for whom all the former creatures were made. . . . Austin saith well *Fecit alia præmissa ut procul stans, at hominem ut prope accedens, porrigens manum.* God framed man out of the earth, as doth the Potter his pot out of the clay, *As the clay is in the potters hand, so is the house of Israel in Gods hand* (Jer. xviii 6). We are not only the sheep of his pasture, but the sheep also of his hands, *He made us and not wee our selves.*' Cp. *Serm. Prayer* vii (v 365): and pp. 88, 211 below. With the whole passage in the text cp. S. Chrys. *ad eos qui scandalizantur* (iii 480); S. Bas. *Reg. fusius tractata* ii 3 sq. (iii 338 D): S. Aug. *de civ. Dei* vii 30, 31, *Enar. in Pss.* lxx[1] 15, cxliv 6; and the thanksgiving of the oriental liturgies, esp. S. James and S. Basil.
—— 12. *Serm. Prayer* vii (v 366) 'When man was fallen from his first estate, God opened to him a door of repentance; which favour He hath not vouchsafed to the angels that fell.'
—— 16. Cp. pp. 40, 211.
—— 23 sq. See *Serm. Nativ.* iv (i 45 sqq.).
—— 25. *Ib.* i (i 1 sqq.).
—— 26 sqq. *Ib.* iv (i 52-57), xii (i 206), *Temptation* i (v 479).
—— 30 sqq. See on p. 4 l. 12. Cp. *Serm. Pent.* iii (iii 148) 'Candlemas-day: He was presented in the Temple, offered as a live oblation for us, that so the obedience of his whole life might be ours. Good-Friday: made a slain sacrifice on the cross, that we might be redeemed by the benefit of his death': *Justif.* (v 120) 'Why should there be a necessary use

of the sacrifice of Christ's death for the one, and not a use full as necessary of the oblation of his life for the other?': *S. Giles* p. 571 'Christ . . was an oblation offered in the morning, when He was presented to God his Father, that He would for us yield obedience to the Law; and in his death was an evening oblation.' Cp. *Nativ.* iv (i 56).

P. 35. 37. See *S. Giles' Serm.* p. 621 sq.

P. 36. 7 sq. *Serm. Res.* ii (ii 210) 'If it [the Resurrection] be not credible, how is it credible that the world could believe it? the world, I say, being neither enjoined by authority, nor forced by fear, nor inveigled by allurements: but brought about by persons, by means less credible than the thing itself.'

—— 11. See *Responsio ad Bellarmin.* p. 457.

—— 19 sqq. *Spittle Sermon* (v 30; preached in 1588) '"That giveth us things to enjoy plenteously." "Plenteously" indeed, may Israel now say, said the Prophet: may England now say, say I, and I am sure upon as great cause. He hath not dealt so with every nation; nay "He hath not dealt so with any nation" (Ps. cxlvii 20). And "plenteously" may England now say, for it could not always; nay, it could not ever have said the like. "Plenteously" indeed, for He hath not sprinkled, but poured his benefits upon us. Not only "blessed be the people whose God is the Lord," that blessing which is highly to be esteemed if we had none besides it, but "blessed be the people that are in such a case." That blessing He hath given us, "all things to enjoy plenteously": we cannot, nay our enemies cannot but confess it. O that our thankfulness to Him, and our bounty to his, might be as plenteous as his gifts and goodness have been plenteous to us.' Cp. *Serm. Lent* iii (ii 56: in 1593), *On giving Cæsar his due* (v 140: in 1601).

—— 28 sq. *Serm. Pentec.* ii (iii 142) 'Intending, as it seemeth, a part of our Pentecostal duty should be, not only to give thanks for them He first sent on the very day, but even for those He sent ever since: for those He still sendeth, even in these days of ours. To thank Him for the Apostles: thank him for the ancient Doctors and Fathers: thank Him for those we have, if we have any so much worth. And are these the "gifts" which Christ sent "from on high"? Was St Paul well advised? Must we keep our Pentecost in thanksgiving for these? Are they worth so much, trow? We would be loath to have the Prophet's way taken with us, that it should be said to us as there it is; If you so reckon of them indeed, let us see the wages you value them at; and when we shall see it is but eight pound a year, and having once so much, never to be capable of more, may not then the Prophet's speech there well be taken up, "A goodly price" (Zech. xi 13) these high gifts are valued at by you! and may not He justly, instead of Zachary and such as he is, send us a sort of foolish shepherds; and send us this senselessness withal, that speak they never so fondly, so they speak, all is well, it shall serve our turn as well as the best of them all? Sure if this be a part of our duty this day to praise God for them, it is to be a part of our care too, they may be such as we may justly praise God for. Which whether we shall be likely to effect by such courses as of late have been offered, that leave I to the weighing of your wise considerations' (1608). For his estimate of the clergy in 1593, see the Convocation sermon, *Opuscula* 31 sqq., especially p. 48: Querela vetus est, nec iam querela sed *clamor:* Sacris initiatos per vos [the bishops] inque ordinem hunc nostrum ascitos *novissimos populi;* nec modo ignaros penitus atque illiteratos, sed et infamiæ notis aspersos ac omni flagitiorum genere contaminatos. Et sane hinc aliquo ab annis, hoc in genere largiter peccatum est. At iam cura id fit et virtute vestra (Patres) ut amoveantur hinc demum multi quo digni sunt. Bonum factum: factum et Deo approbante et cælo favente et hominibus acclamantibus *Fiat, fiat.* Quare ut magis magisque fiat, quod ita factum placet, precibus apud vos summis intercedit Ecclesia.

P. 37. 6. Cp. *Serm. on Absolution* (v 95) 'I take it (S. Jo. xx 23) . . . to be the accomplishment of the promise made, of the power of "the keys" (S. Mt. xvi 19) which here in this place and in these words is fulfilled, and have therein for me the joint consent of the Fathers. Which . . . is that which we all call the act or benefit of absolution, in which . . . there is in the due time and place of it a use for the remission of sins. Whereunto our Saviour Christ, by his sending them doth institute them and give them the key of authority; and by breathing on them and inspiring them doth enable them and give them the key of knowledge to do it well; and having bestowed both these upon them as the stewards of his house, doth last of all deliver them their commission to do it, having so enabled them and authorised them as before.' Cp. pp. 213, 225.

—— 12. For conclusions see pp. 87, 225, 230.

P. 38. 25. See on p. 27 l. 11.

P. 40. 7. *Heb. Morning Prayer* p. 37 'who didst form light . . . didst enlighten the earth.' *Horolog.* p. 82 (final prayer of Prime) ὁ ποιῶν ὄρθρον καὶ φωτίζων πᾶσαν τὴν οἰκουμένην: so Coptic morning prayer, Bute *Coptic morning service* p. 124.

—— 9 sq. *Serm. Gunpowder Tr.* i (iv 217) '"Open me" saith he at the nineteenth verse, "the gates of righteousness," that is the church door—his house would not hold him—thither will "I go in" and there in the congregation, in the great congregation, "give thanks to the Lord." And that so great a congregation, that it may *constituere diem solennem in condensis ad cornua altaris* "that they may stand so thick in the church, as fill it from the entry of the door to the very edge of the altar."' The right rendering of the Hebrew 'Bind the sacrifice with cords, even unto the horns of the altar,' is noticed *ib.* p. 221. On the rendering in the English Primers, see Maskell *Mon. rit.* iii p. 45.

P. 40. 11 sqq. *Serm. Prayer* ii (v 317) 'Because He is that only cause of the visible light which at the first He created, and also of that spiritual light whereby He shineth into our hearts by "the light of the Gospel" (2 Cor. iv 4), the Apostle saith of the whole Trinity *Deus lux est* (1 Jo. i 5).' On the seven lights of which God is 'the Father' (S. Ja. i. 17) see *Serm. Pentec.* xiv (iii 372) esp. "2. There is the light of God's Law: *Lex lux*, saith Solomon *totidem verbis* (Prov. vi 23); and his father, "a lantern to his feet" (Ps. cxix 105). Nay, in the nineteenth Psalm what he saith at the fourth verse of the "sun," at the eighth he saith the same of "the Law of God"—lights both. 3. The light of Prophecy, as of "a candle that shineth in a dark place" (2 Pet. i 19). 4. There is "the wonderful light" of his Gospel, so St Peter calls it (1 Pet. ii 9), the proper light of this day. The tongues that descended—so many "tongues," so many "lights"; for the tongue is a light, and brings to light what was before hid in the heart.'

—— 14. φῶς νοητόν: the spiritual light, 'the light of grace.' Used of God in Dionys. Areop. *de div. nom.* iv 5 (i 557) φῶς νοητὸν ὁ ἀγαθὸς λέγεται διὰ τὸ πάντα μὲν ὑπερουράνιον νοῦν ἐμπιμπλάναι νοητοῦ φωτὸς, πᾶσαν δὲ ἄγνοιαν καὶ πλάνην ἐλαύνειν ἐκ πασῶν αἷς ἂν ἐγγένηται ψυχαῖς. S. Aug. *Solil.* i Deus intelligibilis lux (i 356). S. Bas. *Hexaëm.* i 5, has it of the premundane light; and Andrewes *Serm. Prayer* ii (v 316) calls the angels "the intellectual lights."

—— 16-21. See p. 35 l. 16.

—— 22 I.e. 'the light of glory.' *Serm. Pentec.* xiv (iii 376) '*Ascendat oratio, descendet miseratio* "let our prayer go up to Him that His grace may come down to us," so to lighten us in our ways and works that we may in the end come to dwell with Him, in the light which is φῶς ἀνέσπερον "light whereof there is no eventide," the sun whereof never sets, nor knows tropic.' *Nativ.* xv (i 251) 'Christ "the bright morning Star" of that day which shall have no night.' The phrase occurs in S. Methodius *Convivium* (Migne *P. G.* xviii 209) applied to our Lord: and in *Euchology.* p. 289, *Triodion* p. 27. Cp. S. Bas. *Hexaëm.* ii 8; S. Cæsarius of Pontus *Dial.* iii 116; [S. Aug.] *Solill.* 35: o dies præclara, nesciens vesperum, non habens occasum.

—— 24. From the prayer of Simeon Metaphrastes before communion, *Horolog.* p. 474. μετανοίας τρόπος occurs in S. Bas. *in Ps.* i 2 (i 91 c). Cp. p. 19 l. 15.

—— 25 sqq. *Serm. Res.* xviii (iii 80 sqq.) is in Heb. xiii 20, 21.

P. 41. 5 sqq. The characteristic *troparion* of Terce. See on p. 19.

P. 41. 17, 25. The Hebrew as it stands in the MS. is unintelligible; but it is obviously meant for Job xxxiii 27, which is quoted, with the Hebrew, also in *Serm. Pentec.* xv (iii 399).

— 23. *Serm. Repent.* iii (i 347) '"What have I done?" 1. What, in respect of itself! what a foul, deformed, base, ignominious act! which we shame to have known, which we chill upon, alone and nobody but ourselves. 2. What, in regard of God, so fearful in power, so glorious in majesty! 3. What, in regard of the object! for what a trifling profit, for what a transitory pleasure! 4. What, in respect of the consequent! to what prejudice of the state of our souls and bodies, both here and forever! O what have we done? How did we it? Sure, when we thus sinned, we did we know not what.'

— 30. Andrewes quotes Hos. xiii 9 as *perditio tua ex te Israel* (*Serm. Gowries* vi [iv 142], *Prayer* i [v 308]). So also S. Thomas quotes it, *Summa* ii^{2} 112 § 3 ad 2. It is not the reading of any Biblical text, but it represents the traditional interpretation; see *Homilies* i 2 fin., *Glossa ordinaria*, Hugo, a Lapide, Pusey *ad loc.*

P. 42. 1. *Euchologion* p. 556 *νικησάτω τὸ πλῆθος τῶν οἰκτιμῶν σου τὸ τῶν ἁμαρτιῶν ἡμῶν πονηρὸν σύστημα*: 373 *σὺ γὰρ εἶ ὁ γινώσκων τὸ πολὺ τῶν ἁμαρτιῶν μου πλῆθος ἀλλ' ἡ σὴ εὐσπλαγχνία νικήσει τούτων τὸ ἄμετρον*: cp. 226.

— 17 sqq. This is a favourite topic with Andrewes: see pp. 146, 173: *Serm. Prayer* vii (v 365 sq.), xvii (457), xviii (462), *Pentec.* vii (iii 228).

— 23. *Eucholog.* p. 229 (prayer against evil thoughts) *πλάσμα σόν εἰμι· μὴ παρίδῃς ἔργον χειρῶν σου.*

— 25 sqq. *Serm. Nat.* xi (i 180) 'And her [mercy's] plea is *nunquid in vanum?* "What, hath God made all men for nought?" "What profit is there in their blood?" It will make God's enemies rejoice. Thither it will come if God cast them clean off. What then, "will He cast them off for ever, will He be no more entreated?"'

P. 43. 7. See *Serm. Prayer* iv (v 332 sqq.).

— 10. Cp. *Serm. Gunpowder Tr.* iv (iv 272) 'But in this word of the Prophet's there is yet more than "bowels." *Ma'îm* were enough for them: *rahmîm* are more, are the bowels or vessels near the womb, near the loins; in a word, not *viscera* only, but *parentum viscera*, the bowels of a father or mother, those are *rahmîm*, which adds more force a great deal. See them in the parable of the father towards his riotous lewd son; when he had consumed all viciously, his fatherly bowels of compassion failed him not though. See them in the story of David towards his ungracious imp Absalom, that sought his crown, sought his life, abused his concubines in the sight of all Israel; yet hear the bowels of a father, "Be good to the youth Absalom, hurt him not, use him well for my sake" (2 Sam. xviii. 8). See them in the better harlot of the twain; out of her motherly bowels, rather give away her child quite, renounced it rather than see it hurt. This is mercy, here is compassion indeed. *O paterna viscera miserationum!* When we have named them, a multitude of such mercies as come from a father's bowels, we have said as much as we can say or can be said. Cp. *ib.* p. 276, 322, S. Bern. *Serm.* i *in Annunc.* 9: *paterna viscera;* F. Bacon *Prayer* 'fatherly compassions.'

P. 43. 20 sqq. Cp. *S. Giles' Lect.* p. 549: 'Because we are by nature inclined to forget them which we commit in our youth, and have been committed in former time by our Fathers; therefore we must beware that we provoke not God to punish us for them. *When the wicked Servant forgot his old debt, which his Lord forgave him and began again to deal cruelly with his fellow,* this forgetfulness made God to reverse his purgation (S. Mt. xviii)' S. Chrys. *hom.* xxxi *in Heb.* 3 (xii 289 B) μέγα ἀγαθὸν ἐπιγινώσκειν τὰ ἁμαρτήματα καὶ μιμνήσκεσθαι αὐτῶν διηνεκῶς· οὐδὲν οὕτω θεραπεύει πλημμέλειαν ὡς μνήμη διηνεκής . . μὴ ἁμαρτωλοὺς καλῶμεν ἑαυτοὺς μόνον ἀλλὰ καὶ τὰ ἁμαρτήματα ἀναλογιζώμεθα κατ' εἶδος ἕκαστον ἀναλέγοντες.

—— 27. 'I am weary': προσοχθίζω in the lxx represents several Heb. words in the O.T.: Gen. xxvii 46 (be weary), Lev. xviii 25 (vomit out), xxvi 44 (abhor), 1 Chr. xxi 6 (be abominable to), Ps. xxii 24 (abhor), xxxvi 4 (abhor) xcv 10 (be grieved with).

—— 28. *Serm. Repent.* iv (i 372) 'So was Job, "Therefore I abhor myself." "Myself," saith he; not so much the sin which was done and past and so incapable of anger, but myself for the sin. Which if it be indignation indeed in us, and not a gentle word, will seek revenge some way or other.'

—— 29. Cp. pp. 130, 161, 165. *Notes on Book of Common Prayer* (*Minor Works* p. 147) '*That be penitent:* that desire to be penitent, wish they were, would be glad if they were so, fear they are not enough; are sorry that they are no more.' Cp. *Primer* 1545, f. KK. 3 b 'my soule mourneth for sorow, most merciful father, that I am not a thousand times sorier then I am' (*Three Primers* p. 525): *Form of Prayer* 1572 (*Lit. Services of Q. Elizabeth* p. 543) 'we are sorry therefore, o Lord, yea we are most sorry, that we are no more sorry for our sins.'

—— 30 sq. Cp. *Serm. Pent.* iii (iii 153) '"We keep, Lord, help our not keeping" as well as "I believe, Lord, help my unbelief."'

—— 33. Cp. p. 127, 160. *Serm. Repent.* iv (i 372) '"Grind to powder, break in pieces," at least make a "rent." *Contritio, confractio, conscissio, compunctio,* somewhat it will be': *S. Giles' Lect.* p. 613 'There are three degrees of operation in Gods word: Contrition, when *the heart is broken,* Ps. li. Comfort, when *it is rent in two pieces,* Joel ii. Compunction, when *it is pricked only,* Acts ii. The first is the perfection.

The second is a degree under it. And the last and lowest degree is Compunction, which we see was not rejected in Peters hearers.'

P. 43. 35. Ἄνες ἄφες συγχώρησον is a common combination in the Greek service-books.

— 36. See on p. 28 l. 21.

P. 44. 8 sqq. A verse from each of the Penitential Psalms. It is related that S. Augustine in his last sickness had the 'very few' penitential psalms written out and affixed to the wall beside his bed where he could see and read them (Possidius *Vita Aug.* 31); but it is not said which or how many they were ('seven' in *Serm. Temptation* iii [v 505] is Andrewes' addition). The seven are first enumerated in Cassiodorus (c. 490) *in Ps.* vi (Migne *P.L.* lxx 60 A); and a *Comment. in psalmos poenitent.* is among the works of S. Gregory the Great (iii pars 2, p. 467) but is probably not his. Cp. *Serm. Repent.* viii (i 443) 'The Penitential Psalms shew this, that they were chosen for no other end but to be a task for penitential persons.'

— 28 sqq. *Serm. Res.* xviii (iii 98) 'But in the doing of all or any, beside our part, εἰς τὸ ποιῆσαι, here is also ποιῶν ἐν ὑμῖν, a worker besides [Heb. xiii 21] . . He leaves us not to ourselves . . but to that outward application of ours joins his ποιῶν ἐν ὑμῖν, an inward operation of his own inspiring, his grace, which is nothing but the breath of the Holy Ghost. Thereby enlightening our minds, inclining our wills, working on our affections, making us *homines bonæ voluntatis;* that when we have done well, we may say with the Prophet, *Domine universa opera nostra operatus es in nobis*, "Lord all our good works Thou hast wrought in us."'

— 32 sqq. A paraphrase of the X Commandments. The *Pattern of Catechistical Doctrine* is mainly a detailed exposition of the decalogue.

— 33 sq. *Cat. doct.* p. 82 'The first commandment hath in it three things, 1. We must have a God, 2. Him for our God, 3. Him alone and none else.' 'Beside' or 'apart from' (παρεκτός) apparently represents Ex. xx 3 '*al-pānāi*, πλήν ἐμοῦ, *coram me*, and Is. xlv 5 *zûtāthî*, πλήν, *extra:* 'with' (σύν) Deut. xxxii 39 '*immādî*, πλὴν ἐμοῦ, *praeter me*. *Resp. ad Bellarm.* p. 274: utrumque vero in vitio est, tam cum Creatore, quam pro Creatore, creaturam adorare.

— 35 sqq. *S. Giles' Lect.* p. 637: 'For as in the first Commandment of the Law, we must serve God in the truth of the spirit; so in the second Commandment, in the service of the body; in the third with the blessing of the mouth, we must blesse and praise God, that is, we must professe our Godlinesse at all times and all occasions; not only privately, but publiquely, in the fourth Commandment, that is, intirely, by all the parts of the body, even with the tongue which is our glory, especially on the day of our publique profession; not only to have a reverent opinion of God, but as the Church calls us, *Come, let us fall down before the Lord*, Ps. xcv; not only to say with the Apostle, Rom. vii, *I serve God in my spirit*, but Eph. iii, *I bow my knees to God the Father*.' On 'blessing of mouth' see *Serm. Gunpowder Tr.* ix (iv 376).

P. 45. 1. *Serm. Imaginations* (v 60) 'Imaginations touching the ceremony. First I take it to be a fancy to imagine there needs none; for without them neither comeliness nor orderly uniformity will be in the Church. Women will "pray uncovered" (an uncomely sight) unless the Apostle enjoin the contrary (1 Cor. xi 13): therefore, "Let everything be done decently and in order" (1 Cor. xiv 40) . . . And the custom of each Church is peaceably to be observed by the members of it. In a matter ceremonial, touching the veiling of women—after some reasons alleged, which yet a troublesome body might quarrel with—thus doth St Paul determine the matter definitively: "If any list to be contentious *nos non habemus talem consuetudinem nec Ecclesiae Dei.*"' Cp. *Pestilence* (v 231).

—— 14. Ἀληθεύειν ἐν ἀγάπῃ is so rendered in *Cat. doct.* p. 265. R.V. marg. 'deal truly.'

—— 18. The 'Hedge of the Law' was the name given to the mass of rabbinic casuistical ordinances directed 'to prevent any breach of the Law or customs, to ensure their exact observance or to meet peculiar circumstances and dangers' (Edersheim *Life and Times of Jesus the Messiah* i p. 101) *i.e.* to fence men off from the danger of violating the Law. *Pirqê abhôth* i 1: 'Moses received the Law on Sinai and handed it down to Joshua; Joshua to the elders; the elders to the prophets; and the prophets handed it down to the men of the Great Synagogue. They said three things: Be deliberate in judgement, raise up many disciples and make a hedge to the Law'; iii 17 'Rabbi Aqiba said . . The Massorah [oral tradition] is a hedge to the Law; tithes are a hedge to riches; vows are a hedge to abstinence: silence is a hedge to wisdom.' In *S. Paul's Lectures* p. 135 Andrewes says of ceremonies: 'some were appointed as closures or fences, to inclose or defend or aid the Law, as the sixth Precept had this Ceremonie for his fence *That men should eat no blood, to signifie unto them how greatly they should abhor murder.*' In *Cat. doct.* p. 7 he mentions another use of the phrase: 'One calleth the two heads to which Christ drew the Law and the prophets [S. Mt. xxii 37 sqq.] *sepem legis* "the hedge of the Law," lest we might waver and wander *in infinito campo* "in an infinite field."'

—— 19. *S. Giles' Lect.* p. 692 'By the Serpent's head is meant the first suggestion whereby he stirreth up to sinne; which albeit in the beginning it were strong when he tempted *Eve*, yet since the promise Christ hath weakned it notwithstanding, as Christ resisted the first suggestion (S. Mt. iv), so must we, after his example, begin at the weakest part, even at the first suggestions and provocations, which seem to us to be nothing; which the Prophet signified by *the children of Babel, which he would have dashed to the stones* (Ps. cxxxvii). In that respect it is that the Church would have the little Foxes destroyed that hurt the Vines (Cant. ii 12). And the Prophets counsel is, *That we tread upon the Cockatrice egge, lest it prove a Serpent* (Is. lix 5). . . . The Nettle if it be lightly touched will sting and prick, but if it be crushed hard in a mans hand, it looseth the power. So if we dally with sinne, it will sting us, but if we bruise the very head of it, that is, the first motions, then it shall not hurt us.' Cp. S. Greg. Mag. *Mor. in Job.* i 53 caput quippe serpentis observare est initia suggestionis eius aspicere et manu sollicitæ considerationis a cordis aditu funditus extirpare. Cp. Cassian *Instit.* iv 37: S. Aug. *Enarr. in Ps. xlviii* i 6.

P. 45. 20. *Serm. Lent.* v (ii 93) '*Utinam novissima providerent* (Deut. xxxii 29) "Would God," saith Moses, "men would remember the four *novissima*"; 1. that there is a death; 2. there is a judgment: 3. there is a Heaven: 4. there is a hell. But of all the four *Novissima inferni* in the same chapter (*ib.* 22), "the nethermost"; *Nunc igitur cruciaris* "the place of torments" [S. Lk. xvi 25]. The Prophets said as much. Jeremy—Ever think that an end there will be, *Et quid fiet in novissimo*, "what shall become of us in that end?" (Jer. v 31). "Who among us," saith Esay, "can endure devouring fire?" who can dwell with *ardores sempiterni*, "everlasting burnings" (Is. xxxiii 14).' Cp. *Cat. doct.* p. 89.

—— 21. *S. Giles' Lect.* p. 692: "The Fathers out of *Adams* temptation made four degrees of our spiritual battail, the Man, the Woman, the Serpent, the Tree. By Man they understand reason; by the Woman, the sensuality and carnall affections of our mindes; by the Serpent, the Devil; by the Tree, the occasion. Concerning which, as it is good counsel to hear this spoken, "Command *Eve*"; so it is better counsel, "Take heed of the Serpent, and thou shalt be safe; but if thou doe not look upon the tree, thou shalt be safer." For if we avoid the occasion of sinne, then shall not our concupiscence be stirred up; but he that maketh no conscience to shun the occasion, he loveth danger, and as the Wise man saith, *he shall perish therein*': *ib.* p. 402 sq. '*We may not plough for sin* (Prov. xxi 4), as if he should say, sinne will come fast enough in the fallow grounds; therefore we need not to provoke ourselves by pictures, lewd songs, enterludes, and such like means to draw it to us, but to abandon them all. It is this which the Apostle exhorts all men to (2 Cor. xi 12), *to cut off all occasions to sinne*, observing what that is that provoketh them to sinne, and cut that off that we draw not sinne to our selves and so be accessary to sinne and cause of our own woe: If the water be comming, that we give no passage to it; if the coals lye before you, spit on it you may, but beware you blow it not: and if sinne would have passage, stop it.' Cp. *Repent.* iv (i 365).

P. 45. 22. *Serm. Temptation* ii (v 491) 'And as at all times we are to use watchfulness and carefulness, so then especially, when we look that the devil will be most busy.'

—— 23. *S. Giles' Lect.* p. 526: 'To avoid all temptations, we must occupie our selves in godly meditation, as Augustine saith *Semper te diabolus inveniat occupatum*': *Temptation* i (v 483) 'The state of a man regenerate by baptism is not a standing still. "He found others standing idle in the market place and He said to them, Why stand ye idle all day?" (S. Matt. xx 6). We must not only have a mortifying and reviving, but a "quickening" and stirring "spirit," which will move us and cause us to proceed; we must not lie still like lumps of flesh, laying all upon Christ's shoulders.' Cp. *Cat. doct.* p. 239 sq.

—— 24. 'The evil' i.e. evil persons. *Repent.* iv (i 365) 'For conversion hath no greater enemy than conversing with such of whom our heart telleth us, there is neither faith nor fear of God in them.' Cp. *Res.* vii (ii 306).

—— 25. *S. Giles' Lect.* p. 638 'If we esteem of places and times of godlinesse aright, and cleave to the persons that professe godlinesse, as Acts xvii 34 *Dionysius* and *Damaris*; they that doe so, shew Godlinesse.' Cp. the quotation κολλᾶσθε τοῖς ἁγίοις ὅτι οἱ κολλώμενοι αὐτοῖς ἁγιασθήσονται in S. Clem. Rom. *ad Cor.* xlvi 2, Clem. Al. *Strom.* v 8 § 53 (p. 677): cp. Hermas *Pastor* Vis. iii 6, Sim. viii 8, 9, ix 20, 26.

—— 26. *Serm. Prayer* xvi. (v 447) 'Therefore, if we will not be led into temptation . . . we must make "a covenant with our eyes," so we shall not be tempted.'

—— 27. *Serm. Repent.* viii (i 445 sq.) '*Castigo corpus* serves for what hath been done: *in servitutem redigo* serves, that he do it no more. . . . This latter we call "amendment of life"; which is not repentance, for it pertains rather to πρόνοια than to μετάνοια, being yet to come, but it never fails to follow it infallibly, insomuch as if it do not, nothing is done. For I report me to you; let it be but known to the flesh that this same light or slight repentance shall not serve the turn, but to a round reckoning it shall come and make full account to taste of these fruits throughly, without hope of being dispensed with, whether it will not take off the edge of our appetite, and make it more dull and fearful to offend?'

—— 28, 29. *Serm. Prayer* xvi (v 447) 'As we must forbear the occasion of sin, so must we use the means that may keep us from it, that is prayer.' *Repent.* viii (i 452 sq.) 'There be two words, words of weight; one is St Peter's, and that is χωρῆσαι εἰς μετάνοιαν "to withdraw, go aside, to retire and be private, to sequester ourselves to our repentance";

the other is St Paul's σχολάζειν προσευχῇ καὶ νηστείᾳ, "to take us a time, nay to make us a time, a vacant time, a time of leisure to intend fasting and prayer," two fruits of repentance. . . . I doubt ours hath been rather a flash, a qualm, a brunt, than otherwise; rather a gourd of repentance than any growing tree (Jonah iv 10).' Cp. *ib.* iii p. 350, iv p. 369, v p. 380, 390.

P. 45. 30 sqq. S. Gregory the Great combines Hos. ii 6 and S. Lk. xiv 24 in *Hom.* xxxvi *in Evang.* 9.

—— 33 sqq. *Serm. Prayer* xi (v 401) '*In chamo et fraeno constringe maxillas meas*, saith an ancient Father; and upon the words of Christ "Compel them to enter in that my house may be full," saith he, *Compelle me Domine intrare, si vocare non est satis*.'

P. 46. 6. 'Natural affection,' στοργή. Cp. *Serm. Gunpowder Tr.* vii (iv 322) '*Raḥmîm* are the bowels of a parent, so we said the word signifies, and this adds much: adds to "mercy" στοργήν "natural love."'

—— 11. Διὰ τὴν ἡμετέραν σωτηρίαν S. Clem. Rom. *Cor.* 7 § 4, and then commonly in Greek Creeds.

—— 21. *Resp. ad Bellarm.* p. 34: nondum enim *ubique* obtinuit Ecclesia (non modo *simul* sed neque *per successionem*) *in universo quidem mundo. Genti* iam non est, vel *loco* (ut olim) astricta; late patet, καθ' ὅλου per universum esse potest, (eam enim vim habet vox illa καθ' ὅλου) etsi non sit.'

'Called out.' The etymological interpretation of ἐκκλησία is patristic: e.g. S. Cyril of Jerusalem *Cat.* xviii 24 ἐκκλησία δὲ καλεῖται φερωνύμως διὰ τὸ πάντας ἐκκαλεῖσθαι καὶ ὁμοῦ συνάγειν (cp. [S. Ath.] *Quaestt. in parab. evang.* 37 [ii 316], S. Aug. *Expos. ad Rom.* 2, *Enarr. in Ps.* lxxxi 1). Originally ἐκκλησία meant a body of persons 'called out' of the mass of the people for purposes of state; but already in classical usage it has come to mean a formal assembly of qualified citizens without reference to their selection, and later any assembly (Acts xix 32, 41: Hesych. *s.v.*). By the lxx it was adopted to represent the *qāhāl* or 'congregation' of Israel (Dt. Chr. Ezra: cp. Acts vii 38); and hence its Christian use. Thus the idea of 'calling' was already absorbed before it meant the 'Church.'

—— 23. S. Isidore of Pelusium *Ep.* ii 246 τὸ ἄθροισμα τῶν ἁγίων, τὸ ἐξ ὀρθῆς πίστεως καὶ πολιτείας ἀρίστης συγκεκροτημένον.

—— 25 sqq. S. Aug. *Serm.* ccxxiii 8: *remissionem peccatorum:* hæc in ecclesia si non esset, nulla spes esset: remissio peccatorum si in ecclesia non esset, nulla futuræ vitæ et liberationis æternæ spes esset. gratias agimus Deo qui ecclesiæ suæ dedit hoc donum. See Pearson *on the Creed* art. x note 10. *Serm. Absolution* (v 93) 'Now as by committing this power [of absolution] God doth not deprive or bereave Himself of it, for there is a *Remittuntur* still, and that chief, sovereign and absolute; so on the other side where God proceedeth by the Church's act as ordinarily He doth, it being his own ordinance, then whosoever will be partaker of the Church's act must be partaker of it by the Apostles' means.' *Ib.* p. 98 'The conditions to be required, to be of *quorum remittuntur* are two: First, that the party be within the house and family whereto those keys belong, that is, be a member of the Church, be a faithful believing Christian. . . . And to end this point, the Angel when he interpreteth the name of Jesus, extendeth it no further than thus, that "He shall save his people from their sins." To them there is the benefit of remission of sins entailed and limited: it is *sors Sanctorum* and *dos Ecclesiæ*."

P. 46. 37 sqq. Cp. *Serm. Nativ.* vii (i 115) 'Our duty then is, for his excellency to honour Him [Christ]; for his power to fear Him; for his love shewed, reciprocally to love Him again; for his hope promised, truly to serve Him.' *Prayer* vii (v. 369) '"Behold what great love He hath shewed us, that we should be called the sons of God" (1 S. Jo. iii 1). This dignity requireth this duty at our hands, that we reverence our Father. "If I be your Father, where is my love?"' (Mal. i 6).'

P. 47. 1 sqq. *Serm. Res.* i (ii 205) 'In Christ, dropping upon us the anointing of his grace: in Jesus, Who will be ready as our Saviour to succour and support us with his *auxilium speciale*, "his special help."'

—— 5 sq. *Serm. Nativ.* ii (i 30) 'He is given us, saith St Peter *εἰς ὑπογραμμόν*, "for an example" to follow. In all; but—that which is proper to this day—to do it in humility. . . . As faith to his conception, *beata quæ credidit;* so humility to his birth, *et hoc erit signum. Fieri voluit in vitâ primum quod exhibuit in ortu vitæ* (it is Cyprian;) that "He would have us first to express in our life, that He first shewed us in the very entry of his life."' Cp. *ib.* xii (i 205 sq.) The passage attributed to S. Cyprian really belongs to Arnold of Chartres *de nativitate Christi*, in *S. Cypriani Opera* Oxon 1682 p. 25.

—— 11. Simeon the Metaphrast's prayer before communion, *Horolog.* p. 473 *νέκρωσόν μου τὰ ψυχοφθόρα πάθη τοῦ σώματος· ὁ τῇ ταφῇ σου τὰ τοῦ ᾅδου σκυλεύσας βασίλεια θάψον μου διὰ τῶν ἀγαθῶν λογισμῶν τὰ πονηρὰ διαβούλια.* Cp. *Serm. Res.* iii (ii 237) 'leaving whatsoever formerly hath been amiss in Christ's grave as the weeds of our dead estate, and rising to newness of life, that so we may have our parts "in the first resurrection."'

—— 13. S. Gregory Nazianzen *Orat.* xlv 24 *ἂν εἰς ᾅδου κατίῃ συγκάτελθε· γνῶθι καὶ τὰ ἐκεῖσε τοῦ Χριστοῦ μυστήρια.*

—— 24. *Serm. Pentec.* ix (iii 265 sq.) 'First, breath is air; and air, the most subtile and, as I may say, the most bodiless body that is, approaching nearest to the nature of a spirit, which is quite devoid of all corporeity. So in that it suits well. . . . And, as the breath and the spirit, so Christ's breath and the Holy Spirit. *Accipe Spiritum* gives to man the life of nature: *Accipe Spiritum Sanctum*, to the Christian man, the life of grace.' See the whole sermon. Cp. xv (iii 390).

P. 47. 28. *Serm. Pentec.* vii (iii 235) '"The spoils are divided to them of the household" (Ps. lxviii 12), come not all to one man's hand; they be *μερισμοί*, by proportion and measure, part and part.' *Ib.* xv (iii 385) 'From the Spirit then they came, but by way of division. Not so, as some, all; some, never a whit; but by way of division. The nature whereof is, neither all gifts to one, nor one gift to all; but as it follows, *ἑκάστῳ*, *unicuique*, "to each" some (1 Cor. xii 7): neither *donum hominibus* "one gift to all men"; nor *dona homini* "all gifts to one man"; but *dona hominibus* [Ps. lxviii 18] "gifts to men"; every one his part of the dividend, for such is the law of dividing. Which division is of two sorts: 1. either of the thing itself in kind, 2. or of the measure.' See the whole sermon.

—— 29. Cp. pp. 75, 186. *Sanctorum*, in *Communionem sanctorum*, is here taken as neuter. Cp. *Visit. infirmorum* (Sarum *Manuale* in Maskell *Mon. rit.* i p. 92): et *sanctorum communionem*: id est omnes homines in caritate existentes esse participes omnium bonorum gratiæ quæ fiunt in ecclesia: *A goodly Prymer* 1535 (*Three Primers put forth in the reign of Henry viii* Oxford 1848 p. 43) 'I believe that in this communion or Christianity, all the prayers and good works of this congregation do necessarily help me, weigh on my side, and comfort me, in all times of life and death.' But this corresponds rather to *communio sacramentorum*, which is included in *com. sanctorum* as in part at least its ground and expression, but is not identical with it. *Com. sanctorum* means primarily the fellowship of the saints which the Creed asserts to exist in the Church in spite of the mixture of good and evil in it. See Swete *The Apostles' Creed* London 1894, pp. 82 sqq.

—— 30. Cp. *Horae* f. 96 (in agonia mortis) fac me participem omnium orationum et beneficiorum quæ sunt in ecclesia tua sancta.

P. 49. 3 sq. Andrewes' standing prayer for the Church of England: cp. p. 60.

—— 27. *Serm. before two kings* (v. 238) 'the name θεοφυλάκτου agrees to the King more than others.' It is an ordinary Byzantine epithet of the Emperor.

P. 50. 5. 'Sabaoth' apparently first of the army of Israel (1 Sam. xvii 45); later of the hosts of heaven—angels and stars.

—— 6 sq. cp. p. 92. There is a reference here no doubt to the Turks. During Andrewes' lifetime, under Suleiman the Magnificent (1520-1566) they were repulsed at Malta, 1565; in 1566 they took Chios and invaded Hungary. Under Selim ii (1566-1574) they captured Cyprus; in 1571 were defeated at Lepanto: 1574 recovered Tunis. Under Mohammed iii (1596-1603) and Achmet i (1603-1617) they suffered a decline. See *Liturgical Services in the reign of Elizabeth* (Parker Soc.) pp. 509, 527, 524. Cp. *Homilies* ii 8 Of the place and time of prayer (1562) 'Alas, how many churches, countries and kingdoms of Christian people have of late years been plucked down, overrun and left waste, with grievous and intolerable tyranny and cruelty of the enemy of the Lord Christ, the great Turk, who hath so universally scourged the Christians, that never the like was heard or read of. Above thirty years past, the great Turk had overrun, conquered and brought into his dominion and subjection twenty Christian kingdoms, turning away the people from the faith of Christ, poisoning them with the devilish religion of wicked Mahomet and either destroying their churches utterly or filthily abusing them with their wicked and detestable errors; and now this great Turk, this bitter and sharp scourge of God's vengeance is even at hand in this part of Christendom, in Europe, at the borders of Italy, at the borders of Germany, greedily gaping to devour us, to overrun our country, to destroy our churches also.' Bacon's fragment, *Advertisement touching a Holy War* (*Works* vii p. 12), written in 1622, is addressed to Andrewes, who is probably represented by *Eusebius* in the list of interlocutors. Cp. Becon *The Policy of War* p. 239 (ed. Parker Soc.). There is probably also a reference here to Spain.

P. 50. 12 sq. 'Husbandmen, graziers, fishermen'—the characteristic English industries. See Green *English People* pp. 387 sqq.; Creighton *Age of Elizabeth* p. 19 sq.

—— 17. 'Beggars.' Cp. *Spittle Sermon* (v. 43) 'There are others [of the poor], such as should not be suffered to be in Israel, whereof Israel is full: I mean beggars and vagabonds able to work; to whom good must be done by not suffering them to be as they are, but to employ them in such sort as they may do good. This is a good deed no doubt; and there being, as I hear, an honourable good purpose in hand for the redress of it, God send it good success. I am as one, in part of my charge, to exhort you by all good means to help and further it.' Elizabeth's Poor Law was passed in 1601. Cp. Green *Eng. People* p. 384 sq.

—— 39. S. Aug. *Conff.* iv 9: Hoc est quod diligitur in amicis, et sic diligitur, ut rea sibi sit humana conscientia, si non amaverit redamantem, aut si amantem non redamaverit.

P. 51. 9. Cp. *Lit. S. James* (*Litt. E. and W.* p. 45) *τῶν ἐντειλαμένων ἡμῖν ὥστε μνημονεύειν αὐτῶν ἐν ταῖς προσευχαῖς*: *Lit. S. Bas.* ib. p. 408.

—— 21 sqq. col. 2. The objects of the seven corporal works of mercy: see p. 128 and note. Most of the first col., and down to p. 52 l. 6, is from *Lit. S. Bas.* ib. p. 408.

P. 52. 7. 'In galleys' *ἐν τριήρεσι*—added by Andrewes—refers to the slaves in the Genoese, Venetian, French and Spanish galleys, and those of the Turks and Barbary corsairs. For their condition, which was apparently no better in the Christian than in the Turkish galleys, see S. Lane Poole, *The Barbary Corsairs*, pp. 200, 235. Cp. *Serm. Pent.* vii (iii 230) 'For all the world as an English ship takes a Turkish galley, wherein are held many Christian captives at the oar. . . . The poor souls in the galley, when they see the English ship hath the upper hand, are glad, I dare say, so to be taken: they know it will turn to their good and in the end to their letting go': cp. x (iii. 292). After the battle of Lepanto 1571, 15,000 Christian slaves were liberated.

P. 52. 8. In *Lit. S. Bas.* p. 407, τῶν ἐν ἐρημίαις refers to the anchorets of the desert, but Andrewes' τῶν ἐν ἐρημίᾳ is general in its reference.

—— 14 sqq. *Serm. Prayer* xviii (v 463) 'In the blessings of the Law the Name of God is thrice repeated . . . to teach that there are three Persons in the Godhead.' For the use of the blessing cp. *Horae* 1514 f. 107 b.

—— 20 sqq. Cp. the old English commendation in Maskell *Mon. rit.* iii 305. The refs. in the margin give the source of all in the text, except 'and all my vows,' 'my life and my death,' 'and their children,' 'my country.' Cp. p. 277.

—— 32 sqq. See on p. 25 l. 12.

—— 35—p. 53 l. 9 col. 1. The Names of God in the Pentateuch: *'Elōhîm; Jehovah (Yahweh), The Name* (Lev. xxiv 11: 'the incommunicable Name,' Wisd. xiv 23); *'Elyôn*; *'Adhōnai* ('my Lord,' substituted for *Jehovah* in reading, whence the vowels of the latter); *Shaddai; 'Ôlām; Ḥai rō'î*. On these names see Ottley *Bampton Lectures* pp. 182 sqq.; Burney *Outlines of O.T. Theology* ch. i.

Col. 2. Titles of God in respect of his operations: *Bôr'ē* as absolute Creator (Gen. i 1); *Qônēh*, combining the idea of creating and possessing; *Pôdheh*, looser, liberator; *Gō'ēl*, 'redeemer,' used of the nearest blood-relation on whom devolved the duties of redemption and blood revenge (Ruth ii 20, Num. xxxv 19) on behalf of one deceased, and often of God as redeeming His people from captivity (Is. xl-lxvi) or individuals from distress (Gen. xlviii 16, Ps. ciii 4); *Meḥayyeh* 'quickening' or 'preserving alive'; *Meqaddēsh* 'sanctifying,' characteristic of the 'Law of Holiness' (Lev. xvii-xxvi), and in Ezek.

P. 53. 14-20. The abstract attributes corresponding to the first column above.

—— 21. Titles with *'El*. *Serm. Justif.* (v. 110) 'His name *'El* which is his name of power.'

—— 22. 'The Holy One': cp. Job vi 10, Hab. iii. 3: the common Rabbinic title by which God is referred to. 'God of hosts': the form *'El-tsebhā'ôth* here used does not occur in O.T.; the phrase there is *'Elōhîm* or *'Elôhê*, or *Jehovah*, or *'Adhōnê, tsebhā'ôth*.

P. 53. 38 sqq. Largely collected from the *berakoth* or blessings scattered throughout the Synagogue forms of prayer, with additions from the Psalter etc. A few of them I have been unable to trace. Cp. S. Aug. *Serm.* 216 § 11.

P. 54. 28 sqq. An eucharistic Preface and *Sanctus*, largely from the Liturgy of S. James.

P. 55. 7. Quoted also by Hooker *E.P.* v 53 § 1.

—— 17 sqq. The *Sanctus* here combines Is. vi 3, Rev. iv 8, and that of *Te Deum*, which is perhaps the Gallican form.

—— 22. The addition of Ezek. iii 12 is probably suggested by the Jewish formula, on which perhaps the Christian Preface and Sanctus was originally founded: (*Heb. Pr. Bk.* Morning service p. 39, Sabbath morning p. 138).

—— 24-30. From the Sabbath services (*Heb. Pr. Bk.* pp. 117, 120, 139, 163, 176) according to the Sephardic text, *Daily Prayers* pp. 95, 131, 142, 154.

—— 31 sqq. From the service of the New Year.

P. 56. 9 sqq. The angels were created on the second day according to the Jerusalem Targum on Gen. i 26: 'and the Lord said to the angel who ministered to Him, who had been created on the second day of the creation of the world, *Let us make*' etc.; and *Shemoth rabba* xv c. xii 12 (ed. Wünsche p. 120): 'after He had formed the firmament, He formed the angels and that on the second day.' (The Jerus. Targum was printed in *Biblia Rabbinica* Venice 1516-7.) In *S. Paul's Lect.* p. 46 Andrewes follows S. Aug. *de civ Dei* xi 9 in the view that they were created on the first day, so agreeing with *Book of Jubilees* ii 2 (see Charles *Apocalypse of Baruch* xxi 6). The Fathers speculated on the subject and held various views.

—— 12 sqq. Cp. *S Paul's Lect.* pp. 43, 49 sq., 148.

—— 31 sq. *Serm. Res.* v (ii 253) 'Moses . . in his ordinary prayer, the ninetieth Psalm, as it were his *Pater noster.*' See title of Ps. xc.

P. 57. 1. Job is placed with Moses as his supposed contemporary. *Serm. Res.* v (ii 253) 'as old as Job's time and that as old as Moses'; *ib.* p. 256 'Moses and Job are holden to have lived at one time.'

—— 9. Andrewes here corrects the Septuagint by the Vulgate. For his Greek, cp. 2 Reg. (2 Sam.) xxi 3. Cp. *Serm. Nativ.* xi (i 184).

P. 58. 2-16. Against violations of the Ten Commandments.

—— 3 sq. *Serm. Res.* vii (ii 304) 'Christ willed his Disciples to "beware of the leaven of the Pharisees and Sadducees" . . . 1. The Pharisees', of the leaven of superstition, consisting in phylacteries, phrases and observances, and little else. 2. The Sadducees', of a leaven that smelt strong of profaneness, in their liberty of prophesying, calling in question Angels and Spirits and the Resurrection itself.' Cp. *S. Giles' Lectt.* p. 586.

P. 58. 5. *Serm. Res.* xii (ii 387) 'Not with idolatry perhaps, but, which is an evil and differs but a letter, with idiolatry; for to worship images, and to worship men's own imaginations, comes all to one.' See *Serm. on the Worshipping of Imaginations* (v 54 sqq.); *Cat. doct.* p. 123 'The general thing here forbidden is the making of images. But a further thing is set down, Col. ii 23, invented worship; for "to make" in this place signifieth "to invent" . . . So that ἐθελοθρησκεία "will-worship," Col. ii 23, is forbidden; man must not think himself so wise to devise a worship for God, nor must he be so humble as to bow down to any representation of God; this honour is only due to one Lord God.' Cp. S. Vincent. Lirin. *Commonitorium* 10 (15) nova dogmata quæ Vetus Testamentum allegorico sermone deos alienos appellare consuevit, eo quod scilicet ita ab hæreticis ipsorum opiniones sicut a gentibus dii sui observentur.

—— 6. Cp. *Cat. doct.* pp. 150 sq. Tertull. *de Pudicit.* 19 facile maledicere aut temere iurare.

—— 7. 'Withdrawal, ὑποστολή. *Serm Pentec.* i (iii 114): 'Both "in the unity of the Spirit," that is, inward, and "in the bond of peace" too, that is, outward (Eph. iv. 3). An item for those whom the Apostle calleth *filii subtractionis* (Heb. x 39), that forsake the congregation, as even then in the Apostles' times "the manner of some" was "and do withdraw themselves to their perdition," to no less matter': *ib.* ix. (iii 273): 'They be *hypostles*—so doth S. Paul well term them, as it were the mock-apostles—and the term comes home to them, for υἱοὶ ὑποστολῆς they be, *filii subtractionis* right; work all to subtraction, to withdraw poor souls, to make them forsake the fellowship, as even then the manner was. This brand hath the Apostle set on them, that we might know them and avoid them.' Cp. *S. Giles' Lect.* p. 638.

'Indecency' ἀσχημον. *Serm. Pestilence* (v 232) 'And to present them (our bodies) "decently" (1 Cor. xiv 40). For that also is required in the service of God. Now "judge in yourselves" (1 Cor. xi 13) is it comely to speak unto ourselves, sitting? *Sedentem orare extra disciplinam est* saith Tertullian (*de orat.* 12), To pray sitting or sit praying is against the order of the Church. The Church of God never had nor hath any such fashion. All tendeth to this, as Cyprian's advice is, *etiam habitu corporis placere Deo* (*de orat. dom.* 4) "even by our very gesture to behave ourselves so as with it we may please God." Unreverent, careless, undevout behaviour, pleaseth Him not.'

—— 8. ἀκηδές 'heedlessness,' viz. of those belonging to us. Cp. 1 Tim. v 8.

—— 13-16. From the introduction to the Lord's Prayer in *Lit. S. James* (*Litt. E. and W.* p. 59).

—— 21. *Serm. of Swearing* (v 71 sqq).

—— 22. Cp. *Serm Gunpowder Tr.* ix (iv 373 sqq).

—— 28. *Yetser tôbh* 'good imagination' (1 Chr. xxviii 9: Is.

xxvi 3) 'inclination,' 'impulse.' According to the doctrine of the Talmud, founded on Gen. vi 5, viii 21, man was created with two 'impulses,' one to good, *yetser tôbh*, the other to evil, *yetser ha-ra'*; his moral life consists in the conflict between the two, and it is within his power to conquer the evil and to attain to perfect righteousness. Cp. *Heb. Pr. Book* p. 7 'make us to cleave to the good impulse'; *Daily Prayers* p. 84 'make the good impulse to prevail in me, and suffer not the evil impulse to prevail.' See Edersheim *Life and times* i pp. 52, 167, ii pp. 441, 757. The evil impulse is referred to below p. 66. Andrewes of course uses the phrases to represent the observed impulses of men as they are, the true regenerate nature and the concupiscence or φρόνημα σαρκός, without accepting the Talmudic doctrine. Cp. *Cat. doct.* p. 284.

—— 29. *Serm. Lent* iv (ii 72) '1. That which we should draw out [from the example of Lot's wife] is perseverance, *Muria virtutum*, as Gregory calleth it, 'the preserver of virtues,' without which, as summer fruits, they will perish and putrify; the salt of the covenant, without which the flesh of our sacrifice will take wind and corrupt But St Augustine better *Regina virtutum*, 'the Queen of virtues'; for that, however the rest run and strive and do masteries, yet *perseverantia sola coronatur*, "perseverance is the only crowned virtue" [S. Bern. *Ep.* 32 § 3, 109 § 2]. 2. Now perseverance we shall attain, if we can possess our souls with the due care, and rid them of security. Of Lot's wife's security, as of water, was this salt here made. And, if security, as water, do but touch it, it melts away presently. But care will make us fix our eye and gather up our feet and "forgetting that which is behind" *tendere in anteriora* "to follow hard toward the prize of our high calling" (Phil. iii 13). 3. And to avoid security and to breed in us due care, St Bernard saith "Fear will do it." *Vis in timore securus esse? securitatem time*; "the only way to be secure in fear is to fear security" (cp. *de donis Sp. S.* 1). St Paul hath given the same counsel before that to preserve *si permanseris*, no better advice than *noli altum sapere sed time* (Rom. xi 20-22).'

P. 60. 1, 20. 'Restoration,' 'readjustment,' καταρτισμός. On the meanings of the word see *Serm. Res.* xviii (iii 94).

—— 18. I.e. its deliverance from the Turk, and its union with the West.

—— 33. See on p. 14 l. 19.

—— 35. See on p. 50 l. 12.

P. 61. 1-3. For Andrewes' interest in education see Isaacson's *Life and death of Lancelot Andrewes* in *Minor Works* p. xviii. Contrast Bacon (Abbott *Bacon's Essays* i p. cliv, ii p. 158).

—— 15. 'Ordained' τελειωθέντων. Τελειοῦν is used ecclesiastically for 'to consecrate' in any sense, whether of baptism and confirmation (S. Ath. *c. Arian.* i 34, ii 41) or of ordination (Dion. Ar. *Eccl. hierarch.* v) or of the eucharist (*Lit. S. Mark* invoc.). Either baptised and confirmed, or ordained, or both might be meant here: but the Latin has *ordinati.*

P. 62. 4. Cp. the prayer *For all christian souls:* 'animabus quæ singulares apud te non habent intercessores' *Horae* 1514 f. 161 b.

—— 23-28. From the Greek Matins and Compline *Horolog.* pp. 16, 170; and the Coptic Lauds (Bute *Coptic morning service* p. 124).

—— 29-32. From the first prayer of S. Chrysostom in Ἀκολουθία τῆς ἁγ. μεταλήψεως.

—— 35 sqq. *Serm. Gunpowder Tr.* vii (iv 324) 'God's own style framed and proclaimed by Himself, Exodus the thirty-fourth chapter, consisting of thirteen titles, *middôth*, measures or degrees.' Pesiqta *Eth-qorbani* init. 'R. Simon said "Thirteen degrees (*middôth*) of mercy are written concerning the Holy One, blessed be He: this is what is said *And the Lord passed*"' etc. [Exod. xxxiv 6, 7]. Cp. *Heb. Daily Prayers* p. 2 'O God, Thou hast taught us to repeat the Thirteen attributes. Remember unto us this day the covenant of the Thirteen, as Thou didst reveal them of old to the meek [i.e. Moses, Num. xii 3]; for thus it is written in thy law [Ex. xxxiv 5-7].'

P. 63. 19 sqq. From *O inflammati seraphim:* cp. p. 221. The nine orders of the angelic hierarchy are deduced from the nine names which occur in Holy Scripture: Angels (*angeli* ἄγγελοι 1 S. Pet. iii 22), archangels (*archangeli*, ἀρχάγγελοι 1 Th. iv 16, S. Ju. 9), virtues (virtutes δυνάμεις Eph. i 21, 1 S. Pet. iii 22), powers (*potestates* ἐξουσίαι Eph. i 21, Col. i 16, 1 S. Pet. iii 22), principalities (*principatus* ἀρχαί Eph. i 21, Col. i 16), dominations (*dominationes* κυριότητες Eph. i 21, Col. i 16), thrones (*throni* θρόνοι Col. i 16), cherubim (*cherubim* χερουβίμ Gen. iii 24), seraphim (*seraphim* σεραφίμ Isa. vi. 2). They are first enumerated by S. Cyril of Jerusalem, *Cat.* xxiii 6 (quoted from Lit. S. James). There are two lines of speculation as to their relations and functions, developed respectively by the pseudo-Dionysius the Areopagite (c. 500 A.D.) and by S. Gregory the Great († 604), characterised by S. Thomas Aquinas *Summa* i 108 § 5 Dionysius exponit ordinum nomina secundum convenientiam ad spirituales perfectiones eorum: Gregorius vero in expositione horum nominum magis attendere videtur exteriora ministeria (cp. Dante *Par.* xxviii 130-133). Some elements of the latter are found in Origen *de principiis* i 5 § 3, 6 § 2 and in Cassian *Collat.* viii 15; but the complete scheme occurs first in S. Gregory *hom.* xxxiv *in Evangel.* 8, 10, and he is followed by S. Isidore of Seville *Etym.* vii 5, S. Anselm *Med.* xiii 2, Peter Lombard *Sentt.* ii 9, S. Bernard *de Consid.* v 4 §§ 8, 10, Gerson *de mendacitate spirituali* (iii 512), and by the prayer quoted by Andrewes in the text. (S. Thomas Aq. *Summa* i 108 § 5, 6 combines Dionysius and Gregory; S. Bonaventura *Eccl. hierarch.* 1-3 follows Dionysius).

1. Angels in this scheme are generally regarded simply as the divine messengers announcing lesser events—qui minima nunciant (Greg.); but in S. Anselm and S. Bern., as in the text, the care and charge of men is dwelt on (Ps. xci 11, Heb. i 14).

2. Archangels 'illuminate' men as to the more important divine purposes—'qui summa annunciant' (Greg.: Dan. ix 21, xi, S. Lk. i 26, 1 Th. iv 16). 'Illumination' (ἀπαυγασμός, *illuminatio*) is Andrewes' own substitute for, as here, or addition to, as p. 221, the word 'annunciation.'

3. Virtues—per quos signa et miracula frequentius fiunt (Greg.).

4. Thrones. Orig. *de princ.* i 6 § 2 iudicandi vel regendi . . habentes officium. Greg.: qui tanta divinitatis gratia replentur ut in eis Dominus sedeat et per eos sua iudicia decernat. Cp. Dante *Par.* ix 61 sqq. They appear to correspond to the Jewish *ophannim* 'wheels' (Ezek. i 16).

5. Dominations—quæ mira potentia præeminent (over the orders beneath them), Greg. But Andrewes' source has 'dominantes largitione,' and εὐποιΐα apparently represents 'largitione,' which however would seem to mean 'by divine bestowal.'

6. Principalities — governing other angels (Greg.) or 'præsidentes gubernationis gentium et regnorum' (Thom.: cp. Dan. x 13, xii 1).

7. Powers—restraining evil spirits 'ne corda hominum tantum tentare prævaleant quantum volunt' (Greg.)—'sicut per potestates terrenas arcentur malefactores [Rom. xiii]' (Thom.).

8. Cherubim. Philo. Jud. *de vita Mosis* iii 8 χερουβὶμ ὡς δ' Ἕλληνες εἴποιεν ἐπίγνωσις καὶ ἐπιστήμη πολλή: Clem. Al. *Strom.* v 6 § 36 ἐθέλει δὲ τὸ ὄνομα τῶν χ. δηλοῦν ἐπίγνωσιν πολλήν: and so later writers generally. The ground of this interpretation is uncertain: but it is illustrated by the 'eyes' of the living creatures (Ez. i, Rev. iv), who are identified with the cherubim: S. Jer. *Ep.* liii 8 cherubim quod interpretatur *scientiæ multitudo* per totum corpus oculati sunt. Cp. *S. Giles' Lect.* p. 347.

9. Seraphim. Dion. Ar. *cael. hier.* 7 τὴν μὲν ἁγίαν τῶν σεραφὶμ ὀνομασίαν οἱ τὰ Ἑβραίων εἰδότες ἢ τὸ ἐμπρηστὰς ἐμφαίνειν ἢ τὸ θερμαίνοντας. *Sāraf*=to burn; interpreted symbolically of the warmth of love. Cp. Euseb. *Dem. ev.* vii 1: S. Chrys. *de incompr.* iii 5.

P. 63. 28 sqq. The connexion of this is obscure. Perhaps it is unfinished.

P. 64. 9, 13, 17. The three words of Gen. i 2 *thehôm*, *thōhû* and *bhōhû* represent the chaotic beginnings which in the six days were shaped and organised into the forms enumerated under each head. Cp. *S. Paul's Lect.* p. 2 'In which six dayes the proceeding of God in this worke consisteth in these three points. First, the creating of all Creatures, of and after an indigest, rude and imperfect matter, and manner: for, the first day *was made a rude masse or heape*, which after *was the Earthe:* secondly, *a bottomless huge gulfe, which was the Waters:* thirdly, *over both was a foggie obscure myst of darknesse which was the Firmament.* After that, in the second place, is set downe the distinction, which is in three sorts: first, *of Light from darknesse;* secondly *of the nether Waters from the upper Waters*, viz. *of the Seas and Clouds;* thirdly, *of the Waters from the Earth.* After the distinction and dividing of this, ensueth in the third place, Gods worke in beautifying and adorning them after this order which we now see; first, *the Heaven with Starres;* secondly, *the Ayre with Fowles:* thirdly, *the Earth with Beasts, Herbs and Plants of all sorts;* fourthly, *the Sea and Waters with Fishes.*'

P. 64. 10-12. *S. Paul's Lect.* p. 11 'At the first he sheweth touching the waters, that they were a bottomless gulfe; afterward, he made them quiet waters; and at last, made them salt Seas and fresh Waters, Fountains and Springs, in most necessary and orderly sort.' Cp. *ib.* pp. 56-63.

—— 14-16. *Ib.* p. 11 'And for the Earth, first the beginning ot them (which were the matter of all earthly things) it was a desolate and disordered, rude and deformed mass, covered with water; after, God set it above the Waters, and made it dry ground, as the word signifieth': p. 13 'the earth was both *Tohu* and *Tobohu*, without deformed, and within void and empty; not that it had no form, for that were against reason, but it was such a form as was altogether deformed.' Cp. *ib.* pp. 63-65.

—— 18. *Ib.* p. 12 'And at the last he brought it to its perfection, making it fruitfull and sanctifying it in all necessary things.' Cp. *ib.* 65-72.

—— 22-24. Cp. *Ap. constt.* viii 40 πρὸς χρῆσιν . . ὑγείαν . . τέρψιν.

—— 35. That is, apparently, volcanoes.

P. 65. 25. *Serm. Pentec.* x (iii 294) 'Without any worldly cross this [viz. to be humbled aright] we might have, if we loved not so to absent ourselves from ourselves, to be even *fugitivi cordis*, to run away from our own hearts, be ever abroad, never within; if we would but sometimes *redire ad cor*, return home thither and descend into ourselves; sadly and seriously to bethink us of them, and the danger we are in by them.' In the text Andrewes has changed the Heb. 'bring back to their heart' (ἐπιστρέψωσιν καρδίαν αὐτῶν, conversi in corde suo) of 2 Chr. vi 37, to ἐπιστρ. ἐπὶ τὴν καρδίαν (Bar. ii 30).

—— 26. *Serm. Repent.* iv (i 364) '"With the heart" and "with the whole heart." . . . The devil to hinder us from true turning, turns himself like Proteus into all shapes. First, turn not at all, you are well enough. If you will needs turn, turn whither you will, but not to God. If to God, leave your heart behind you, and turn and spare not. If with the heart, be it *in corde*, but not *in toto*, with some ends or fractions, with some few broken affections, but not entirely. *In modico*, saith Agrippa, "somewhat";—there is a piece of the heart. *In modico et in toto*, saith St Paul, "somewhat and altogether";—there is "the whole heart." For which cause, as if some converted with the brim or upper part only, doth the Psalm call for it *de profundis* (Ps. cxxx 1) and the Prophet "from the bottom of the heart (Joel ii 12).""

P. 66. 10. On the rendering of Ps. xxx 5 see Kirkpatrick *in loc.*

—— 30 sqq. Several names for sin in the O. T.

'Imagination' (*yetser*) cp. on p. 58 l. 28. 'Error' (*shegāgah*, from *shāgag* 'to wander'), sin by inadvertence; cp. Eccl. v 6. 'Trespass' (*'āshām*, from *'āshem* 'to be guilty') sin of negligence; cp. Lev. iv 22. 'Sin' (*ḥaṭa'ah*, from *ḥāṭ'a* 'to miss, err from the mark') sin as a missing of the mark; cp. Eph. v 15. 'Transgression' or rebellion (*peshā'*, from *pāsha'* 'to transgress, rebel') sin as against a person or persons. 'Iniquity' (*'āvōn*, from *'āvāh* 'to bend, distort') sin as perversity, depravity, Gen. xliv 16 (but see Driver on 1 Sam. xx 30). 'Abomination' (*tō'ebhah* from *tā'abh* 'to abhor') sin as that which is abhorrent to God, as forbidden by religion, *nefas*; used esp. of idols and all that belongs to them, Prov. iii 32, xxi 27, Gen. xliii 32, 1 Ki. xiv 24. Cp. *Serm. Repent.* iii (i 343) 'There is sin, a fall: men fall against their wills; that is sin of infirmity. There is sin, an error: men err from the way of ignorance; that is sin of ignorance. The one for want of power, the other for lack of skill. But rebellion, the third kind, that hateful sin of rebellion, can neither pretend ignorance nor plead infirmity; for wittingly they revolt from their known allegiance, and wilfully set themselves against their lawful Sovereign;—that is the sin of malice.'

—— 38 sqq. The effect of godly sorrow. Causæ, effectus, partes, præparationes, signa pænitentiæ, Calvin *in 2 Cor.* vii 11 and *Instit.* iii 3 § 15: opera pænitentiæ, Lorinus *in Ps.* vi init.: effectus, fructus pænitentiæ, Corn. a Lapide *in 2 Cor.* vii 11. *Serm. Repent.* viii (i 452) 'Those seven degrees in 2 Cor. 7, which may serve to assure ourselves and to shew the world, we dally not with repentance, but make a serious matter of it and go to it in good earnest': *ib.* v (i 386) 'Now mark these four well; 1. fear, 2. sorrow, 3. anger, 4. desire, and look into 2 Cor. 7, 11, if they be not there made, as it were, the four elements of repentance, the constitutive causes of it. 1. Fear, the middle point, the centre of it. 2. Sorrow that works it. And, if sorry for sin, then of necessity 3. angry with the sinner, that is ourselves, for committing it. It is there called indignation, and no slight one, but proceeding *ad vindictam*, to be wreaked on ourselves for it. 4. And desire is there too, and zeal joined with it to give it edge. These four, the proper passions all of repentance, and these four carry everyone, as we say, his fast on his back. Much more, where they all meet, as in true earnest repentance they all should.' Cp. *ib.* iv (i 372 sq.), v (i 380), viii (i 441), *Absolution* (v 100 sq.), *S. Giles* p. 626.

P. 67. 7 sqq. The Apostles' Creed translated into abstract terms. Cp. the Sunday creed above.

P. 69. 27 sqq. From the morning prayer *O bone Jesu:* also in *Horae* 1494 f. 3.

P. 70. 2. 'Goodness,' ἀγαθωσύνη. *Serm. Nat.* xiii (i 230) 'And the Apostle tells us, the εὐδοκία that is in God is εὐδοκία ἀγαθωσύνης (2 Th. i 11): it is not but regulate by his goodness'—where, as the A.V., Andrewes takes ἀγαθωσύνη of the divine goodness (contrast R.V.) as in Neh. ix 25, 35, Pr. of Manas. 14. Elsewhere not used of God in lxx or N.T.

—— 17. πολυευσπλαγχνία, the reading of S. James v 11 in the Complutensian text.

—— 23 sqq. I.e. punishing.

—— 24. *Serm. Rep.* iii (i 345) 'I for my part fain would, saith God; it is their "not" and not mine. My *nolo* is *nolo ut moriatur*; my *volo* is *volo ut convertatur*, "I will not their death, I will their conversions" (Ezek. xviii 32, xxxiii 11); this is my *volo*. Nay, *quoties volui?* "How often would I?" *et noluistis* "and ye would not" (S. Mt. xxiii 37).'

—— 30. Andrewes apparently takes Is. xl 2 to mean that the Return is a double compensation for what Israel has suffered for its sins; whereas it obviously means that in the Exile it has suffered a double retribution, Jer. xvi 18.

—— 31 sqq. *Serm. Pentec.* x (iii 298) 'There is much in this term "accepting." . . . Three degrees there are in it: 1. Accepted to pardon—that is συγγνώμη. 2. Accepted to reconciliation—that is καταλλαγή. And further, 3. Accepted to repropitiation, that is ἱλασμός, to as good grace and favour as ever, even in the very fulness of it. They show it by three distinct degrees in Absalom's receiving. 1. Pardoned he was when he was yet in Geshur (2 Sam. xiii 39); 2. Reconciled, when he had leave to come home to his own house (2 Sam. xiv 23); 3. Repropitiate, when he was admitted to the king's presence and kissed him (33).' Cp. pp. 136, 153.

P. 71. 6 sqq. See *S. Paul's Lectt.* pp. 72-84.

—— 9-11. *S. Paul's Lectt.* p. 81 'As touching the fixed starres, God saith in *Job* in his 38. chapter 32. *Canst thou bring forth Mazaroth in their time?* This Mazaroth is taken for the Zodiack. *Canst thou guide Arcturus with his sonnes?* The starre Arcturus is the Northern Pole, in the tayle of *Ursa maior.* . . . There is mention of Orion and the Pleiades, *Job* 38 31. Orion, when it appeareth, bringeth in Winter: sweet are the influences of the Pleiades, *delitiæ sunt Pleiadum:* When those seven starres appear, the same being in *Taurus*, they bring in the spring and pleasant flowers.' The meaning of *Mazzaroth* is uncertain. Perhaps it is the *Mazzaloth* of 2 Ki. xxiii 5, meaning either the signs of the Zodiac or the planets. The *chambers of the south* 'are probably the great spaces and deep recesses of the southern hemisphere of the heavens, with the constellations which they contain.' See Davidson on Job ix 9 and xxxviii 31.

P. 71. 19. The Earthquake. 'On Easter Wednesday, being the sixt of April, 1580, somewhat before six of the clock in the afternoon, happened this great Earthquake, whereof this discourse treateth: I mean not great in respect of long continuance of time, for (God be thanked) it continued little above a minute of an hour, rather shaking God's rod at us, then smiting us according to our deserts: Nor yet in respect of any great hurt done by it within this Realm: For although it shook all houses, castles, churches, and buildings, every where as it went, and put them in danger of utter ruin; yet within this Realm (praised be our Saviour Christ Jesus for it) it overthrew few or none that I have yet heard of, saving certain stones, chimneys, walls and pinnacles of high buildings, both in this City and in divers other places: Neither do I hear of any Christian people that received bodily hurt by it, saving two children in London, a boy and a girl. . . . But I term it great in respect of the universalness thereof almost at one instant, not only within this Realm, but also without, where it was much more violent and did far more harm; and in respect of the great terror which it then strake into all men's hearts when it came. . . .' *The Report of the Earthquake*, appended with an admonition to *The Order of Prayer for Wednesdays and Fridays*, for the provinces of Canterbury and York, 1580 (*Liturgical services*, Parker Soc. p. 567). Cf. *Romeo and Juliet* I iii 23 ''Tis since the earthquake now eleven years.' Andrewes must have been in London at the time; since from 1574 onwards, so long as he was in Cambridge, he visited his parents for a fortnight before Easter and a fortnight after (*Minor Works* p. v).

P. 72. 6. 'With us' ('*immanû*) added from the Greek (ἡμῖν).

P. 74. 7-13. The seven capital or principal sins. The history of this list can be gathered sufficiently from the following writers: Evagrius of Pontus († 398) *de octo vitiosis cogitationibus* (Migne *P.G.* xl 1272); John Cassian († c. 430) *Instit.* v 1, *Collat.* v 2; S. Nilus Asceta († c. 430) *de octo spiritibus nequitiæ* (Migne *P.G.* lxxix 1145); Eutropius of Valentia (vi cent.) *de octo vitiis* (Migne *P.L.* lxxx 9); S. Gregory the Great († 604, *Moralia* xxxi 87; S. Isidore of Seville († 636) *Quæst. in V.T. Deut.* xvi; S. John of Damascus († c. 760) *de octo spiritibus nequitiæ* (i 506 ed. Lequien); Alcuin († c. 800) *de virtutibus et vitiis* 27; pseudo-Alcuin (xi cent.) *de officiis* 13:

Peter Lombard († 1164) *Sentent.* ii 42; S. Thomas Aquinas († 1272) *Summa* ii[1] 84 § 4; and the homily *de verbo Venite ad me* among the works of Gerson (iii 735).

1. They are called *vitia* or *peccata principalia* or *originalia* or *capitalia* and *λογισμοὶ γενικώτατοι* — as the root-sins, the fountain-heads from which the rest flow: cf. Alcuin *loc. cit.* sunt vitia principalia vel originalia omnium vitiorum; ex quibus quasi radicibus omnia corruptæ mentis vel incasti corporis diversarum vitia pullulant iniquitatum (cp. S. Thom. Aq. *Summa* ii[1] 84 § 3). Also *criminalia* and *πνεύματα τῆς πονηρίας*. The later name 'the mortal or deadly sins' (R. Rolle [1340] 'hede or deadlyche sins': Chaucer *Parson's Tale*: Æneas Sylvius *de liberorum educatione* 'mortis peccata'; *Prymer* ap. Maskell *Mon. rit.* iii 255 'seuen dedeliche synnes': *Prymer* Regnault 1537 *septem peccata mortalia*, 'seuen deadly sins': Shakespeare *Measure for Measure* III i 111 'the deadly seven': Cosin *Private devotions* 'seven deadly sins, as they are commonly called'; etc.) is popular and not strictly correct. Mortal or deadly sins in the strict sense cannot be enumerated, since the deadly character of sins depends upon the state of the will.

2. Eastern writers generally, and the early westerns (Cass., Eutrop.) and some later westerns (Alc., Gers. and others) enumerate eight principal vices: viz.

(1) Gluttony (*γαστριμαργία, gastrimargia, ventris ingluvies, gulæ concupiscentia, gula*).

(2) Fornication (*πορνεία, ἐπιθυμία, fornicatio*).

(3) Avarice (*φιλαργυρία, philargyria, avaritia, amor pecuniæ*).

(4) Sadness (*λυπή, tristitia*).

(5) Wrath (*ὀργή, ira*).

(6) Accidy (*ἀκηδία, acedia, anxietas, tædium cordis*).

(7) Vainglory (*κενοδοξία, cenodoxia, vana* or *inanis gloria, iactantia*).

(8) Pride (*ὑπερηφανία, superbia*).

Westerns for the most part distinguish between guilty sorrow on one's own account (*tristitia* or *acedia*) and that on account of others' good (*invidia*), and accordingly for 'sadness' and 'accidy' substitute 'sadness or accidy' and 'envy'; and they generalise 'fornication' into 'luxuria.' So modified the list appears in Greg., pseudo-Alc., and [Gerson]. Besides this Greg., followed by pseudo-Alc., treats pride as the root of all the rest, so that the seven are the *principalia* issuing out of pride. Then in Pet. Lomb. these seven appear simply as 'the seven capitals': S. Thomas treats 'pride' and 'vainglory' as identical, and so the list becomes finally *inanis gloria* or *superbia, invidia, ira, tristitia* or *acedia, avaritia, gula, luxuria* (cp. Dante *Purg.* x-xxvii) and in English *pride, envy, wrath* or *ire, accidy* or *sloth, avarice* or *covetise, gluttony, lechery* (Chaucer *Parson's Tale; Prymer* 1537 f. 167 b.; Maskell *Mon. rit.* iii p. 255). A *memoria technica* of the list is contained in the verse *Luxus gustus avet tristis furit invidet ambit* (S. Raymund of Pennafort *Summa* iii 34 § 4), and again in the word SALIGIA, formed of the initial letters, with its meaning pointed in the verse *Vt tibi sit vita semper* saligia *vita* (S. Antonine of Florence *Summa* III xvii 17 § 3). For an analysis and rationale of the list see S. Thom. Aq. *Summa* ii^{1} 84 § 4.

Andrewes' list is the same, except that it is expressed in biblical words or phrases: *τύφος* 1 Tim. iii 6, vi 4, 2 Tim. iii 4: *φθόνος* Gal. v 21: *ὀργίλον* Tit. i 7: *πλησμονή* Col. ii 23: *ἀσέλγεια* (=*luxuria*) S. Mk. vii 22, Gal. v 19: *περισπασμοὶ βιωτικοί* (=*avaritia*) S. Lk. x 40, xxi 34 (the complete phrase occurs in the introduction to the Lord's Prayer in *Lit. S. James* p. 31 (59): cp. S. Cyr. Al. *hom. pasch.* xxx 5 *τοῦ παρόντος βίου περισπασμοί*): *τὸ χλιαρὸν τῆς ἀκηδίας* Rev. iii 16, Ps. cxix 28, Is. lxi 3, Ecclus. xxix 5 (on Accidy see Paget *Spirit of discipline*, introd. and serm. i). Andrewes' order is not the usual one, and it seems to be accidental.

3. Origen *in Jes. Nav.* i 7 (cp. viii 6) interprets the nations of Canaan as symbolising our spiritual enemies, sins to be conquered; Eutropius *u.s.* as symbolising the eight principal vices. Cassian makes Egypt the symbol of gluttony (Ex. xvi 3) and the seven Canaanite nations of the other seven principal vices. In S. Isidore of Seville *u.s.*, in the *Glossa ordinaria* on Deut. vii 1, in Peter Lombard *u.s.*, and in Card. Hugo on Deut. vii 1 (quoting the *Glossa*), the seven nations correspond generally to the seven capital sins of the western list. In the 'moral' addition to the *Glossa ordinaria* on Deut. vii. 1, the seven nations are made to correspond one by one to the seven sins, on the ground of the supposed etymological meaning of the national names, and in [Gerson] a different set of correspondences is made out, also on etymological grounds, between the eight nations and the eight sins. Andrewes agrees with the *Glossa* in assigning avarice to the Canaanite, and with [Gerson] in assigning pride to the Amorite and accidy to the Jebusite. Since the names do not occur in any biblical order, it is probable that he intended them to correspond one by one to the sins. It is obvious to make the Amorite correspond to pride, since the name means 'mountaineer,' and the Canaanite to 'the distractions of this life,' since, from the commercial pursuits of the Canaanites (Phenicians), the name was used for any merchant, Job xli 6, Prov. xxxi 24, Hos. xii 7; and the Jebusite to accidy or a crushed spirit, by deriving the word from *bûs* 'to trample, tread down' (*Jebus*=a trodden place, a threshing floor). The rest do not seem to be explicable.

P. 74. 15-21. The virtues opposed to the capital sins. S. Nilus *de vitiis quæ opposita sunt virtutibus* (Migne *P.G.* lxxix 1141) gives a list of virtues opposed to the eight vices. Cp. Dante *Purg.*; Chaucer *Parson's Tale; Prymer* Regnault 1537 f. II virtutes et remedia contra septem vitia capitalia: Sis humilis largus castus patiens moderatus compatiens fortis: septem mortalia tollis; Martene *de ant. eccl. rit.* iii 681 ed. Antw. 1737. Andrewes' list is again in N.T. language.

P. 74. 34. *Serm. Nativ.* ix (i 141) 'Our conception being the root as it were, the very groundsill of our nature; that He might go to the root and repair our nature from the very foundation, thither He went; that what had been there defiled and decayed by the first Adam, might by the Second be cleansed and set right again. That had our conception been stained, by Him therefore *primum ante omnia*, to be restored again. He was not idle all the time He was an embryo—all the nine months He was in the womb; but then and there He even eat out the core of corruption that cleft to our nature and us and made both us and it an unpleasing object in the sight of God.' Cp. S. Bernard *Serm.* ii *in Pentec.* 4 (i 937) Christus ergo ibi primum medicinam apposuit ubi primus vulneri patebat locus et substantialiter utero virginis illapsus de Spiritu sancto conceptus est, ut conceptionem nostram mundaret, quam spiritus malus, si non fecerat, tamen infecerat: ut non esset etiam in utero vita ipsius otiosa dum novem mensibus purgat vulnus antiquum, scrutans ut dicitur usque ad imum putridinem virulentam ut sanitas sempiterna succederet.

—— 35. *Serm. Nativ.* vii (i 114) 'To purge our sins He began this day, the first day, the day of His birth; wherein He purified and sanctified by His holy Nativity the original uncleanness of ours.'

—— 36. *Serm. Passion* ii (ii 157) 'What this day the Son of God did and suffered for us: and all for this end that what He was then we might not be, and what He is now we might be for ever.'

P. 75. 1-3. Cp. S. Athan. *de incarn. adv. Apollin.* i 5 *τῆς μὲν ἁμαρτίας τὴν κατάκρισιν ἐπὶ γῆς ἐποιήσατο, τῆς δὲ κατάρας τὴν καθαίρεσιν ἐπὶ ξύλου, τῆς τε φθορᾶς τὴν ἀπολύτρωσιν ἐν τῷ τάφῳ καὶ τοῦ θανάτου τὴν κατάλυσιν ἐν τῷ ᾅδῃ, παντὶ ἐπιβὰς τόπῳ ἵνα τοῦ σύμπαντος ἀνθρώπου τὴν σωτηρίαν κατεργάσηται.*

—— 4. *Serm. Res.* xviii (iii 89) 'Brought thither He was to the dead: so, it lay us upon; if He had not, we should. We were even carrying thither; and that we might not, He was. Brought thence He was, from the dead: so it stood us in hand; if He had not been brought thence, we should never have come thence, but been left to have lain there world without end.' Cp. *ib.* 93. Tertullian *de animâ* 55 sed in hoc, inquiunt, Christus inferos adiit, ne nos adiremus: S Aug. *in Ps. lxxxv* 17 ille pervenit usque ad infernum ne nos remaneremus in inferno.

—— 5 sq. *Serm. Pentec.* iii (iii 148) 'Easter day: opened us the gate of life, "as the first fruits of them" that rise again. Ascension-day: opened us the gate of heaven; thither as "our forerunner entered," to prepare a place for us.' *Serm. Res.* ii (ii 206 sqq.) is on 1 Cor. xv 20.

—— 11-13. *Serm. Pentec.* xi (iii 309) 'That we may know the grace of the Spirit, they are *ἔξωθεν*, "from without." In us, that is, in our flesh, they grow not; neither they nor any good thing else. And not only ἔξωθεν "from without"; but St James' ἄνωθεν too, "from above, from the Father of lights." Both these are in *super* (Acts ii 16); and but for these, we might fall into a phantasy they grew within us and sprung from us; which, God knoweth, they do not.' Cp. *ib.* vi (iii 211), ix (iii 272), xiv (iii 368). On the evident effects of the coming of the Holy Ghost see *ib.* xiii (iii 356-8), vi (204 sq.).

P. 75. 19. 'Mutual' (ἀλλεπάλληλον), not merely 'common,' because intercessions, alms, etc. are included in the 'hallowed things.' Cp. on p. 47 l. 29.

P. 77. 13 sq. The phrase ὁ ἐν ἁγίοις N. generally means 'N. among saints' i.e. 'Saint N.'; but Andrewes habitually uses it in the present sense.

—— 39. Cp. on p. 52 l. 7.

P. 78. 25. Andrewes has altered the 'war' of the original into 'factiousness.'

P. 79. 6 sqq. Imitated from *Domine Iesu Christi apud me sis ut me defendas*, etc. (also in *Horae* 1494 f. 151). Cp. the benedictions of the sick in *Ordo Rom.* x 33; Menard *Sacr. Greg.* annot. p. 354; *Liber Evesham.* c. 114; *Hort. an.* Lyons 1516 f. 193 b; Gerson *de verbis Venite ad me* (iii 736).

—— 23 sq. Alternative renderings of *hôdh* = majesty.

—— 27 sq. Sept. has this (cp. Isa. lxiv 1) in place of the next three lines which represent the Hebrew.

P. 81. 6 sqq. Cp. *S. Paul's Lectt.* 84-92.

—— 14. L has ἀναστάσεως apparently by mistake for ἀναβάσεως.

—— 16 sq. *Serm. Res.* viii (ii 309 sqq.) is on this text.

—— 20. The day of Andrewes' birth in 1555 is unknown. Sept. 25, which is sometimes given, seems to arise from a misunderstanding of a passage in Buckeridge's funeral sermon: 'Yea, then his life did begin, when his mortality made an end; that was *natalis*, "his birthday," September the twenty-fifth' (*Sermons* v 297)—where the allusion is to *natale*, the technical name for the day of a Saint's death. Besides, Sept. 25 1555 was a Wednesday. The meaning of this petition is not clear; perhaps διὰ τῆς ἡμέρας is a mistake for δ. τὴν ἡμέραν, 'because of.'

P. 82. 17 sq. Heb. 'according to all thy righteousness,' Sept. κατὰ τὴν δικαιοσύνην σου. Andrewes combines Theodotion's ἐν πάσιν ἡ ἐλεημοσύνη σου and Vulg. *in omnem iustitiam tuam* (representing *bekol* instead of *kekol*), but correcting ἐλεημοσύνη.

—— 25-27. This follows exactly neither Heb., Sept., Theodt. nor Vulg.

—— 29, 33. These passages from S. James and S. John are similarly combined in *Serm. Rep.* iii (i 339), *Pent.* iii (iii 153), ix (iii 270), *Absol.* (v 91), *Prayer* xiv (v 428).

P. 82. 31. Cp. *Hebrew daily prayers* p. 9 'let thy mercies rejoice over thine attributes.'

P. 83. 14. *Serm. Res.* ii (ii 219) 'this sin that "cleaveth so fast" to us (Heb. xiii 1)': *S. Giles' Lect.* p. 623 'εὐπερίστατος ἁμαρτία an imbracing sinne.'

—— 20 sq. From the introd. to the Lord's Prayer (59). Cp. *Euchologion*. p. 283 ἐν οἱᾳδήποτε κινήσει σαρκὸς καὶ πνεύματος τοῦ σοῦ ἀπηλλοτριώθη θελήματος καὶ τῆς σῆς ἁγιότητος.

P. 84. 9 sq. *Serm. Res.* v (ii 262) 'That Job's flesh should be admitted upon the Septuagint's reason in the forepart of the verse, τὸ ἀναντλοῦν ταῦτα, that it hath gone through, joined in the good, endured all the evil, as well as the soul.'

—— 20. On *Paraclete* see *Serm. Pentec.* iv (iii 175 sqq.). *Ib.* iii (iii 158) 'If we look up we have a Comforter in heaven, even Himself; and if we look down, we have a Comforter on earth, his Spirit; and so we are at anchor in both.'

—— 25-85, l. 11. The Μεγάλη συναπτή or great litany of the orthodox eastern rite, said by the deacon at the beginning of the Liturgy, at Vespers and at Lauds. The ℟ Κύριε ἐλέησον is said by the choir after each suffrage, except the last, to which the ℟ is Σοὶ κύριε retained by Andrewes. The last line 'for unto Thee' etc. is the beginning of the doxology said by the priest. 'Mother of God' is of course θεοτόκος, *deipara*, 'she who brought forth (as man) Him who is (personally) God.'

P. 85. 28 sqq. This thanksgiving, being a review of life, is appropriate to the weekly commemoration of Andrewes' birthday. Cp. pp. 229, 233, and the thanksgiving in *Hort. animae* 1516 f. 79, quoted below.

—— 29-31. S. Aug. *de civ. Dei* vii 31: quanquam enim quod sumus, quod vivimus, quod cælum terramque conspicimus, quod habemus mentem atque rationem, qua eum ipsum qui hæc omnia condidit inquiramus, nequaquam valeamus actioni sufficere gratiarum.

P. 86. 5. *Serm. Pent.* xii (iii 331) 'His gifts of nature; outward—beauty, stature, strength, activeness; inward—wit to apprehend, memory to retain, judgement to discern, speech to deliver.'

—— 9. 'Instruction' i.e. catechising (κατηχήσεως). See *Cat. doct.* p. 6.

—— 23 sqq. *Horolog.* p. 16 διὰ τῆς ἐπαγγελίας τῶν μελλόντων ἀγαθῶν: p. 90 τῆς τῶν μελλόντων . . ἀπολαύσεως . . θησαυρῶν.

—— 27 sqq. On Andrewes' 'honest and religious parents' see H. Isaacson *Life and death of Lancelot Andrewes* (Andrewes *Minor Works* p. iii); on his 'thankfulness to all from whom he had received any benefit' *ib.* p. xx sq.; on his friends, R. L. Ottley *Lancelot Andrewes* ch. vi; on his bequests to his servants, Isaacson p. xiv. With this passage cp. Marcus Aurelius *Med.* i.

P. 86. 30. 'Colleagues' συμμυστῶν; Newman 'religious intimates': Whyte 'fellow-ministers.' Συμμύστης 'one who is initiated into the mysteries with others': see examples in Lightfoot on S. Ignat. *ad Eph.* 12; and add S. Jer. *Ep.* lviii *ad Paulin.* 11 ad teipsum veniam symmysten, sodalem meum et amicum; and cp. *symmuses*, *symmistæ* as the title of the priests who concelebrate with the archbishop at Lyons (de Moleon *Voyages liturgiques* p. 47). Andrewes probably means simply 'colleagues,' who in fact at most stages of his life would be in orders.

P. 87. 1-6. Preface of *Lit. S. Chrys.* (384) ὑπὲρ τούτων ἁπάντων εὐχαριστοῦμέν σοι . . ὑπὲρ πάντων ὧν ἴσμεν καὶ ὧν οὐκ ἴσμεν, τῶν φανερῶν καὶ ἀφανῶν εὐεργεσιῶν τῶν εἰς ἡμᾶς γεγενημένων: S. Chrys. *hom.* vi *in* 1 *Tim.* 1 εἰ δὲ ὑπὲρ τῶν τοῦ πέλας εὐχαριστεῖν δεῖ, πολλῷ μᾶλλον ὑπὲρ τῶν εἰς ἡμᾶς καὶ τῶν λάθρα γινομένων καὶ ἑκόντων καὶ ἀκόντων καὶ ὑπὲρ τῶν δοκούντων εἶναι λυπηρῶν. Cp. *hom.* x *in Col.* 2.

P. 88. 5 sqq. Cp. *S. Paul's Lect.* pp. 669-672.

—— 14-18. *Serm. Gunpowder Tr.* vii (iv 330) 'We divide his works, as we have warrant, into his works of *Fiat*, as the rest of his creatures; and the work of *Faciamus*, as man, the masterpiece of his works, upon whom He did more cost, shewed more workmanship, than on the rest; the very word *Faciamus* sets him above all. 1. God's προβούλια, that He did deliberate, enter into consultation, as it were, about his making, and about none else. 2. God's αὐτουργία, that Himself framed his body of the mould, as the potter the clay. 3. Then that He breathed into him a two-lived soul, which made the Psalmist break out *Domine quid est homo* etc. "Lord, what is man, that Thou shouldest so regard him," as to pass by the heavens and all the glorious bodies there, and passing by them, breathe an immortal soul, put thine own image upon a piece of clay? 4. But last, God's setting him *super omnia opera manuum suarum*, "over all the works of his hands." His making him, as I may say, Count Palatine of the world; this shews plainly his setting by man more than all of them.' Cp. on p. 35 l. 3: *S. Paul's Lect.* pp. 93-111: S. Clem. Rom. *ad Cor.* 33 § 4, S. Iren. *Hær.* iii 22 § 1.

—— 14, 15. S. Cyr. Al. *Glaph.* i *in Gen.* p. 5 προβουλίοις ἐτίμα καὶ αὐτουργίᾳ τὸ τέχνημα: cp. *in Esai.* i 2 p. 44, *adv. Iulian.* i p. 22.

—— 16. *Serm. Pentec.* vi (iii 206) 'They count them [the gifts of the Holy Ghost]. 1. His *meraḥepheth* or "agitation" (Gen. i 2), which maketh the vegetable power in the world. 2. His *nephesh ḥayāh* "spirit or soul of life" (Gen. i 20), in the living creatures. 3. His *nishmath ḥayyîm* "heavenly spirit of a double life" (Gen. ii 7) in mankind.' Cp. *S. Paul's Lect.* p. 151; and above on ll. 12-16 'a two-lived soul.' *Serm. Res.* ii (ii 217) 'Two lives here be: in the holy tongue, the word which signifieth life [*ḥayyîm*] is of the dual number, to shew us there is a duality of lives, that two there be, and that we to have an eye to both. . . . The Apostle doth after at the forty-fourth verse [1 Cor. xv 44], expressly name them both. 1. One a natural life, or life by the "living soul"; the other, 2. a spiritual life, or life by the "quickening Spirit." Of these two, Adam at the time of his fall had the first, of a "living soul" [*nephesh ḥayāh*], was seized of it; and of him all mankind, Christ and we all, receive that life. But the other, the spiritual, which is the life chiefly to be accounted of, that he then had not, not actually; only a possibility he had, if he had held him in obedience and "walked with God," to have been translated to that other life. . . . Now Adam by his fall fell from both, forfeited both estates. Not only that he had in reversion, by not fulfilling the conditions, but even that he had in *esse* too. For even on that also did death seize after *et mortuus est*.' This interpretation of *ḥayyîm* (an abstract plural, not a dual) is fanciful: the word simply means 'life.'

P. 88. 17. *S. Paul's Lect.* p. 95, 'The lineaments hereof by the Fathers are said to be first, The essence of the soul is in the body, *in omni & unaquaque parte*, as God is in the world. Secondly, the soul is immortal: God is so. Thirdly, there is a triple power of the soul, Understanding, Memory, and Freewill. Understanding is every where, in Heaven, in Earth, in the deep, on this side and beyond the Seas; there is an ubiquitie of the soul, as of Gods presence, every where. Memory, the infinitenesse thereof is as that of God, who is without limitation; *quæ est hæc immensa hominum capacitas?* saith a Father; the will and conscience cannot be bound, but is free to think: so God what him pleaseth, that can he doe. God, by his power, createth man, and maketh a natural World: And Man, likewise, maketh *artificialem mundum*, as ships for carriage, temples for service, lights and candles as artificial starres: *creavit etiam homo alteram quasi naturam*.' Cp. the following context.

—— 18. *S. Paul's Lect.* p. 96 'After God hath crowned man with knowledge and love, in the latter part of this verse [Gen. i 26], he giveth him a Scepter and maketh him Vicegerent over the Sea, the Aire, the Earth; over all the fishes, fowls, beasts, and creeping things therein, bidding him *to rule over them*. . . . *Miscen* saith, *Fecit Deus hominem nudum*, to shew that he needed the help of other Creatures for cloathing and for meat: Mans soveraigntie is to have at his command, and to serve him, the whole earth and the furniture thereof. If God bid him to rule over the fowls, fishes, and the beasts, over the better sort, then surely over the worser: Yea, God hath made the Sunne, the Moon and Starres, with all the hoste of Heaven, to serve man, *and hath distributed them to all People*, Deut. iv 19. *He hath given him dominion over the beasts*, that is, the priviledge of hunting into what parts he please; *and dominion over the Earth*, which is the priviledge of Husbandry. Oh let us live after the similitude of him whose Image we are; and let us not be like, nay worse than beasts, *pejus est comparari bestiæ, quam nasci bestiam.*'

P. 88. 20. *S. Paul's Lect.* pp. 155-167.

—— 21 sqq. col. 3. Cp. pp. 35, 40.

—— 31 sq. It is an early speculation that the Fall and the promise of the victory of the Seed happened on Friday, the day of the fulfilment of the promise. S. Irenæus *Hær.* v 23 § 2 Si quis velit diligenter discere qua die ex septem diebus mortuus est Adam, inveniet ex Domini dispositione. Recapitulans enim universum hominem in se ab initio usque ad finem, recapitulatus est et mortem eius. Manifestum est itaque, quoniam in illa die mortem sustinuit Dominus obediens Patri in qua mortuus est Adam inobediens Deo. In qua antem mortuus est, in ipsa et manducavit. Dixit enim Deus *In qua die manducabitis ex eo, morte moriemini.* Hunc itaque diem recapitulans in semetipsum Dominus venit ad passionem pridie ante sabbatum, quæ est sexta conditionis dies in qua homo plasmatus est, secundam plasmationem ei, eam quæ est a morte, per suam passionem donans. Cp. [Tertullian] *adv. Marcion.* ii 161: [S. Ath.] *Quæst. ad Antioch.* 49: Ludolph. Sax. *Vita Christi* ii 66 § 7: Dante *Par.* xxvi 139 sqq. The correspondence is also extended to the hour of the day, Bede *in Marc. Evang.* xv 33: Theophylact *in Matt.* xxvii 45: *Synaxarion* of Sunday of the Tyrophagos: *Golden Legend* Passion.

P. 90. 22-36. Modelled upon and largely quoted from the *Salve tremendum . . caput* (*Horae* 1514 f. 70); cp. p. 216 below. L omits 'given to drink,' 'shamefully befouled,' 'loaded,' which are supplied by W, apparently from the Latin text (on the opposite page in the ed. of 1675). Cp. *Serm. Res.* x (ii 355) 'They loosed Him not, but rudely they rent and rived Him, one part from another, with all extremity; left not one piece of the *continuum* whole together. With their whips they loosed not, but tore his skin and flesh all over; with their hammers and nails they did not *solvere* [S. Jo. ii 19], but *fodere* [Ps. xxii 17] his hands and feet; with the wreath of thorns they loosed not, but gored his head round about; and with the spear-point rived the very heart of Him, as if He had said to them *Dilaniate*, and not *solvite.* For as if He had come *e lanienâ*, it was not *corpus solutum*, but *lacerum:* "his body not loosed, but mangled and broken," *corpus quod frangitur:* and his blood not easily let out, but spilt and poured out, *sanguis qui funditur* (1 Cor. xi 24, S. Mt. xxvi 28) even like water upon the ground.' *Passion* ii (ii 143) 'His skin and flesh rent with the whips and scourges, his hands and feet wounded with the nails, his head with the thorns, his very heart with the spear-point; all his senses, all his parts laden with whatsoever wit or malice could invent. His blessed body given as an anvil to be beaten upon with the violent hands of those barbarous miscreants.'

—— 22. *Serm. Passion* ii (ii 144) 'No manner violence offered

Him in body, no man touching Him or being near Him; in a cold night, for they were fain to have a fire within doors, lying abroad in the air and upon the cold earth, to be all of a sweat, and that sweat to be blood; and not as they call it *diaphoreticus* "a thin faint sweat," but *grumosus* "of great drops"; and those so many, so plenteous, as they went through his apparel and all; and through all streamed to the ground, and that in great abundance;—read, enquire, and consider, *si fuerit sudor sicut sudor iste* "if ever there were sweat like this sweat of His."'

P 90. 24. *Serm. Passion* iii (ii 170) 'They did not put on his wreath of thorns and press it down with their hands, but beat it on with bats to make it enter through skin, flesh, skull and all.' *Res.* vi (ii 277) 'When "they made furrows on his back" with the scourges, when "they platted the crown of thorns and made it sit close to his head," when "they digged his hands and feet," He felt all.' So Ludolph of Saxony *Vita Christi* ii 62 § 19 *et acceperunt arundinem* de manu eius et *percutiebant* sacrum *caput eius:* et ratione doloris infligendi ut aculei spinarum fortius infigerentur capiti: and the *Golden Litany* (Maskell *Mon. rit.* iii p. 268) 'thi crowne of thornes violently pressed on thi hede.' This seems to be only an interpretation of S. Matt. xxvii 30, and perhaps is not intended by the Evangelist. Its treatment in art, often with painful emphasis, is familiar: see Mrs. Jameson *The History of our Lord* ii pp. 87 sq.

— 26. *Serm. Res.* vi (ii 277) 'And for *reprobaverunt* [Ps. cxviii 22], that is as true. For how could they have entreated a reprobate worse than they entreated Him? in his thirst, in his prayer, in the very pangs of death, what words of scorn and spiteful opprobry!' *Golden Litany* (Maskell *Mon. rit.* iii p. 271) 'for tho opprobrious and scornefull wordes whych hangyng on the crosse Thou herdist spokyn vnto Thee.'

— 30 sq. *Serm. Passion* iii (ii 170) 'In Gabbatha they did not whip Him, saith the Psalmist, "they ploughed his back and made," not stripes but "long furrows." . . . They did not in Golgotha pierce his hands and feet, but made wide holes like that of a spade, as if they had been digging in some ditch (Ps. xxii 16).'

— 32. Ludolph of Saxony *Vita Christi* ii 63 § 41 de qua oratione videtur loqui apostolus dicens de Christo *Qui in diebus carnis suæ* etc. Cp. *S. Giles' Lect.* p. 691. *Serm. Pass.* ii (ii 146) 'His most dreadful cry, which at once moved all the powers in heaven and earth "My God, my God, why hast Thou forsaken Me?" Weigh well that cry, consider it well and tell me *si fuerit clamor sicut clamor iste* "if ever there were cry like that of his."' *Res.* xvi (iii 55) 'That we might cry "Abba Father," He was content to cry that strange cry *Eli Eli*, "My God, my God," on the cross.' *Golden Litany* (Maskell *Mon. rit.* iii p. 271) 'for that grete and myserable crye that Thou madist to thi Father.'

P. 90. 35 sq. The words of Institution are here applied to the Passion, as in *Serm. Res.* vii (ii 300). But 'broken' is probably no part of the N.T. text, but a liturgical addition; and in any case it refers, not to what was done in the passion, but to the 'breaking' of our Lord's body for distribution as food (cp. Is. lviii 7). And it is questionable whether 'outpoured' refers to the shedding of our Lord's blood on the cross, and not rather to its application, the antitype of the levitical outpouring, sprinkling etc. (1 S. Pet. i 2: Heb. ix 19-26).

P. 91. 24 sqq. *Serm. Pentec.* i (iii 129) 'There be nine of them set down, nine "manifestations of the Spirit"—some of them nine; there be nine more set down, nine "fruits of the Spirit"—some of them nine, some gift He will give.' *Ib.* vii (233) 'Great variety of gifts there are in it, and all are feathers of the dove mentioned in this Psalm, verse thirteen [Ps. lxviii 13]; either the silver feathers of her wing, or the golden of her neck, for all are from her. They are reduced all to two; 1. "The gifts," 2. "the fruits." "The gifts," (1 Cor. xii 4) known by the term *gratis data;* "the fruits" pertaining to *gratum faciens.* But the *gratum faciens* bring to every man for himself, the *gratis data* for the benefit of the Church in common; these latter are ever reckoned the proper, and most principal, *dona aedit* of this day.'

—— 24-27. *Serm Pentec.* vii (iii 238) 'We said even now: to "dwell among us," He must dwell *in* us; and in us He will "dwell," if the fruits of his Spirit be found in us. And of his fruits the very first is love. And the fruit is as the tree is. For He Himself is love, the essential love, and love-knot of the undivided Trinity.' In the West, the fruits of the Spirit are commonly counted as twelve, in accordance with the text of the Vulgate. The Old Latin version has nine: *caritas*, *gaudium*, *pax*, *patientia*, *bonitas*, *mansuetudo*, *fides*, *lenitas*, *continentia castitatis.* The Vulgate adds *benignitas* before *bonitas*, and *longanimitas* before *mansuetudo*, apparently as preferable renderings of χρηστότης and ἀγαθωσύνη, and for *lenitas* reads *modestia*, and for *continentia castitatis* reads *continentia*, *castitas.* Cp. S. Thom. Aq. *Summa* ii[1] 70.

—— 28-30. The Gifts of the Holy Ghost, *dona Spiritus Sancti.* *Serm. Pentec.* ii (iii 134) 'These "gifts" and "graces" be of many points, more points of this wind than there be of the compass, and as it were many Spirits in One; six, saith Esay (Is. xi 2); "seven," saith St John (Rev. i 4, iii 1).' *Ib.* xii (iii 335) 'And care not for them that talk, they know not what, of "the spirit of bondage." Of the seven Spirits, which are the divisions of one and the same Spirit . . . the last and chiefest of all is "the Spirit of the fear of God" (Is. xi 2).' Cp. *Prayer* ix (v 388). The seven are derived from Is. xi 2, 3 through the Sept., which renders 'the fear of the Lord,' in v. 2 by εὐσέβεια, and in v. 3 by φόβος θεοῦ. Cp. S. Thom. Aq. *Summa* ii[1] 68.

—— 31-39. The spiritual gifts, τὰ πνευματικά, *spiritualia*, χαρίσματα, *gratiæ* (1 Cor. xii 1, 4). *Serm. Pentec.* xv (iii 384) 'The word is χαρίσματα. It is a word of the Christian style; you shall not read it in any heathen author. We turn it "gifts." "Gifts" is somewhat too short, χάρισμα is more than a gift. But first, a gift it is. It is not enough with us Christians that a thing be had; with the heathen man it is, he cares for no more, he calls it ἕξις. Sure he is he hath it, and that is all he looks after. The Christian adds further, how he hath it; hath it not of himself, spins not his thread as the spider doth, out of himself, but hath it of another, and hath it of gift. It is given him. *Unicuique datur*, it is the eleventh verse [1 Cor. xii 11]. "To everyone is given." So instead of Aristotle's word ἕξις habit [*Eth. Nic.* ii 6 § 15] he puts St James' word, δόσις or δώρημα—it is "a gift" unto him. And how a gift? Not *do ut des;* give him as good a thing for it, and so was well worthy of it. No, but of free gift. And so to St James' word, δώρημα, which is no more but a gift, he adds St Paul's here, χάρισμα wherein there is χάρις, that is, "grace," and so a grace-gift, or gift of grace. This word the pride of our nature digests not well, φύσις and φυσίωσις touch near, nature is easily puffed or blown up; but χάρισμα hath a prick in it for the bladder of our pride, as if either of ourselves we had it and received it not, or received it but it was because we earned it. No, it is *gratis accepistis* on our part, and *gratis data* on his; freely given of Him, freely received by us; and that is χάρισμα right.' *Ib.* p. 380 'By "Gifts" is meant the inward endowing, enabling, qualifying, whereby one, for his skill, is meet and sufficient for aught.' Cp. the whole *Serm. Pentec.* xv (iii 377 sqq.) on 1 Cor. xii 4-7.

P. 92. 3-5. *Serm. Prayer* xviii (v 462) 'We are thy workmanship created by Thee; therefore "despise not the works of thy own hands."' *Prymer* 1557 f. P1 'O most mighty maker, despise not thi work.' *Euchology.* p. 229 πλάσμα σόν εἰμι, μὴ παρίδῃς τὸ ἔργον τῶν χειρῶν σου. Erasmus *Precatio* (ap. *Orarium* 1546 f. 256 b) Tu factor es, refice opus tuum quod formasti.

—— 6-8. *Serm. Prayer* xviii (v 462) 'Besides, we are the "likeness" of God's "image"; therefore suffer not thine own image to be defaced in us, but repair it.' Cassiodorus *de Instit.* 33 imaginem tuam in nobis non sinas obscurari.

—— 9-11. *Serm. Prayer* xviii (v 462) 'Secondly, in regard of Christ, we are the price of Christ's blood. *Empti estis pretio*, "Ye are bought with a price"; therefore suffer not so great a price to be lost, but deliver us and save us.' S. Aug. *Serm.* 274 potens homo non potest perdere quod emit auro suo et Christus perdit quod emit sanguine suo?: Erasmus *Precatio* (*Orarium* 1546 f. 256 b) Tu redemptor es, serva quod emisti: *Prymer* 1557 f. P1 'O most prudent redemer, suffer not to perish the price of thy redempcion.'

—— 12-14. *Serm. Prayer* xviii (v 462) 'Again, we carry his name, for as He is Christ, so we are of Him called Christians. Seeing, therefore, that "thy name is called upon us," be gracious to us and grant our request.' S. Anselm *Med.* xi 26 christianum me fecisti vocari de nomine tuo.

P. 92. 27-93. l. 9. From the Greek Mattins, *Horolog.* p. 21 sq.

P. 93. 11-21. From *The Book of Common Order* ('Knox's Liturgy') 1564 (ed. Sprott, 1901, p. 191); thence in Sternhold and Hopkins *Psalms* 1566 (*Lit. Services of the reign of Q. Elizabeth* Parker Soc. p. 265); H. Bull *Christian prayers and holy meditations* 1566 (ed. Parker Soc. p. 54); *Christian prayers* 1578 (*Private prayers of the reign of Q. Elizabeth* Parker Soc. p. 559). The last words seem to be copied in Francis Bacon's 'grant them patience and perseverance in the end and to the end.' (*Works* ed. Ellis and Spedding, vii p. 262).

—— 22-28. The *Anima Christi* is at least of the xivth century. Harl. MS. 1260 f. 158, of about 1370, and later books note that an indulgence was attached to the saying of it at the Elevation, by John XXII who died in 1334. The variations in the text of it may be illustrated from the following groups of authorities: A. Brit. Mus. MSS. *Harl.* 1260 f. 158 (*Horae*, written in England, c. 1370), *Add.* 28962 f. 419 b (Spanish Dominican *Horae* of beginning of xvth cent.): B. *Heures de Lengres* Vostre, Paris 1502, f. 86 b, *Prymer of Salisbury* N. Le Roux, Rouen 1537, f. 18 b: C. *Prymer of Salisbury* N. Le Roux, Rouen 1537, f. 142 b; Regnault, Rouen, 1537, dd f. 2: D. *Hortulus animae* Strassburg 1503 f. v 5, Lyon 1513 f. 165, Lyon 1516 f. 170: E. S. Ignatius Loyola *Exercitia spiritualia* Toulouse 1593 title page *verso*: F. the current text, e.g. in *Horae diurnae*, Tournai 1889. Taking the last as the standard, the results of collation are as follows:—

1. Anima Christi sanctifica me	Harl. MS. *prefixes* 'O.'
2. corpus Christi salva me	
3. sanguis Christi inebria me	
4. aqua lateris Christi lava me	*add.* splendor vultus Christi illumina me C.
5. passio Christi conforta me	*add* sudor vultus Christi virtuosissimi sana me B.
6. o bone Jesu exaudi me	*Prymer* Le Roux 1537 *omits* 'o.'
7. *intra tua vulnera absconde me*	*om.* AB. in vulneribus tuis C. vulnera tua D.
8. *ne permittas me separari a te*	*om* C. et ne ABD.
9. ab hoste maligno defende me	
10. in hora mortis *meæ* voca me	*om.* meæ AB.
11. *et iube me venire ad te*	*om.* et E. et pone me iuxta te AB. protege me et pone me iuxta te C.
12. ut cum *sanctis* tuis *laudem te*	sanctis angelis C. sanctis et angelis E. angelis et sanctis B. angelis A. *om.* laudem te C. te dominum salvatorum meum B.
in saecula *saeculorum.* Amen.	saeculorum laudem te C.

In the first (Rome 1548) and second (Vienna 1563) editions of the *Exercitia spiritualia* the *Anima Christi* is frequently referred to, as a familiar devotion, but its text is not given till the Toulouse ed. of 1593. In the first ed. of Wil. Nakatenus *Cæleste palmetum* 1668 and in that of 1699 it is called *brevis et pia oratio S. P. Ignatio fundatori Societatis Jesu olim familiaris*, but in the later editions published after Nakatenus' death it is called *brevis et pia oratio S. Ignatii*, and since then its authorship has commonly been ascribed to Ignatius. See J. Mearns and Linke in *Blätter für Hymnologie* 1, Jan. 1894.

Andrewes uses with modifications vv. 1-5, 7, and the clause interpolated between 5 and 6 by B. With his 3, 4 cp. *Serm. Pentec.* xiii (iii 359) 'Come, o blessed Spirit, and bear witness to our spirit, that Christ's water and his blood, we have our part in both': with 5, 6 cp. *Serm. Passion* ii (ii 153) '"By his stripes we are healed," by his sweat we refreshed, by his forsaking we received to grace.'

P. 93. 30 sqq. This blessing first appears as a blessing after communion in the *Order of Communion* of 1548. In the book of 1549 it was prefixed to the final blessing of the mass, where it has since remained.

—— 35 sqq. Cp. p. 35 l. 10 sqq; Neh. ix; Wisd. xix 22; *Litt. E. and W.* p. 51.

P. 94. 8 sqq. See on p. 35 l. 30.

—— 14. *Serm. Nativ.* i (i 6) 'but when men fell, He did all.' S. Chrys. *ad eos qui scandalizantur* 8 (iii 483) *οὐ διέλιπεν ἐξ ἀρχῆς ἕως τέλους πάντα ποιῶν καὶ πραγματευόμενος ὑπὲρ τοῦ γένους τοῦ ἡμετέρου*: *Euchol.* p. 312 *ὁ πάντα ποιῶν καὶ πραγματευόμενος ἐπὶ σωτηρίᾳ τοῦ γένους τῶν ἀνθρώπων.*

P. 96. 6-9. Cp. *S. Paul's Lect.* pp. 122-130.

—— 10-15. *S. Paul's Lectt.* p. 135 'The Ceremonie of the Sabbath taught us a double Lesson and Document, the one of a benefit already past and exhibited [i.e. conferred], as of the Creation done on the seventh day. The other of a benefit to be exhibited hereafter and perfected also on the seventh day, that is, the work of Redemption and Regeneration. So now the promised Saviour being come, that Ceremony of the set seventh day surceaseth and the first day of the week is in its stead. There was also another Ceremonie, *Heb.* 4. 9. and that taught us to rest from sinne in this life and also it was a type of the eternall rest in the life to come, *Revel.* 14. 13': S. Thom. Aq. *Summa* ii² 122 § 4 ad 1: similiter etiam cærimoniale est (viz. the 4th Commandment) secundum allegoricam significationem, prout fuit signum quietis Christi in sepulchro quæ fuit septima die: et similiter secundum moralem significationem, prout significat cessationem ab omni actu peccati et quietem mentis in Deo: . . similiter etiam cærimoniale est secundum significationem anagogicam, prout scilicet præfigurat quietem fruitionis Dei quæ erit in patria.

Serm. Res. xii (ii 397) 'For his body it was the day of rest, the last sabbath that ever was; and then his body did rest,

rest in hope': *Against Mr Traske* (*Minor Works* p. 91) 'It hath ever been the Church's doctrine that Christ made an end of all sabbaths by his sabbath in the grave. That sabbath was the last of them. And that the Lord's Day presently came in place of it.'

P. 96. 11. 'An intermittent rest' ἀναπαύσεως ἀμοιβαίας. Newman renders 'the Christian rest instead of it' (cp. Andrewes above 'in its stead,' 'in the place of it'); but ἀμοιβαίας cannot bear this meaning. Drake has 'the rest in the returns thereof,' Peter Hall 'our intervals of rest in its return,' Medd 'recurring'; and these are no doubt right. 'Αμοιβ. must mean 'alternating with' or the like: and may be represented by 'recurrent,' 'intermittent.' Cp. *S. Paul's Lectt.* p. 161 'if we beware of this fall and losse, we shall at last not only come to that *Sabbatum cum intermissione*, which was but once a week, but to that *Sabbatum sine intermissione*, which Christ hath appointed for us . . . an everlasting Sabbath of repose and rest without any ceasing.' The clause commemorates the *principle* of a day of rest.

P. 97. 27. The *Prayer of Manasses*, purporting to be that alluded to in 2 Chr. xxxiii 12, 13, is first quoted at length in the 3rd cent. in *Didascalia apostolorum* (=*Ap. Constt.* ii 22). It is commonly included in Greek MS. Bibles (*e.g.* Cod. Alex.) among the hymns suffixed to the Psalter; and in the Old Latin version (Sabatier iii 1038 sq.); and it was printed in R. Stephen's Vulgate of 1540. While not admitted into the Tridentine Canon, it is added along with 3 and 4 Esdras as an appendix to post-Tridentine editions of the Vulgate. And it is included among the so-called Apocrypha of the English and of Luther's Bible. It is recited in the Greek 'Απόδειπνον or Compline (*Horolog.* p. 164); and since Andrewes' text agrees almost exactly with that of the *Horologion*, which differs considerably from that of *Ap. Constt.* (first printed in 1583), and since the first edition of the Septuagint text which included the Prayer was Walton's Polyglott of 1657, Andrewes must have derived it from the *Horologion*. It occurs in Latin in the *Horae* and *Prymer*, e.g. *Horae* 1514 f. 109 b, and in English among the *Prayers* appended to Sternhold and Hopkins' metrical Psalms and afterwards to editions of the Book of Common Prayer (*Lit. Services of the reign of Q. Elizabeth* pp. xix, 270).

P. 98. 28-34. A series of neuter plurals, expressing concrete acts of sin in its various aspects. Where the word occurs both in the O.T. and the N.T. a ref. is given to each; where a ref. is given only to one of the two, it is meant that the word does not occur in the other; where more than one ref. is given to the O.T., the Greek represents different Hebrew words. 'Αμάρτημα ('sin') and ἀνόμημα ('iniquity') are used very generally in O.T. to represent many different Heb. words, but only one O.T. ref. is given for each. Πταῖσμα ('fault') is not used in either O.T. or N.T., but only the verb πταίειν.

P. 98. 36-99. l. 26. When the Greek in the second column is used in the Sept. to represent the Hebrew of the first, the same ref. is given in both columns, and where the word is used also in the N.T. a ref. is added. *Serm. Pent.* xiii (iii 347) 'To take away sin, two things are to be taken away. For in sin are these two; 1. *Reatus*, and 2. *Macula*, as all Divines agree, 'the guilt,' and 'the soil' or spot. The guilt, to which punishment is due; the spot, whereby we grow loathsome in God's eyes, and even in men's too.'

—— 36. *Nāthan* (give) is not used in this sense in O.T.; while *nāthan 'al* (give upon) is used in the opposite sense, 'to impute' Ezek. vii 3, Jon. i 14; cp. Deut. xxi 8.

P. 99. 28 sqq. *S. Giles' Lect.* p 626 'As they that are partakers of the Divine nature, are a body compact of many joynts and sinnews; so the divine spirit is not one alone, but as the ancient Fathers define the eleventh verse of the seventh chapter of *Isaiah*, and the fourth chapter of the *Apocalyps*. Secondly, This is not *promiscuè*, confusedly; but orderly as in a Quier, one begins, another follows: This multitude of virtues is *Acies ordinata*, *Canticles* the sixt chapter, like the marching of Soldiers; for it comes from God, *who is the God of order and not of confusion.* Thirdly, All at once doe not break out, but there is a successive bringing in one of the other. In that order there are degrees, First, *Faith:* Secondly, *Virtue:* Thirdly, *Knowledge.* The number of virtues be eight, as eight parts of repentance, in the second epistle to the *Corinthians* the seventh chapter. Those contain our separation from the Devils nature: As the other are our union with Gods nature, which are usually compared to those eight steps, in *Ezekiel* the fourtieth chapter, from the thirty first to the fourty first verse, they are our assents, whereby we approach to the Altar; so the promises of blessednesse which our Saviour speaketh of, are eight, *Matthew* the fift chapter. Another thing to be observed is, That of these eight there are four pair; for to a theologicall virtue is added ever more a moral: *Faith*, *knowledge*, *godlinesse*, and *charity*, are theologicall; to every one of these there is a moral virtue.' This and the following lectures (pp. 626-639) are on these virtues.

—— 36 sqq. *S. Giles' Lect.* pp. 544-549 is on 2nd Pet. i 9, 10.

P. 100. 18-21. *Serm. Res.* i (ii 205) 'He is our Lord who, having come to save that which was lost, will not suffer that to be lost which He hath saved': cp. *ib.* v (ii 258): Erasmus *Precatio* (*Orarium* 1546 f. 256 b) Tu servator es, ne sinas perire qui tibi innituntur. See on p. 92 l. 11.

—— 22. *Serm. Pent.* xiv (iii 372) 'Good things come from Him as kindly as do they: therefore said to be, not the Author, the Lord and Giver, but even the very Faither of them.' It is curious that Andrewes seems to be misled by the English rendering 'the Lord and Giver of life' of the τὸ κύριον καὶ τὸ ζωοποιόν of the Constantinopolitan creed. But perhaps he has in mind the phrase of the post-sanctus of *Lit. S. James* πάσης ἁγιωσύνης κύριος καὶ δωτήρ (*Litt E. and W*. p. 51).

P. 100. 24. *Serm. Pent.* xv (iii 398) 'To know that end then, that we run not in vain, labour not in vain, have not the gifts, take not on us the calling, do not the works in vain, "receive not the grace of God in vain," nay receive not our own souls in vain': *Prayer* iii (v 326) 'If we ask we shall have grace, whereby it shall appear we have not received our soul in vain.' 'To receive the soul in vain' λαβεῖν ἐπὶ ματαίῳ τὴν ψυχήν is the Sept. rendering of 'to lift up the mind to vanity' Ps xxiv 4 (Vulg. 'accepit in vano animam'). See the Latin commentators *in loc.*

P. 101. 2-13. From the Greek Lauds (*Horolog.* p. 73) and Evensong (*ib.* p. 148).

—— 15-17. From the *Benedicat me imperialis maiestas*—but with the verbs of the second and third lines interchanged, no doubt rightly.

—— 20-30. From *Obsecro te domina*—some of the verbs being changed. Cp. the episcopal benedictions in the *Gregorian Sacramentary* in *Opp. S. Greg. Mag.* iii 624, 628, 635: Alcuin *Confessio* iv 18 (=S. Ans. *Or.* xvi, *Med.* xviii 17).

P. 102. 7-16. col. 2, 17-26. From *Oratio de omnibus sanctis* O mitissime Deus. Cp. p. 221 sq.

—— 14. 'Ascetics' is substituted for 'penitents' of the original.

—— 16. 'Sweetening,' γλυκασμοῦ. The construction does not admit of Newman's rendering 'infants, darlings of the world.' Γλυκασμός is used not infrequently of the Blessed Virgin in the Greek service-books.

—— 17-26. This corresponds line by line with the list above.

—— 23. Τῆς σπουδῆς should perhaps be rendered 'study': it represents *studia* of the original.

P. 104. 2, 3. These lines, R. Drake's translation of Dean Nowell's couplet:—

> ὅς δὲ σὺ νῦν νυκτὸς κατὰ πάντα κάλυψας ὀμίχλῃ
> ἀμπλακίας ἡμῶν σοῖς οἰκτιρμοῖσι κάλυπτε,

together with the original, and a Latin rendering, also by Drake, is written on the last page of W and on p. 142 of B.

—— 18 sqq. The hymn Φῶς ἱλαρόν, like the Morning Hymn, was appended to the *Preces* by the first editor of the text, being derived from Ussher *de Romanæ ecclesiæ symbolo apostolico vetere* p. 43. It was already ancient and popular in 374, as appears from S. Basil *de Spiritu sancto* 29. By a mistaken inference from the context, in which S. Basil speaks of 'the hymn of Athenogenes,' the Φῶς ἱλαρόν is sometimes attributed to S. Athenogenes the Martyr (fl. 196), as in the *Horologion* where it is headed ποίημα παλαιὸν ἤ ὥς τινες λέγουσιν Ἀθηνογένους τοῦ Μάρτυρος; and there is also a mistaken tradition attributing it to S. Sophronius of Jerusalem (†c. 637). It forms part of the Greek Evensong, *Horolog.* p. 145, where, as in S. Basil, it is called ἡ ἐπιλύχνιος εὐχαριστία: it is used also in the Armenian evensong. The most interesting of the many English translations are J. Keble's 'Hail gladdening Light' in *Brit. Mag.* 1834 and *Lyra Apostolica* 1836 (*H. A. and M.* 18), and H. W. Longfellow's 'O gladsome Light of the Father immortal' in *The Golden Legend* 1851. See *Dictionary of Hymnology* s. v. Φῶς ἱλαρόν.

P. 105 sq. *S. Paul's Lect.* p. 21 (on Gen. i 4) '*Examen in mente est quod visus in oculo.* Therefore we must consider often of our doings, to see whether they be good or bad, which thing is contrary and against a humour of ours; for when we have done any thing, we never consider whether it be good or bad, we have no regard of it afterwards. Therefore, the Prophets oftentimes beat upon this exhortation, *Vadite in cor vestrum.* Consider your own doing in your hearts, *Esay* 46. 8. *Preach.* 2. 12. The wise man, often saith, that he returned to consider the fruit and labor of his hands, to see the vanity or good of them: And if we thus consider our waies and works, whether they be good or evill, and repent, or rejoyce, approve or disprove them, then we doe, like Children, imitate our Father: If God return to behold his light, how much more should we return to see and consider of our works of darknesse, and to acknowledge with repentance, how evill they are.' Cp. *ib.* p. 110.

—— 21. Virgil *Georg.* iii 454 alitur vitium vivitque tegendo: S. Chrys. *hom.* xxxi *in Heb.* 3 ἁμαρτία γὰρ ὁμολογουμένη ἐλάττων γίνεται, μὴ ὁμολογουμένη δὲ χείρων. Cp. Ovid *Remed. am.* 91 sq.; Machiavelli *Il principe* 3.

P. 106. 4. Cicero *de senect.* 11: Pythagoreorumque more exercendæ memoriæ gratia, quid quoque die dixerim audierim egerim commemoro vesperi. Cp. Woolton *Christian Manual* 1576 p. 101 (ed. Parker Soc.).

—— 7 sq. The Greek which Ausonius translates is (*Poetæ min. græc.* Cambr. 1667 p. 421)

> μηδ' ὕπνον μαλακοῖσιν ἐπ' ὄμμασι προσδέξασθαι
> πρὶν τῶν ἡμερινῶν ἔργων τρὶς ἕκαστον ἐπελθεῖν.

—— 11. According to Lucian, trials before the Areopagus were held at night, in order that the judges might not be moved to partiality by the sight of the speakers: *Hermotimus* 64 (ed. Dindorf, i p. 314) κατὰ τοὺς Ἀρεοπαγίτας αὐτὸ ποιοῦντα οἳ ἐν νυκτὶ καὶ σκότῳ δικάζουσιν ὡς μὴ ἐς τοὺς λέγοντας ἀλλ' ἐς τὰ λεγόμενα ἀποβλέποιεν: cp. *de domo* 18 (iii p. 91).

—— 26. 'Rabbi J.', perhaps Jonah of Gerunde (13th cent.), whose *Portæ pænitentiæ* and *Liber timoris* were printed at Venice in 1544.

P. 107. 3 sq. The opening words (with διαβάς of v. 3 substituted for διελθών) of the *troparia* in the Greek Ἀπόδειπνον or Compline, which are the original of 'The day is past and over' (*H. A. and M.* 21), translated by J. M. Neale and first published in *The Ecclesiastic and Theologian* 1853 and *Hymns* *of the Eastern Church* 1862 and amended into its present shape in the 2nd ed. of the latter, 1862. See *Dict. of Hymnology* s.v. Τὴν ἡμέραν διελθών. The troparia occur also in the Coptic Compline (Bute *Coptic Morning Service* p. 135).

P 107. 28. *Cat. Doct.* p. 216 '*Cor sanum* "a sound heart," which is the true *lignum vitæ*, the life of the body, Prov. xiv 30, and without it our life is but a dying life, ἄβιος βίος.' Cp. Empedocles *de natura* prœm. 38 παῦρον δὲ ζωῆς ἀβίου μέρος ἀθρήσαντες ὠκύμοροι.

—— 31. Θάνατος ἀθάνατος here seems to mean 'death from which there is no return.' Elsewhere (p. 244) it is used of hell.

P. 108. 15. L ends abruptly here. For lines 14, 15, W reads 'To remember the days of darkness that they are many, that so we be not cast into outer darkness: to remember withal to prevent the night by doing some good thing.' Cp. Eccl. xi 8, S. Mt. xxii 13.

—— 35. *Heb. even. pr.* p. 96 'Thou createst day and night.'

P. 109. 17. Eur. *Hippol.* 255 πρὸς ἄκρον μυελὸν ψυχῆς. Cp. S. Aug. *Serm.* 330 § 1: medullisque intimis cordis: S. Ans. *Orat.* x: totis medullis cordis, toto nisu mentis te rogo.

—— 39. From the second prayer of S. Basil in Ἀκολ. τῆς ἁγ. μεταλήψεως.

P. 110. 5. Pr. of S. Ephraim in Greek Mattins πνεῦμα . . . ἀργολογίας μή μοι δῷς.

—— 7 sq. See the 4th troparion of the first ode of the Κανὼν ἱκετήριος, *Horolog.* p. 489 αἰσχρῶν ἐνθυμήσεων ἐν ἐμοὶ πηγάζει πλημμύρα βορβορώδης καὶ ζοφερά.

—— 11. See on p. 113 l. 32.

—— 14. From the second collect of the English Litany, itself derived from the collect in *Processionale Sarisburiense* (ed. Henderson p. 121) Infirmitatem nostram quæsumus Domine propitius respice et mala omnia quæ iuste mereamur omnium sanctorum tuorum intercessione averte.

—— 21. Cp. the prayer of Antiochus the Monk in Compline, *Horolog.* p. 172 καὶ δὸς ἡμῖν δέσποτα πρὸς ὕπνον ἀπιοῦσιν ἀνάπαυσιν σώματος καὶ ψυχῆς.

P. 111. 7 sqq., 19. From the same prayer.

—— 13-18, 21. From a troparion in the Greek Compline.

P. 113. 32 sqq. Also in *Primer in Latin and English according to the reformed Latin* Antwerp, Arnold Conings, 1604, p. 200: si quid dignum laude egimus propitius respice, et quod negligenter actum est clementer ignosce.

P. 114. 13 sq. Cp. *Hort. an.* 1516 f. 76: *oratio dicenda a dormituro:* . . . nunquam cor obdormiat sed semper tecum vigilet.

—— 36 sq. *S. Paul's Lect.* p. 20 '*Sive Lucerna ardet, videt te: sive extincta est, videt te* saith one.'

P. 115. 29 sqq. See on p. 113 l. 32.

P. 116. 38 sq. From the collect of the mass of the Five Wounds. Cp. *Horae* 1514, f. 69; S. Ans. *Med.* i 51; the intercession of the Mass, and the last prayer in the Burial of the Dead, of 1549. P. 251 below.

P. 117. 21 sqq. Cp. p. 225. *Serm. Gunpowder Tr.* vii (iv 340) 'Glory be to Thee, o Lord, glory be to Thee; glory be to Thee, and glory be to thy mercy, the *super omnia* (Ps. cxlv. 9), the most glorious of all thy great and high perfections. Glory be to Thee and glory be to it—to it in Thee and to Thee for it; and that by all thy works, in all places and at all times. And of all thy works, and above them all, by us here; by the hearts and lungs of us all, in this place, this day, for this day, for the mercy of this day; for the mercy of it above all mercies, and for the work of this day above all the works of it. And not this day only, but all the days of our life, even as long as thy mercy endureth, and that "endureth for ever"—for ever in this world, for ever in the world to come; *per*, "through" the cistern and conduit of all thy mercies, Jesus Christ.'

—— 30. sqq. Cp. *Serm. Gunpowder Tr* vii (iv 325) 'All the tongues of saints and angels must say this verse with us *Misericordia Domini super omnia opera eius.*'

P. 121. 2-17. From 'the third prayer, of S. Chrysostom,' in Ἀκολουθία τῆς ἁγ. μεταλήψεως.

—— 10. Cp. *Serm. Nativ.* vi (i 99) 'The house would be somewhat handsome, as handsome as we could, that is to receive Him. We blame them that this day received Him in a stable; take heed we do not worse ourselves.' Cp. ii (i 29).

—— 12. *S. Giles' Lectt.* p. 596 'And that no unworthinesse by means of any filth, either of body or soul, doth keep Him from us, we see, for bodily uncleannesse, He was content to be received by *Simon* the leper (Mk. xiv 3); And in regard of spiritual pollution, howsoever a man know himself to be a sinner, that is, to have an unclean soul, yet not to despair, because Christ, by the confession of his enemies, is such a one as doth not only receive sinners, but *eats with them* (Luke xv 3).'

—— 18. *S. Giles' Lectt.* p. 601 'Now we receive Christ, and therefore there is great hope, that if we come, He will receive us: Now we celebrate the memory of his death, when He was content to receive the thief that came unto Him; and therefore it is most likely that He will receive us, if we come to Him.'

—— 20 sqq. Cp. *Lit. S. Jas.* p. 38 (*Litt. E. and W.* p. 65) *κατηξίωσας ἡμᾶς τοὺς ἁμαρτωλοὺς καὶ ἀναξίους δούλους σου ἐν ἀπολαύσει γενέσθαι τῶν ἀχράντων σου μυστηρίων*: *Lit. S. Bas.* p. 66 (340) *καταξίωσον ἀκατακρίτως μετασχεῖν τῶν ἀχράντων τούτων καὶ ζωοποιῶν μυστηρίων*: p. 65 (338) *τῶν φρικτῶν σου τούτων καὶ ἐπουρανίων μυστηρίων.*

—— 30 sqq. From the Prayer of the Elevation before the Fraction and Communion in the Byzantine Liturgy (S. Bas. and S. Chrys.): *Litt. E. and W.* pp. 341, 392.

P. 122. 3. Invocation of *Liturgy of S. Basil* (*Litt. E. and W.* p. 406) ἐλθεῖν τὸ Πνεῦμά σου τὸ ἅγιον ἐφ' ἡμᾶς καὶ ἐπὶ τὰ προκείμενα δῶρα ταῦτα καὶ εὐλογῆσαι αὐτὰ καὶ ἁγιάσαι.

—— 4. From the Great Intercession of *Lit. S. Bas.* (*ib.* p. 407).

—— 7 sqq. From the thanksgiving after Communion in *Lit. S. Bas.* (*ib.* p. 411).

—— 14 sqq. From the Introduction to the Lord's Prayer in *Lit. S. Bas.* (*ib.* p. 410): 'unalloyed' is added from a similar passage in the first prayer (of S. Basil) in Ἀκ. τῆς ἁγίας μεταλήψεως *Horolog.* p. 467.

—— 23 sq. The *Agnus Dei* was inserted in the Roman Liturgy as a hymn during the Fraction by Pope Sergius I, A.D. 687 (Anastasius *Vit. pontiff.* 85); and was retained as a communion hymn in the mass of 1549. *Ecce Agnus Dei* etc. is also used at the communion of the people in the Roman rite.

—— 26 sqq. This passage, expanding ll. 7-13, is added apparently to supply points of meditation if the offertory is long.

—— 26. Σύμβολον τῆς συνάξεως. *Serm. Nat.* xvi (i 282) 'It is well known that the Eucharist itself is called *Synaxis*, by no name more usual in all antiquity, that is, a "collection or gathering." For so it is in itself; for at the celebration of it, though we gather to prayer and to preaching, yet that is the principal gathering the Church hath, which is itself called a "collection" too by the same name as the chief (Heb. x 25); for "where the body is there the eagles will be gathered" [S. Mt. xxiv 28] . . . The very end of the Sacrament is to gather again to God and his favour, if it happen, as oft it doth, we scatter and stray from Him. And to gather us as close and near as *alimentum alito*, that is as near as near may be. And as to gather us to God, so likewise each to other mutually; expressed lively in the symbols of many grains into the one [S. Cyp. *Ep.* lxiii 13] and many grapes into the other. The Apostle is plain that we are all "one bread and one body, so many as are partakers of one bread" [1 Cor. x 17], so moulding us as it were into one loaf altogether.' Cp. *Serm. Pent.* i (iii 128), iii (iii 239).

—— 27. 'The Dispensation' (ἡ οἰκονομία) is applied technically to the Incarnation (Theodoret *Dial.* ii p. 93 τὴν ἐνανθρώπησιν δὲ τοῦ θεοῦ Λόγου καλοῦμεν οἰκονομίαν) and its issues in the Life, Passion, Death and Resurrection of our Lord (id. *de oraculis* p. 979 ἐνανθρωπήσας δὲ καὶ τὴν οἰκονομίαν τελέσας εἰς ἅπασαν τὴν οἰκουμένην τοὺς ἀποστόλους ἐξέπεμψεν) regarded as the divine 'scheme of redemption.' *Serm. Nativ.* iii (i 43) 'Nothing sorteth better than these two mysteries [the Eucharist and the Incarnation] one with the other; the dispensation of a mystery [1 Cor. iv 1] with the mystery of dispensation. It doth manifestly represent, it doth mystically impart what it representeth. There is in it even by the very institution both a manifestation, and that visibly, to set before us this flesh; and a mystical communication to infeoffe us in it or make us partakers of it.' Cp. p. 124 l. 16.

P. 122. 27-29. *Serm. Res.* vii (ii 300) 'Two things Christ there gave us in charge: 1. ἀνάμνησις "remembering" and 2. λῆψις "receiving." The same two St Paul, but in other terms, 1. καταγγελλία "shewing forth"; 2. κοινωνία "communicating" (1 Cor. xi 26, x 16). Of which, "remembering" and "shewing forth" refer to *celebremus*, "receiving" and "communicating" to *epulemur*' (1 Cor. v 8).

—— 28. *Serm. Res.* vii (ii 301) 'It was the will of God that so there might be with them [the Jews] a continual foreshewing, and with us a continual shewing forth, the "Lord's death till He come again." Hence it is that what names theirs carried, ours do the like, and the Fathers make no scruple at it—no more need we. The Apostle in the tenth chapter (1 Cor. x 21 sqq.) compares this of ours to the *immolata* of the heathen; and the Hebrews *habemus aram* (Heb. xiii 10), matcheth it with the sacrifice of the Jews. And we know the rule of comparisons, they must be *eiusdem generis*.' Cp. *Serm. Imagin.* (v 66).

—— 30. *Serm. Pentec.* ix (iii 278) '*Accipite corpus*, upon the matter, is *Accipite Spiritum*, inasmuch as they two never part, nor possible to sever them one minute. Thus when or to whom we say *Accipite corpus*, we may safely say with the same breath *Accipite Spiritum*; and as truly every way. For that body is never without this Spirit: he that receives the one, receives the other; he that the body, together with it the Spirit also.' Cp. *Serm. Res.* xviii (iii 102), *Pentec.* iii (iii 162), v (iii 199), xi (iii 322), *S. Giles' Lectt.* p. 618.

—— 31. *Serm. Res.* xii (ii 402) 'The holy mysteries . . . do work to this, even to the raising of the soul with "the first resurrection" (Rev. xx 5). And . . . they are a means for the raising of our soul out of the soil of sin—for they are given us, and we take them expressly for the remission of sins.' Cp. xiii (ii 427), *Pentec.* ix (iii 279), *Absolution* (v 94).

—— 33. *Serm. Pent.* iii (iii 162) 'By the holy mysteries . . . the heart is "established by grace" (Heb. xiii 9) and our soul endued with strength, and our conscience made light and cheerful, that it faint not but "evermore rejoice in his holy comfort"': *ib.* ix (iii 279) 'to the stablishing of our hearts with grace, to the cleansing and quieting our consciences.' Cp. *S. Giles' Lect.* p. 597. *Homilies* ii 15 (Of the worthy receiving of the Sacrament) 'Here they may feel wrought the tranquillity of conscience.'

—— 35 sq. *Serm. Pent.* xiii (iii 359) 'His blood is not only drink to nourish, but medicine to purge. To nourish the new man, which is faint and weak, God wot; but to take down the old, which is rank in most. It is the proper effect of his blood; it doth "cleanse our consciences from dead works to serve the living God" (Heb. ix 14).'

—— 37. *Serm. Res.* iv (ii 251) 'This day therefore the Church never fails, but sets forth her peace-offering;—the body whose hands were here shewed and the side whence issued *sanguis crucis* "the blood that pacifieth all things in earth and heaven" (Col. i 20), that we in it and by it may this day renew the covenant of our peace': *Pent.* iii (iii 161) 'To a covenant there is nothing more requisite than to put the seal. And we know the Sacrament is the seal of the new covenant as it was of the old.'

P. 122. 38. *Serm. Nat.* ii (i 31) 'St Augustine put all four together, so will I and conclude; *Sequamur* 1 *exemplum; offeramus* 2 *pretium; sumamus* 3 *viaticum; expectemus* 4 *præmium;* let us follow Him for our pattern, offer Him for our price, receive Him for our sacramental food, and wait for Him as our endless and exceeding great reward.' *Viaticum* (ἐφόδιον) = provision for a journey.

—— 39 sq. *Serm. Pent.* vii (iii 239) 'His body the Spirit of strength, His blood the Spirit of comfort, both the Spirit of love.' Cp. *ib.* iii (iii 161 sq.).

P. 123. 6. *Serm. Imaginations* (v 67) 'It is an imagination to think that this "breaking of bread" can be severed from the other, which is Esay's breaking of "bread to the needy" (Is. lviii 7). Whereby, as in the former Christ communicateth Himself with us, so we in this latter communicate ourselves with our poor brethren, that so there may be a perfect communion. For both in the sacrifice which was the figure of it it was a matter of commandment (Deut. xvi 10), insomuch as the poorest were not exempt from God's offerings; and our Saviour Christ's practice was at this feast to command somewhat "to be given to the poor" (Jo. xiii 29). And last of all the *agapæ* or lovefeasts of the Christians for relief of the poor do most plainly express that I mean. In place of which, when they after proved inconvenient, succeeded the Christian offertory.'

—— 8. *Serm. Nativ.* iv (i 62) 'Our thanks are surely not full without the Holy Eucharist, which is by interpretation, thanksgiving itself. Fully we cannot say *Quid retribuam Domino?* but we must answer *Calicem salutaris accipiam* "we will take the cup of salvation" and with it in our hands give thanks to Him, render Him our true Eucharist, or real thanksgiving indeed.'

—— 10. *Serm. Res.* vi (ii 289) 'First, uniting us to Christ the "Head," whereby we grow into one frame of building, into one body mystical, with Him. And again, uniting us also as living stones, or lively members, *omnes in ia ipsum*, one to another and all together in one, by mutual love and charity. *Qui comedit de hoc Pane, et bibit de hoc Calice, manet in Me, et Ego in illo* "He that eateth of this bread, and drinketh of this cup, abideth in Me, and I in him" (Jo. vi 56). There is our corner [Ps. cxviii 22] with Him. And again, *Unum corpus omnes sumus, qui de uno pane participamus* "All we that partake of one bread or cup, grow all into one body mystical" (1 Cor.

x 17). There is our corner, either with other.' Cp. *Nativ.* vi (i 100), *Res.* i (ii 205).'

P. 123. 11. *Serm. Res.* xii (ii 402) 'As [the holy mysteries] are a means for the raising of our soul out of the soil of sin—for they are given us and we take them expressly for the remission of sins—so are they no less a means also for the raising of our bodies out of the dust of death. The sign of that body which was thus "in the heart of the earth," to bring us from thence at the last. Our Saviour saith it *totidem verbis* "Whoso eateth my flesh and drinketh my blood, I will raise him up in the last day" (Jo. vi 54):' *ib.* v (ii 268) 'The Church offereth us a notable pledge and earnest of this hope [of the resurrection] there to bestow; even the Holy Eucharist.' Cp. *ib.* xiv (iii 22), xvi (iii 38).

—— 13. *Serm. Res.* xviii (iii 102) '*Quidquid Testamento legatur, Sacramento dispensatur*, "what the testament bequeatheth, that is dispensed in the holy mysteries."' Cp. Hooker *E.P.* v 56 § 11 'the pledge of our heavenly inheritance.'

—— 14. *Serm. Pent.* vi (iii 219) 'And by and with these [the body and the blood], there is grace imparted to us; which grace is the very breath of this Holy Spirit, the true and express character of his seal, to the renewing in us the image of God whereunto we are created. . . . Be careful to "stir it up" (2 Tim. i 6), yea "to grow" and increase in it (2 Pet. iii 18), more and more, even to the consummation of it, which is glory—glory being nothing else but grace consummate, the figure of this stamp in his full perfection.'

—— 16 sqq. The Commemoration, with which the Invocation of the Holy Ghost, following the recital of the Institution, opens in the Lit. of S. Basil (*Litt. E. and W.* p. 405). It is of the same type in all liturgies, except in some instances of Gallican masses and the English since 1552. It is restored in the Scottish and American.

—— 27 sqq. From the preface to the Lord's Prayer in Lit. S. Bas. (*Litt. E. and W.* p. 410) and the first prayer, of S. Basil, in 'Ακολ. τῆς ἁγ. μεταλήψεως, *Horolog.* p. 467.

P. 124. 3 sqq. From the third prayer, of S. Chrys., in 'Ακολ. τῆς ἁγ. μεταλ.

—— 13 sqq. The prayer in the sacristy at the end of Lit. S. Bas. (*Litt. E. and W.* p. 411: cp. p. 344).

—— 24 sqq. Cp. *Serm. Pent.* iii (iii 152) 'Why should concupiscence to evil be reputed sin on the worst part, and a like desire, *concupivi desiderare mandata tua* (Ps. cxix 40), not be as well reckoned for as much as the better part, though it be not full out "according to the purification of the sanctuary"?'

P. 127. *Serm. Gowries* vii (iv 164) 'Will ye see David do penance indeed for it? Penance, I say, in all the parts the schoolmen make of it: 1. *contritio cordis*, in this verse [1 Sam. xxiv 5] his heart smites him for it; 2. *confessio oris*, in the next "The Lord keep me" from doing more, this was too much; 3. *satis-*

factio operis in the last verse [8], in making amends, by not suffering his men to rise, but converting them from so sinful a purpose.' In the text there is no heading of the third section; Andrewes generally uses 'fruits' or 'works of repentance' instead of 'satisfaction' (*Serm. Repent.* viii [i 435 sqq.]). The definition of Penance as consisting on the part of the penitent in contrition, confession and satisfaction seems to have begun with the *Decretum*, Peter Lombard and Richard of S. Victor in the xiith cent. and it has since been the accepted teaching of the schools: see Pet. Lomb. *Sentt.* iv 16 § 1; Richard a S. Victore *de potestate ligandi* 5; S. Thom. Aq. *Summa* iii 90 § 1; Conc. Trident. *Sess.* xiv; *Catech. Rom.* ii 5 § 21; Hooker *Eccl. Pol.* vi. From the *Decretum* onwards a homily attributed to S. Chrysostom (*Opp. lat.* Basel 1547, v 901) is commonly quoted: pœnitentia . . in corde eius contritio, in ore confessio, in opere tota humilitas. Cp. Cassian *Coll.* xx.

P. 127. 5-7. See on p. 43 l. 33.

—— 9. See on p. 28 l. 19.

—— 10. *Serm. Repent.* viii (i 437) 'Now if affections give life, the quicker the affection the more life it gives. And there is none quicker than that of anger. For which cause when time was you may remember we made it the chief ingredient into repentance. Even anger at ourselves, we were so evil advised as to bring ourselves into the anger of God.'

—— 13 sq. *Serm. Prayer* xvi (v 442) 'Sin consists not only of an offence or guilt, but of an issue or inclination to sin, so that our care must be as well that we pray that this running issue may be stopped, as that punishment due to us for sins past be remitted; and to this end both parts of repentance are required of us, that is, sorrow for sins past, and provident care to avoid sin to come; we must by prayer seek for grace of God *non modo quo deleatur debitum sed ne contrahatur debitum*, "not only that our debt be done away, but that it may not be contracted."'

—— 22. The meaning of this is not clear; but perhaps it is explained by *S. Giles' Lectt.* p. 398 'Secondly . . . there is another *dore* whereat sin is said to lye, that is "the dore or gate of death" (Ps. ix 13), "I am going to the gate of death" (Is. xxxviii 10)'—so that the meaning would be, that there is room for repentance in this life, but not after; unrepented sin waits at death's door to seize us. Cp. *Targum of Onqelos* in Gen. iv 7: si non bene egeris opera tua, in diem iudicii peccatum servatum est: in qua futurum est ut ulciscatur de te si non converteris. Elsewhere Andrewes interprets *peccatum cubans* as temptation (*S. Giles' Lectt.* p. 402 'Forasmuch as we shall be continually provoked and assaulted by sinne, and sin will run to us and ly at the dore, yet we are not to goe and meet it'), or as sin unrealised 'while it is committed' as opposed to *peccatum vigilans*, sin realised in 'the remorse after' (*ib.* 403); or again as sin 'enticing gently at the first' as opposed to *peccatum clamans* 'pulling a man by the throat' and accusing him (*ib.* 427).

P. 127. 25. The editions read *sanctio*, obviously by mistake for *sanatio*: cp. *Serm. Rep.* viii (i 445) 'Repentance is the physic of the soul and body both. *Sit obsecro sanatio* saith Daniel (iv 27) "let there be a cure done," when he exhorted him to repent.' Cp. *Prayer* iv (v 333). See margin of Dan. iv 27 in A.V. and R.V.

—— 26. 'A city of refuge.' S. Jerome *c. Pelagian.* i 33 (ii 716 c) qui ligna cædit, si securi ac ferro fugiente de ligno homo fuerit occisus, pergere iubetur ad urbem fugitivorum et tandiu ibi esse quandiu sacerdos maximus moriatur (Num. xxxv 11 sqq.), id est redimatur sanguine Salvatoris, aut in domo baptismatis aut in pœnitentia, quæ imitatur baptismatis gratiam—where S. Jer. is referring to 'ignorance' or unintentional sin. Cp. S. Bernard *de Conversione* 21: fugite de medio Babylonis; fugite et salvate animas vestras; convolate ad urbes refugii ubi possitis et de præteritis agere pœnitentiam et in præsenti obtinere gratiam et futuram gloriam fiducialiter præstolari. In *Serm. Pent.* vi (iii 209) and *Passion* ii (ii 153), Andrewes uses the death of the high priest, which freed the refugee from his captivity in the city of refuge, as a type of our Lord's death; but otherwise he does not seem to use the figure in the text.

—— 27. Tertullian compares penance to a plank on which the shipwrecked swims to shore: *de pœnitentia* 4: eam [sc. pœnitentiam] tu peccator . . . ita invade, ita amplexare ut naufragus alicuius tabulæ fidem; hæc te peccatorem fluctibus mersum prolevabit et in portum divinæ clementiæ protelabit. So S. Jerome *Epp.* 147 § 3, 79 § 10, 122 § 4. In *Ep.* 130 § 9, 84 § 6, he calls it a *secunda tabula*, meaning, not 'a second' in addition to 'a first,' but 'a plank which is a second resource' after the wreck of the first resource, 'the ship' of the normal Christian life in the Church; in other words, penance is a second resource where Baptism and the Eucharist have so far failed. *Secunda tabula* becomes the traditional phrase. Cp. S. Ambr. *de virg. laps.* 38, S. Cæsarius of Arles *Hom.* xvii, Pet. Lomb. *Sentt.* iv 14, S. Tho. Aq. *Summa* iii 84 § 6, S. Bonavent. *in Sentt.* iv 22 § 3 (2); Luther *Babylonish Captivity* Baptism; *Conc. Trident.* xiv de poen. c. 2; *Catech. Rom.* ii 5 § 1. Dr Neale omits lines 26, 27 in his translation (but he mentions 'the plank' in *Lect. on Church difficulties* xvi p. 241): Mr Venables misunderstands *secunda tabula* and renders 'the second table.'

—— 28 sqq. Cp. Tertullian *de pœnit.* 4: bonum est pœnitentia an non? quid revolvis? Deus præcipit: at enim ille non præcipit tantum sed etiam hortatur: invitat præmio, salute: iurans etiam *Vivo* dicens: cupit credi sibi.

P. 128, 2 sqq. *Serm. Rep.* viii (i 441) 'We sort the works of repentance as they may best answer and suit with the works of sin. Now all sins grow out of these three heads and may be reduced to one of them, the 1 spirit, the 2 flesh, 3 and the world, and are corrected each of them by his contrary. . . . All may be comprised under these three: 1. works of devotion, as prayer; 2. works of chastisement of the body, as fasting; 3. works of mercy, as alms. These three between them make up the corrective or penal part of penitence.' See the whole passage, and cp. *ib.* v (i 381) 'They are all of one assay these three; alms, prayer and fasting. If the other two, if alms be a sacrifice—"with such sacrifices God is pleased" (Heb. xiii 6); if prayer be one—one, and therefore called "the calves of our lips" (Hos. xiv 6); no reason to deny fasting to be one too. If "a troubled spirit be a sacrifice to God" (Ps. li 17), why not a troubled body likewise? . . . And these three, to offer to God our 1. soul by prayer, 2. our body by abstinence, 3. our goods by almsdeeds, hath been ever counted *tergemina hostia* "the triple or threefold Christian holocaust or whole burntoffering."' Cp. *Pent.* xii (iii 338), where notice 'Our alms, alas, they are shrunk up pitifully; prayer swallowed up with hearing lectures; and for the third, feast if you will continually, but fast as little as may be; and of most I might say, not at all. The want of these, the bane of our age.' Cp. Pet. Lomb. *Sentt.* iv 16 pars 1: S. Thom. Aq. *Summa* suppl. xv 3: S. Bonav. *in Sentt.* iv 15: Ludolphus *vita Christi* i 20 § 13, 36 § 2.

P. 128. 10 sqq. Theophylact (11th cent.) *in Mat.* xxv (i 141 E) in the East, and Rupert of Deutz (†1135) *de gloria et honore Filii hominis* v (ii 46) in the West, reckon six corporal works of mercy, those enumerated by our Lord in S. Mt. xxv 35 sq., and Theophylact adds six spiritual works (τὰ ἕξ εἴδη τῆς ἀγάπης . . σωματικῶς . . ψυχικῶς). In the xiiith cent. in the West, seven of each are reckoned, the burial of the dead being added to the six corporal works from Tobit xii 13; and the lists are summarised in such mnemonic verses as are here quoted by Andrewes—visito poto cibo redimo tego colligo condo (S. Thom. Aq. *Summa* ii² 32 § 2; S. Bonavent. in *Sentt.* iv 15 pars 2; *Hortulus animae* Lyons 1516 f. 160 b; *Prymer of Salisbury* Rouen, Regnault 1537, f. Il 4); doce consule castiga (Andrewes, consule plecte doce) solare remitte fer ora (S. Thomas and S. Bonav. *ib.*; that in *Hort. an.* and *Prymer* is of a different type). The translation of the second verse given in the text is that of MS Douce 246 printed in Maskell *Mon. rit.* iii p. 256. The Latin enumeration is adopted by the Greeks in *Confessio Orthodoxa* ii 40-54, of 1672. Andrewes treats the works of mercy under the heads *Of outward mercy* and *Of inward mercy* under the 4th Commandment in *Cat. doct.* pp. 163 sq. As satisfaction they are treated of by S. Bonavent. *loc. cit.*

P. 130. 15. Cp. *Serm. Pent.* iv (iii 173) 'When men grow faint in seeking and careless in keeping Him, as in Canticles the third (iii 1) "lie in bed and seek Him."' Cp. *Repent.* i (i 312, 315).

P. 130. 19 sq. *Serm. Repent.* iv (i 368) 'Two kinds of fasting we find in Scripture. 1. David's, who fasted "tasting neither bread" nor ought else "till the sun was down" (2 Sam. iii 35), no meat at all;—that is too hard. 2. What say you to Daniel's fast? "He did eat and drink," but not *cibos desiderii* "no meats of delight," and namely ate no flesh (Dan. x 33). The Church, as an indulgent mother, mitigates all she may; enjoins not for fast that of David, and yet *qui potest capere capiat* (Mt. xix 12) for all that; she only requires of us that of Daniel, to forbear *cibos desiderii*, and "flesh" is there expressly named—meats and drinks provoking the appetite, full of nourishment, kindling the blood; content to sustain nature, and not "purvey for the flesh to satisfy the lusts thereof" (Rom. xiii 14). And thus by the grace of God we may, if not David's, yet Daniel's. For if David's we cannot, and Daniel's we list not, I know not what fast we will leave, for a third I find not.'

P. 131. 3, 9-11. Ascendat ad te Domine Deus oratio mea et peto ut non revertatur ad me vacua, sed sicut vis et scis miserere mei in omnibus animæ et corporis necessitatibus: also in *Horae* 1494 f. A 3. Cp. *Stowe Missal* f. 13 b.

P. 132. 10 sqq. From the prayer *Dona mihi quæso* after the *Psalterium S. Hieronymi*, also in *Horae* 1494 f. 131.

—— 33. 'Of them' i.e. of sinners. Dr Neale, not noticing the quotation of S. Mt. xxvi 73, rendered this 'I am made of sins.'

—— 35. From the *Conditor cæli et terræ;* also in *Horae* Paris, J. Philippe, 1495; Hilsey's *Primer* 1539 (*Three Primers* p. 369).

P. 133. 6 sqq. With nos. 3, 4, 6-9, 13, 14 cp. Fisher of Rochester's *Psalmus* i (*Private prayers of the reign of Q. Elizabeth*, Parker Soc., p. 318), which Andrewes seems to be following.

—— 23 sqq. This represents the medieval enumeration of the 'circumstances' or 'conditions, aggravating' the gravity of sins, which from the xiiith cent. were summarised in the mnemonic lines

> Aggravat ordo, locus, persona, scientia, tempus,
> ætas, conditio, numerus, mora, copia, causa:
> est modus in culpa, status altus, lucta pusilla.

See S. Bonavent. *in Sentt.* iv xvi 1 § 9; cp. *Hort. an.* 1516 f. 154: *Prymer* Le Roux 1537 f. 168 'Whiche ben the circumstaunces augmentynge synnes? Ordre: tyme: scyence: age: condicyon: nombre: abydynge: abondaunce: cause: maner: dignyte: and weke resistence &c.'; and cp. *Hort. an.* 1516 f. 153 b: Circumstantiæ peccatorum: Quis, quid, ubi, per quas, quotiens, cur, quomodo, quando. *Serm. Repent.* iv (i 369) 'Consider the motives, the bad motives, and weigh the circumstances, the grievous circumstances, and tell over our many flittings, our oft relapsing, our wretched continuing in them . . . These and these sins I have committed, so many, so heinous, so oft iterate, so long lain in': cp. *ib.* iii (i 347), *S. Paul's Lectt.* pp. 286 sq.; ⌊S. Aug.⌋ *de vera et falsa pœnitentia* 29.

P. 134. 2 sq. Cp. Kimchi *in Is.* v 18 'evil desire is in the beginning like a spider's thread, and in the end like the ropes of a wain' (quoted in Pusey *Paroch. and Cath. Serm.* p. 434).

—— 4 sq. *Serm. Prayer* xvi (v 444) 'Human temptations are such as are necessary and cannot be avoided by reason of the corruption of nature; of which the prophet speaketh when he prayeth *Libera me de necessitatibus meis* (Ps. xxv 16). The Apostle doth more plainly express when he calls it "the infirmity of the flesh" (Rom. vi 19) and the "sin that dwells in us" (Rom. vii 17), which causeth this necessity, that while we remain in the body the "flesh will ever lust against the spirit" (Gal. v 17). But there is another kind of temptation which is devilish, when we do not sin of infirmity or through the necessary weakness of the flesh, but of malicious purpose, that whereof the prophet speaketh "Be not merciful unto them that trespass of malicious wickedness" (Ps. lix 5) and "Keep thy servant from presumptuous sins" (Ps. xix 13). These sins proceed not from that necessity of sinning which doth accompany our nature, but from that corruption of nature which the Apostle doth call the "superfluity of wickedness" (Jas. i 21). These proceed not from sin that dwells in us, but from that sin which reigneth in us.' Cp. S. Aug. *c. duas epp. Pelagian.* i 10 (x 420 E): *Si autem quod nolo, hoc facio, consentio legi quoniam bona est.* Magis enim se dicit legi consentire, quam carnis concupiscentiæ: hanc enim peccati nomine appellat. Facere ergo se dixit et operari, non affectu consentiendi et implendi, sed ipso motu concupiscendi. . . . Deinde dicit *Nunc autem iam non ego operor illud sed id quod habitat in me peccatum.* Quid est *nunc autem*, nisi 'iam nunc sub gratia quæ liberavit delectationem voluntatis a consensione cupiditatis'? Cp. also *de perfectione iustitiæ hominis* 4: per arbitrii libertatem factum ut esset homo cum peccato; sed iam pœnalis vitiositas subsecuta ex libertate fecit necessitatem. Unde ad Deum fides clamat *De necessitatibus meis educ me;* sub quibus positi vel non possumus quod volumus intelligere, vel quod intellexerimus volumus nec valemus implere. Cp. [S. Prosper] *de vita contempl.* iii 2 § 2. 'Necessities' are therefore partly the *concupiscentia* 'the lust of the flesh' or φρόνημα σαρκός, which, if it has 'of itself the nature of sin' (Art. ix), is yet not properly sin but only becomes so when consented to or acquiesced in by the will; partly what results from the absence of grace or the neglect to 'stir up the gift that is in us' (2 Tim. i 6).

—— 6-9. *Prymer* Le Roux 1537 f. 167 b.

—— 10 sqq. *Eucholog.* p. 378 τὰ ἑκούσια καὶ τὰ ἀκούσια, τὰ ἐν γνώσει καὶ ἐν ἀγνοίᾳ τὰ πρόδηλα, τὰ λανθάνοντα, τὰ ἐν πράξει, τὰ ἐν διανοίᾳ, τὰ ἐν λόγῳ, τὰ ἐν πάσαις ἡμῶν ταῖς ἀναστροφαῖς καὶ τοῖς κινήμασι: *Horolog.* p. 102 ἄνες ἄφες συγχώρησον ὁ Θεὸς τὰ παραπτώματα ἡμῶν τὰ ἑκούσια καὶ τὰ ἀκούσια, τὰ ἐν ἔργῳ καὶ λόγῳ, τὰ ἐν γνώσει καὶ ἀγνοίᾳ, τὰ ἐν νυκτὶ καὶ ἐν ἡμέρᾳ, τὰ κατὰ νοῦν καὶ διάνοιαν. Cp. S. Cyr. Hier. *Cat.* i 5.

P. 134. 18, 19. I.e. carelessly or by inadvertence, and deliberately.

—— 40-135 l. 7. From *Confiteor tibi domine Iesu Christe* (also in *Horae* 1494 f.A 5 b).

P. 135. 28. See on p. 128 l. 10.

—— 29. The treatise *de vera et falsa pœnitentia*, which is of some importance in the history of penance, is quoted from the xith cent. onwards and attributed to S. Augustine: Gratian *Decretum* II xxxiii 3; Pet. Lomb. *Sentt.* iv 14 § 2; S. Thom. Aq. *Summa* iii 84 § 9; Ludolphus *Vita Christi* i 20 § 7. Its spuriousness began to be recognised in the xvith cent. and the Benedictines put it among the *spuria*. The passage in the text is found in all the above references.

P. 136. 14-16. These three—*placabilis*, *præstabilis*, *deprecabilis*—are the Vulgate renderings of *hinnāḥēm* or *niḥam* in Ex. xxxii 12 (repent of), Joel ii 13 (repent of) and Ps. xc (lxxxix) 13 (be gracious) respectively.

—— 17 sq. From *Confiteor tibi domine Iesu Christe*: cp. on p. 134 l. 40.

—— 20. From *Domine Iesu Christe Fili Dei vivi pone passionem*.

—— 21 sqq. From the prayer 'for thy frende that is dede' *Suscipe piissime Deus*.

P. 137. 15. *Serm. Pent.* ix (iii 266) 'Ye may call to mind that the Scriptures speak of sin sometime, as of a frost; otherwhile, as of a mist or fog (Is. xliv 22) that men are lost in, to be dissolved and so blown away. For as there be two proceedings in the wind, and according to them two powers observed by Elihu (Job xxxvii 9); forth of the south, a wind to melt and dissolve; out of the north, a wind to dispel and drive away: and as in the wind of our breath there is *flatus* "a blast," which is cooler and which blows away; and *halitus* "a breath," that is warm, and by the temperate moist heat, dissolves; answerable to these, there is in the breath of Christ [Jo. xx 22] a double power conferred, and both for the remission of sins; and that in two senses, set down by St John. 1. The one of *ne peccetis*, astringent, to keep men from sin and so *remissio peccandi*; 2. the other *si quis autem peccaverit* "but if any do sin" (1 Jo. ii 1) to loose men from it, and so *remissio peccati*. Shewing them the way, and aiding them with the means to clean their conscience of it, being done; remitting that is past, making that more remiss that is to come; as it were to resolve the frost first and turn it into vapour; and after it is so, then to blow it away.'

—— 16. The text has κάλαμον κατεάγης, which is unintelligible as it stands.

—— 36 sqq. *Serm. Res.* i (ii 197) 'Why but once? Because once was enough *ad auferenda* saith St John (Jo. i 29), *ad abolenda* saith St Peter (Acts iii 19), *ad exhaurienda* saith St Paul (Heb. ix 28); "to take away, to abolish, to draw dry" and utterly to exhaust all the sins of all the sinners of all the world. The excellency of his Person that performed it was such; the excellency of the obedience that He performed, such; the excellency both of his humility and charity wherewith He performed it, such; and of such value every of them, and all of them much more; as made that his once dying was *satis superque* "enough and enough again"; which made the prophet call it *copiosam redemptionem* [Ps. cxxx 7]. But the apostle, he goeth beyond all in expressing this; in one place terming it ὑπερβάλλων (Eph. ii 7), in another ὑπερεκπερισσεύων (Eph. iii 20), in another πλεονάζων (1 Tim. i 14),—mercy, rich, exceeding; grace overabounding, nay, grace superfluous, for so is πλεονάζων, and superfluous is enough and to spare; superfluous is clearly enough and more than enough. Once dying then being more than enough, no reason He should die more than once.' Cp. *Pent.* xiv (iii 371); *Prayer* ii (v 318) quoted above on p. 25 l. 26; Erasmus *Concio de immensa Dei misericordia*, London, Berthelet, 1533.

P. 138. 2. See *Serm. Gunpowder Tr.* vii (iv 318) on the text Ps. cxlv 9.

—— 6. See *ib.* iv (iv 261) on Lam. iii 22.

—— 8-10. See *ib.* iv (iv 267); *Cat. doct.* p. 96. Cp. p. 153 above.

—— 22. *Tenera* seems to represent σπλάγχνα in the phrase σπλ. ἐλέους rendered 'tender mercy' in the *Benedictus* S. Lk. i 78.

—— 32. *Serm. Gunpowder Tr.* vii (iv 326) '*Naturas rerum minimarum non destituit Deus:* the very *minims* of the world his mercy leaves not destitute. Not "the wild asses" without a place "to quench their thirst" (Ps. civ 11). Not the young ravens crying on Him. Not the sparrow of half a farthing, lets not them light on the ground without his providence. Even these, even such his mercy is over also.'

P. 139. 36. *Serm. Prayer* i (v 304) 'The inchoation or beginning of that which is good is denied us: though we purpose in our hearts to perform those duties of godliness that are required, yet we have not the power to put them in practice. *Filii venerunt ad partum et non sunt vires pariendi* "the children are come unto the birth and there is no strength to bring forth." If we begin to do any good thing it is *Deus qui coepit in nobis bonum opus* (Phil. i 6).'

P. 140. 34. I.e. apparently, sin has not yet 'found us out,' vengeance is not yet taken, and there is room for repentance. Cp. on p. 127 l. 22.

—— 36. I.e. at the moment of greatest need, 'at the very pinch' *Serm. Tempt.* iii (v 510) God's help will come. Cp. *ib.* v (v 529), *Gunpowder Tr.* i (iv 213).

P. 143. Cp. [S. Aug.] *Soliloqq.* 2 (vi app. 86 c).

P. 143. 3 sq. *Serm. Pent.* viii (iii 244) 'Being "conceived of unclean seed" Job (xiv 4); and warmed in a sinful womb—David (Ps. li 5);—at their birth "polluted" no less in sin, than "in their blood"—Ezekiel (xvi 6); there is not *infans unius diei super terram*, as the Seventy read it, "not a child of a day old" (Job xiv 4) but needs *baptismus lavacri*, if it be but for *baptismus uteri*, "the baptism of the Church, if it be but for the baptism it had in the womb."' Cp. *S. Giles' Lectt.* p. 621. Confession of original sin is prominent in protestant formulæ of the 16th century, but is carefully avoided in the Book of Common Prayer. On the subject see S. Thomas Aq. *Summa* iii 84 § 2 ad 3: S. Bonaventura *in Sentt.* iv dist. xvi pars 2 § 1.

—— 6. *Serm. Pent.* xvii (iii 71) 'Adam was by God planted a natural vine, a true root, but thereby, by that cup [of devils] degenerated into a wild strange vine, which instead of good grapes, "brought forth" *labruscas*, "wild grapes" (Is. v 4); "grapes of gall," "bitter clusters," Moses calls them (Dt. xxxii 32); *colocynthidas*, the Prophet, *mors in olla* (2 Ki. iv 40) and *mors in calice*; by which is meant the deadly fruit of our deadly sins.'

—— 23 sq. *Serm. Pent.* xv (iii 399) 'As we are forbidden to "hatch cockatrice' eggs" (Is. lix 5), things that will do harm; so are we also in the same place, to weave spiders' webs, things very finely spun but for nobody's wearing; none the better for them. Our ἐνεργήματα must be εὐεργήματα, "works tending to profit with"; else they are not right works.' Cp. *ib.* p. 391; and *ib.* p. 384 'the Christian . . hath it not of himself, spins not his thread as the spider doth, out of himself, but hath it of another and hath it of gift. It is given him. *Unicuique datur*, it is the eleventh verse (1 Cor. xii 11) "to everyone is given." So instead of Aristotle's word ἕξις, "habit," he puts St James' word δόσις or δώρημα (Jas. i 17)': cp. *ib.* ix (iii 272). Cp. S. Greg. Mag. *Mor. in Job.* xv 15: telas quoque araneæ texere est pro huius mundi concupiscentia temporalia quælibet operari; quæ dum nulla stabilitate solidata sunt, ea procul dubio ventus vitæ mortalis rapit.

—— 29. Heb. 'a worm and a grub'—i.e. corruption (Job vii 5) and abjectness (Is. xli 14).

P. 144. 19. See on p. 161, l. 10.

—— 30. *Serm. Pent.* xi (iii 321) 'Our sins . . have a voice, a cry, an ascending cry, in Scripture assigned them. They invocate too, they call for somewhat, even for some fearful judgement to be poured down on us.'

—— 33 sq. *Serm. Rep.* iv (i 367) 'But we in our turning [are] to come before Him all abashed and confounded in ourselves that for a trifle, a matter of nothing, certain carats of gain, a few minutes of delight—base creatures that we be!—so and so often, *sic et sic faciendo* [Josh. vii 20], by such and such sins, have offended so presumptuously against so glorious a Majesty, so desperately against so omnipotent a Power, so unkindly against so sovereign a bounty of so gracious a God and so kind and loving a Saviour.'

P. 145. 2 sq. *Serm. Rep.* iii (i 348) 'All return to sin is brutish; *recidiva peccati*, that is *tanquam canis ad vomitum; volutabrum peccati*, that is *tanquam sus ad lutum* (2 Pet. ii 22); but this fury and fierceness of sin is *tanquam equus ad proelium* (Jer. viii 7).'

—— 35 sq. The form of this quotation, which is not exactly that of the vulgate, seems to be derived from Fisher *Psalm* i (*Private prs. of the reign of Q. Elizabeth*, Parker Soc., p. 320).

P. 146. 8. See on p. 32 l. 14.

—— 25 sq. *Serm. Prayer* vii (v 367) 'Notwithstanding the greatness of our sins, we may be bold to seek to God for favour and say *Etsi amisi ingenuitatem filii, tamen tu non amisisti pietatem Patris.* "Although, Lord, I have lost the duty of a son, yet Thou hast not lost the affection of a Father."' Cp. *ib.* xiv (v 430).

—— 27 sq. [S. Aug.] *Med.* 39 (vi app. 127): licet peccator sim non possum non esse filius tuas, quia tu me fecisti et refecisti.

—— 34. *Triodion* p. 25 φεῖσαι φεῖσαι τότε Σωτὴρ τοῦ πλάσματός σου: cp. p. 107: *Horae* 1494 f. 155: parce, Domine, parce et defende plasma tuum in eis: S. Bern. *in fest. S. Martini* 2 (i 1055): pepercisti ergo creaturæ tuæ, pepercisti gloriæ nominis tui.

P. 147. 1, 11. Cp. [S. Aug.] *Solill.* 24 (vi app. 96 B): Tu nosti figmentum nostrum Domine Deus noster: num, Deus inæstimabilis fortitudinis, contra folium quod vento rapitur ostendere vis potentiam tuam et stipulam siccam persequi?

—— 17 sqq. *Serm. Gowries* vii (iv 173) 'Thou [David] hast a testimony in holy writ to have been "a man after God's own heart," what was in God's heart was in thine.' Cp. p. 177.

P. 149. 27 sqq. *Serm. Gunpowder Tr.* vii (iv 321) 'Goodness *in merentes*, that is justice: goodness *in immerentes*, yea and sometimes a degree farther, *in male merentes*, that is mercy properly.'

P. 150. 7 sq. In *Serm. Absolution* (v 89), Is. xxviii 21 is given as ref. for 'that to "remit" is more proper to Him and that He is more ready to it and that it is first; first in his purpose, first in his grant; and that to the other [sc. to "retain"] He cometh but secondarily, but by occasion, when the former cannot take place.' Cp. p. 171 l. 28.

P. 151. 1. See *Serm. Gunpowder Tr.* vii (iv 318 sqq.)

—— 8, 9. S. Aug. *Enarr. in Ps.* lviii² 11: O nomen, sub quo nemini desperandum est: *Deus meus* inquit *misericordia mea*. Cp. *Serm. Justification* (v 111).

—— 10 sqq. *Serm. Gunpowder Tr.* vii (iv 328) '*Grande est barathrum peccatorum meorum*, it is Chrysostom, *sed maior est abyssus miseri-*

cordiæ Dei—"Great is the whirlpool."' The passage referred to is apparently S. Chrys. *Orat.* 2 (xii 802 B) *οἶδας τὸ πλῆθος τῶν ἀνομιῶν μου ὅτι πολὺ καὶ ἀριθμῷ μὴ ὑποκείμενον. ἀλλ' οἶδα καὶ τὸ πέλαγος τῆς φιλανθρωπίας σου ὅτι ἀνείκαστον καὶ ἀνίκητον.* Cp. *S. Giles' Lectt.* p. 440.

P. 152. 1 sq. *Serm. Prayer* vii (v 367) 'Fathers stand thus affected towards their children, that they are hardly brought to chasten them; and if there be no remedy, yet they are ready to forgive or soon cease punishing. *Pro peccato magno paullulum supplicii satis est patri*, "For a great offence, a small punishment is enough to a father."' Cp. *Gunpowder Tr.* vii (iv 326) 'This is sure: *Deus præmiat ultra, punit citra*, "God ever rewards beyond, but punishes on this side," short still of that we deserve; that his very punishment is tempered with mercy, that even in his wrath He remembereth mercy.'

P. 153. 2 sqq. See on p. 70 l. 31.

—— 29 sq. S. Chrys. *ad Theod. laps.* i 6 (i 8) *κἂν γὰρ μὴ πᾶσάν τις ἐπιδείξηται τὴν μετάνοιαν οὐδὲ τὴν βραχεῖαν καὶ πρὸς ὀλίγον γεγενημένην παραπέμπεται ἀλλὰ καὶ ταύτῃ τίθησι πολὺν τὸν μισθόν*: quoted in Pet. Lomb. *Sentt.* iv 14 § 2.

P. 154. 16 sqq. The Heb. and Vulg. of Ps. cxix 49 are here combined.

—— 38 sq. S. Anselm *Med.* iii 9 (=[S. Aug.] *Med.* 39) Domine noli sic attendere malum meum ut obliviscaris bonum tuum.

P. 155. 4 sqq. S. Aug. *Serm.* 382 § 2: nam et modo orat pro nobis, orat in nobis, et oratur a nobis: ut sacerdos noster orat pro nobis, ut caput nostrum orat in nobis, ut Deus noster oratur a nobis. Cp. *Enarr. in Ps. lxxxv* 1

—— 24. Omitted by mistake in the text of the *Anglo-Catholic Library* p. 423.

P. 156. 6-11. For this *Instit. piae* has 'which be pleased to grant for thy great and many mercies, thy Name's sake, the glory of thy Name, thy promise' sake, thy practice' sake, my misery, my infirmity, even for thy Son Jesus Christ's sake.'

P. 157. S has some differences of order and some omissions, as compared with O, in this Act.

—— 29 sqq. Cp. p. 25.

P. 158. 1-8. See on p. 26 l. 3.

—— 19 sq. From the Litany.

—— 22 sqq. See p. 169.

—— 36 sqq. From the prayer *Conditor cœli et terræ.*

P. 159. 17 sq. S. Chrys. *Orat.* 2 (xii 802) *πολλὰ ἐποίησας ἀπὸ τοῦ αἰῶνος, μεγάλα καὶ θαυμαστὰ, ἔνδοξά τε καὶ ἐξαίσια ὧν οὐκ ἔστιν ἀριθμός* [Job v 9, ix 10]· *ἀλλ' εἰ ἐμὲ τὸν ἄσωτον σώσεις, εἰ ἐμὲ τὸν ἀνάξιον παραστήσεις, πλείω καὶ μείζω θαυμαστωθήσῃ.*

—— 22 sqq. *Serm. Pent.* iv (iii 168) 'St Augustine prayeth well

Domine da mihi alium Te: alioqui non dimittam Te "Give us another as good as Yourself or we will never leave that or consent that You leave us."' I have not found the words in the works of S. Augustine.

P. 159. 26 sq. From the prayer *Conditor cæli et terræ*.

—— 38. *Serm. Rep.* iv (i 370) 'Complain we can and bemoan ourselves as doth the prophet, with a very little variation from him; "My leanness, my leanness," saith he, "woe is me!" "My dryness, my dryness," may each of us say, "woe is me! The transgressors have offended, the transgressors have grievously offended. Grievously offend we can, grievously lament we cannot, my dryness, my dryness, woe is me!" Nay, we need not vary, we may even let leanness alone, his own word. For dry and lean both is our sorrow, God wot: God help us! this mourn we can.'

P. 160. 6 sq. Cp. *Horae* 1514 f. 131 b: infunde cordibus nostris fontem lacrymarum (in *Per horum omnium sanctorum* after the Litany).

—— 9 sqq. *Serm. Pent.* xii (iii 340) '"And Thou, Lord, never failest them that seek Thee," but "acceptest them, not according to that they have not, but according to that they have," though it be but a "willing mind" they have. God forbid but concupiscence should be of equal power to good that it is to evil.'

—— 21 sqq. [S. Aug.] *Solill.* 24 (vi app. 96) alioquin desperarem, nisi quia spes mea es tu qui creasti me.

—— 25 sqq. *Serm. Absolution* (v 96) 'Christ teaching us that we ourselves should forgive "until seventy times seven" doth thereby after a sort give us to understand that He will not stick with us for the like number in ours. For God forbid we should imagine He taught us to be more merciful or of greater perfection than He will be Himself. That number amounteth to ten jubilees of pardon.' Cp. S. Thom. Aq. *Summa* iii 84 § 10: Petro quærenti *Quoties peccabit* etc. respondit Jesus *Non dico tibi* etc. Ergo etiam Deus sæpius per pœnitentiam veniam peccantibus præbet: Savonarola *in Ps. l 2*: Qui Petro interroganti *Quoties peccabit* etc. respondisti *Non dico* etc., numerum finitum pro infinito accipiens. Numquid ergo indulgentia superaberis ab homine? *Euchology.* p. 554 ἀλλ' ἔτι καὶ ἔτι μακροθύμησον . . . ὁ ἑβδομηκοντάκις ἑπτὰ συγχωρεῖν τοῖς ἀδελφοῖς κελεύων τὰ ἁμαρτήματα: *ib.* 284, 288.

P. 161. 3 sq. *Serm. Gowries* vii (iv 166) 'We use to strike our breasts with the publican, because we cannot come at our heart, to strike it for not striking us when we made a fault. But when the heart needs not be stricken for it, when it strikes us first, when we feel *plagam cordis*, as Solomon calls it in express words (1 Ki. viii 38), upon making a fault, that our heart corrects us, gives us discipline for it; then is our penance begun, then is our contrition in a good way.'

—— 10. Cp. p. 144 l. 18 sq. *Op. imperf. in Mat.* xxxvii (*Opp. S. Chrys.* ed. Montfaucon, vi app. clviii c) Omnis enim homo naturaliter non solum peccator sed etiam totum peccatum, dicente apostolo *Et eramus natura filii iræ* (Eph. ii 3). The *Opus imperfectum*, commonly included among the works of S. Chrysostom, is an incomplete commentary on S. Matthew by a heretical Latin writer. It will be noticed that the statement, whatever be thought of it, is made of man in the state of unregenerate nature, and at least it is extravagant and untrue of the regenerate, still more of the penitent, if only because one who was 'wholly sin' could not possibly be conscious of it. This in view of such remarks as that of Dr Whyte *L. Andrewes* p. 55.

P. 161. 12 sq. Also in [S. Aug.] *Speculum* 20, S. Anselm *Oratio* 16.

—— 28 sqq. See on p. 43 l. 29.

P. 162. 1 sqq. *Serm. Rep.* iv (i 370) 'This too [we can] wish with the prophet and so let us wish "O that my head were full of water and my eyes fountains of tears" (Jer. ix 1), to do it as it should be done! This we can. And pray we can, that He which "turneth the flint stone into a springing well," would vouchsafe us, even as dry as flints, *gratiam lachrymarum*, as the Fathers call it, some small portion of that grace to that end. Though weep we cannot, yet wish for it and pray for it we can.' S. Greg. Mag. *Dial.* iii 34 gratia lachrymarum: Alcuin *Conf. fidei* iv 18 (= [S. Aug.] *Med.* 36, S. Ans. *Or.* 16) da mihi gratiam lachrymarum: *Sacrament. Gregor.* missa pro petitione lachrymarum (Muratori ii 387): 'qui sitienti populo fontem viventis aquæ de petra produxisti, educ de cordis nostri compunctionis lachrymas': *Horolog.* p. 486 χάρισαί μοι τῷ πολλά σοι πταίσαντι δάκρυα κατανύξεως: *ib.* p. 160.

—— 6 sqq. Cp. S. Anselm *Or.* 17: cunctisque terrarum divitiis et honoribus mihi carior.

—— 10-20. *Serm. Repent.* iv (i 369) 'There is, saith the Psalm a flagon provided by God on purpose for them (Ps. lvi 8); therefore some would come, some few drops at least. Not as the Saints of old. No: *humanum dicimus* here too. Job's eyes "poured forth tears to God" (Job xvi 20); David's eye gushed out with water, he all to "wet his pillow" with them (Ps. cxix 136, vi 6); Mary Magdalene wept enough to have made a bath (Lu. vii 38). We urge not these. But if not pour out, not gush forth, *Nonne stillabit oculus noster*, saith Jeremy (xiii 17) "Shall not our eye afford a drop or twain?"'

—— 12. *Horolog.* p. 160 δάκρυά μοι δὸς, ὁ Θεὸς, ὥς ποτε τῇ γυναικὶ τῇ ἁμαρτωλῷ.

—— 23 sqq. *Serm. Repent.* viii (i 438) 'But our anger and generally all our affections are well compared to lime. Out of the water, where they should be hot, no heat appears in them; in water, where they should be cold, there they boil and take on. Used there most where they should be least, and again least where they should be most. For take me a worldly man, and let him but overreach himself in some good bargain, in matter of profit, you shall see him so angry, so out of patience with himself as oft it casts him into some disease. There lo is repentance in kind; there is that which makes it a tree, the spirit of life. Ours for the most part towards God is dull and blockish, neither life nor soul in it.'

P. 162. 29 sqq. *Serm Prayer* iv (v 339) 'If the spirit that quails in us do quail also in the whole Church, yet we have a supply from the tears which our Head, Christ, shed on his Church (Lu. xix 41), and from "the strong cries" (Heb. v 7) which He uttered to God his Father "in the days of his flesh," by which He ceaseth not to make request to God still for us; so that albeit the hardness of our heart be such as we cannot pray for ourselves nor the Church for us, yet we may say *Conqueror tibi, Domine, lachrymis Jesu Christi*': *Repent.* iv (i 371) 'And lastly, this we can, even humbly beseech our merciful God and Father, in default of ours, to accept of the "strong crying and bitter tears which in the days of his flesh his blessed Son in great agony shed for us" (Heb. v 7); for us, I say, that should, but are not able to do the like for ourselves, that what is wanting in ours may be supplied from thence."

P. 163. 6-22. See p. 65.

—— 31. sq. Andrewes seems to use this verse in some such sense as that of S. Augustine's exposition—that 'the thought' is penitence leading to confession and a new life, and 'the residue of his thought' the grateful memory the penitent's delivery (S. Aug. *Enarr. in Ps.* lxxv 11), or of one of Card. Hugo's expositions—that 'thought' or reflexion upon sins committed and on the character of sin and on the mercy of God, leads to inward 'confession' to God, and has as its 'residue,' or consequence a formal penitence in contrition, confession and satisfaction, issuing in a 'keeping festival,' i.e. rest from sin and devotion to God (Hugo di S. Chiaro *in loc.*). As interpretations these are of course wrong, both on other grounds and because ἐξομολογεῖσθαι, *confiteri*, here means 'to praise,' not 'to confess sins.'

Pp. 164-168. The Latin (O 302-307) does not correspond in range with the Greek (O 224-230, S 17-19), and to indicate exactly the relation of the two would require too complicated a marginal apparatus. Only additional matter, therefore, supplied by the Latin, is indicated by square brackets; but it must be noted that in the text these passages are in some cases substituted for what is found in the Greek.

P. 165. 11. *Serm. Rep.* viii (i 447) 'At this beam [i.e. balance] no fruit of ours will hold weight; none so found worthy; no not if we could, I say not shed or pour out, but even melt into tears, and every tear a drop of blood.' Cp. *ib.* iv (i 370).

—— 26 sqq. *Serm. Rep.* iv (i 373) 'Who with great indignation cannot but abhor himself for the manifold indignities offered to God thereby? To the law of his justice, to the awe of his majesty, to the reverend regard of his presence, the dread of his power, the longsuffering of his love, that being a creature of so vile and brittle consistence he hath not sticked for some lying vanity, some trifling pleasure, or pelting profit, to offend so many ways at once, all odious in themselves and able to make a rent in any heart that shall weigh them aright': *Pent.* v (iii 195) 'the rule of his justice, the reverence and majesty of his presence, the awful regard of his power, the kind respect of his bounty and goodness.' The passage seems to be a quotation.

—— 36 sqq. From the Greek Compline: also in the Coptic (Bute *Coptic morning service* p. 137).

P. 166. 10 sqq. Phrases collected from the sermon *de exitu animæ* among the works of S. Cyril of Alexandria, but probably unauthentic. It was published with two sermons of S. John of Damascus, in a tiny volume, Paris, Ch. Wechel, 1538, uniform with the Greek version of the Roman *Horae B.V.M.* of the same date and publisher.

—— 34 sq. See on p. 43 l. 33.

P. 167. 2 sqq. *Serm. Rep.* iv (i 372) 'The very heathen set themselves in passion against vice. That it is a brutish thing, so against the nobleness of reason; that a shameful, so against public honesty; that ignominious, so against our credit and good name; that pernicious, as shutting us out of heaven whither we would come.'

—— 17 sq. Cp. on p. 32 l. 14.

P. 169. 2 sqq. The prayer *O bone Jesu, duo in me cognosco* appears, among English books, only in the editions of the Sarum *Horae* published from 1511 onwards by Byrckmann, Paris. Cp. *Serm. Pent.* xv (iii 392) 'the defect from us, the work from God.'

—— 13 sq. S. Ans. *Med.* ii 8: ne perdat mea iniquitas quod fecit tua omnipotens bonitas.

—— 15 sqq. This extract from two chapters of S. Anselm's third *Meditation* is found in the Byrckmann *Horae* under the title *Oratio S. Anselmi.*

P. 170. 1 sqq. This prayer *Respice ad me* is in the Byrckmann *Horae* attributed to S. Augustine, and it occurs as *Oratio S. Augustini* in Alcuin *Officia per ferias* (ii[1] p. 77).

—— 11 sqq. Mostly from the *Conditor cæli et terræ.*

—— 22 sq. From the prayer *de omnibus sanctis* O mitissime Deus creator omnipotens.

—— 24 sqq. From the invocation *O sancte angele Dei;* also in *Horae* 1494 f. 59.

P. 171. 28. Collect after the Litany *Deus cui proprium est misereri et parcere* ('O God whose nature and property,' etc.): Sacr. Greg. (ed. Muratori) cc. 200, 248. Cp. S. Bernard *hom.* v *in Nativ.* 3: cui vult miseretur et quem vult indurat; sed quod miseretur, proprium illi est.

—— 29. See on p. 150 l. 7.

P. 173. Cp. on p. 42 l. 17.

P. 177. 4 sqq. Cp p. 155 l. 1. *Serm. Gunpowder Tr.* iii (iv 253) 'For whatsoever as the Son of God He may do, it is kindly [natural] for Him as the Son of man to save the sons of men. Specially being the Son of such men as He was; the Son of Abraham, who entreated hard that Sodom might not be destroyed (Gen. xviii 23 sq.); the Son of Jacob who much misliked, yea even cursed the wrath of his two sons, in destroying Shechem (Gen. xlix 7); the Son of David, who complained much of the sons of Zeruiah that they were "too hard" for him (2 Sam. iii 39), as Christ doth here [S. Lk. ix 55] of the sons of Zebedee.'

P. 178. Cp. p. 132.

P. 180. 6 sq. *Serm. Pent.* v (iii 192) '*Sane novum supervenisse Spiritum, nova desideria demonstrant* saith Bernard': *ib.* xiii (iii 357) '*Novum supervenisse Spiritum nova vitæ ratio demonstrat.*' Perhaps the allusion is to S. Bern. *Serm. in Ascens.* iii 8.

—— 9. S. Hilary of Poictiers *in Ps. cxviii* 17 § 11 (347 E) vera peccati confessio est sine intermissione temporis pœnitere.

—— 10 sqq. Cp. S. Bernard *in Pascha Serm.* i 17: sit veræ compunctionis indicium opportunitatis fuga, subtractio occasionis: S. Isidore of Seville *Sentent.* ii 13 § 7: ille pœnitentiam digne agit qui sic præterita mala deploratur ut futura iterum non committat.

—— 14 sq. S. Anselm *Orat.* 10: si iustitia aboletur iusti ruentis, quanto magis pœnitentia peccatoris in idipsum revertentis. Pet. Lomb. *Sentt.* iv 14 and Ludolph. *vita Christi* i 20 § 1 quote, the latter as from S. Augustine, 'inanis est pœnitentia quam sequens coinquinat culpa,' the source of which is perhaps S. Isid. *Synon.* i 77.

Pp. 184-188. Cp. pp. 46 sq., 74 sq. and notes.

P. 186. 28. *Serm. Res.* xvii (iii 66) 'And having thus "spoiled principalities and powers, He made an open show of them, triumphed over them" in *Semetipso* "in his own person"—all three are in Colossians the second [14 sq.]—and triumphantly came thence with the keys of Edom and Bozrah both [Is. lxiii 1], "of hell and of death" [Rev. i 18] both at his girdle, as He shews Himself. And when was this? if ever, on this very day. On which, having made a full and perfect conquest of death, "and of him that hath the power of death, that is the devil" (Heb. ii 14), He rose and returned thence this morning as a mighty Conqueror, saying as Deborah did in her song, "O my soul, thou hast trodden down strength" (Judg. v 21), thou hast marched valiantly.'

—— 31. *Serm. Pent.* vii (iii 226) 'His going up then is not all for Himself; some part and that no small part, "for us." For thither He is gone *ut præcursor noster* (Heb. vi 20), as our "Forerunner" or Harbinger, *pandens iter ante nos*, saith the prophet Micah (ii 13) "to make a way before us," "to prepare a place" (Jo. xiv 2) and to hold possession of it in our names, saith He Himself.'

P. 186. 37 sq. *Serm. before two Kings* (v 239) 'The angel of the bottomless pit, of whom the same John speaks: "His name in Hebrew is Abaddon, in Greek Apollyon," that is, a destroyer. A destroyer; a name directly opposite to God's name. His name is Saviour. And the name of His Son, Jesus, a Saviour also—an Angel interpreting it (Mt. i 21).'

—— 40 sqq. *Serm. Pent.* vii (iii 225) 'There is somewhat still to be done for us. We have our cause there to be handled, and to be handled against a false and slanderous Adversary—so Job found him (i 10, ii 4). By means of his being there "on high," *habemus Advocatum*, saith St John, "we have an Advocate" (1 John ii 1) will see it take no harm.' Cp. *ib.* iii (iii 158).

P. 188. 6. See on p. 21 l. 20.

—— 9. Reading with O, *Pater ungens*, instead of *Patre unigenitum* with H.

—— 38 sqq. *Serm. Pent.* v (iii 193) 'As for what is in the heart, *quis cognoscit illud?* "who knows it?" (Jer. xvii 9). Not we ourselves; our own hearts oft deceive us. And there is a *verbis confitentur*, "confess at the mouth," with a *factis negant*, "deny with the deeds" (Tit. i 16); and that deceives too. But there is *opus fidei*, "the work of faith" (1 Th. i 3) from *fides quæ operatur*, "faith that worketh" (Gal. v 6)—that is St Paul's faith; that can shew itself by working (Jas. ii 18)—that is St James' faith; and there may well be the Spirit. But without works, there it may not be. For without works, St James is flat, it is but "a dead faith" (Jas. ii 17), the carcase of faith, there is no Spirit in it. No Spirit if no work. For *usque adeo proprium est operari Spiritui, ut nisi operetur nec sit*, "so kindly is it for the Spirit to be working, as if It work not It is not." There is none to work. There is none to work; *spectrum est, non Spiritus*, "a flying shadow it is, a Spirit it is not," if work it do not. And yet I cannot deny, works there may be and motion, and yet no Spirit, as in artificial engines, watches and jacks and such-like. And a certain artificial thing there is in religion, we call it hypocrisy, that by certain pins and gins, makes a show of certain works and motions as if there were Spirit, but surely Spirit there is none in them. . . . You shall easily discover these works, that they come not from the Spirit, by the two signs in Psalm the fifty-first, *nākôn* and *nedîbāh* (Ps. li 10, 12), 1. "constant" and 2. "free." . . . Ingenuity and constancy, the free proceeding, the constant continuing of them will soon disclose whether they come from a Spirit or no': *ib.* xii (iii 337 sq.) 'Neither fear, if it be fear alone; nor faith, if it be faith alone, is accepted of Him; but *timet* and *operatur* here with Peter (Acts x 35), and *fides quæ operatur* there with Paul (Gal. v 6). . . And they observe that it is not "that doeth," but "that worketh righteousness." Not *facit*, but *operatur*. And what manner of work? St Peter's word is ἐργαζόμενος here; and for ἐργαζόμενος, ἔργον will not serve; it must be ἐργασία, which is plain "trade." *Discite bene agere*, saith Esay (Is. i 17), learn it, as one would learn a handicraft, to live by; learn it and be occupied in it; make an ἐργασία, that is, even "an occupation" of it. Christ's own occupation, who as St Peter tells us straight after, *pertransiit benefaciendo* "went up and down, went about doing good," practising it and nothing else; for that is ἐργάζεσθαι.'

P. 189. 6. H reads *mundam* 'pure'; O, *vincentem mundum.*

P. 190. 16-18. See on p. 214 l. 20.

P. 192. Thomas Bradwardine was archbishop of Canterbury for five weeks in 1349. His work *de causa Dei contra Pelagium et de virtute causarum*, from which the present passage is taken, won him the name of *Doctor profundus* and was commonly known as *Summa doctoris profundi.* It is a defence of the Augustinian doctrine of grace against what he considered the prevailing Pelagianism of his day. It was edited by Sir Henry Saville in 1618. Andrewes quotes him in 1619 in *Serm. Nativ.* xiii (i 220).

P. 195. The comments, except ll. 24-27, are found only in S, not in O.

—— 7. *Serm. Gunpowder Tr.* vii (iv 331) 'You shall mark therefore at the very next words, when he comes to his thanks, it is *Confiteantur tibi opera Deus*, but *Sancti tui benedicant tibi*; "thy works, let them say *Confiteor*; thy redeemed, thy saints, let them say *Benedictus.*" Thy works let them tell truth and confess, but thy saints, let them speak all good and bless Thee.'

—— 21 sq. Quoted in [S. Aug.] *Med.* 35, *Soliloqq.* 31. Cp. Bright *Select sermons of S. Leo* note 60.

—— 24. The opening words of Ps. lxv in Heb. and Lat. are not in O. For the rendering see A.V. marg. and S. Jerome's *tibi silentium laus. Instit. piae* p. 11 'But in this and all other his attributes *verius cogitatur quam dicitur* [S. Aug. *de Trin.* vii 7]. We may better conceive of them than express them: and we speak best of his worth when with a silent admiration we hold our peace, according to that of the Psalmist, Ps. lxv 1, which S. Hierome hath translated *Tibi silet omnis laus Deus in Sion.*' Cp. the famous passage in Hooker *Eccl. Pol.* i 2 § 2 and Church's note on it; S. Cyril of Jerusalem *Cat.* vi 2; S. Hilary of Poictiers *de Trin.* ii 6.

P. 196. 3. sqq. Adapted from the prayer 'Dona mihi quæso' after the *Psalterium S. Hieronymi*, fac me tuis semper laudibus vacare et ad tuam quandoque dulcedinem misericorditer pervenire (also in *Horae* 1494 f. 131). And see note on p. 45 l. 28.

—— 10. See also *Breviarium Sarisburiense* init.; and *Horae* 1494 f. 2 b.

P. 196. 13. From the responsory of the 7th Lesson of Mattins in the *Officium mortuorum*: cp. p. 231 l. 2.

—— 22. Adapted from *Prayer of S. Ambrose*, gratias tibi referimus licet indignas sed utinam devotas et tibi gratas.

—— 23. From the *Oratio ad Patrem* Domine sancte pater omnip. eterne Deus qui coequalem.

—— 29. From *Sancta Trinitas unus Deus.* Cp. p. 198.

P. 198. 3-19. From the *Orationes speciales* to the three Persons of the Holy Trinity.

—— 20, 22-33. From *Sancta Trinitas unus Deus*, *Horae* f. 101, and *Benedicat me imperialis maiestas*, *ib.* f. c. 2b.

—— 21. From the antiphon of the commemoration of the Holy Name.

P. 202. 15-24. From *The breath of every living being* in the morning service for Sabbaths and festivals. The text of the Spanish rite (*Daily Prayers* p. 122) differs somewhat from that of the German rite (Singer p. 126). Andrewes does not wholly agree with either. 'Extol' in l. 15 is from the German; l. 18 from the Spanish; l. 19 is in neither. The passage is quoted, without l. 19, in *Serm. Gunpowder Tr.* vii (iv 339) 'Wherefore the powers Thou hast distributed in our souls, the breath of life Thou hast breathed into our nostrils, the tongues Thou hast put into our mouths, behold all these shall break forth and confess and bless and thank and praise and magnify and exalt Thee and thy mercy for ever. Yea every mouth shall acknowledge Thee, every tongue be a trumpet of thy praise, every eye look up, every knee bow, every stature stoop to Thee, and all hearts shall fear Thee. And all that is within us . . . even our bones . . . all shall say, "Who is like unto Thee, o Lord," in mercy? "Who is like unto Thee, glorious in holiness, fearful in praises, doing wonders?"'

P. 204. 19, 20, 24. See on p. 196 l. 3, 10, 22.

P. 206-208. Of these, 1-4 are the 'immanent' or 'metaphysical' attributes, the first apparently representing the scholastic *immutabilitas*, the second *infinitas*; 5, 6 'operative' and 7-10 'moral.' The rest are the several forms of mercy; cp. p. 70.

P. 208. 4-12. Cp. on p. 70 l. 30.

—— 16. *Serm. Pent.* iii. (iii. 153) 'A true endeavour with an humble repentance, for so he resolves, and then *omnia mandata facta deputantur quando quod non sit ignoscitur*, "all are accounted as kept, when what is not is pardoned out of his mercy"; and so the rest rewarded out of his bounty that alloweth a day's wages for an hour's work, as to them that came at the eleventh hour to the vineyard, that is at five of the clock after noon.'

—— 18 sqq. Cp. p. 53 l. 38 and note.

P. 211. 9-15, 17-23. Cp. p. 88.

—— 10. *Euchology.* p. 557 τὸν ἄνθρωπον οἰκείαις χερσὶ διαπλάσας.

P. 212. 2 sq. Cp. on p. 35 l. 30.

—— 4. *Serm. Pass.* iii (ii 163) 'His main end (Heb. xii 2) being to exhort them, as they had begun well, so well to persevere; to very good purpose, He willeth them to have an eye to Him and His example, who first and last ἀπὸ φάτνης ἄχρι σταυροῦ "from the cratch to the cross," from S. Luke's time *quo coepit Jesus facere et docere*, "that He began to do and teach" (Acts i 1), to S. John's time that He cried *Consummatum est* (Jo. xix 30), gave them not over *sed in finem usque dilexit eos*, but "to the end loved them" (Jo. xiii 1).' Cp. *Nativ.* xii (i 201).

—— 6. See on p. 122 l. 27.

—— 10 sq. *Serm. Nativ.* iv (i 55) 'When was He "made under the Law" (Gal. iv 4)? Even then when He was circumcised. For this doth St Paul testify in the third of the next chapter "Behold, I Paul testify unto you, whosoever is circumcised" *factus est debitor universæ legis*, "he becomes a debtor to the whole law." At his circumcision then He entered bond anew with us; and in sign that so He did He shed then a few drops of His blood, whereby He signed the bond as it were, and gave those few drops then *tanquam arrham universi sanguinis effundendi* "as a pledge or earnest" that "when the fulness of time came," "He would be ready to shed all the rest."'

—— 12. On the Holy Name see *Serm. Res.* ix (ii 332).

—— 21. *Serm. Pentec.* v (iii 188) 'Distinct in number, as in our Baptism; "The Father, Son, Holy Ghost." And that number distinct to the sense, as at Christ's Baptism; the Father in the voice, the Son in the flood, the Holy Ghost in the shape of a dove." Cp. *ib.* xv (iii 380). Cp. the apolytikion of the Epiphany, *Horolog.* p. 262 ἐν Ἰορδάνῃ βαπτιζομένου σου Κύριε ἡ τῆς Τριάδος ἐφανερώθη προσκύνησις· τοῦ γὰρ Γεννήτορος ἡ φωνὴ προσεμαρτύρει σοι, ἀγαπητόν σε Υἱὸν ὀνομάζουσα καὶ τὸ Πνεῦμα ἐν εἴδει περιστερᾶς ἐβεβαίου τοῦ λόγου τὸ ἀσφαλές: and S. Anselm *Med.* xv 17: *Golden Litany* (Maskell *Mon. Rit.* iii 265) 'thi holy baptyme and thi gloriouse apperyng of the holy trinite.'

—— 25 sqq. *Golden Litany* (Maskell p. 266) 'For thy thirste, hunger, coolde, and hete, whyche thou sufferedist in this vale of miseri . . . thy heuines, labor, and weriness . . . thy wache and prayers . . . thi meke and holy conuersacion.'

—— 41. *Serm. Pass.* iii (ii 172) 'To count Him worse than the worst thief in gaol: to say and to cry *Vivat Barabbas pereat Christus*, "Save Barabbas and hang Christ."'

P. 213. 1 sqq. *Golden Litany* (Maskell p. 266 sq.) 'For thy wache and prayers . . . the wonderfull signes and myracles whyche thou wroughtest . . . thi holi wordis and sermons.'

—— 8 sq. From the prayer *Domine Jesu Christi Fili Dei vivi deprecor te*—where *per omnes* etc., depends upon *deprecor*. What the intended construction is here is not clear, but perhaps 'wrought by' expresses the meaning.

—— 18. 'Sayings,' *sententiis* 'maxims.'

P. 214. 2. Andrewes takes the 'woman' of S. Lk. vii 37 to be S. Mary Magdalen, *Serm. Res.* xiv, xv.

—— 9. This line summarises the point of the preceding examples. The construction of the ablatives of the next 7 lines is not clear; but apparently they are governed by *pro* and given thanks for as examples of our Lord's endurance of the 'contradiction of sinners' Heb. xii 3.

—— 20-22. *Serm. Passion* iii (ii 171) 'Certainly the blood of Gethsemane was another manner of blood than that of Gabbatha or that of Golgotha either; and that was the blood of his internal Cross. Of the three Passions, that was the hardest to endure, yet that did He endure too' (cp. pp. 169-171): *Pentec.* viii (iii 247) 'He had *trinam mersionem*; 1. one in "Gethsemane"; 2. one in "Gabbatha"; 3. and a third in "Golgotha." In "Gethsemane" in his sweat of blood. In "Gabbatha" in the blood that came from the scourges and thorns; in "Golgotha" that which came from the nails and the spear.' Cp. *Res.* xvii (iii 70), *Pentec.* xiii (iii 348).

—— 23-25. *Serm. Pass.* iii (ii 174) 'So have we now the cross, ξύλον δίδυμον "the two main bars of it," 1. Pain, 2. Shame; and either of these again a cross of itself; and that double, 1. outward, and 2. inward. Pain, bloody, cruel, dolorous and enduring—pain He endured. Shame, servile, scandalous, opprobrious, odious—shame He despised. And beside these, an internal cross, the passion of Gethsemane; and an internal shame, the curse itself of the cross, *maledictum crucis*.' Cp. *ib.* p. 167.

—— 31 sqq. From the *Prayer of S. Ambrose* Domine Jesu Christi Fili Dei vivi.

P. 215. 1, 24. The text has the titles *Gethsemane* and *Golgotha* respectively before these lines, but they are obviously out of place and should perhaps stand before p. 214 l. 30 and 217 l. 7.

—— 16 sqq. *Serm. Pass.* iii (ii 173) 'Was it a tragedy, or a Passion trow? A Passion it was, yet by their behaviour it might seem a May-game. Their shouting and outcries, their harrying of Him about from Annas to Caiaphas, from him to Pilate, from Pilate to Herod and from him to Pilate again; one while in purple, Pilate's suit; another while in white, Herod's livery; nipping Him by the cheeks, and pulling off his hair; blindfolding Him and buffetting Him; bowing to Him in derision, and then spitting in his face;—was as if they had not the Lord of glory, but some idiot or dizard in hand. "Died Abner as a fool dieth?" saith David of Abner in great regret (2 Sam. iii 33). O no! Sure our blessed Saviour so died; and that He so died, doth equal, nay surpass even the worst of his torments.' Cp. *Tempt.* iv (v 516).

—— 24 sqq. From the *Versus S. Bernardi*; also in *Horae* 1494 f. 85b.

—— 33 sqq. From the *Prayer of S. Ambrose.*

—— 38. 'Cudgelled' *fustigari.* Not in the Gospels.

P. 216. 1 sqq. From the *Salve tremendum*. Cp. p. 90 and notes.

—— 9. *Serm. Pass.* iii (ii 170) 'Even to stand, as He hung, three long hours together, holding up but the arms at length, I have heard it avowed of some that have felt it, to be a pain scarce credible.'

—— 14. *Serm. Pass.* iii (ii 171) 'In all those [outward sufferings] no blood came but where passages were made for it to come out by, but in this [the internal suffering] it strained out all over, even at all places at once.' *Golden Litany* (p. 268) 'For thi innumerable woundes and the plentuous shedyng of thi blode.'

—— 19. All the passages on this and the next page referred to *Horae* f. 75 b are from the *Prayer of S. Ambrose*.

—— 24. *Serm. Passion* iii (ii 172) 'Was it not yet a more foul disgrace and scandal indeed to appoint Him for his death that dishonest, that foul death, the death of malefactors, and of the worst sort of them? *Morte turpissima*, as themselves termed it; "the most shameful, opprobrious death of all other," that the persons are scandalous that suffer it.'

—— 34. The 'pillar' is inferred from Roman practice: Livy ii 5 stabant deligati ad palum: . . nudatos virgis caedunt [lictores]: Cicero *Verr.* II v 5 ad supplicium traditi, ad palum alligati. In the ivth cent. the pillar of our Lord's flagellation was already shewn in Jerusalem: *Itinerar. Burdigal*, 592; S. Jer. *Ep.* cviii *ad Eustoch.* 9 (i 691 D). *Golden Lit.* (Maskell p. 268) 'the byndynge of thi most holy body to a pilour.'

—— 35. 'Beaten with rods.' The phrase *virgis cædi* (Acts xvi 22, 2 Cor. xi 25), the position of the clause, and the distinction between this and 'to be scourged,' suggests that Andrewes supposes our Lord was beaten with the rods of the *fasces*. But there is no authority for this in the Gospels, and besides Pilate as imperial procurator had no lictors. Ἐράπισαν (S. Mt xxvi 67) probably means 'struck with rods,' but that is in the mockery, not at the formal scourging. The sources Andrewes draws upon here have not the clause.

P. 217. 6. S. Jo. xix 17 says that our Lord 'came forth bearing his cross,' while the other Gospels only notice that Simon of Cyrene was impressed to bear the cross. *Acta Pilati* 10 has ἦλθε μέχρι τῆς πύλης. As late as Hugo di S. Chiaro († 1263) *in S. Jo. xix* 17 the difference is merely noted; and the first attempt to harmonise in detail seems to be S. Bonaventura († 1274) *Vita Christi* 77, Nicolas of Lyra († 1340) *in S. Matt. xxvii* 32 and Ludolphus of Saxony (fl. 1330) *Vita Christi* ii 62 § 35, who suppose that Simon was impressed when our Lord was too weary to carry the cross further: and so even Corn. a Lapide *in S. Mt. xxvii* 32. But Caietan († 1554) *in Mt. xxvii* 32, after mentioning this general view, adds 'hoc quoque apparet rationi consentaneum esse quod Jesus sub onere crucis caderet, nimio pressus onere, ut prædicatur,' i.e. that our Lord's falling had become a topic of the pulpit; and the 34th. of the York Miracle Plays (c. 1430) represents our

Lord as swooning (*York Plays* Oxford 1885, p. 344) and the *Golden Litany* (Maskell, p. 269) has 'bi the grete wereness that thou haddest on thi shuldir beryng the crosse vntill thou fell downe.' In art, our Lord is represented as falling in the directions of the Byzantine Painters' manual (Didron *Christian Iconography*, Engl. tr. Stokes, ii p. 316) of uncertain date, but not earlier than the xii cent., and in the west first in the 'Stations of the Cross' which were introduced from Jerusalem in the xvth cent.; in these, in the earliest example, those at Nürnberg, executed in 1488, seven in number (figured in Kraus *Gesch. d. Christlich. Kunst* ii p. 308), our Lord falls once; in later examples, of fourteen stations, three times. Apart from these, the subject appears first in the engravings of Martin Schön (1420-1486), then in Rafael's *Spasimo*. See Jameson and Eastlake *History of our Lord in Art* ii pp. 114 sqq.

P. 217. 9. S. Bonaventura *Vita Christi* 78 represents our Lord as ascending the cross by a ladder, as in some earlier pictures and even in Fra Angelico (Jameson and Eastlake ii 129 sqq.); but it is certain that He would be stretched on the cross as it lay on the ground: so Ludolphus *Vita Christi* ii 63 § 5 and generally in later art (Jameson and Eastlake ii 132 sqq.).

—— 18. *Serm. Pass.* iii (ii 173) 'Yea in the very time of his prayers deriding Him, even in his most mournful complaint and cry for very anguish of spirit.'

—— 26. *Serm. Pass.* ii (ii 145) 'To very good purpose it was that the ancient Fathers of the Greek Church in their Liturgy, after they have recounted all the particular pains, as they are set down in his Passion, and by all and by every one of them called for mercy, do after all shut up all with this, Δι' ἀγνωστῶν κόπων καὶ βασάνων ἐλέησον καὶ σῶσον ἡμᾶς "By thine unknown sorrows and sufferings" felt by Thee but not distinctly known by us, "have mercy upon us and save us."' Cp. *S. Giles' Lectt.* p. 641. I have been unable to trace the Greek passage quoted, and its form and that of its setting as described is not suggestive of a Greek formula. It may be suspected that Andrewes had met with, and mistaken for original, a Greek translation of the *Golden Litany*, which has (Maskell p. 268) 'for all that labour and tormentis that were secrete and vnknowne whiche thou sufferedist all that nyght.'

—— 27 sq. From the *Deus qui voluisti pro perditione*; also in *Horae* 1494 f. 56 b.

—— 37 sqq. From *A devoute prayer to our Lorde crucifyed in the crosse for the redemptyon of man* 'Qui gloriosum caput'; also in *Horae* 1494 f. 35. They are founded on the forms of anointing the various members of the body in Extreme Unction (Maskell *Mon. rit.* i p. 108).

P. 218. 25. Thanksgiving after Communion from 1549 onwards, 'the most precious death and passion of thy dear Son.'

—— 31. *Triduana*: τῆς τριημέρου ταφῆς in the commemoration of Lit. S. Bas. (*Litt. E. and W.* p. 328).

P. 218. 32 sqq. From the prayers *In the agony* (of death) 'Domine Jesu Christe per agoniam' and 'Domine Jesu Christe qui pro nobis.'

—— 38 sq. Cp. on p. 186 l. 28.

P. 219. 1. From the commemoration in the mass of 1549.

—— 2-11. This list is probably imitated from *Golden Legend* Resurrect. (Ellis i p. 93).

—— 12. *Golden Litany* (Maskell p. 273) 'for thi wondirfull and gloriouse ascension'; *Canon missae* in cœlos gloriosæ ascensionis.

—— 13. *Litt. E. and W.* p. 329 τῆς ἐκ δεξιῶν σοῦ τοῦ Θεοῦ καὶ Πατρὸς καθέδρας.

—— 18 sqq. The *Veni Creator* was probably written in Gaul in the last quarter of the ixth. cent. See *Dict. of Hymnology* s.v. It has been variously used, chiefly in the Office of Pentecost, since the xith. cent. in Ordination of presbyters and bishops, during the vesting of the celebrant for mass (Sarum etc.), at the offertory (York, Hereford), and since the xivth. cent. in Coronations (English, and later French). The longer English version, in its original form probably by Cranmer, appeared first in the Ordinals of 1550 and 1552; in 1661 it was emended, and the shorter version was added, having appeared first in Cosin's *Devotions* 1637 and perhaps been used at the coronation of Charles I (C. Wordsworth *Coronation of K. Charles I*, p. 57).

—— 22 sqq. *Serm. Pent.* vi (iii 206) 'No Person of the Three hath so many, so diverse denominations as He; and they be all to shew the manifold diversity of the gifts He bestoweth on us. They count them, 1. the *meraḥepheth* or "agitation" (Gen. i 2) which maketh the vegetable power in the world. 2. His *nephesh ḥayyah* "spirit or soul of life" (Gen. i 20) in the living creatures. 3. His *nishmath ḥayyîm* "heavenly spirit of a double life" (Gen. ii 7) in mankind [see on p. 88 l. 16]. 4. Then that in Bezaleel (Ex. xxxi 3), that gave him excellency of art. 5. That in the seventy elders (Num. xi 16, 17) that gave them excellency of wisdom to govern. 6. That in Balaam (Num. xxiv 14) and the Sibyls, that gave them the word of prophecy, to foretell things contingent. 7. That of the Apostles this day, that gave them skill to speak all tongues (Acts ii 5, 8).' Cp. *ib.* v (iii 184).

—— 28 sqq. *Serm. Pent.* iv (iii 174) 'We conceive, I trust, after two manners He came as this day: 1. one visible, "in tongues of fire that sat upon their heads"; 2. the other invisible, by inward grace whereby He possessed their hearts.' *Golden Legend* (Ellis i p. 124) 'The Holy Ghost is sent in two manners, visibly and invisibly. As touching into the hearts pure and chaste He descended visibly, when by some sign visible He is showed. Of the sending invisible saith S. John, Johannis iii: *Spiritus ubi vult spirat*.' The following lists are those of the *Legend*, except the first example, which is certainly a very strange one.

—— 31 sqq. *Serm. Pentec.* ix (iii 261) 'Three such comings [in a type or form, by the sense to be perceived] there were in all. Once did our Saviour receive the Holy Ghost and twice did He give It. Give It on earth in the text [Jo. xx 22]; and after from heaven on the day [of Pentecost]. So three in all. At Christ's baptism, "It came upon Him in the shape of a dove" (Lk. iii 22). At this feast It came upon his apostles in the likeness of "tongues of fire." And here now in this, comes breath-wise, having breath for the *symbolum* to represent It': *ib.* p. 264 'Thrice was the Holy Ghost sent and in three forms: 1. of "a dove," 2. of breath, 3. of "cloven tongues." From the Father as a "dove"; from the Son as breath; from both as "cloven tongues."'

P. 219. 31. The figure of the dove is beautifully developed in *Serm. Pentec.* viii (iii 251 sqq.).

—— 33. The editions read *habitus* and *habitu*, and Neale apparently regarding it as unintelligible omits the line in his translation. It is a misprint of course for *halitus*, *halitu*.

—— 38 sqq. *Serm. Pent.* i (iii 127) 'In this book, after this time here three several times, in the fourth, tenth and nineteenth chapters; and at three several places, Jerusalem, Cæsarea, Ephesus, the same Spirit came upon the faithful people, and yet nothing heard nor seen; only discovered after, by the impression It left behind It. . . . 1. In the fourth chapter, the thirty-first verse, "as they prayed" the Spirit came upon them. 2. In the tenth, verse the forty-fourth, "while Peter yet spake, the Spirit fell upon them." 3. In the nineteenth chapter, verse the sixth, as they received the sacrament, the Spirit was sent on them. In which there are plainly set down to us, these three means to procure the Spirit's coming: 1. Prayer, 2. the Word, 3. the Sacraments.'

P. 220. 2-6 col. 2. The compounds of κλῆσις—ἔκκλησις, ἀνάκλησις, ἐπανάκλησις, ἐπίκλησις, παράκλησις.

—— 6. *Serm. Pent.* iv (iii 176) 'When we send for Him, He is *Paracletus*; when He for us, then we are, and not He:—if we be that, if we be *advocati* and not rather *avocati*, every trifling occasion being enough to call us away.'

—— 7-12. See on p. 91.

—— 13 sqq. *Serm. Pentec.* vi (iii 207) 'From the Holy Spirit, or the Spirit as He is holy, cometh the *gratum faciens*, the gift of gifts, the gift of grace, which He bestoweth on his saints and servants, and maketh them such by it. . . . 1. The grace reproving and checking from within, when they are ready to go astray; *spiritus reflans* "the wind against them" (Acts xvi 16), not suffering them to go into Asia or Mysia, when they shall do no good there, but making them even windbound as it were. 2. *Spiritus afflans* 'the wind with them,' "guiding them" and giving them a good pass "into all truth" (Jo. xvi 13). 3. The grace teaching them what they knew not and calling to their minds that they did know and have forgot (Jo. xiv 26). And so *spiritus difflans*, "blowing away and scattering," as it were, the mists of error and forgetfulness. 4. The grace quickening them and stirring them up, when they grow dull and even becalmed. 5. The grace inspiring and inditing their requests, when they know not what or how to pray (Rom. viii 26). 6. The Spirit breathing and "shedding abroad his love in their hearts"; which makes them "go bound in the Spirit" (Acts xx 22), and as it were with full sail to Jerusalem, when it is for his service. 7. And last, the Spirit "sealing" them (2 Cor. i 22) an assurance of their estates to come.'

P 220. 19. *Serm. Pent.* vi (iii 219) 'When we turn ourselves every way, we find not in the office of the Church, what this seal should be but the sacrament; or what the print of it, but the grace there received, a means to make us and a pledge or "earnest" (2 Cor. v 5) to assure us that we are his.'

P. 221. Cp. on p. 63 l. 19.
—— 24-27. From the *Omnes sancti beatorum ordines.*
—— 28. From the prayer 'de omnibus sanctis' *O mitissime Deus.*
—— 29 sq. From the *Deus qui novem.*
—— 31—p. 222 l. 5. See on p. 102.

P. 222. 6. *Therapeutæ.* Used of the Jewish devotees in Egypt (Philo *de vita contempl.* p. 471; Eusebius *Hist. eccl.* ii 17 § 3, 8); then of Christian Monks ('Dionys. Areop.' *Hier. eccl.* vi p. 386 *οἱ θεῖοι καθηγεμόνες ἡμῶν ἐπωνυμιῶν αὐτοὺς ἱερῶν ἠξίωσαν, οἱ μὲν θεραπευτὰς, οἱ δέ μοναχοὺς ὀνομάζοντες ἐκ τῆς τοῦ Θεοῦ καθαρᾶς ὑπηρεσίας καὶ θεραπείας*). On Andrewes' view of monasticism, see *Resp. ad Bellarm.* p. 394.
—— 7-9. From the invocation *Omnes sancti innocentes*, here transferred from Innocents to Virgins.
—— 10. From the prayer *De omnibus sanctis.*
—— 11-13. From the invocation *Omnes sancti confessores*, here transferred from Confessors to Innocents.
—— 14. From the invocation *Omnes sancti patriarchæ et prophetæ.*
—— 15-17. From the *Omnes sancti confessores*, with the change of *manibus*, *verbis*, *actibus* into *corde*, *ore*, *vita.*

P. 223. Cp. p. 272.

P. 224. 31 sqq. From the first prayer, of S Basil, in the Ἀκολουθία τῆς ἁγίας μεταλήψεως. Cp S. Anselm *Med.* iv 5: adhuc patitur expectans tuam emendationem (cp. v 2, vi 4): *Hort. an.* 1516 f. 78 b: ad emendationem expectasti. *Serm. Pent.* i (iii 115) 'He hath waited for us and our conversion more years than we do days for Him.'

P. 225. 16 sqq. Cp. p. 87, 234.
—— 27 sqq. Cp. p. 117.

P. 226. 7-14. From *The breath of every living being*, following the Spanish text (*Daily Prayers* p. 121). Cp. *Serm Gunpowder Tr.* vii (iv 339) 'But we are not able to praise Thee, o Lord, and to extol thy Name, for one of a thousand, nay not for one of the many millions of the great mercies which Thou hast shewed upon us and upon our children.'

P. 226. 15-20. I have not found the source of this, and perhaps it is Andrewes' own composition. With the last line cp. Singer *Daily Prayer Book* pp. 44, 56, 137.

P. 227. 10. The MS here has 'Isaac,' but it must be a mistake for Moses.

P. 229. 16. The *divinitatem* of the Vulg. is apparently a mistake for *divitias*.
—— 23 sqq. See on p. 231 l. 13 sqq.

P. 231. 2. Cp. on p. 196 l. 13.
—— 13 sqq. Cp. *Hort. an.* Lyons 1516 f. 79: Tibi ago laudes . . . in quo mihi indigno famulo tuo N. corpus et animam contulisti et me imaginis tuæ similitudine decorasti mihique dedisti esse et vivere, me non bestiam, non terræ vermiculum, non rem insensatam, sed creaturam rationalem, æternæ beatitudinis cum sanctis angelis tuis capacem fecisti. Secundum corpus me non claudum, cæcum, monstruosum vel defectuosum, sed sanum, integrum et robustum formasti, meque in utero matris meæ et in infantia, in igne aqua aut aliis in periculis diversis, prout multis contingit, ante legitimam ætatem interire non permisisti, et me a multis animæ et corporis periculis per totam vitam meam preservasti . . . parentes etsi simplices et pauperes, honestos tamen et catholicos mihi providisti. . . Mihi quoque secundum animam ingenium bonum, memoriam tenacem, rationem perspicacem, litterarum scientiam competentem virtutesque naturales et morales cæteraque bona omnia si quæ habeo gratis absque meo merito contulisti.
—— 13 sq. S. Anselm *Med.* iv 5: et quod te non pecus aut creaturam insensibilem sed eam creaturam fecit quæ eum posses intelligere.
—— 14. *Serm. Lent* ii (ii 27) 'For there is in *tuus* (Ps. lxxvii 20), not only that they be men and not beasts; freemen and not villains; Athenians or Englishmen, that is, a civil, not a barbarous people—the three considerations of the heathen ruler, but that they be God's own people and flock.' Diogenes Laertius *vitae philosophorum* i 33 (of Socrates) ἔφασκε γὰρ . . . τριῶν τούτων ἕνεκα χάριν ἔχειν τῇ τύχῃ. πρῶτον μὲν ὅτι ἄνθρωπος ἐγενόμην καὶ οὐ θήριον· εἶτα ὅτι ἄνηρ καὶ οὐ γυνή· τρίτον ὅτι Ἕλλην καὶ οὐ βάρβαρος: cp. Plutarch *Marius* 46: Lactantius *Institt.* iii 19 § 17.
—— 16, 25. *Hebrew Morning Service* (Singer, p. 5) 'Blessed art Thou, o Lord our God, King of the universe, who hast not made me a heathen . . a bondman.'
—— 18. *Mali corvi malum ovum*, the Greek proverb κακοῦ κόρακος κακὸν ᾠόν. See Leutsch & Schneidewin *Paræmiographi græci* i pp. 107, 259, ii. pp. 73, 466; Erasmus *Adagia* s. v. *Originis*.
—— 28. *Hort. an.* 1516 f. 78 b, 'tranquillitatem temporum' in *Gratias tibi ago tibi*.

P. 235. 13 sqq. From the prayer of the Trisagion Ὁ Θεὸς ὁ ἅγιος

(*Litt. E. and W.* p. 313) ὁ καταξιώσας ἡμᾶς τοὺς ταπεινοὺς καὶ ἀναξίους δούλους σου καὶ ἐν τῇ ὥρᾳ ταύτῃ στῆναι κατενώπιον τῆς δόξης τοῦ ἁγίου σου θυσιαστηρίου καὶ τὴν ὀφειλομένην σοι προσκύνησιν καὶ δοξολογίαν προσάγειν.

P. 235. 16 sqq. Adapted from the offertory prayer Κύριε ὁ Θεὸς ἡμῶν (*ib.* p. 401) ἵνα γενώμεθα ἄξιοι τοῦ προσφέρειν σοι τὴν λογικὴν ταύτην καὶ ἀναίμακτον θυσίαν . . . ἣν προσδεξάμενος εἰς τὸ ἅγιον καὶ νοερόν σου θυσιαστήριον εἰς ὀσμὴν εὐωδίας, ἀντικατάπεμψον ἡμῖν τὴν χάριν τοῦ ἁγίου σου Πνεύματος. But Andrewes seems to follow the text of the prayer as it has been inserted into Lit. S. Jas. (*ib.* p. 47) since he reads *ss.* (i.e. *sanctissimi*) *Spiritus* (παναγίου for ἁγίου).

—— 20 sqq. From the prayer of the Trisagion (*ib.* p. 313), ἐπίσκεψαι ἡμᾶς ἐν τῇ χρηστότητί σου, συγχώρησον ἡμῖν πᾶν πλημμέλημα ἑκούσιόν τε καὶ ἀκούσιον; and the prayer of Propitiation, Κύριε Ἰησοῦ Χριστοῦ, appended to some texts of S. James: συγχώρησον αὐτοῖς πᾶν πλημμέλημα ἑκούσιόν τε καὶ ἀκούσιον· ἀπάλλαξον αὐτοὺς τῆς αἰωνίου κολάσεως; and the prayer of the Trisagion Οἰκτίρμον καὶ ἐλέημον (*L. E. and W.* p. 34) σῶσον ἡμᾶς ὁ Θεὸς ἐκ τῶν δυσχερῶν τοῦ κόσμου τούτου. The prayer of Propitiation is the first prayer of the Byzantine administration of penance (*Euchology*. p. 221), but it was used in the Liturgy of S. James for those about to communicate (Swainson *Greek Liturgies* p. 331).

—— 24. From the prayer at the Entrance Ὁ Θεὸς ὁ παντοκράτωρ and the prayer of the Veil Εὐχαριστοῦμέν σοι Κύριε (*L. E. and W.* pp. 33, 48), ἁγίασον ἡμῶν τὰς ψυχὰς καὶ τὰ σώματα καὶ τὰ πνεύματα καὶ ἀλλοίωσον τὰ φρονήματα ἡμῶν πρὸς εὐσέβειαν; the prayer of the Trisagion of S. Basil (p. 314) ἁγίασον ἡμῶν τὰς ψυχὰς καὶ τὰ σώματα καὶ δὸς ἡμῖν ἐν ὁσιότητι λατρεύειν σοι πάσας τὰς ἡμέρας τῆς ζωῆς ἡμῶν; and the prayer of Incense Δέσποτα παντοκράτωρ, βασιλεῦ τῆς δόξης of S. James (*L. E. and W.* p. 41), σῴζων εἰς τὸ πάντοτε εὐαρεστεῖν καὶ προσκυνεῖν καὶ δοξάζειν σε.

P. 239. This is imitated from the form in the *Ordo de extrema unctione* (Maskell *Mon. rit.* i p. 129) as commonly in mediæval prayers, e.g. Alcuin *Officia per ferias* iv (ii[1] 83), v (*ib.* 87), *Horae* 1514 f. 99.

P. 240. Cf. *Horae* 1514, f. c. vii b.

P. 241. 8 sqq. The antiphon *Ne reminiscaris* (Tobit iii 3) is that of the Penitential Psalms in the Breviary and the Prymer; the *Parce Domine* is said after the same Psalms in the office *de extrema unctione* (Maskell *Mon. rit.* i p. 122); the two combined are the antiphon of the Penitentials in *Ordo ad visitandum infirmum* (*ib.* p. 84). This last form was adopted as the first suffrage of the English Litany of 1544 and is so used here.

—— 18. *Litan. Sarisb.* propitius esto: parce nobis Domine.

P. 241. 20. *Euchology.* p. 517 ἵλεως ἵλεως γενοῦ ἡμῖν Δέσποτα ἐπὶ ταῖς ἁμαρτίαις ἡμῶν καὶ ἐλέησον ἡμᾶς.

—— 22. 'Full sore,' ἕως ἄλις, apparently to represent the Heb. '*ad m'ōd*'; the vulg. has *satis*, sept. σφόδρα.

P. 242. 2 sq. The Greek is apparently meant to render these clauses of the English Litany.

—— 16. S. Ans. *Med.* xvii 10: lucet eis (the righteous) vultus Jesu, non terribilis sed amabilis, non amarus sed dulcis, non terrens sed blandiens.

—— 18. S. Ans. *Med.* i 50: vox illa terribilis . . *Discedite a Me* Cp. Aspera vox *Ite*, sed vox est blanda *Venite* (Trench *Proverbs* p. 188).

—— 39. I.e. the four sins which in Holy Scripture are said to cry to God. *S. Giles' Lectt.* p. 426 'First, wilfull murther, as *Cains* in this place (Gen. iv 10). Secondly, the sinne of *Sodom* against nature which cried to God for vengeance (Gen xviii 20, xix 13). . . . Thirdly, the oppression of the poor (Ex. ii 23), which crieth to God. . . . The fourth is Deut. xxiv 14, that of other poor, *the poor Labourer must not be oppressed, nor his hire delayed from him when he hath taken pains*; for the Apostle saith (Jas. v 4) *ecce merces operantis clamat in auribus domini.* There are the sinnes that speak not, but crie to God for vengeance.' Nicolas of Lyra *in S. Jas.* v 4 reckons only three crying sins; but in the Primers the four are reckoned: e.g. *Prymer of Salisbury* Le Roux 1537 f. 167 b 'Whiche ben the synnes cryenge before God for vengeaunce? Manslaughter, synne agaynst nature, oppression of poore people and with holdynge of dettes'; *Prymer*, Regnault 1537 f. II 7 has the mnemonic lines Clamitat ad Dominum vox sanguinis et sodomorum, vox oppressorum, merces detenta laborum: Marshall's *Primer* 1535 (*Three Primers* p. 34) mentions them without enumeration, 'the sins which are called dumb and cry for vengeance to God, are contrary to the sixth and seventh commandments.' The Greeks adopt the list in *Confessio Orthodoxa* (1672) iii 42 In *Cat. doct.* p. 247 Andrewes somewhat modifies the application of the name—'To defend the sin [against the 7th commandment] maketh it a crying sin, Gen. xviii 21: the Sodomites, Gen. xix 9, cried out upon Lot when he reproved them, "Away hence," say they, "thou art but a stranger and shalt thou judge and rule?" and Prov. xxx 20 the adulterous woman saith "I have not committed iniquity": of these the Apostle saith, Phil. iii 19, they "glory in their shame."' And in *Serm. Pent.* xi (iii 321) he generalises it: 'For whether we respect our sins, they have a voice, a cry, an ascending cry, in Scripture assigned them. They invocate too, they call for somewhat, even for some fearful judgment to be poured down on us.'

—— 40. In medieval writers, the sins against the Holy Ghost are counted as six, viz. despair, presumption, impenitence, obstinacy, impugning known truth, and envy of another's grace. See S. Thom. Aq. *Summa* ii[2] 14 § 2, S. Bonavent. in *Sentt.* II xliii 2 art. 3 qu. 1, Hugo *in Mt.* xii 31, etc. They are summarised in the verses

Impugnans verum, præsumens, spemque relinquens,
hinc duratus : odiens quoque fratris amorem,
emendam sperans (*leg.* spernens), impugnans Pneuma beatum.

Prymer Regnault 1537, f. II 7; *Hort. an.* Lyons 1516, f. 163. Cp. *Prymer* Le Roux 1537 f. 167 b: 'pertinacite: strynynge against trynyte, bycause God is mercyfull to synners: despere of the forhyueness of God: obstynacion in euyll hatred and enuy of thy neyghbours vertue: inuydence: despysynge of penaunce.' It is apparently these which are here called 'the six which forerun'—certainly, in the case of some of them at least, with some propriety. It is possible that Andrewes means to identify the six states of mind described in lines 33-36 with 'the sin against the Holy Ghost' and 'the sin unto death'; they seem better chosen than the medieval list as a whole. See S. Bernard's description of hardness of heart in *de Consideratione* i 2.

P. 243. 2. From the prayer of the Trisagion (*L. E. and W.* p. 34) *σῶσον ἡμᾶς ὁ Θεὸς ἐκ τῶν δυσχερῶν τοῦ κόσμου τούτου.*

—— 3 sq. From the Great intercession (*ib.* p. 408).

—— 5. 'The plague of immoderate rains,' from the thanksgiving for fair weather inserted in the Book of Common Prayer at the end of the Litany after the Hampton Court Conference, 1604.

—— 10. *Litan. Sarisb.*: a subitanea et improvisa morte. *Serm. Gunpowder Tr.* x (iv 390) 'Against a lingering death we pray not, *ab improvisa morte*, we do.'

—— 12. Private interpretation. *Serm. Pent.* ii (iii 133) 'There is a "spirit" in a man, saith Elihu (Job xxxii 8), that is, our own spirit; and many there be *qui sequuntur spiritum suum* (Ezek. xiii 3) "that follow their own ghost" instead of the Holy Ghost; for even that ghost taketh upon it to inspire, and "flesh and blood" we know have their revelation (Mt. xvi 17) . . . St Peter opposeth [this spirit] "of private resolution" to the Holy Ghost (2 Pet. i 20)': *Imagin.* (v 57) 'All that are after [the Apostles] speak not by revelation, but by labouring in the word and learning; are not to utter their own fancies and to desire to be believed upon their bare word—if this be not *dominari fidei* "to be lords of their auditors' faith" [1 Pet. v 3], I know not what it is—but only on condition that the sense they now give be not a feigned sense, as St Peter termeth it, but such a one as hath been before given by our fathers and forerunners in the Christian faith.' Cp. *Nativ.* xv (i 260), *Pent.* ix (iii 275), xii (iii 328).

—— 13. Innovation. For the two types of innovation Andrewes

would have specially in view see *Serm. Gunpowder Tr.* vi (iv 306).

P. 243. 15. *Serm. Nativ.* xi (i 191): see on p. 259 l. 23.

—— 17 sq. *Serm. Pr.* ix (v 388) 'As we may not usurp God's honour for ourselves, so we may not deify princes, for we see how ill that voice was taken *Vox Dei et non hominis* "the voice of God and not of man."' Cp. and contrast Bacon: 'the king's voice was the voice of God in man, the good Spirit of God in the mouth of man: I do not say the voice of God and not of man: I am not one of Herod's followers: a curse fall upon him that said it, a curse on him that suffered it' (Church *Bacon* p. 74). On Andrewes' attitude to James I. see the anecdote in *Minor Works* p. xii note a.

—— 19, 20. Saul, Michal. *Serm. Lent* i (ii 11) 'The Wise Man saith that "evil looking to will decay the principals of any building"; and that was Saul's defect, as the Scripture recordeth. Religion first: instead of *Celebrabimus*, *Negligimus Jehovam*. King David in his oration to the states of his realm before his first Parliament testifieth "the ark was not sought to in the days of Saul"; that pillar was not looked to. Sought to it was, after a sort, religion: but nothing so as it should. "Come let us have the ark," saith he; and then "Go to, it skills not greatly, carry it back again" (1 Sam. xiv 18, 19); which, what was it but to play fast and loose with religion? To intend Paul, as Felix saith, at our idle time (Acts xxiv 25); and not to "redeem time" (Eph. v 16) to that end? Judge of Religion's case by the reverence of the Ephod. A daughter of his own bringing up, Michal, saw David for honour of the ark wear it, and "despised him in her heart" (2 Sam. vi 16). Judge of it by the regard of the Priest, the keeper of the ark: for very love to it, that calling was kept so low and bare that they were tied to the allowance of their shewbread: the High Priest had not a loaf in his house besides (1 Sam. xxi 4). This was the first root of his kingdom: the ark not sought to, the ephod in contempt, the priesthood impoverished; *et Saulo nihil horum curæ* "and Saul regarded not any of these things" [cp. Acts xviii 17].' Cp. *Res.* vi (ii 284); *Spittle* (v 17); *Prayer* iii (v 323).

—— 21. Clerical arbitrariness and exaction. *Serm. Pent.* iv (iii 166 sq.). 'There was amongst the heathen one that would have his will stand for reason [Juvenal *Sat.* vi 222]. And was there none such among the people of God? Yes; we find one of whom it was said This it must be, for Hophni will not have it so, but thus. His reason is "for he will not"; and God grant none such be found among Christians.' Cp. *Of giving Cæsar his due* (v 134) 'Cæsar hath *vim coactivam*. Hophni hath a flesh-hook and can say *Date vel auferetur a vobis*; and therefore to part with it as one delivereth a purse, or to bear it as a porter doth his load, groaning under it. . . But we must offer it as it were a gift, voluntarily, willingly, cheerfully, ἐκ χάριτος, ἐκ ψυχῆς, not ἐξ ἀνάγκης, ἐκ λύπης (Col.

iii 23, 2 Cor. ix 7). Δια τὸν Κύριον, saith St Peter (1 Pet. ii 13), διὰ τὴν συνείδησιν, saith St Paul (Rom. xiii 5); even "for the Lord," even "for conscience' sake"; though Hophni had no flesh-hook, though Cæsar had no publican to take a stress'—from which it would seem that Andrewes intends also to pray against the withholding of ecclesiastical dues and the necessity of levying them by distraint.

P 243. 22. Plunder of the Church. In the *Concio ad clerum pro gradu doctoris* (*Opuscula* pp. 19, 22), on Prov. xx 25 'It is a snare to the man who observeth not that which is holy,' Athaliah is used as a type of the *violent* 'devouring' of sacred things, and her violent death *in the Temple*, of the appropriate 'snare.' This petition is probably not without reference to Elizabeth's plunder of the Church.

—— 23. Amateur adventures in religion. *Serm. Coronation* (v 170) 'One Micah, a private man of Mount Ephraim, he and his old mother, it took them in the heads they would have a new religion by themselves, and that was plain idolatry; and up with an idol they went. And because they lacked a priest, it came into Micah's head to give orders, and so he did': *ib.* (v 179) 'One would think this were impertinent and we were free from Micah. We are not. Even to this day do men still cast images or imaginations (all is one) in the mould of their conceits and up they set them, at least for their own household to adore. And then if they can get such a fellow as is hereafter described, a Levite for ten shekels and a suit (or because now the world is harder, ten pounds) they are safe, and there they have and hold a religion by themselves.' Cp. *Serm before two Kings* (v 240).

—— 24. Trafficking in sacred things—simony and sacrilege. *Serm. Pent.* xv. (iii 395) 'Those gifts hold not of this feast, not of Pentecost; but hold of the feast of Simon and Jude, they. The Church hath joined these two Saints in one feast; and the devil, in many things else God's ape, hath made a like joining of his two, in imitation of the true. His Simon is Simon Magus, not Simon Zelotes; and Jude, Judas Iscariot, not Judas the brother of James—no kin to him. Simon, he came off roundly, προσήνεγκε χρήματα (Acts viii 18), offered frankly, would come to the price. And Judas, he would know what they would give, how thankful they would be (Mt. xxvi 15); and it was done; and there goeth a bargain. These two are like enough to agree. And thus is the Holy Ghost defeated; bought out, He and his gifts, by Simon still. And thus is Christ betrayed in his places, and that by Judas still. This wicked fraternity of Simon and Jude are the bane of the Church unto this day. Judas that sold Christ, like enough to make sale of Christ's places. Simon that would buy the Holy Ghost, had He been to be sold, as like to buy out the Holy Ghost's gifts, as the Holy Ghost Himself': *Concio ad clerum in Synodo Provinciali* (*Opusc.* 48) Proxime post hos, attentionem vestram requirit scelerata illa Simonis et Judæ fraternitas . . . Nec hoc solum in nobis *minoritis* [i.e. presbyters], qui sic rectorias nostras fere paciscimur; sed et apud vos *Majoritas* [i.e. bishops], quos sic *cathedras* vestras, nempe vel pecuniarum summis, vel Ecclesiarum spoliis foede cauponari vulgo dictitant. Quo morbo male iam diu et habet et audit Ecclesia nostra.

P. 243. 25 sq. See on p. 32 l. 36.

—— 28. A censorious laity. *Serm. Coron.* (v 176) 'There were priests: would they not serve? It seemed they would not. Phinehas was to look to their eyes: but somewhere there be some such as Osee speaks of; *Populus hic quasi qui contradicit sacerdoti*, This people will look to Phinehas' eyes; set their priests and preachers to school, and not learn of them, but learn them divinity.'

—— 29. Anarchy. *Serm. Coron.* (v 182 sq.) '"The shout of a king" (Num. xxiii. 21) is a joyful shout, was a true saying out of the mouth of a false prophet, Balaam, but forced thereto by God. That a joyful shout, and this a woeful cry, *Nonne ideo nobis nullus Rex, quia non timemus Dominum?* (Hos. x. 3) "Are we not therefore without any King at all, because we fear not God?" . . . Far better any than an anarchy; better anyone a King than everyone a King; and everyone is more than a King, if he do what he lists": *Gunpowder Tr.* v (iv 286) 'It is better for us not to be at all, than not to be under rule. Better no creation, than no government.' Cp. *Lent* ii (ii 20), *Before two Kings* (v 241), *Opusc.* 60.

Multiplicity of rulers. *Serm. Coron.* (v 183) 'Secondly, [thanks shall be] for this, that *a* King, not many. For to have many, is a plague for the people's sins.' Πολυκοιρανία is from the well-known Homeric line (*Il.* ii 204) οὐκ ἀγαθὸν πολυκοιρανίη· εἷς κοίρανος ἔστω.

Tyranny. *Serm. Gunpowder Tr.* v (iv 286) 'But what if [kings] take too much upon them, Korah's exception (Num. xvi 3)? Then it is *Dedi vobis regem in irâ*, saith God by the Prophet. Angry I was when I gave him, but I gave him though. *Per me iratum* it is, but *per me* it is still: per me though with a difference (Prov. viii 15)'—where '*Tyranny*' is the marginal heading.

—— 30. *Serm. Lent.* ii (ii 20) '"The Lord is Ruler, let the people tremble" (Ps xcix 1). For if they fall to be unruly . . . He can send them a Rehoboam without wisdom, or a Jeroboam without religion, or Ashur a stranger to be their king.'

'Asshur,' foreign domination. *Serm. Coron.* (v 183) '"For this cause Ashur shall be your King" (Hos. xi 5), is a fearful threat God useth to his people for their unkindness. To have a mere alien, one from beyond the water, as Nebuchadnezzar was, out of a people whose speech they did not understand.' The thought of Spain would be in Andrewes' mind. Cp. the allusions to the Armada in *Gunpowder Tr.* viii (iv 357), ix (iv 366 sq., 369). In 1588 one Christopher Stile published a violent 'Godly Prayer' against 'the Spanish Assyrians' (quoted in *Lit. services of the reign of Q. Elizabeth* p. 609 note).

'Jeroboam,' irreligious rule: *Serm. Lent.* ii (ii 20) quoted above: or the rule of one of an alien religion: *Coron.* (v 184) 'No stranger in birth he, but one addicted to strange worship, a stranger in religion; (and it was even Micah's religion just; as Micah's countryman he was, for both were of Ephraim) who did that which was evil in God's eyes, by doing that which was good in his own, and so "made Israel sin" (1 Ki. xv 26)': or religious indifference in rulers: *Lent.* i (ii 12) 'Such another indifferency for Church matters we find in Jeroboam. "Tush," said he jestingly, "let them kiss the calves and spare not" (Hos. xiii 2). Let it go which way it will. But therefore God sends him word by Ahijah "that Israel should be as a reed in the water" (1 Ki. xiv 15), bowing to and fro, at the devotion of every wave and every wind, without any steadiness.' In *Of giving Cæsar his due* (v 128), Jeroboam is the type of rebellion against láwful taxation: 'rather rise and take arms, as Jeroboam did. The people's ears itched after this doctrine. The best religion for the purse is the best for them, and they ready to hold with Jeroboam or Judas [of Galilee, Acts v 37] or any that will abrogate payments': and in *Concio ad clerum pro gradu doctoris* (*Opusc.* 19) he represents the alienation of ecclesiastical revenues: '*publica magnificentia* visus est facere Jeroboam: exstruxit inde Shechemum et Phenuelem; sed in *sanguinibus*, quippe spoliato *Templo* et alienato iure *decimarum*'—which seems to be groundless. Probably 'alien religion' is chiefly in view—and the petition may be illustrated by the apprehension caused by the project of Prince Charles' Spanish marriage.

'Rehoboam,' foolish rule. *Serm. Coron.* (v 184) 'Rehoboam . . . was indeed well for his religion, but otherwise not able to advise himself, and so ready to be advised for the worse. One that was full of great words, but so faint-hearted as not able to resist ought; that under him every one did what he would, for all the King. . . . It is otherwise where princes are intelligent, learned, and as David was, both religious and wise; wise "as an angel of God" to discern good and evil (2 Sam. xix 27).' Though in 1606 Andrewes congratulates England on not being ruled by a Rehoboam so described, perhaps it is not difficult to see in this petition a reference to the practical displacement of the Council by such ministers as Carr and Villiers, after Robert Cecil's death in 1614. Charles IX and Henry III of France were contemporary Rehoboams.

'Gallio,' indifference to ecclesiastical affairs. *Concio ad clerum in Synodo provinc.* (*Opusc.* 35) neque vero tetra magis aut funesta facies Ecclesiæ quam cum Galliones habuit, quibus *nihil illorum curæ* [Act. xviii 17], quibus susque deque quid fieret Ecclesiæ. Cp. on l. 19 sq.

'Haman' represents worldliness in dealing with religion—like 'the men of Shechem' p. 247—*Serm. Lent* iii (ii 46)

'It was the very reason whereby Haman went about to persuade Ahashuerus to suppress the Jews' religion: Let it be done and I will weigh so many thousands to the King's coffers (Esth. iii 9)':—and this in its extreme form of conspiracy to assassinate: *Serm. Gunpowder Tr.* x (iv 385) is the application of Haman's project to the Gunpowder Plot, and the same application is made in passing *ib.* i (iv 204). The assassinations of Henry III and Henry IV of France are alluded to in *Gowries* ii, iii, vi, vii (iv 36, 47, 65, 71, 74, 145, 166) and *Gunpowder Tr.* v (iv 289) and the massacre of S. Bartholomew *ib.* x (iv 393). Besides the attempts on Elizabeth's life, Andrewes would remember also the assassinations of the two Guises (1563 and 1588) and of William of Orange (1584).

P. 243. 31-37. These fall into three groups—perversion and lack of counsel (31 sq.), evils in legislation and in the administration of the law (33 sq.), and military evils (35 sqq.).

—— 31. 'Ahitophel,' wisdom perverted by worldliness. *Serm. Gunpowder Tr.* vi (iv 308) 'How many ways may one be or be said to be a meddler [Prov. xxiv 21]? That may be many ways, as many ways as one may be partakers of another man's sins. . . . By giving them shrewd advice, how to manage their matters, as did Ahitophel to Absalom': *ib.* (iv 313) 'There was one . . . whose counsel in his time was holden as the oracle of God; yet this great wise man for meddling in this, contrary to it, proved a fool, and made up the number of those that come to this untimely and unknown ruin and destruction': *ib.* v (iv 291) 'Ahitophel's and Jeroboam's go for wisdom in the world; but, indeed, such wisdom, as St James termeth it, is "earthly, sensual," and hath somewhat of the devil in it (Jas. iii 15).' Cp. *ib.* vi (iv 299), vii (iv 332).

—— 32. 'Zoan,' foolish counsel. Is. xix 11.

—— 33. 'Omri' seems naturally in this context to stand for secularism in legislation; elsewhere Andrewes uses it for the acceptance of secular legislation as the motive or sufficient standard of morality, i.e. secularism in morality: *Serm. Pent.* v (iii 195) 'I do forbear to sin: what is my motive? Because, as Micah saith, it is against "Omri's statutes," some penal law; I shall incur such a penalty, be liable to such an action, if I do not. It is well; but all this is but the spirit of the world; *e Prætorio, non e Sanctuario*, bloweth "out of Westminster Hall, not out of the Sanctuary"': *Gunpowder Tr.* ix (iv 379) 'A third, and that very common [error is that] of them that make the law of man a scantling [measure] of their "righteousness," and, further than that will compel them, they will not go, not an inch; not so far neither, *sine timore*, but for fear. Yea not only our "righteousness" to men, but even our fear to God is taught us by man's precepts (Is. xxix 13); and in both, so "the statutes of Omri be observed," all is well. But whatsoever a man else may make sure, he cannot make sure his soul by the law of the land': and perhaps for the intrusion of secular law into the Church: *Pent.* ix (iii 276) 'I know not how, but as if Christ's mouth were stopped and his breath like to fail Him, the world begins to fare as if they had got a new mouth to draw breath from; to govern the Church as if *spiritus Prætorii* would do things better than *Spiritus Sanctuarii*, and man's law become the best means to teach the fear of God, and to guide religion by.' Cp. *Nativ.* xvii (i 297), *Pent.* i (iii 119), ix (iii 275), *Gowries* vi (iv 131), *Prayer* xviii (v 464).

P. 243. 34. 'Jezreel,' the perversion of justice. Andrewes touches on abuses in the courts in *Serm. Spittle* (v 10: corruption) and *Gunpowder Tr.* ix (iv 380: interference of jurisdictions).

—— 35-37. These three military evils, among others, are treated together in *Serm. Rep.* ii (i 321) delivered Feb. 21, 1599 'at what time the Earl of Essex was going forth upon the expedition for Ireland' to quell the insurrection of Hugh O'Neil Earl of Tyrone. Cp. Donne *Serm.* xii (i p. 238 ed. Alford).

—— 35. 'The overflowings of Belial' or 'of ungodliness': military licence. *Serm. Repent.* ii (i 329) 'For the most part . . even they that are goers forth [to war] seem to persuade themselves that *then* they may do what they list; that at that time any sin is lawful, that war is rather a placard than an inhibition to sin. A thing so common that it made the heathen man hold that between *militia* and *malitia* there was as little difference in sense as in sound; and the prophet David to call Saul's companies in his days, *torrentes Belial* "the land-floods of wickedness"': *ib.* p. 335 'arming themselves with a mind to cease from sin, keeping their vessels holy; having pay wherewith they may be content, and being content with their pay; *et neminem concutientes*, saith St John Baptist; not being *torrentes Belial* "land-floods of wickedness."'

—— 36. 'The Plague of Peor.' *Serm. Pestilence* (v 227) 'This Plague here, as appeareth by the twenty-eighth verse . . . came for the sin of Peor, that is for fornication, as you may read.' Cp. *Repent.* ii (i 335), where it is regarded especially as besetting the army.

—— 37. 'The Valley of Achor': defeat through sin, especially sacrilege. *Serm. Repent.* ii (i 327) 'Let us then, as advice leadeth us, make up our period with taking a course for restraint of sin. For what sin unrestrained can work, the valley of Achor may teach us, where the inhabitants of the poor town of Ai put to flight Joshua with all his forces, and all because this second point was not well looked to': *ib.* p. 335 'Achan's sin, that is sacrilege; *Anathema in medio tui, non poteris stare coram hostibus tuis*, God's own words to Joshua (Josh. vii 11, 12)—the cause of the army's miscarrying before Ai. To keep them from that wickedness.'

—— 38. Perhaps the allusion here is indicated by *Cat. doct.* p. 232 '[Adultery] is when both are married, and that is worst; or the woman only, and the man single; or the man only, and the woman single; and the second is the less evil than the third, because in the third there is *corruptio prolis* "a corrupting of posterity."'

P. 244. 5. Aristophanes *Plutus* 969 ἀβίωτον εἶναί μοι πεποίηκε τὸν βίον: cp. Clem. Al. *Protrept.* ii 39, Euseb. *H.E.* i 2 § 18.

—— 13. See on p. 107 l. 31.

P. 245. 2 sq. From the prayer of the Elevation Πρόσχες Κύριε, *L. E. and W.* p. 341.

—— 17. The suffrage *ab ira tua: Libera nos Domine* is in the Roman Litany and in that of the Sarum *Ordo de extrema unctione*, but not in the ordinary Sarum Litany.

P. 246. 12 sqq. Phrases collected up and down in the homily *de exitu animæ*: see on p. 166 l. 10. The two columns are only so arranged for convenience, and do not correspond as Neale's paraphrase attempts to make them do. The corresponding phrases describing the blessedness of the righteous are collected on p. 253.

—— 28 sqq. *De exitu an.* p. 411 δεινὸν τὸ χωρισθῆναι ἀπὸ τῶν ἁγίων, ἀργαλεώτερον τὸ χωρισθῆναι ἀπὸ τοῦ Θεοῦ· ἄτιμον το δεθῆναι χεῖρας καὶ πόδας καὶ εἰς τὸ πῦρ βληθῆναι· θλιβερὸν τὸ ἐκπεμφθῆναι εἰς τὸ σκότος τό ἐξώτερον . . . ἀσυμπαθὲς τὸ αἰτεῖν ῥαγνίδα ὕδατος καὶ μὴ λαμβάνειν πικρὸν τὸ ἐν πυρὶ εἶναι καὶ βοᾷν καὶ μὴ βοηθεῖσθαι.

—— 38-41. See on p. 243 l. 29, 37.

P. 247. 1. 'Shechem,' worldliness under the guise of religion: *Serm. Lent.* iii (ii 46) 'It is no new thing but common and usual, in all exceptions to religion: the true cause is ἀγάνακτησις "a thinking all too much," a thinking all is *perditio*, all lost that cometh not to us, that we gain not by. We see it was the true reason the men of Shechem made among themselves why they would become of Jacob's religion and be circumcised: *Nonne omnia quæ habent nostra erunt?* "Shall not all they have be ours?"': *Pent.* ix (iii 276) 'The Shechemites—oh set forward that point of divinity, for then "all they have is ours." See we not whence this wind blows, from what spirit this breath comes? From *spiritus mundi*.'

—— 2. From the *Auxilietur nobis pie Domine.*

—— 3-5, 8, 9. From the *Sancta Maria regina celi et terre.*

—— 6 sq. From the *Domine Iesu Xpe fili dei vivi te deprecor.*

—— 17 sq. From *Deus misericordiæ Deus pietatis.*

—— 19-22. Cp. the invocation *Obsecro te domina sancta Maria, Horae* f. 39 b: in omnibus orationibus et requisitis meis et in omnibus angustiis et necessitatibus meis festines in auxilium et consilium meum: S. Anselm *Orat.* 1 propitiare mihi in omnibus angustiis et tribulationibus, in necessitatibus et tentationibus, in omnibus periculis et infirmitatibus meis.

P. 251. 2. Cp. on p. 15 l. 13. *Serm. Gunpowder Tr.* i (iv 220) 'To save us with the true saving health—it is the word whereof our Saviour Jesus hath his Name—it importeth the salvation of the soul; properly to that it belongeth and hath joined to it Hosanna in the Gospel, *Hosanna in excelsis*, to shew it is a high and heavenly salvation.' 'Hosanna in the highest' then means petition for spiritual blessings. Cp. p. 259 l. 2.

P. 251. 12. W, which has ll. 4-8 in Greek only and omits 9-11, has here 'But there is glory to be revealed, for when the Judge' etc.

— 13. Cp. *Serm. Res.* v (ii 264) 'So that this word [*videbo* Job xix 27] is all in all: which God after expounds *videbit faciem meam in iubilo* "with joy and jubilee shall he behold my face" (Job xxxiii 26); as a Redeemer, not as a Revenger; and as it followeth, with hope and not with fear in his bosom.'

— 15 sq. See on p. 116 l. 38.

— 19-21. *S. Giles' Lectt.* p. 622 'In this life we must seek for God's grace and glory: and He hath promised to give both (Ps. lxxxiv 12), and then we shall *intrare in gaudium Domini* (Mt. xxv 21) and so *we shall be alwaies with Him* (1 Th. iv 17) and *see Him as He is* (1 Jo. iii 1).'

— 20. *Serm. Nativ.* xv (i 251) 'Christ "the bright morning star" (Rev. xxii 16) of that day which shall have no night; the *beatifica visio* "the blessed sight" of which day is the *consummatum est* of our hope and happiness for ever': *Res.* iii (ii 237) 'They that came to anoint Him, with joy and lifting up their heads they shall see Him; with that sight shall they see Him, that shall evermore make them blessed.'

— 30 sq. *Serm. Gunpowder Tr.* ix (iv 381) 'If we will serve Him to please Him—and as good not serve as serving not please—if we will so serve Him, we must do it "with reverence and fear"; λατρεῦσαι εὐαρέστως μετ' αἰδοῦς καὶ εὐλαβείας (Heb. xii 28). Neither rudely then without fear, nor basely with fear; but reverently with fear, and cheerfully without fear; that is the meaning.'

— 32. Cp. *Serm. Rep.* iii (i 351) 'Opportunity itself is a great favour, even to have it; but a second grace it is, to discern when we have it, and a third better than both, when we discern it to observe and take it': cp. *ib.* p. 355.

P. 252. 1 sqq. *Serm. Pent.* vi (iii 220) 'This grace we are thus to receive there; only, that we "receive it not in vain" (2 Cor. vi 1); "be not wanting to it" (Heb. xii 15) after; "neglect it not" (1 Ti. iv 14); "quench it not" (1 Th. v 19); "fall not from it" (Gal. v 4); but "stand fast" (Rom. v 2) and "continue in" (Acts xiii 43) it; be careful to "stir it up" (2 Ti. i 6); yea, "to grow" (2 Pet. iii 18) and increase in it, more and more even to the consummation of it, which is glory—glory being nothing else but grace consummate.'

— 15 sqq. S. Aug. *Confess.* iv 9: beatus qui amat Te et amicum in Te et inimicum propter Te. Quoted also in *S. Giles' Lectt.* p. 638, *Cat. doct.* p. 108.

— 18 sq. *Serm. Pent.* v (iii 196) 'That we therefore pray to

Him that "giveth grace to the humble" to give us the grace to be humble, that so we may be meet to receive Him.'

P. 252. 20 sqq. On the fear of God see *Serm. Pent.* xii (iii 333 sqq.).

—— 21 sq. Cp. Jer. xxxii 39. Sept., Syr. and Vulg., perhaps rightly, read *yiḥad* for *yaḥēd*; hence the rendering of l. 22.

—— 27 sq. S. Gregory of Nazianzus *Or.* xi 5 (on S. Gregory of Nyssa) ἓν φοβηθῶμεν μόνον, τὸ φοβηθῆναί τι Θεοῦ πλέον. Cp. Prov. vii 2 τίμα τὸν Κύριον καὶ ἰσχύσεις, πλὴν δὲ αὐτοῦ μὴ φοβοῦ ἄλλον: the imperial *Laudes* in Goldast *rerum Alemannicarum scriptores* ii p. 176 te timeant ut mortalia non pavescant; p. 177 te timeant ut nihil metuant: N. Brady *Psalm* 34 'Fear Him ye saints, and you will then Have nothing else to fear': Racine *Athalie* I i 64.

P. 253. 1-10. From the *Prayer of S. Gregory* Dominator Domine Deus omnipotens: also in Alcuin *Officia per ferias* (ii[1] p. 111), *Book of Cerne* (Cambr. 1902) p. 105. Cp. [S. Aug.] *Med.* 40.

—— 18 sqq. See on p. 166 l. 10: cp. p. 246. The columns are only a convenient arrangement, and do not correspond as Neale makes them.

P. 254. 1-3. *Serm. Tempt.* iii (v 504) 'The Scripture is the broad plate that is to bear off "the darts" (Eph. vi 16); our faith is the braces or handle whereby we take hold and lift it up to defend ourselves withal. For the Scripture is a shield *non quod dicitur sed quod creditur. Dicitur*—there is the strong broad matter, fit to bear off; and *creditur*—that is the handle or braces to it, "God spake once, or twice I have heard it, power belongeth unto God" (Ps. lxii 11).'

—— 4. *Serm. Rep.* ii (i 328) 'Prayer then is of use; and though we be, saith St Paul, armed at all points from hand to foot, yet must we *super omnia*, "over all" (Eph. vi 18), draw this, and arm our very armour with "prayer and supplications."'

—— 5 sq. Adapted from the *Omnipotens sempiterne Deus precor* (also in *Horae* 1494 f. 3 b) 'concede mihi spacium vitæ et possibilitatem et voltuntatem bene vivendi, ut ante diem exitus mei per veram pœnitentiam merear' etc.

—— 11-14. The first prayer after the *Versus S. Bernardi* Omnip. sempit. Deus qui Ezechiæ regi Judæ . . . terminum suæ vitæ protendisti, concede mihi . . . tantum vitæ spacium saltem quoad mensuram ut peccata mea valeam deplorare.

—— 17 sq. From *Precor te amantissime Domine.*

P. 255. 15 sq. *S. Giles' Lectt.* p. 633 'Thus wee see what is the object of temperance, which virtue performes two things: First to bee able to want those things, as Phil. iv 12 *possum deficere;* then, having them to use them moderately; as the Apostle counsels in *Timothie* (1 Tim. v 23) *modico vino utere;* for many comming to have the possession of these things, exceede in Ryot. For the first, it is a dangerous lust how pleasant soever it bee; not to bee able to want them, if wee make necessary lusts of them, so as wee must have our lusts satisfied though it cannot bee without sinne, wee bring ourselves under the power, as it is in [1 Cor. vi 12], if we make ourselves debtors to the flesh so farre (Rom. viii 12). *A man that cannot refraine his appetite, hee is like a City broken downe and without walls* (Prov. xxiii 28).'

P. 255. 19 sq. S. Anselm *Orat.* 16: ut nihil terrenum, nihil carnale desiderem vel cogitem (=[S. Aug.] *Med.* 36).

—— 21. 'Ingenuity' (*ingenuitas*, the condition of a freeborn person, a gentleman, cp. p. 229 l. 28; so the corresponding character, highmindedness, p. 146 l. 25, *Serm. Pent.* v [iii 194]) seems to represent what Andrewes means here by *καλοκαγαθία*. Cp. Hooker *Eccl. Pol.* i 8 § 1 'That which is good in the actions of men doth not only delight as profitable, but as amiable also. In which consideration the Grecians most divinely have given to the active perfection of men a name expressing both beauty and goodness (καλοκαγαθία), because goodness in ordinary speech is for the most part applied only to that which is beneficial'; and see Church's note *in loc.*: S. Luke viii 15 ἐν καρδίᾳ καλῇ καὶ ἀγαθῃ: p. 86 l. 27 καλοις καὶ ἀγαθοῖς (p. 230 l. 16 bonis et honestis).

P. 256. 12, 15-18. From the Great Intercession (*Litt. E. and W.* p. 408) μνήσθητι Κύριε τοῦ περιεστῶτος λαοῦ κ.τ.λ.

—— 13 sq. From the litany at the Offertory (*ib.* p. 46).

—— 19 sqq. See on p. 93 l. 4.

P. 257. 18 sqq. Stokes *Verus Christianus* append. p. 4 'These I found written with his [Andrewes'] own hand (in his Hebrew Bible, in a little *quarto sine punctis*).' S. Fulgentius was bishop of Ruspe in Numidia, 508-533.

P. 258. 17. Δός μοι λόγον ὁ Λόγος τοῦ Πατρός occurs in a troparion quoted by Daniel, *Codex hymnologicus* iii p. 133, from Pelargus. I have not been able to trace it to its source: it is probably in the *Menaea*.

—— 21. Adapted from a combination of two forms of the prayer for the reader of the Gospel in the Latin rite—Roman, 'Dominus sit in corde tuo et in labiis tuis ut digne et competenter annuncies evangelium suum,' and Sarum, 'Dominus sit in corde tuo et in ore tuo ad pronunciandum sanctum evangelium.'

—— 24. From the prayer of Incense Δέσποτα Κύριε Ἰησοῦ Χριστέ (cp. *Litt. E. and W.* p. 32) ὁ διφυὴς ἄνθραξ ὁ τῇ λαβίδι τῶν τοῦ προφήτου χειλέων ἀψάμενος καὶ τὼς ἁμαρτίας αὐτοῦ ἀφελόμενος, ἅψαι καὶ ἡμῶν τῶν ἁμαρτωλῶν τῶν αἰσθήσεων καὶ καθάρισον ἡμᾶς ἀπὸ πάσης κηλίδος . . . καὶ ἁγίασον ἡμᾶς τῇ ἁγιαστικῃ δυνάμει τοῦ παναγίου σου Πνεύματος.

—— 26. *S. Giles' Lectt.* p. 517 'There are two natures in a Cole, that is the Cole it selfe, which is a dead thing, and the burning nature and heate that it hath; which setteth out, first, Christs humane nature, which is dead in it selfe; And then his divine nature containing the burning force of that is represented in this burning Cole.' Cp S Cyril of Alexandria in *in Esaiam* i 4 (ii

107 E: incorporated by Procopius *in loc.*) *ὥσπερ οὖν ὁ ἄνθραξ ξύλον ἐστὶ τῇ φύσει, πλὴν ὅλος τοῦ ὅλου μεμέστωται τοῦ πυρὸς καὶ τὴν αὐτοῦ δύναμίν τε καὶ ἐνέργειαν ἔχει, κατὰ τοῦτον οἶμαι τρόπον νοοῖτ' ἀνεικότως καὶ αὐτὸς ὁ κύριος ἡμῶν Ἰησοῦς ὁ Χριστός· γέγονε γὰρ σὰρξ ὁ λόγος καὶ ἐσκήνωσεν ἐν ἡμῖν, ἀλλ' εἰ καὶ ἦν καθ' ἡμᾶς ὁρώμενος ἄνθρωπος οἰκονομικῶς, ἀλλ' οὖν ἅπαν τὸ τῆς θεότητος πλήρωμα κατῴκηκεν ἐν αὐτῷ.* Cp. *adv. Nest.* ii (vi 32 B).

P. 259. 2. The title *Ὥσαννα ἐν ἐπιγείοις* is only in W and the texts derived from it. It indicates a petition for earthly things, as *Ὡσ· ἐν τοῖς ὑψίστοις* p. 251 for spiritual things.

—— 3. W. begins 'Remember, o Lord, to crown the year with thy goodness, for the eyes,' etc., omits l. 8 sq. and continues 'and to us, o Lord, grant the precious things of heaven,' etc. 'From' i.e. the source or means of the blessing asked for.

—— 18, 19, 21. From the *Μεγάλη συναπτή*; cp. on p. 84 l. 25.

—— 23 sqq. *Serm. Nativ.* xi (i 191) 'Now mark the order how they stand (Ps. lxxxv 10, 11). Mercy leads to Truth and the knowledge of it; and Truth to Righteousness and the practice of it; and Righteousness to Peace and the ways of it—"guides our feet" first "into the ways of Peace" (Lk. i 79). And such a way shall there always be, do all the controversy writers what they can, a fair way agreed upon of all sides, questioned by none, in which "whoso orders his steps aright may see the salvation of God" (Ps. l 23). Even the way here chalked out before us; to shew Mercy, and speak Truth; do Righteousness and follow Peace. And by this rule proceeding in the points whereto we are come already, even those truths wherein we are otherwise minded would in due time be revealed unto us': *Pentec.* xii (iii 329) 'Conclude then, if we happen to be in "some points otherwise minded God will bring us to the knowledge even of them." "Only in these whereto we are come and whereof we are agreed on all sides, that we proceed by one rule," make a conscience of the practice of such truths as we agree of, "and those we do not shall soon be revealed unto us," and we shall say even of them *in veritate comperi* (Acts x 34).' Cp. *Nativ.* iii (i 35 sq.).

—— 31. 'Decency' *ευσχημοσυνη*. *Serm. Pentec.* xv (iii 387) 'And order is a thing so nearly concerning us, as break order once and break both your "staves," saith God in Zachary (Zech. xi 7); both that of "beauty" and that of "bands." The "staff of beauty"; for no *εὐσχημοσύνη*, no manner of "decency or comeliness" without it, but all out of fashion. The "staff of bands"; for no *στερέωμα*, no kind of "steadiness or constancy," but all loose without it. All falls back to the first *tohu* and *bohu* (Gen. i 2). For all is *tohu* "empty and void" if the spirit fill not with his gifts; and all is *bohu* "a disordered rude chaos of confusion," if Christ order it not by his places and callings. Every body falls to be doing with every thing, and so nothing done; nothing well done, I am sure. Every man therefore, whatever his gift be, to stay till he have his place and standing by Christ assigned him.' Cp. *Cat. doct.* p. 168.

P. 260. 2-8. These represent a series of compounds with εὐ-, which it is difficult to render satisfactorily. The translation largely follows Newman.

—— 9-18. *Serm. before two Kings* (v 244) 'But why seek I for these examples abroad, seeing we have them growing at home here in our Psalm [cxliv 12-14], and surely far more abundantly? . . . By account indeed there are eight—which the Fathers from the words of the Psalm "Blessed are the people who are in such a case," have called them the eight felicities of this life, the eight earthly beatitudes.' So Caietan *in loc.* 'octo partes felicitatis politicæ.'

—— 20. Caietan *in loc.* 'nona pars beatitudinis adiungitur, hoc est vera religio.'

—— 22 sqq. Cp. the old Greek grace, Εὐλογητὸς ὁ Θεὸς ὁ ἐλεῶν *καὶ τρέφων ἡμᾶς ἐκ νεότητος ἡμῶν· ὁ διδοὺς τροφὴν πάσῃ σαρκί, πλήρωσον χαρᾶς καὶ εὐφροσύνης τὰς καρδίας ἡμῶν, ἵνα πάντοτε πᾶσαν αὐτάρκειαν ἔχοντες περισσεύωμεν εἰς πᾶν ἔργον ἀγαθόν*, in S. Chrys. *hom.* lv *in Mat.* 5 (vii 561 A), where it is said to be the grace after supper of the monks in the desert: *Constt. ap.* vii 49, [S. Athanasius] *de Virginitate* 12, and *Horologion* p. 130; in Latin in *Hymni et collectae* Cologne 1586 p. 639; and in *Preces privatae* 1564 (*Private prayers of the reign of Q. Elizabeth*, Parker Soc., p. 400). Cp. Lit. S. Mark (*Litt. E. and W.* pp. 128, 168).

—— 28 sqq. In S the first three lines are placed at the end, with the opening words of each quotation added in Hebrew.

P. 265. 15 sqq. *Serm. Prayer* iv (v 339) on Rom. viii 26: 'Albeit we pray but faintly and have not that supply of fervency that is required in prayer, yet we have comfort that ever when we most faint in prayer there are of God's saints that pray for us with all instancy, by which it comes to pass that being all but one body their prayers tend to our good as well as their own, for the faithful howsoever they be many and dispersed into divers corners of the world, yet they are but one body; and as they are the members of one body, so they pray not privately for themselves but for the whole body of the Church; so that the weakness of one member is supplied by the fervent and earnest prayer of the other. Therefore when the Apostle saith, "The Spirit maketh intercession for us" *gemitibus inenarrabilibus*, Augustine asketh, What groanings are these? are they thine or mine? No they are the groanings of the Church, sometime in me, sometime in thee.' I cannot find the passage of S. Aug. here referred to, which is the source of lines 16-19 of the text, but lines 19-21 are from *contra Maximum Arianum* i 9: ne credamus Spiritum sanctum nunquam esse sine gemitibus posse, quoniam nullus dies, nulla hora, nullum momentum temporis invenitur, quo non a sanctis orationes Deo ubicunque fundantur, ab aliis hic, ab aliis alibi

. . . gemitibus sanctorum desideriorum interpellare sanctos facit, quibus affectum pium gratiæ spiritalis infundit. The 'one Dove,' i.e. the Church : *Serm. Pent.* viii (iii 254) 'The Holy Ghost is a Dove and He makes Christ's Spouse, the Church, a Dove; a term so oft iterate in the Canticles (ii 14, v 2, 5, 12, vi 9) and so much stood on by Saint Augustine and the Fathers, as they make no question, No Dove, no Church': *ib.* p. 252 'Esay's dove, for the voice *gemebat ut columba* (Is. xxxviii 14, [cp. lix 11]); in patience mourning, not in impatience murmuring or repining; for *carmen amatorium*, her voice. And no other voice to be heard from the first Church.' Cp. S. Bern. *in Cant.* lix 6.

P. 266. 2 sq. Great Intercession (*Litt. E. and W.* p. 389) ὑπὲρ τῆς οἰκουμένης· ὑπὲρ τῆς ἁγίας καθολικῆς καὶ ἀποστολικῆς ἐκκλησίας.

—— 7 sqq. S. Basil, Great Intercession (*ib.* p. 408) τὰ νήπια ἔκθρεψον, τὴν νεότητα παιδαγώγησον, τὸ γῆρας περικράτησον: S. James, Litany at Offertory (*ib.* p. 45) ὑπὲρ τῶν ἐν γήρᾳ καὶ ἀδυναμίᾳ ὄντων.

—— 9 sqq. S. Basil, Great Intercession (*ib.* p. 408) τοὺς ὀλιγοψύχους παραμύθησαι . . . τοὺς ὀχλουμένους ὑπὸ πνευμάτων ἀκαθάρτων ἐλευθέρωσον· τοῖς πλέουσι σύμπλευσον, τοῖς ὁδοιποροῦσι συνόδευσον· χηρῶν πρόστηθι, ὀρφανῶν ὑπεράσπισον, αἰχμαλώτους ῥῦσαι, νοσοῦντας ἴασαι: (p. 407) τῶν ἐν ἐρημίαις: S. James, Lit. at Offertory (p. 46) ἐν πικραῖς δουλείαις.

P. 267. With this Act, cp. p. 59 sq., 32 sqq. and notes.

P. 268. 11 sqq. Cp. on p. 243.

—— 15. 'Urijah' *i.e.* public apostasy in compliance with the civil power, as 'Micah' represents private adventurers in religious corruption. S. reads 'Michal' evidently by mistake for 'Micah.'

—— 24, 34. These are biddings of the deacon in the preparatory office before the Liturgy (*Litt. E. and W.* p. 32). The second is properly addressed to the priest, 'Sir, give a blessing' like *Jube domne benedicere.*

—— 37 sq. From the Offertory litany (*ib.* p. 45) and elsewhere.

P. 269. 12 sqq. From the same: ὑπὲρ πάσης ψυχῆς χριστιανῆς θλιβομένης καὶ καταπονουμένης, ἐλέους καὶ βοηθείας Θεοῦ ἐπιδεομένης (p. 46).

—— 17 sqq. With this Act, cp. p. 59 sqq., 32 sqq. and notes.

P. 271. 26. *Serm. Gunpowder Tr.* vii (iv 326) 'His very punishment is tempered with mercy, . . . "even in his wrath He remembereth mercy (Hab. iii 2).' Cp. Erasmus *de misericordia Domini concio* f. 22 b (Lond. 1533) 'excepte that . . . the punysshement of the wicked synners were tempered with the great mercye of god.'

—— 28. S. Aug. *Conff.* iv 9: ut rea sibi sit humana conscientia, si non amaverit redamantem aut si amantem non redamaverit.

P. 273. 2-6. From the *Omnipotens sempiterne Deus qui vivorum*, found also in the Gregorian Sacramentary as postcommunion of a *missa propria sacerdotis* (Muratori *Lit. vet. rom.* ii 385), in the modern Roman missal as the collect for a mass *pro vivis et defunctis* (*Orationes ad diversa* 35), and as the last prayer of the Roman Litany.

—— 7-10. From the *Domine Jesu Christe Fili Dei vivi pone passionem*: et largiri digneris vivis misericordiam et gratiam, defunctis requiem et veniam, ecclesiæ tuæ sanctæ pacem et concordiam, et nobis peccatoribus vitam et gloriam sempiternam. The alteration in the second line is derived from the common petition for the dead (e.g. in the *preces* of the Sarum Hours) 'Dona eis requiem æternam et lux perpetua luceat eis (cp. 4 Esdr. ii 34, 35); in the third line from Isa. xxxix 8 veritas et pax.

—— 20 sqq. From *A general and deuowte prayer for the gode state of our moder the churche milytante here in erth* Omnip. et misericors Deus rex cœli et terræ. Lines 23-29 also occur approximately in the *Oratio Isidori pro omnibus christianis* in Alcuin *Officia per ferias* v (ii[1] 86) and the Fleury *Libellus precum* (Martene *Eccl. ant. rit.* Antw. 1637, iii 660).

—— 32-34. Cp. p 253.

P. 274. 2. *Serm. Lent.* ii (ii 33) 'Moses may not be spared from sitting and deciding the causes which are brought before him. No more may Aaron, whose *Urim* giveth answer in doubts no less important; and who not only with his *Urim* and *Thummim* giveth counsel, but by his incense and sacrifice obtaineth good success for all our counsels.' Cp. *Serm. Pr.* ix (v 384).

—— 15 sqq. *Serm. Lent.* ii (ii 35) 'And Moses, for his part, is not behind, but a most jealous preserver of Aaron's honour and right everywhere. Everywhere mild save in Aaron's quarrel, and with those only that murmured against Aaron, and said he took too much upon him. Take but his prayer for all, because I would end, his prayer made for Aaron by name, in the thirty-third of Deuteronomy, and these three points in it. "Bless, o Lord, his substance";—therefore he would never have heard, *ut quid perditio hæc?* (Mat. xxvi 8) that all is lost that is spent on Aaron's head. Then, "accept the work of his hands";—therefore he would never easily have excepted to, or with hard construction scanned, all the doings of Aaron. Last of all, "smite through the loins of them that rise up against him";—therefore he would never have strengthened the hand of his evil willers, or said with Saul to Doeg "Turn thou and fall upon the priests" (1 Sam. xxii 17).'

P. 277. Cp. on p. 52 l. 20.

P. 281. *Serm. Pr.* vi (v 360) 'Albeit to set forth the desire of our hearts we use other forms of prayer, and that in more words, yet we must conclude our prayers with this prayer of Christ': *Imagin.* (v 68) 'Our Saviour Christ thus willeth us: "When ye pray, say, Our Father," etc. A most fond imagination is started up in our times, never once dreamed of before, that telleth us in no case we must say "Our Father," etc., with which form, if St Augustine be to be believed as a witness of antiquity, the universal Church of Christ hath ever used to begin and end all her prayers, as striving indeed by divers other forms more largely to express the sense of that prayer; but not being able to come near the high art and most excellent spirit of perfection in that pattern, they always conclude with it, as being sure, howsoever they may for divers defects not attain to the depth of it, [that] by it they shall be sure to beg all things necessary at God's hands.' The passage of S. Aug. referred to is *Ep.* 149 § 16, where he says of the prayer of consecration in the liturgy—quam totam petitionem fere omnis ecclesia dominica oratione concludit. It is not the case that the Church has always begun with the Lord's Prayer, but it has almost uniformly so ended its most characteristic prayer, the eucharistic action; the old Roman vespers and lauds ended with the Lord's Prayer, as the Benedictine office still does (Batiffol *Hist. du Brév. Rom.* p. 87, 100); and so matins and vespers in Spain (*Conc. Gerund.* c. 11). The initial *Paternoster* of modern offices is only a private prayer; and that of the English mass is indefensible.

P. 281. 2. 'Last': this passage forms the conclusion of the intercession on p. 267 sqq.

—— 3-5. From the Great Intercession, *Litt. E. and W.* p. 409.

—— 6 sq. From the prayer Οὐδεὶς ἄξιος at the Great Entrance, *ib.* p. 318.

—— 8-10. From the Offertory prayer Ὁ ἐπισκεψάμενος ἡμᾶς in Lit. S. James, *ib.* p. 45 and in the Egyptian Greek S. Gregory (Renaudot *Lit. orient. coll.* i p. 85).

—— 11, 12. From the Invocation, *Litt. E. and W.* p. 53.

—— 14-16. From the Invocation of S. James, *ib.* καὶ μὴ δι' ἐμὲ καὶ διὰ τὰς ἐμὰς ἁμαρτίας ἀθετήσῃς τὸν λαόν, and the Great Intercession of S. Basil, *ib.* p. 409 καὶ μὴ διὰ τὰς ἐμὰς ἁμαρτίας κωλύσῃς τὴν χάριν τοῦ ἁγίου σου Πνεύματος ἀπὸ τῶν προκειμένων δώρων: and the Οὐδεὶς ἄξιος *ib.* p. 318 σὲ δυσωπῶ τὸν μόνον ἀγαθὸν καὶ εὐήκοον.

—— 19-25. The conclusion of the preface to the Lord's Prayer, *ib.* p. 59: all liturgies have words of the same sort.

—— 31 sq. *Serm. Pr.* xii (v 405) '*In earth as it is in heaven.* Which words are an appendix to the three first petitions; for though it be added to the third which concerneth the doing of his will, yet the ancient Fathers refer it also to the two former; so that we are to pray no less that God's Name may be sanctified in earth as it is in heaven, and that his kingdom may be consummate in earth as it is in heaven, than that his will be accomplished on earth as it is in heaven.' Cp. *Catech. Rom.* iv 10 § 3; Chase *The Lord's Prayer in the Early Church* p. 40.

P. 283. 3 sq. 'Holy art Thou, holy is thy Name' is the opening of the 3rd of the Hebrew 'Eighteen Benedictions' (*Shmone 'Esreh*).

P. 283. 17. S. Chrys. *hom.* xix *in Mat.* 4 (vii 250 D) καταξίωσον γὰρ φησὶν οὕτως ἡμᾶς βιοῦν καθαρῶς ὡς δι' ἡμῶν ἅπαντάς σε δοξάζειν.

—— 20. S. Greg. Nyss. *de or. dom.* iii (Migne *P.G.* xliv. 1156 c) ἀγαθοῦ δὲ παντὸς τὸ κεφάλαιον τὸ ὑπὸ τὴν ζωοποιὸν ἐξουσίαν ὑποτέταχθαι.

—— 21 sq. Ludolphus *vita Christi* i 37 § 5: nec possumus ad Deum venire per gloriam nisi ipse primo veniat ad nos per gratiam.

—— 28 sq. *Serm. Prayer* xi (v 400) 'The will of the flesh wills one thing, and the will of God another; therefore that God's will may take place, we must renounce our own will and, as Christ saith, willingly "deny ourselves" (Mt. xvi 24). We must oppose God's will to "the will of the flesh" and "the will of man" (Jo. i. 13). We must pray unto God, *Converte meum nolle in tuum velle* "convert my froward and unwilling will into thy will"; and because thy will is the true will, *insere oleam voluntatis tuæ oleastro voluntatis meæ* "ingraft the true olive of thy will into the wild olive of my will."'

—— 32 sq. *Serm. Prayer* xii (v 411) 'We are everyone of us particularly to apply to ourselves, for to man it was said by God *Terra es* (Gen. iii 19): to man it was said "Earth, earth, earth, hear the word of the Lord" (Jer. xxii 29). So we desire that God's will may especially be done and fulfilled in that part of the earth whereof God hath made us, that is, that in these our earthly vessels . . we may be careful to do that which God requireth at our hands.'

P. 284. 1 sqq. *Serm. Prayer* xiii (v 418) 'Under this petition is contained, not only that God would give us bread by causing the earth to bring forth corn, and all good seasons for that purpose, but that withal He will give us health of body, and not plague us with sickness as He did the Israelites (Ps. cvi 29). Then, that we may have peace, without which these outward blessings would afford us no comfort; and that as He fills our bellies with food, so He will give us *lætitiam cordis* (Acts xiv. 17), that is all manner of contentment in this life.'

—— 4. *Serm. Nativ.* x (i 173) 'The Church in this sense is very Bethlehem no less than the town itself For that the town itself never had the name rightly all the while there was but bread made there, bread (*panis hominum*), "the bread of men." Not till this Bread was born there, which is *Panis angelorum*, as the Psalm calleth it, "and man did eat angels' food" (Ps. lxxviii 25). Then and never till then was it Bethlehem; and that is in the Church, as truly as ever in it.' Cp. *ib.* xii (i 213).

—— 7 sqq. *Serm Rep.* iv (i 369) 'Our many flittings, our often relapsing, our wretched continuing in them.'

—— 21. *Serm. Prayer* xvii (v 452) 'To be delivered from his [Satan's] jaws, that he swalloweth us not down—for then there is no help for us—that is, that God would save us from "the nethermost hell," that which is called "the second death" (Rev. xx 6) and αἰωνία κόλασις [Mt. xxv 46].'

P. 284. 29. 'Suffer me not to be led,' *ne me induci sinas*, represents the reading *ne patiaris nos induci in tentationem* found in some Latin writers, first in S. Cyprian *de or. dom.* 25, and in some Latin texts of the N.T. See Chase *The Lord's Prayer in the Early Church* p. 64. *Necessary Erudition for any Christian man* 1543 ("the King's book") 'and let us not be led into temptation.'

— 34 sqq. *Serm. Prayer* xvii (v 451) 'Cyprian's exposition [*de or. dom.* 27] is, when we pray *Libera nos a malo*, "deliver us from evil," we desire not to be delivered from this or that evil, but generally from all evil.' Cp. Ludolphus *vita Christi* i 37 § 10: *Sed libera nos a malo*, scilicet omni, vel innato quod contrahimus, scilicet originali; vel adiecto quod committimus, scilicet actuali; vel inflicto quod sustinemus, scilicet pœnali, id est pœna consequenti: vel, a malo omni, visibili et invisibili, id est culpæ et poenæ; vel, a malo omni, scilicet præterito præsenti atque futuro.

— 34. *Serm. Prayer* xvii (v 451) 'If we desire to be delivered from whatsoever is evil, then from ourselves, saith Augustine; for we are evil and so have need to pray . . when we say *Libera nos a malo* "deliver us from evil," it is from that infirmity of the flesh and necessity of sinning which doth accompany our nature, in regard whereof the Apostle saith *Quis me liberabit de hoc corpore mortis?* "Who shall deliver me from this body of death?" (Rom. vii 24).'

— 36. *Ib.* 'Touching the evil from which we desire to be delivered, Chrysostom and the rest of the Greek Church expound it of the devil, who is *lerna malorum* or the greatest evil that can befall us, which exposition is grounded upon the article ἀπὸ τοῦ. But this exposition is too narrow.' Cp. A.V. with R.V.; and see Chase *Lord's Prayer in Early Church* p. 116 *sqq*.

— 37. *Serm. Prayer* xvii (v 450) 'In the [preceding petition] we pray against *malum culpæ*, "the evil of sin," in [this] the second against *malum pœnæ*, "the evil of punishment."'

— 40 *Serm. Lent* v (ii 91) 'And of evil: if it must come here or there, with St Augustine *Domine, hic ure, hic seca, ibi parce* "Let my searing and smart be here: there let me be spared."' The petition is also quoted as S. Augustine's in *Speculum artis bene moriendi* f. A 5 [Colon. 1495?] and in Fisher of Rochester *in Ps.* xxxi 10 (*Opera* Würzburg 1597, c. 1489).

— 41. *Serm. Prayer* xvii (v 457) 'We are to pray . . . at the least, if He take us not presently out of the world, yet "to keep us from the evil of the world" (Jo. xvii 15), till that day when there shall be "no more death, nor sorrow, nor crying, nor pain" (Rev. xxi 4), but God shall be all in all to us for ever.'

P. 285. 4 sq. Isaacson *Life and death of Lancelot Andrewes* (*Minor Works* p. xxix) 'He was not often sick, and but once [1612] till his last sickness in thirty years before the time he died; which was at Downham in the Isle of Ely; the air of that place not agreeing with the constitution of his body . . Of his death he seemed to presage himself a year before he died.' On May 27, 1626, Mede writes to Sir Martin Stuteville 'The Bishop of Winchester is also very ill and hath long been sick' (*ib.* xxix note b). He was also prevented by illness from visiting James I on his deathbed (*Minor Works* p. lix). This passage therefore seems to belong to 1612 or to the last two years of his life.

P. 285 8. *Libera* (after Lord's Prayer): Libera nos quaesumus Domine ab omnibus malis præteritis præsentibus et futuris. So used also in S. Ans. *Or.* i.

—— 12. *Serm. Prayer* xix (v 469) 'There is no petition in the Lord's Prayer which is not found in the Old Testament, used by the Church of the Jews.' These paraphrases seem to be suggested by S. Augustine *Ep.* 130 *ad Probam* 22, where to illustrate that all right and spiritual prayers are included in the *Paternoster* he collects a series of verses like these, corresponding to the seven petitions, viz. (1) Ecclus. xxxvi 4, 18: (2) Ps. lxxx 4: (3) Ps cxix 133: (4) Prov. xxx 8: (5) Ps. cxxxii 1, vii 4: (6) Ecclus. xxiii 6: (7) Ps. lix 2 In the sermon quoted above, Andrewes has another set: (1) Ps. lvii 6, lxvii 2: (2) Ps. cvi 4, 5: (3) Ps. cxliii 10: (4) Ps. cxlv 15, Prov. xxx 8: (5) Ps. lxv 3, vii 3-5: (6) Ps. cxix 37, cxli 3: (7) Ps. xxv 21.

P. 286. 16 sq. These are quoted in illustration of this petition (time and place) in *Serm. Pr.* ix (v 386).

—— 23 sqq. Quoted to illustrate this petition *ib.* xiii (v 421).

—— 34. Quoted on this petition *ib.* ix. (v 383)

P. 287 3, 4. Similarly used *ib.* xiii (v 415), xix (v 469).

—— 13 *sq.* S. Paul's citation (Rom. ii 25) of this is similarly used *ib.* ix (v 387).

—— 24. *Serm. Pr.* xvi (v 447) 'That we be not led into temptation, the means that we are to use is, that we put from before our face "the stumbling-blocks of iniquity" (Ezek. xiv 3), that we restrain our eyes and mouths from beholding or speaking that which is evil, that we restrain our feet, as the Wise Man saith, "Keep thy way far from her, and come not into the door of her house" (Prov. v 8). "For can a man take fire in his bosom, and his clothes not be burnt?" (Prov. vi 27).' Cp. *Repent.* ii (i 334).

INDEX OF NON-SCRIPTURAL MARGINAL REFERENCES

TURNBULL AND SPEARS, PRINTERS, EDINBURGH.

A SELECTION FROM

MESSRS. METHUEN'S PUBLICATIONS

This Catalogue contains only a selection of the more important books published by Messrs. Methuen. A complete catalogue of their publications may be obtained on application.

Bain (F. W.)—
A DIGIT OF THE MOON: A Hindoo Love Story. THE DESCENT OF THE SUN: A Cycle of Birth. A HEIFER OF THE DAWN. IN THE GREAT GOD'S HAIR. A DRAUGHT OF THE BLUE. AN ESSENCE OF THE DUSK. AN INCARNATION OF THE SNOW. A MINE OF FAULTS. THE ASHES OF A GOD. BUBBLES OF THE FOAM. A SYRUP OF THE BEES. THE LIVERY OF EVE. THE SUBSTANCE OF A DREAM. *All Fcap.* 8*vo.* 5*s. net.* AN ECHO OF THE SPHERES. *Wide Demy.* 12*s.* 6*d net.*

Balfour (Graham). THE LIFE OF ROBERT LOUIS STEVENSON. *Fifteenth Edition. In one Volume. Cr.* 8*vo. Buckram,* 7*s.* 6*d. net.*

Belloc (H.)—
PARIS, 8*s.* 6*d. net.* HILLS AND THE SEA, 6*s. net.* ON NOTHING AND KINDRED SUBJECTS, 6*s. net.* ON EVERYTHING, 6*s. net.* ON SOMETHING, 6*s. net.* FIRST AND LAST, 6*s. net.* THIS AND THAT AND THE OTHER, 6*s. net.* MARIE ANTOINETTE, 18*s. net.* THE PYRENEES, 10*s.* 6*d. net.*

Bloemfontein (Bishop of). ARA CŒLI: AN ESSAY IN MYSTICAL THEOLOGY. *Seventh Edition. Cr.* 8*vo.* 5*s. net.*
FAITH AND EXPERIENCE. *Third Edition. Cr.* 8*vo.* 5*s. net.*
THE CULT OF THE PASSING MOMENT. *Fourth Edition. Cr.* 8*vo.* 5*s. net.*
THE ENGLISH CHURCH AND RE-UNION. *Cr.* 8*vo.* 5*s. net.*
SCALA MUNDI. *Cr.* 8*vo.* 4*s.* 6*d net.*

Chesterton (G. K.)—
THE BALLAD OF THE WHITE HORSE. ALL THINGS CONSIDERED. TREMENDOUS TRIFLES. ALARMS AND DISCURSIONS. A MISCELLANY OF MEN. *All Fcap.* 8*vo.* 6*s. net.* WINE, WATER, AND SONG. *Fcap.* 8*vo.* 1*s.* 6*d. net.* THE USES OF DIVERSITY. 6*s. net.*

Clutton-Brock (A.). WHAT IS THE KINGDOM OF HEAVEN? *Fourth Edition. Fcap.* 8*vo* 5*s. net.*
ESSAYS ON ART. *Second Edition. Fcap.* 8*vo.* 5*s. net.*
ESSAYS ON BOOKS. *Fcap.* 8*vo.* 6*s. net.*
MORE ESSAYS ON BOOKS. *Fcap.* 8*vo.* 6*s. net.*

Cole (G. D. H.). SOCIAL THEORY. *Cr.* 8*vo.* 5*s. net.*

Conrad (Joseph). THE MIRROR OF THE SEA: Memories and Impressions. *Fourth Edition. Fcap.* 8*vo.* 6*s. net.*

Einstein (A.). RELATIVITY: THE SPECIAL AND THE GENERAL THEORY. Translated by ROBERT W. LAWSON. *Third Edition. Cr.* 8*vo.* 5*s. net.*

Eliot (T. S.). THE SACRED WOOD: ESSAYS ON POETRY. *Fcap.* 8*vo.* 6*s. net.*

Fyleman (Rose.). FAIRIES AND CHIMNEYS. *Fcap.* 8*vo. Eighth Edition.* 3*s.* 6*d. net.*
THE FAIRY GREEN. *Third Edition. Fcap.* 8*vo.* 3*s.* 6*d. net.*

Gibbins (H. de B.). INDUSTRY IN ENGLAND: HISTORICAL OUTLINES. With Maps and Plans. *Tenth Edition. Demy* 8*vo.* 12*s.* 6*d. net.*
THE INDUSTRIAL HISTORY OF ENGLAND. With 5 Maps and a Plan. *Twenty-seventh Edition. Cr.* 8*vo.* 5*s.*

Gibbon (Edward). THE DECLINE AND FALL OF THE ROMAN EMPIRE. Edited, with Notes, Appendices, and Maps, by J. B. BURY. Illustrated. *Seven Volumes. Demy* 8*vo.* Illustrated. *Each* 12*s.* 6*d. net. Also in Seven Volumes. Cr.* 8*vo. Each* 7*s.* 6*d. net.*

Glover (T. R.). THE CONFLICT OF RELIGIONS IN THE EARLY ROMAN EMPIRE. *Ninth Edition. Demy* 8*vo.* 10*s.* 6*d. net.*
POETS AND PURITANS. *Second Edition. Demy* 8*vo.* 10*s.* 6*d. net.*
FROM PERICLES TO PHILIP. *Third Edition. Demy* 8*vo.* 10*s.* 6*d. net.*
VIRGIL. *Fourth Edition. Demy* 8*vo.* 10*s.* 6*d. net.*
THE CHRISTIAN TRADITION AND ITS VERIFICATION. (The Angus Lecture for 1912.) *Second Edition. Cr.* 8*vo.* 6*s. net.*

Grahame (Kenneth). THE WIND IN THE WILLOWS. *Eleventh Edition. Cr.* 8*vo.* 7*s.* 6*d. net.*

Hall (H. R.). THE ANCIENT HISTORY OF THE NEAR EAST FROM THE EARLIEST TIMES TO THE BATTLE OF SALAMIS. Illustrated. *Fifth Edition. Demy* 8*vo.* 21*s. net.*

Hawthorne (Nathaniel). THE SCARLET LETTER. With 31 Illustrations in Colour by HUGH THOMSON. *Wide Royal* 8*vo.* 31*s.* 6*d.* net.

Holdsworth (W. S.). A HISTORY OF ENGLISH LAW. *Vols. I., II., III. Each Second Edition. Demy 8vo. Each* 15*s. net.*

Inge (W. R.). CHRISTIAN MYSTICISM. (The Bampton Lectures of 1899.) *Fourth Edition. Cr. 8vo.* 7*s.* 6*d. net.*

Jenks (E.). AN OUTLINE OF ENGLISH LOCAL GOVERNMENT. *Fourth Edition.* Revised by R. C. K. ENSOR. *Cr. 8vo.* 5*s. net.*

A SHORT HISTORY OF ENGLISH LAW: FROM THE EARLIEST TIMES TO THE END OF THE YEAR 1911. *Second Edition, revised. Demy 8vo.* 12*s.* 6*d. net.*

Julian (Lady) of Norwich. REVELATIONS OF DIVINE LOVE. Edited by GRACE WARRACK. *Seventh Edition. Cr. 8vo.* 5*s. net.*

Keats (John). POEMS. Edited, with Introduction and Notes, by E. DE SÉLINCOURT. With a Frontispiece in Photogravure. *Fourth Edition. Demy 8vo.* 12*s.* 6*d. net.*

Kidd (Benjamin). THE SCIENCE OF POWER. *Ninth Edition. Crown 8vo.* 7*s.* 6*d. net.*

SOCIAL EVOLUTION. *Demy 8vo.* 8*s.* 6*d. net.*

Kipling (Rudyard). BARRACK-ROOM BALLADS. 208*th Thousand. Cr. 8vo. Buckram,* 7*s.* 6*d. net. Also Fcap. 8vo. Cloth,* 6*s. net; leather,* 7*s.* 6*d. net.*
Also a Service Edition. *Two Volumes. Square fcap. 8vo. Each* 3*s. net.*

THE SEVEN SEAS. 157*th Thousand. Cr. 8vo. Buckram,* 7*s.* 6*d. net. Also Fcap. 8vo. Cloth,* 6*s. net; leather,* 7*s.* 6*d. net.*
Also a Service Edition. *Two Volumes. Square fcap. 8vo. Each* 3*s. net.*

THE FIVE NATIONS. 126*th Thousand. Cr. 8vo. Buckram,* 7*s.* 6*d. net. Also Fcap. 8vo. Cloth,* 6*s. net; leather,* 7*s.* 6*d. net.*
Also a Service Edition. *Two Volumes. Square fcap. 8vo. Each* 3*s. net.*

DEPARTMENTAL DITTIES. 94*th Thousand. Cr. 8vo. Buckram,* 7*s.* 6*d. net. Also Fcap. 8vo. Cloth,* 6*s. net; leather,* 7*s.* 6*d. net.*
Also a Service Edition. *Two Volumes. Square fcap. 8vo. Each* 3*s. net.*

THE YEARS BETWEEN. *Cr. 8vo. Buckram,* 7*s.* 6*d. net. Also on thin paper. Fcap. 8vo. Blue cloth,* 6*s. net; Limp lambskin,* 7*s.* 6*d. net.*
Also a Service Edition. *Two Volumes. Square fcap. 8vo. Each* 3*s. net.*

HYMN BEFORE ACTION. Illuminated. *Fcap. 4to.* 1*s.* 6*d. net.*

RECESSIONAL. Illuminated. *Fcap. 4to.* 1*s.* 6*d. net.*

TWENTY POEMS FROM RUDYARD KIPLING. 360*th Thousand. Fcap. 8vo.* 1*s. net.*

Lamb (Charles and Mary). THE COMPLETE WORKS. Edited by E. V. LUCAS. *A New and Revised Edition in Six Volumes. With Frontispieces. Fcap. 8vo. Each* 6*s. net.*
The volumes are:—
I. MISCELLANEOUS PROSE. II. ELIA AND THE LAST ESSAY OF ELIA. III. BOOKS FOR CHILDREN. IV. PLAYS AND POEMS V. and VI. LETTERS.

THE ESSAYS OF ELIA. With an Introduction by E. V. LUCAS, and 28 Illustrations by A. GARTH JONES. *Fcap. 8vo.* 5*s. net.*

Lankester (Sir Ray). SCIENCE FROM AN EASY CHAIR. Illustrated. *Thirteenth Edition. Cr. 8vo.* 7*s.* 6*d. net.*

MORE SCIENCE FROM AN EASY CHAIR. Illustrated. *Third Edition. Cr. 8vo.* 7*s.* 6*d. net.*

DIVERSIONS OF A NATURALIST. Illustrated. *Third Edition. Cr. 8vo.* 7*s.* 6*d. net.*

SECRETS OF EARTH AND SEA. *Cr. 8vo.* 8*s.* 6*d net.*

Lodge (Sir Oliver). MAN AND THE UNIVERSE: A STUDY OF THE INFLUENCE OF THE ADVANCE IN SCIENTIFIC KNOWLEDGE UPON OUR UNDERSTANDING OF CHRISTIANITY. *Ninth Edition. Crown 8vo.* 7*s.* 6*d. net.*

THE SURVIVAL OF MAN: A STUDY IN UNRECOGNISED HUMAN FACULTY. *Seventh Edition. Cr. 8vo.* 7*s.* 6*d. net.*

MODERN PROBLEMS. *Cr. 8vo.* 7*s.* 6*d. net.*

RAYMOND; OR LIFE AND DEATH. Illustrated. *Twelfth Edition. Demy 8vo.* 15*s. net.*

Lucas (E. V.).
THE LIFE OF CHARLES LAMB, 2 *vols.*, 21*s. net.* A WANDERER IN HOLLAND, 10*s.* 6*d. net.* A WANDERER IN LONDON, 10*s.* 6*d. net.* LONDON REVISITED, 10*s.* 6*d. net.* A WANDERER IN PARIS, 10*s.* 6*d. net* and 6*s. net.* A WANDERER IN FLORENCE, 10*s.* 6*d. net.* A WANDERER IN VENICE, 10*s.* 6*d. net.* THE OPEN ROAD: A Little Book for Wayfarers, 6*s.* 6*d. net* and 7*s.* 6*d. net.* THE FRIENDLY TOWN: A Little Book for the Urbane, 6*s. net.* FIRESIDE AND SUNSHINE, 6*s. net.* CHARACTER AND COMEDY, 6*s. net.* THE GENTLEST ART: A Choice of Letters by Entertaining Hands, 6*s.* 6*d. net.* THE SECOND POST, 6*s. net.* HER INFINITE VARIETY: A Feminine Portrait Gallery, 6*s. net.* GOOD COMPANY: A Rally of Men, 6*s. net.* ONE DAY AND ANOTHER, 6*s. net.* OLD LAMPS FOR NEW, 6*s. net.* LOITERER'S HARVEST, 6*s. net.* CLOUD AND SILVER, 6*s. net.* A BOSWELL OF BAGHDAD, AND OTHER ESSAYS, 6*s. net.* 'TWIXT EAGLE AND DOVE, 6*s. net.* THE PHANTOM JOURNAL, AND OTHER ESSAYS AND DIVERSIONS, 6*s. net.* SPECIALLY SELECTED: A Choice of Essays. 7*s.* 6*d. net.* THE BRITISH SCHOOL: An Anecdotal Guide to the British Painters and Paintings in the National Gallery, 6*s. net.* TRAVEL NOTES.

McDougall (William). AN INTRODUCTION TO SOCIAL PSYCHOLOGY. *Sixteenth Edition. Cr. 8vo.* 8*s. net.*
BODY AND MIND: A HISTORY AND A DEFENCE OF ANIMISM. *Fifth Edition. Demy 8vo.* 12*s.* 6*d. net.*

Maeterlinck (Maurice)—
THE BLUE BIRD: A Fairy Play in Six Acts, 6*s. net.* MARY MAGDALENE; A Play in Three Acts, 5*s. net.* DEATH, 3*s.* 6*d. net.* OUR ETERNITY, 6*s. net.* THE UNKNOWN GUEST, 6*s. net.* POEMS, 5*s. net.* THE WRACK OF THE STORM, 6*s. net.* THE MIRACLE OF ST. ANTHONY: A Play in One Act, 3*s.* 6*d. net.* THE BURGOMASTER OF STILEMONDE: A Play in Three Acts, 5*s. net.* THE BETROTHAL; or, The Blue Bird Chooses, 6*s. net.* MOUNTAIN PATHS, 6*s. net.* THE STORY OF TYLTYL, 21*s. net.*

Milne (A. A.). THE DAY'S PLAY. THE HOLIDAY ROUND. ONCE A WEEK. *All Cr. 8vo.* 7*s. net.* NOT THAT IT MATTERS. *Fcap 8vo.* 6*s. net.* IF I MAY. *Fcap. 8vo.* 6*s. net.*

Oxenham (John)—
BEES IN AMBER; A Little Book of Thoughtful Verse. ALL'S WELL: A Collection of War Poems. THE KING'S HIGH WAY. THE VISION SPLENDID. THE FIERY CROSS. HIGH ALTARS: The Record of a Visit to the Battlefields of France and Flanders. HEARTS COURAGEOUS. ALL CLEAR! WINDS OF THE DAWN. *All Small Pott 8vo. Paper,* 1*s.* 3*d. net; cloth boards,* 2*s. net.* GENTLEMEN—THE KING, 2*s. net.*

Petrie (W. M. Flinders). A HISTORY OF EGYPT. Illustrated. *Six Volumes. Cr. 8vo. Each* 9*s. net.*
VOL. I. FROM THE IST TO THE XVITH DYNASTY. *Ninth Edition.* (10*s.* 6*d. net.*)
VOL. II. THE XVIITH AND XVIIITH DYNASTIES. *Sixth Edition.*
VOL. III. XIXTH TO XXXTH DYNASTIES. *Second Edition.*
VOL. IV. EGYPT UNDER THE PTOLEMAIC DYNASTY. J. P. MAHAFFY. *Second Edition.*
VOL. V. EGYPT UNDER ROMAN RULE. J. G. MILNE. *Second Edition.*
VOL. VI. EGYPT IN THE MIDDLE AGES. STANLEY LANE POOLE. *Second Edition.*
SYRIA AND EGYPT, FROM THE TELL EL AMARNA LETTERS. *Cr. 8vo.* 5*s. net.*
EGYPTIAN TALES. Translated from the Papyri. First Series, IVth to XIIth Dynasty. Illustrated. *Third Edition. Cr. 8vo.* 5*s. net.*
EGYPTIAN TALES. Translated from the Papyri. Second Series, XVIIITH to XIXTH Dynasty. Illustrated. *Second Edition. Cr. 8vo.* 5*s. net.*

Pollard (A. F.). A SHORT HISTORY OF THE GREAT WAR. With 19 Maps. *Second Edition. Cr. 8vo.* 10*s.* 6*d. net.*

Price (L. L.). A SHORT HISTORY OF POLITICAL ECONOMY IN ENGLAND FROM ADAM SMITH TO ARNOLD TOYNBEE. *Tenth Edition. Cr. 8vo.* 5*s. net.*

Reid (G. Archdall). THE LAWS OF HEREDITY. *Second Edition. Demy 8vo.* £1 1*s. net.*

Robertson (C. Grant). SELECT STATUTES, CASES, AND DOCUMENTS, 1660–1832. *Third Edition. Demy 8vo.* 15*s. net.*

Selous (Edmund). TOMMY SMITH'S ANIMALS. Illustrated. *Nineteenth Edition. Fcap. 8vo.* 3*s.* 6*d. net.*
TOMMY SMITH'S OTHER ANIMALS. Illustrated. *Eleventh Edition. Fcap. 8vo.* 3*s.* 6*d. net.*
TOMMY SMITH AT THE ZOO. Illustrated. *Fourth Edition. Fcap. 8vo.* 2*s.* 9*d.*
TOMMY SMITH AGAIN AT THE ZOO. Illustrated. *Second Edition. Fcap. 8vo.* 2*s.* 9*d.*
JACK'S INSECTS. *Popular Edition. Cr. 8vo.* 3*s.* 6*d.*
JACK'S OTHER INSECTS. *Cr. 8vo.* 3*s.* 6*d.*

Shelley (Percy Bysshe). POEMS. With an Introduction by A. CLUTTON-BROCK and Notes by C. D. LOCOCK. *Two Volumes. Demy 8vo.* £1 1*s. net.*

Smith (Adam). THE WEALTH OF NATIONS. Edited by EDWIN CANNAN. *Two Volumes. Second Edition. Demy 8vo.* £1 10*s. net.*

Stevenson (R. L.). THE LETTERS OF ROBERT LOUIS STEVENSON. Edited by Sir SIDNEY COLVIN. *A New Rearranged Edition in four volumes. Fourth Edition. Fcap. 8vo. Each* 6*s. net.*

Surtees (R. S.). HANDLEY CROSS. Illustrated. *Ninth Edition. Fcap. 8vo.* 7*s.* 6*d. net.*
MR. SPONGE'S SPORTING TOUR. Illustrated. *Fifth Edition. Fcap. 8vo.* 7*s.* 6*d. net.*
ASK MAMMA: OR, THE RICHEST COMMONER IN ENGLAND. Illustrated. *Second Edition. Fcap. 8vo.* 7*s.* 6*d. net.*
JORROCKS'S JAUNTS AND JOLLITIES. Illustrated. *Seventh Edition. Fcap. 8vo.* 6*s. net.*
MR. FACEY ROMFORD'S HOUNDS. Illustrated. *Fourth Edition. Fcap. 8vo.* 7*s.* 6*d. net.*
HAWBUCK GRANGE; OR, THE SPORTING ADVENTURES OF THOMAS SCOTT, ESQ. Illustrated. *Fcap. 8vo.* 6*s. net.*
PLAIN OR RINGLETS? Illustrated. *Fcap. 8vo.* 7*s.* 6*d. net.*
HILLINGDON HALL. With 12 Coloured Plates by WILDRAKE, HEATH, and JELLICOE. *Fcap. 8vo.* 7*s.* 6*d. net.*

Tilden (W. T.). THE ART OF LAWN TENNIS. Illustrated. *Cr. 8vo.* 6*s. net.*

Tileston (Mary W.). DAILY STRENGTH FOR DAILY NEEDS. *Twenty-seventh Edition. Medium 16mo.* 3*s.* 6*d. net.*

Underhill (Evelyn). MYSTICISM. A Study in the Nature and Development of Man's Spiritual Consciousness. *Eighth Edition. Demy 8vo.* 15*s. net.*

Vardon (Harry). HOW TO PLAY GOLF. Illustrated. *Thirteenth Edition. Cr. 8vo.* 5*s. net.*

Waterhouse (Elizabeth). A LITTLE BOOK OF LIFE AND DEATH. *Twentieth Edition. Small Pott 8vo. Cloth,* 2*s.* 6*d. net.*

Wells (J.). A SHORT HISTORY OF ROME. *Seventeenth Edition.* With 3 Maps. *Cr. 8vo.* 6*s.*

Wilde (Oscar). THE WORKS OF OSCAR WILDE. *Fcap. 8vo. Each* 6*s.* 6*d. net.*

I. LORD ARTHUR SAVILE'S CRIME AND THE PORTRAIT OF MR. W. H. II. THE DUCHESS OF PADUA. III. POEMS. IV. LADY WINDERMERE'S FAN. V. A WOMAN OF NO IMPORTANCE. VI. AN IDEAL HUSBAND. VII. THE IMPORTANCE OF BEING EARNEST. VIII. A HOUSE OF POMEGRANATES. IX. INTENTIONS. X. DE PROFUNDIS AND PRISON LETTERS. XI. ESSAYS. XII. SALOMÉ, A FLORENTINE TRAGEDY, and LA SAINTE COURTISANE. XIII. A CRITIC IN PALL MALL. XIV. SELECTED PROSE OF OSCAR WILDE. XV. ART AND DECORATION.

A HOUSE OF POMEGRANATES. Illustrated. *Cr. 4to.* 21*s. net.*

Yeats (W. B.). A BOOK OF IRISH VERSE. *Fourth Edition. Cr. 8vo.* 7*s. net.*

PART II.—A SELECTION OF SERIES

Ancient Cities

General Editor, SIR B. C. A. WINDLE

Cr. 8vo. 6*s. net each volume*

With Illustrations by E. H. NEW, and other Artists

BRISTOL. CANTERBURY. CHESTER. DUBLIN. EDINBURGH. LINCOLN. SHREWSBURY. WELLS and GLASTONBURY.

The Antiquary's Books

General Editor, J. CHARLES COX

Demy 8vo. 10*s.* 6*d. net each volume*

With Numerous Illustrations

ANCIENT PAINTED GLASS IN ENGLAND. ARCHÆOLOGY AND FALSE ANTIQUITIES. THE BELLS OF ENGLAND. THE BRASSES OF ENGLAND. THE CASTLES AND WALLED TOWNS OF ENGLAND. CELTIC ART IN PAGAN AND CHRISTIAN TIMES. CHURCHWARDENS' ACCOUNTS. THE DOMESDAY INQUEST. ENGLISH CHURCH FURNITURE. ENGLISH COSTUME. ENGLISH MONASTIC LIFE. ENGLISH SEALS. FOLK-LORE AS AN HISTORICAL SCIENCE. THE GILDS AND COMPANIES OF LONDON. THE HERMITS AND ANCHORITES OF ENGLAND. THE MANOR AND MANORIAL RECORDS. THE MEDIÆVAL HOSPITALS OF ENGLAND. OLD ENGLISH INSTRUMENTS OF MUSIC. OLD ENGLISH LIBRARIES. OLD SERVICE BOOKS OF THE ENGLISH CHURCH. PARISH LIFE IN MEDIÆVAL ENGLAND. THE PARISH REGISTERS OF ENGLAND. REMAINS OF THE PREHISTORIC AGE IN ENGLAND. THE ROMAN ERA IN BRITAIN. ROMANO-BRITISH BUILDINGS AND EARTHWORKS. THE ROYAL FORESTS OF ENGLAND. THE SCHOOLS OF MEDIEVAL ENGLAND. SHRINES OF BRITISH SAINTS.

The Arden Shakespeare

General Editor, R. H. CASE

Demy 8vo. 6s. net each volume

An edition of Shakespeare in Single Plays; each edited with a full Introduction, Textual Notes, and a Commentary at the foot of the page.

Classics of Art

Edited by DR. J. H. W. LAING

With numerous Illustrations. Wide Royal 8vo

THE ART OF THE GREEKS, 15s. *net*. THE ART OF THE ROMANS, 16s. *net*. CHARDIN, 15s. *net*. DONATELLO, 16s. *net*. GEORGE ROMNEY, 15s. *net*. GHIRLANDAIO, 15s. *net*. LAWRENCE, 25s. *net*. MICHELANGELO, 15s. *net*. RAPHAEL, 15s. *net*. REMBRANDT'S ETCHINGS, Two Vols., 25s. *net*. TINTORETTO, 16s. *net*. TITIAN, 16s. *net*. TURNER'S SKETCHES AND DRAWINGS, 15s. *net*. VELAZQUEZ, 15s. *net*.

The 'Complete' Series

Fully Illustrated. Demy 8vo

THE COMPLETE AMATEUR BOXER, 10s. 6d. *net*. THE COMPLETE ASSOCIATION FOOTBALLER, 10s. 6d. *net*. THE COMPLETE ATHLETIC TRAINER, 10s. 6d. *net*. THE COMPLETE BILLIARD PLAYER, 12s. 6d. *net*. THE COMPLETE COOK, 10s. 6d. *net*. THE COMPLETE CRICKETER, 10s. 6d. *net*. THE COMPLETE FOXHUNTER, 16s. *net*. THE COMPLETE GOLFER, 12s. 6d. *net*. THE COMPLETE HOCKEY-PLAYER, 10s. 6d. *net*. THE COMPLETE HORSEMAN, 12s. 6d. *net*. THE COMPLETE JUJITSUAN. *Cr. 8vo.* 5s. *net*. THE COMPLETE LAWN TENNIS PLAYER, 12s. 6d. *net*. THE COMPLETE MOTORIST, 10s. 6d. *net*. THE COMPLETE MOUNTAINEER, 16s. *net*. THE COMPLETE OARSMAN, 15s. *net*. THE COMPLETE PHOTOGRAPHER, 15s. *net*. THE COMPLETE RUGBY FOOTBALLER, ON THE NEW ZEALAND SYSTEM, 12s. 6d. *net*. THE COMPLETE SHOT, 16s. *net*. THE COMPLETE SWIMMER, 10s. 6d. *net*. THE COMPLETE YACHTSMAN, 16s. *net*.

The Connoisseur's Library

With numerous Illustrations. Wide Royal 8vo. 25s. net each volume

ENGLISH COLOURED BOOKS. ENGLISH FURNITURE. ETCHINGS. EUROPEAN ENAMELS. FINE BOOKS. GLASS. GOLDSMITHS' AND SILVERSMITHS' WORK. ILLUMINATED MANUSCRIPTS. IVORIES. JEWELLERY. MEZZOTINTS. MINIATURES. PORCELAIN. SEALS. WOOD SCULPTURE.

Handbooks of Theology

Demy 8vo

THE DOCTRINE OF THE INCARNATION, 15s. *net*. A HISTORY OF EARLY CHRISTIAN DOCTRINE, 16s. *net*. INTRODUCTION TO THE HISTORY OF RELIGION, 12s. 6d. *net*. AN INTRODUCTION TO THE HISTORY OF THE CREEDS, 12s. 6d. *net*. THE PHILOSOPHY OF RELIGION IN ENGLAND AND AMERICA, 12s. 6d. *net*. THE XXXIX ARTICLES OF THE CHURCH OF ENGLAND, 15s. *net*.

Health Series

Fcap 8vo. 2s. 6d. net

THE BABY. THE CARE OF THE BODY. THE CARE OF THE TEETH. THE EYES OF OUR CHILDREN. HEALTH FOR THE MIDDLE-AGED. THE HEALTH OF A WOMAN. THE HEALTH OF THE SKIN. HOW TO LIVE LONG. THE PREVENTION OF THE COMMON COLD. STAYING THE PLAGUE. THROAT AND EAR TROUBLES. TUBERCULOSIS. THE HEALTH OF THE CHILD, 2s. *net*.

Leaders of Religion

Edited by H. C. BEECHING. *With Portraits*

Crown 8vo. 3s. net each volume

The Library of Devotion

Handy Editions of the great Devotional Books, well edited.
With Introductions and (where necessary) Notes

Small Pott 8vo, cloth, 3s. net and 3s. 6d. net

Little Books on Art

With many Illustrations. Demy 16mo. 5s. net each volume

Each volume consists of about 200 pages, and contains from 30 to 40 Illustrations, including a Frontispiece in Photogravure

ALBRECHT DÜRER. THE ARTS OF JAPAN. BOOKPLATES. BOTTICELLI. BURNE-JONES. CELLINI. CHRISTIAN SYMBOLISM. CHRIST IN ART. CLAUDE. CONSTABLE. COROT. EARLY ENGLISH WATER-COLOUR. ENAMELS. FREDERIC LEIGHTON. GEORGE ROMNEY. GREEK ART. GREUZE AND BOUCHER. HOLBEIN. ILLUMINATED MANUSCRIPTS. JEWELLERY. JOHN HOPPNER. Sir JOSHUA REYNOLDS. MILLET. MINIATURES. OUR LADY IN ART. RAPHAEL. RODIN. TURNER. VANDYCK. VELAZQUEZ. WATTS.

The Little Guides

With many Illustrations by E. H. NEW and other artists, and from photographs

Small Pott 8vo. 4s. net, 5s. net, and 6s. net

Guides to the English and Welsh Counties, and some well-known districts

The main features of these Guides are (1) a handy and charming form; (2) illustrations from photographs and by well-known artists; (3) good plans and maps; (4) an adequate but compact presentation of everything that is interesting in the natural features, history, archæology, and architecture of the town or district treated.

The Little Quarto Shakespeare

Edited by W. J. CRAIG. With Introductions and Notes

Pott 16mo. 40 Volumes. Leather, price 1s. 9d. net each volume

Cloth, 1s. 6d.

Plays

Fcap. 8vo. 3s. 6d. net

MILESTONES. Arnold Bennett and Edward Knoblock. *Ninth Edition.*

IDEAL HUSBAND, AN. Oscar Wilde. *Acting Edition.*

KISMET. Edward Knoblock. *Fourth Edition.*

TYPHOON. A Play in Four Acts. Melchior Lengyel. English Version by Laurence Irving. *Second Edition.*

WARE CASE, THE. George Pleydell.

GENERAL POST. J. E. Harold Terry. *Second Edition.*

Sports Series

Illustrated. Fcap. 8vo

ALL ABOUT FLYING, 3*s. net.* GOLF DO'S AND DONT'S, 2*s. net.* THE GOLFING SWING. 2*s.* 6*d. net.* HOW TO SWIM, 2*s. net.* LAWN TENNIS, 3*s. net.* SKATING, 3*s. net.* CROSS-COUNTRY SKI-ING, 5*s. net.* WRESTLING, 2*s. net.* QUICK CUTS TO GOOD GOLF, 2*s.* 6*d. net.* HOCKEY, 4*s. net.*

The Westminster Commentaries

General Editor, WALTER LOCK

Demy 8vo

THE ACTS OF THE APOSTLES, 16*s. net.* AMOS, 8*s.* 6*d. net.* I. CORINTHIANS, 8*s.* 6*d. net.* EXODUS, 15*s. net.* EZEKIEL, 12*s.* 6*d. net.* GENESIS, 16*s. net.* HEBREWS, 8*s.* 6*d. net.* ISAIAH, 16*s. net.* JEREMIAH, 16*s. net.* JOB, 8*s.* 6*d. net.* THE PASTORAL EPISTLES, 8*s.* 6*d. net.* THE PHILIPPIANS, 8*s.* 6*d. net.* ST. JAMES, 8*s.* 6*d. net.* ST. MATTHEW, 15*s. net.*

Methuen's Two-Shilling Library

Cheap Editions of many Popular Books

Fcap. 8vo

PART III.—A SELECTION OF WORKS OF FICTION

Bennett (Arnold)—
CLAYHANGER, 8*s. net.* HILDA LESSWAYS, 8*s.* 6*d. net.* THESE TWAIN. THE CARD. THE REGENT: A Five Towns Story of Adventure in London. THE PRICE OF LOVE. BURIED ALIVE. A MAN FROM THE NORTH. THE MATADOR OF THE FIVE TOWNS. WHOM GOD HATH JOINED. A GREAT MAN: A Frolic. *All* 7*s.* 6*d. net.*

Birmingham (George A.)—
SPANISH GOLD. THE SEARCH PARTY. LALAGE'S LOVERS. THE BAD TIMES. UP, THE REBELS. *All* 7*s.* 6*d. net.* INISHEENY, 8*s.* 6*d. net.*

Burroughs (Edgar Rice)—
TARZAN OF THE APES, 6*s. net.* THE RETURN OF TARZAN, 6*s. net.* THE BEASTS OF TARZAN, 6*s. net.* THE SON OF TARZAN, 6*s. net.* JUNGLE TALES OF TARZAN, 6*s. net.* TARZAN AND THE JEWELS OF OPAR, 6*s. net.* TARZAN THE UNTAMED, 7*s.* 6*d. net.* A PRINCESS OF MARS, 6*s. net.* THE GODS OF MARS, 6*s. net.* THE WARLORD OF MARS, 6*s. net.*

Conrad (Joseph). A SET OF SIX, 7*s.* 6*d. net.* VICTORY: An Island Tale. *Cr. 8vo.* 9*s. net.* THE SECRET AGENT: A Simple Tale. *Cr. 8vo.* 9*s. net.* UNDER WESTERN EYES. *Cr. 8vo.* 9*s. net.* CHANCE. *Cr. 8vo.* 9*s. net.*

Corelli (Marie)—
A ROMANCE OF TWO WORLDS, 7*s.* 6*d. net.* VENDETTA: or, The Story of One Forgotten, 8*s. net.* THELMA: A Norwegian Princess, 8*s.* 6*d. net.* ARDATH: The Story of a Dead Self, 7*s.* 6*d. net.* THE SOUL OF LILITH, 7*s.* 6*d. net.* WORMWOOD: A Drama of Paris, 8*s. net.* BARABBAS: A Dream of the World's Tragedy, 8*s. net.* THE SORROWS OF SATAN, 7*s.* 6*d. net.* THE MASTER-CHRISTIAN, 8*s.* 6*d. net.* TEMPORAL POWER: A Study in Supremacy, 6*s. net.* GOD'S GOOD MAN: A Simple Love Story, 8*s.* 6*d. net.* HOLY ORDERS: The Tragedy of a Quiet Life, 8*s.* 6*d. net.* THE MIGHTY ATOM, 7*s.* 6*d. net.* BOY: A Sketch, 7*s.* 6*d. net.* CAMEOS, 6*s. net.* THE LIFE EVERLASTING, 8*s.* 6*d. net.* THE LOVE OF LONG AGO, AND OTHER STORIES, 8*s.* 6*d. net.*

Doyle (Sir A. Conan). ROUND THE RED LAMP. *Twelfth Edition. Cr. 8vo.* 7*s.* 6*d. net.*

Hichens (Robert)—
TONGUES OF CONSCIENCE, 7*s.* 6*d. net.* FELIX: Three Years in a Life, 7*s.* 6*d. net.* THE WOMAN WITH THE FAN, 7*s.* 6*d. net.* BYEWAYS, 7*s.* 6*d. net.* THE GARDEN OF ALLAH, 8*s.* 6*d. net.* THE CALL OF THE BLOOD, 8*s.* 6*d. net.* BARBARY SHEEP, 6*s. net.* THE DWELLERS ON THE THRESHOLD, 7*s.* 6*d. net.* THE WAY OF AMBITION, 7*s.* 6*d. net.* IN THE WILDERNESS, 7*s.* 6*d. net.*

Hope (Anthony)—
A CHANGE OF AIR. A MAN OF MARK. THE CHRONICLES OF COUNT ANTONIO. SIMON DALE. THE KING'S MIRROR. QUISANTÉ. THE DOLLY DIALOGUES. TALES OF TWO PEOPLE. A SERVANT OF THE PUBLIC. MRS. MAXON PROTESTS. A YOUNG MAN'S YEAR. BEAUMAROY HOME FROM THE WARS. *All 7s. 6d. net.*

Jacobs (W. W.)—
MANY CARGOES, 5*s. net.* SEA URCHINS, 5*s. net* and 3*s.* 6*d. net.* A MASTER OF CRAFT, 5*s. net.* LIGHT FREIGHTS, 5*s. net.* THE SKIPPER'S WOOING, 5*s. net.* AT SUNWICH PORT, 5*s. net.* DIALSTONE LANE, 5*s. net.* ODD CRAFT, 5*s. net.* THE LADY OF THE BARGE, 5*s. net.* SALTHAVEN, 5*s. net.* SAILORS' KNOTS, 5*s. net.* SHORT CRUISES, 6*s. net.*

London (Jack). WHITE FANG. *Ninth Edition. Cr. 8vo. 7s. 6d. net.*

Lucas (E. V.)—
LISTENER'S LURE: An Oblique Narration, 6*s. net.* OVER BEMERTON'S: An Easy-going Chronicle, 6*s. net.* MR. INGLESIDE, 6*s. net.* LONDON LAVENDER, 6*s. net.* LANDMARKS, 7*s.* 6*d. net.* THE VERMILION BOX, 7*s.* 6*d. net.* VERENA IN THE MIDST, 8*s.* 6*d. net.*

McKenna (Stephen)—
SONIA: Between Two Worlds, 8*s. net.* NINETY-SIX HOURS' LEAVE, 7*s.* 6*d. net.* THE SIXTH SENSE, 6*s. net.* MIDAS & SON, 8*s. net.*

Malet (Lucas)—
THE HISTORY OF SIR RICHARD CALMADY: A Romance. THE CARISSIMA. THE GATELESS BARRIER. DEADHAM HARD. *All 7s. 6d. net.* THE WAGES OF SIN. 8*s. net.*

Mason (A. E. W.). CLEMENTINA. Illustrated. *Ninth Edition. Cr. 8vo. 7s. 6d. net.*

Maxwell (W. B.)—
VIVIEN. THE GUARDED FLAME. ODD LENGTHS. HILL RISE. THE REST CURE. *All 7s. 6d. net.*

Oxenham (John)—
A WEAVER OF WEBS. PROFIT AND LOSS. THE SONG OF HYACINTH, and Other Stories. LAURISTONS. THE COIL OF CARNE. THE QUEST OF THE GOLDEN ROSE. MARY ALL-ALONE. BROKEN SHACKLES. "1914." *All 7s. 6d. net.*

Parker (Gilbert)—
PIERRE AND HIS PEOPLE. MRS. FALCHION. THE TRANSLATION OF A SAVAGE. WHEN VALMOND CAME TO PONTIAC: The Story of a Lost Napoleon. AN ADVENTURER OF THE NORTH: The Last Adventures of 'Pretty Pierre.' THE SEATS OF THE MIGHTY. THE BATTLE OF THE STRONG: A Romance of Two Kingdoms. THE POMP OF THE LAVILETTES. NORTHERN LIGHTS. *All 7s. 6d. net.*

Phillpotts (Eden)—
CHILDREN OF THE MIST. SONS OF THE MORNING. THE RIVER. THE AMERICAN PRISONER. DEMETER'S DAUGHTER. THE HUMAN BOY AND THE WAR. *All 7s. 6d. net.*

Ridge (W. Pett)—
A SON OF THE STATE, 7*s.* 6*d. net.* THE REMINGTON SENTENCE, 7*s.* 6*d. net.* MADAME PRINCE, 7*s.* 6*d. net.* TOP SPEED, 7*s.* 6*d. net.* SPECIAL PERFORMANCES, 6*s. net.* THE BUSTLING HOURS, 7*s.* 6*d. net.*

Rohmer (Sax)—
THE DEVIL DOCTOR. THE SI-FAN MYSTERIES. TALES OF SECRET EGYPT. THE ORCHARD OF TEARS. THE GOLDEN SCORPION. *All 7s. 6d. net.*

Swinnerton (F.). SHOPS AND HOUSES. *Third Edition. Cr. 8vo. 7s. 6d. net.*

SEPTEMBER. *Third Edition. Cr. 8vo. 7s. 6d. net.*

THE HAPPY FAMILY. *Second Edition. 7s. 6d. net.*

ON THE STAIRCASE. *Third Edition. 7s. 6d. net.*

Wells (H. G.). BEALBY. *Fourth Edition. Cr. 8vo. 7s. 6d. net.*

Williamson (C. N. and A. M.)—
THE LIGHTNING CONDUCTOR: The Strange Adventures of a Motor Car. LADY BETTY ACROSS THE WATER. SCARLET RUNNER. LORD LOVELAND DISCOVERS AMERICA. THE GUESTS OF HERCULES. IT HAPPENED IN EGYPT. A SOLDIER OF THE LEGION. THE SHOP GIRL. THE LIGHTNING CONDUCTRESS. SECRET HISTORY. THE LOVE PIRATE. *All 7s. 6d. net.* CRUCIFIX CORNER. 6*s. net.*

Methuen's Two-Shilling Novels

Cheap Editions of many of the most Popular Novels of the day

Write for Complete List

Fcap. 8vo

Ingram Content Group UK Ltd.
Milton Keynes UK
UKHW011835100723
424887UK00002B/27